Lecture Notes in Computer Science   9991

Commenced Publication in 1973
Founding and Former Series Editors:
Gerhard Goos, Juris Hartmanis, and Jan van Leeuwen

Editorial Board

More information about this series at http://www.springer.com/series/7409

Jan Hodicky (Ed.)

Modelling and Simulation for Autonomous Systems

Third International Workshop, MESAS 2016
Rome, Italy, June 15–16, 2016
Revised Selected Papers

 Springer

Editor
Jan Hodicky
NATO Modelling and Simulation Centre
  of Excellence
Rome
Italy

ISSN 0302-9743   ISSN 1611-3349 (electronic)
Lecture Notes in Computer Science
ISBN 978-3-319-47604-9   ISBN 978-3-319-47605-6   (eBook)
DOI 10.1007/978-3-319-47605-6

Library of Congress Control Number: 2016953663

LNCS Sublibrary: SL3 – Information Systems and Applications, incl. Internet/Web, and HCI

Printed on acid-free paper

This Springer imprint is published by Springer Nature
The registered company is Springer International Publishing AG
The registered company address is: Gewerbestrasse 11, 6330 Cham, Switzerland

Preface

This volume contains the full papers presented at the 2016 MESAS Workshop: Modelling and Simulation for Autonomous Systems, held during June 15–16, 2016, in Rome. The initial idea to launch the MESAS project was introduced by the Concept Development and Experimentation Branch at the NATO Modelling and Simulation Centre of Excellence in 2013, namely, by LTCDR Alessandro Cignoni, who wanted to bring together the Modelling and Simulation and the Autonomous Systems communities and to collect new ideas for concept development and experimentation in this domain. From that time, the event gathers together — in keynote, regular, poster, and way ahead sessions — fully recognized experts from different technical communities in military, academia, and industry. The main topic of the 2016 edition of MESAS was "M&S for Human and Autonomous System Integration and Cooperation." The community of interest submitted 38 papers for consideration. Each submission was reviewed by three Program Committee members. The committee decided to accept 32 papers to be presented in the four regular streams and in one poster session. Main streams were built upon the following topics: integration, interaction and interfaces, frameworks and architectures, AS principles and algorithms, and UAVs and RPAS operational use. The plenary session and way ahead included an extra four invited presentations. Following a thorough review process after the event, 33 papers were accepted to be included in the proceedings.

August 2016   Jan Hodicky

Organization

General Chair

Antonio Bicchi   University of Pisa, Italy

Technical Program Committee Chair

Lucia Pallottino   University of Pisa, Italy

Technical Program Committee

Filippo Arrichiello	University of Cassino and Southern Lazio, Italy
Richard Balogh	Slovak University of Technology in Bratislava, Slovak Republic
Luca Bascetta	Politecnico di Milano, Italy
Agostino Bruzzone	DIME University of Genoa, Italy
Alessandro Cignoni	NATO Center for Maritime Research and Experimentation, Italy
Mark Coeckelbergh	University of Vienna, Austria; De Montfort University, UK
Andrea D'Ambrogio	University of Rome Tor Vergata, Italy
Marek J. Druzdzel	University of Pittsburgh, USA
Jan Hodicky	NATO Modelling and Simulation Centre of Excellence, Italy
Piotr Kosiuczenko	Military University of Technology in Warsaw, Poland
Miroslav Kulich	Czech Technical University in Prague, Czech Republic
Corrado Guarino Lo Bianco	University of Parma, Italy
Giacomo Marani	West Virginia Robotic Technology Center – NASA, USA
Jan Mazal	University of Defence in Brno, Czech Republic
Pierpaolo Murrieri	Finmeccanica, Italy
Lucia Pallottino	University of Pisa, Italy
Stefan Pickl	University of the Bundeswehr in Munich, Germany
Lorenzo Pollini	University of Pisa, Italy
Libor Preucil	Czech Technical University in Prague, Czech Republic
Paolo Proietti	Finmeccanica and MIMOS, Italy
James Sidoran	US Air Force Research Laboratory, USA
Richard Stansbury	Embry-Riddle Aeronautical University in Daytona Beach, USA
Julie Stark	Office of Naval Research Global, USA
Peter Stutz	University of the Bundeswehr in Munich, Germany

Andreas Tolk   Mitre and Old Dominion University in Norfolk, USA
Alberto Tremori   NATO Center for Maritime Research and
                        Experimentation, Italy
Fumin Zhang   Georgia Institute of Technology, USA

MESAS 2016 Logo

MESAS 2016 Organizer

NATO MODELLING AND SIMULATION CENTRE OF EXCELLENCE
(NATO M&S COE)

The NATO M&S COE is a recognized international military organization activated by the North Atlantic Council in 2012, and does not fall under the NATO Command Structure. Partnering Nations provide funding and personnel for the Centre through a memorandum of understanding. The Czech Republic, Italy, and the United States are the contributing nations, as of this publication.

The NATO M&S COE supports NATO Transformation by improving the networking of NATO and nationally owned M&S systems, promoting cooperation between Nations and organizations through the sharing of M&S information and serving as an international source of expertise.

The NATO M&S COE seeks to be a leading world-class organization, providing the best military expertise in modelling and simulation technology, methodologies, and the development of M&S professionals. Its state-of-the-art facilities can support a wide range of M&S activities including but not limited to: Education and Training of NATO M&S professionals on M&S concepts and technology with hands-on courses that expose students to the latest simulation software currently used across the alliance; Concept Development and Experimentation using a wide array of software capability and network connections to test and evaluate military doctrinal concepts as well as new simulation interoperability verification; and the same network connectivity that enables the COE to become the focal point for NATO's future Distributed Simulation environment and services.

https://www.mscoe.org/

NATO M&S CoE Director

Vincenzo Milano

MESAS 2016 Event Director

John Ferrell, NATO M&S COE Deputy Director

MESAS 2016 Event Manager and Proceedings Chair

Jan Hodicky, Doctrine Education and Training Branch Chief in the NATO M&S COE

MESAS 2016 Organizing Committee

Paolo DI BELLA - NATO M&S COE
Carmine DI BLASI - NATO M&S COE
Felice DAIELLO - NATO M&S COE
Paolo Proietti – MIMOS

MESAS 2016 Technical Co-sponsors

IEEE Robotics and Automation Society

IEEE RAS Italian Chapter

IEEE Italy Section Systems Council Chapter

IEEE RAS Multi-robot Systems Technical Committee

IEEE RAS Networked Robots Technical Committee

Movimento Italiano Modellazione e Simulazione

Simulation Team

MESAS 2016 Commercial Sponsors

Contents

Autonomous Systems Principles and Algorithms

Unmanned Aerial Vehicles and Remotely Piloted Aircraft Systems

Modelling and Simulation Application

Human Machine Integration, Interaction and Interfaces

Challenges in Representing Human-Robot Teams in Combat Simulations

Curtis Blais^(✉)

Naval Postgraduate School, Monterey, USA
clblais@nps.edu

Abstract. Unmanned systems are changing the nature of future warfare. Combat simulations attempt to represent essential elements of warfare to support training, analysis, and testing. While combat simulations have rapidly incorporated representations of unmanned systems into their capabilities, little has been done to distinguish unmanned systems from human systems in these simulations. This is making it difficult to impossible to consider questions of future manned/unmanned system mix, levels of unmanned system autonomy required for most effective operational success, and other relevant questions. One might think that replacing humans with fully autonomous unmanned systems, such as in unmanned convoys, results in identical mission performance with the added benefit of a decrease in loss of human life. However, this is a naïve line of reasoning when one considers that unmanned systems cannot react to the battlespace environment with the same level of flexibility as humans. Unfortunately, we have not yet been able to capture such distinctions in combat models. This paper discusses the challenges we face in developing improved models of human systems, robotic systems, and human-robot teams in combat simulations, with examples posed in the context of the Combined Arms Analysis Tool for the 21st Century (COMBATXXI), a discrete-event simulation developed and employed by the U.S. Army and U.S. Marine Corps to address analytical questions about future warfighting capabilities.

Keywords: Human-robot teams · Modeling · Simulation · Unmanned systems · Robotic forces · Autonomous systems · Combat modeling

1 Introduction

Based on the evidence of the first 16 years of the 21st Century, we could very well call this the "Century of Unmanned Systems". While robotic systems have long played a significant role in manufacturing, we are now seeing a widespread proliferation of unmanned systems across all industries, including the military. In [1], Secretary of the United States Navy Ray Mabus is quoted as saying the F-35 Joint Strike Fighter "should be, and almost certainly will be, the last manned strike fighter aircraft the Department of the Navy will ever buy or fly." While this may or may not strictly come to pass, there is clear determination on the part of the United States government to move in this direction. The recent House of Representatives Department of Defense (DoD) Appropriations Bill for 2017 states the following [2, p. 104]:

© Springer International Publishing AG 2016
J. Hodicky (Ed.): MESAS 2016, LNCS 9991, pp. 3–16, 2016.
DOI: 10.1007/978-3-319-47605-6_1

"Section 220 of the Floyd D. Spence National Defense Authorization Act for Fiscal Year 2001 (Public Law 106-398) mandated a goal, regarding unmanned advanced capability combat aircraft and ground combat vehicles, that by the year 2010, one-third of the aircraft in the operational deep strike force fleet would be unmanned, and that by year 2005, one-third of the operational ground combat vehicles would be unmanned."

Furthermore, the House report calls for an update from the DoD on progress toward these congressionally mandated goals by no later than 15 September 2016, requesting a briefing that "shall include an assessment of progress towards meeting the goals identified for the subset of unmanned air and ground systems established in Section 220 of Public Law 106-398, as well as an assessment of existing, viable unmanned ground vehicle technologies that can be economically used for making significant progress toward the achievement of the 2001 goal within the next 5 years." The budget authorizes funds to address such issues as manned-unmanned system teaming, human-machine autonomous command and control environment, carrier-based operations for unmanned aerial vehicles, immersive operator control stations for unmanned systems, unmanned advanced capability combat aircraft and ground combat vehicles, armed robotic platforms deployable with manned platforms, and many other related areas.

In light of the growing commitment to research, development, and deployment of unmanned systems, the Naval Postgraduate School (NPS), Monterey, California, has performed tasking over the past two years to investigate the representation of unmanned systems in Naval combat simulation systems. Initial tasking was sponsored by the NPS Consortium for Robotics and Unmanned System Education and Research (CRUSER) with the objective of investigating the representation of unmanned systems in Naval analytical models, such as the Synthetic Theater Operations Research Model (STORM) and the Combined Arms Analysis Tool for the 21st Century (COM-BATXXI) [3]. The CRUSER program (see http://my.nps.edu/web/CRUSER/) is working to advance the application of robotics systems in military operations through research, education, and field experimentation. A follow-on project, sponsored by the U.S. Office of the Secretary of Defense Joint Ground Robotics Enterprise (JGRE), is exploring enhancement of robotics education, improvement of the representation of robotic systems in combat simulations, and interoperability standards for military robotics systems. The JGRE is the principal organization in DoD for providing oversight, policy, and program direction to establish definitive robotics operational requirements and to pursue critical technologies to satisfy those requirements. The organization focuses on interoperability, modeling and simulation, and test and evaluation.

This paper discusses the challenges we face in developing improved models of human systems, robotic systems, and human-robot teams in combat simulations, with examples posed in the context of the Combined Arms Analysis Tool for the 21st Century (COMBATXXI), a discrete-event simulation developed and employed by the U.S. Army and U.S. Marine Corps to address analytical questions about future warfighting capabilities. In this discussion, we will use the term "robot" or "unmanned system" somewhat interchangeably to refer to the general class of automated systems possessing some mobile capability, whether under direct human control (as in remote-controlled or tele-operated systems) or through semi-autonomous or fully autonomous control (we will look at definitions for these terms later in the paper). Section 2 states the problem under investigation. Section 3 establishes some basic terminology to guide the discussion and to illustrate various dimensions of concern in modeling unmanned systems. Section 4 discusses challenges faced in modeling unmanned systems and human systems separately, elaborating on current deficiencies in modeling humans in combat, and leading to a discussion in Sect. 5 of the challenges in distinguishing human systems from unmanned systems in combat models. This is followed by a brief discussion in Sect. 6 of synergies that will need to be represented in human-robot teams. Section 7 provides a summary and recommendations of possible actions for moving forward to begin addressing the challenges presented herein.

2 Problem Statement

According to many sources, unmanned systems are changing the nature of future warfare. USAF Chief of Staff Gen Mark A Welsh III is quoted as saying, "Increased levels of system autonomy will ensure enhanced capabilities in responding to a range of operations and global challenges" [4]. Such statements have been made in this workshop (Modeling and Simulation for Autonomous Systems) as well, such as: "The more and more frequent adoption of Robotic & Autonomous Systems (RAS) into operations improves the operational efficiency and the soldiers safety" [5, p. 78]. As we saw in the introduction, there is a clear commitment to unmanned systems and related technologies in the U.S. military, and a growing concern over threats from unmanned systems employed by other actors. The Unmanned Systems Integrated Roadmap FY2013-2038 [6, p. 3] indicates the Presidential Budget for Fiscal Year 2014 was over four billion dollars (covering research, development, test and evaluation, procurement, and operations and maintenance), with similar authorizations each year through 2018.

Even with these many claims and the significant commitment to system acquisitions and employments, one wonders if the projections are well ahead of the analysis of operational effectiveness. Some may argue that the veracity of these statements is self-evident; but if so, then how do we quantify the effects? What is the extent of improvement in soldier efficiency? On the surface, it is clear the introduction of unmanned systems (at anything below fully autonomous operation) requires new and challenging activities that soldiers did not perform previously. Regarding safety, there are clear benefits in employment of robotic systems for activities such as explosive ordnance demolition (EOD) and other applications in clearly dangerous environments; but are there other dangers? Some have been surprised that pilots of remotely operated unmanned aircraft can experience significant stress even though they may be thousands of miles from the operating area [7]. If unmanned systems (UMS) and increasing levels of autonomy are truly game-changers, do we have the means to substantiate Gen. Welsh's statement or these other claims? Can we quantify this change in warfighting capability through our principal simulations used to conduct major service and joint analyses? With respect to our analytical combat models, we are ill-equipped currently to validate those claims through modeling and simulation.

Combat simulations attempt to represent essential elements of warfare to support training, analysis, and testing, among other purposes. For example, combat simulations are used in major assessments such as Quadrennial Defense Reviews for Naval system acquisition and future force structure decisions. For several years, the Navy has been adding capabilities to the Synthetic Theater Operations Research Model (STORM) originally developed by the U.S. Air Force. Similarly, the Army and Marine Corps employ a specific analytical model called the Combined Arms Analysis Tool for the 21st Century (COMBATXXI) to evaluate major proposed changes in materiel and associated warfighting operations and tactics. In a review of these simulations in FY15, we found very little explicit representation of unmanned systems. In particular, we found very little capability to distinguish the performance of unmanned systems from human systems in these simulations. This is making it difficult to impossible to consider questions of future manned/unmanned system mix, levels of unmanned system autonomy required for most effective operational success, and other relevant questions. One might think that replacing humans with fully autonomous unmanned systems, such as in unmanned convoys, results in identical mission performance with the added benefit of a decrease in loss of human life. However, this is a naïve line of reasoning when one considers that unmanned systems cannot react to the battlespace environment with the same level of flexibility as humans. Unfortunately, we have not yet been able to represent and explore such distinctions in combat models. It would appear, then, that significant decisions regarding procurement and employment of unmanned systems are being made without an analytical basis that can show the benefits, limitations, and challenges (manpower, training, logistics, combat service support, vulnerabilities, etc.) of introduction of such systems into the battlespace.

Interestingly, the initial research into the representation of unmanned systems in primary analytical simulations raised a new thesis—that current analytical models actually possess, though unintentionally, a higher fidelity representation of autonomous systems than they do of human-operated systems! If this is true, users of current models must change their perspectives considerably. It is well recognized that a major challenge in modeling and simulation is representation of the human element in combat, reflecting human characteristics such as training, fatigue, unit cohesion, intuition, etc. The lack of such modeling extends to the operation of systems by humans, including the operation of unmanned systems (e.g., remote-controlled, tele-operated, etc.). In many respects, it may be argued that current models of the battlespace provide a reasonably accurate depiction of diverse land, air, and sea *autonomous* systems interacting in the battlespace, while poorly representing the human element in the operation of warfare systems. How this change in perspective in understanding the capabilities and validity of current models will affect the analytical and modeling and simulation communities remains to be seen but clearly needs further study. A key issue becomes determining how to better distinguish humans and human-operated systems from autonomous systems so that the models can more correctly represent the effectiveness of all of these systems, and their interactions, in the battlespace.

Having posed this problem, the purpose of this paper is not to solve it, but to illuminate relevant issues and considerations to enable the modeling and simulation community to see the need and to begin efforts in earnest to address the problem.

3 Terminology

In a vision of the future of unmanned systems, Paul Scharre spoke of human-inhabited and uninhabited systems, with the statement that incorporation of increasing automation in uninhabited systems helps them become "true robotic systems" [8]. Such perspectives make one wonder how to classify the emerging "driverless" automobiles that transport humans and allow human override, or autonomous medical evacuation aircraft transporting human casualties – are those "true robotic systems"? In 2008, the National Institute of Standards and Technology issued Special Publication 1011-I-2.0 [9] in an attempt to standardize terminology for this field. Below, we examine key terms and their respective NIST definitions in light of our interest in improving the representation of human and unmanned systems in combat simulations (this was also presented in the June 2015 CRUSER Newsletter, see [10]).

a. **Unmanned System.** NIST defines an *unmanned system* as: "A powered physical system, with no human operator aboard the principal components, which acts in the physical world to accomplish assigned tasks. It may be mobile or stationary. It can include any and all associated supporting components such as OCUs [Operator Control Units, the computer(s), accessories, and data link equipment that an operator uses to control, communicate with, receive data and information from, and plan missions for one or more UMSs]. Examples include unmanned ground vehicles (UGV), unmanned aerial vehicles/systems (UAV/UAS), unmanned maritime vehicles (UMV)—whether unmanned underwater vehicles (UUV) or unmanned water surface borne vehicles (USV)—unattended munitions (UM), and unattended ground sensors (UGS). Missiles, rockets, and their submunitions, and artillery are not considered the principal components of UMSs."

b. **Autonomy.** NIST defines *autonomy* as: "A UMS's own ability of integrated sensing, perceiving, analyzing, communicating, planning, decision-making, and acting/executing, to achieve its goals as assigned by its human operator(s) through designed Human-Robot Interface (HRI) or by another system that the UMS communicates with. UMS's Autonomy is characterized into levels from the perspective of Human Independence (HI), the inverse of HRI. Autonomy is further characterized in terms of Contextual Autonomous Capability (CAC). A UMS's CAC is characterized by the missions that the system is capable of performing, the environments within which the missions are performed, and human independence that can be allowed in the performance of the missions."

c. **Autonomous.** NIST defines *autonomous* as: "Operations of a UMS wherein the UMS receives its mission from either the operator who is off the UMS or another system that the UMS interacts with and accomplishes that mission *with or without* [emphasis mine] further human-robot interaction."

d. **Fully Autonomous.** NIST defines *fully autonomous* as: "A mode of UMS operation wherein the UMS accomplishes it assigned mission, within a defined scope, without human intervention while adapting to operational and environmental conditions."

e. **Semi-Autonomous.** NIST defines *semi-autonomous* as: "A mode of UMS operation wherein the human operator and/or the UMS plan(s) and conduct(s) a mission and requires various levels of HRI. The UMS is capable of autonomous operation in between the human interactions."

f. **Remote Control.** NIST defines *remote control* as: "A mode of UMS operation wherein the human operator controls the UMS on a continuous basis, from a location off the UMS via only her/his direct observation. In this mode, the UMS takes no initiative and relies on continuous or nearly continuous input from the human operator."

g. **Teleoperation.** NIST defines *teleoperation* as: "A mode of UMS operation wherein the human operator, using sensory feedback, either directly controls the actuators or assigns incremental goals on a continuous basis, from a location off the UMS."

From the above definitions, one might consider if the definitions can be applied to humans, as in: "Should human warfighters be considered as fully autonomous or semi-autonomous entities?" Human warfighters (soldier, sailor, Marine, airman, etc.) are often considered as fully autonomous entities, even though they report to some higher command and their actions can be overridden by modified orders from higher command (and, those orders are subject to interpretation, which may or may not correctly align with the commander's intent, and even so are not guaranteed to be obeyed). It may be reasonable to consider humans as semi-autonomous systems when trained to operate in a strict hierarchy, as in military operations, but tending toward greater autonomy when the chain of command breaks down for some reason. We are not advocating a particular point of view here, but suggesting that there are important considerations that should go into representation of humans, just as the different kinds of control over unmanned systems should be an important consideration in the representation of those systems.

Before we turn to the question of modeling human-robot teams, let's consider the state of modeling of human systems and unmanned systems taken separately.

4   Challenges in Modeling Unmanned Systems and Human Systems

In the following subsections, we discuss some of the considerations that may be important in modeling human systems and unmanned systems, as well as in determining distinctive characteristics that will enable us to distinguish human system performance from unmanned system performance in future combat simulations.

4.1   Modeling Unmanned Systems

Although explicit representation of unmanned systems may be lacking from current combat simulations, there is active research and development in the use of simulation to represent robotic systems in synthetic environments. Many recent activities in the international community have been well reported in the 2014 and 2015 proceedings of this workshop. In [11, p. 281], the authors describe synthetic environments as "a powerful tool to perform system testing," providing a "cost-effective option when facing large and/or complex system testing." They go on to state that "simulation-based testing reduces resources use, eliminates risks of failure on real experimentation and increments the safety level." Such sentiments are shared by numerous authors. Tolk [12] points out the preeminent role of modeling and simulation in autonomous systems, even to forming the very "brain" of the autonomous system. One perspective is that this is a result of the idea that the cognitive system of an autonomous unmanned system must form a mental model, just as is the case for human cognition [13]. Tolk also intimates that robotic systems will likely have numerous unexpected failure modes due to the fundamental computational limitations of software, a consideration unique to unmanned systems that will need representation in future simulations.

Several papers from previous Modeling and Simulation for Autonomous Systems Workshops provide useful lists of robotic system simulation frameworks (e.g., see [14–16]), with experimental frameworks and their drawbacks discussed in [17]. Given that modeling and simulation is clearly a key component of the systems engineering process, one path forward for improving the representation of these systems in combat models is to employ the system's internal decision-making logic directly in the combat model. That is, there is no reason to simulate a robotic system when the actual decision-making logic of a particular robotic system is already available in software. The challenge becomes how to represent the objects and characteristics of the synthetic environment with sufficient fidelity to drive effectively the internal robotic system logic. This is, of course, exactly what the robotic systems engineers are doing in their test environments. There needs to be greater intellectual cross-over between the military modeling and simulation community and the robotics engineering community.

4.2 Deficiencies in Modeling Human Behaviors

To reiterate the earlier concern, we assert that combat simulations have long been representing autonomous (unmanned) systems, but doing so under the guise of representing human systems. In the U.S. Marine Corps, for example, combat simulations developed to support command staff training have represented human systems in a highly constrained way, enabling very limited (if any) representation of the variations in human performance from one individual to another and, perhaps more importantly, across different force sides (a singular exception may be considered to be the difference in hit probabilities for different weapon systems used by different forces; such probabilities can be considered to reflect systemic characteristics of the weapons themselves as well as the aggregated skill level of the weapon operators). We turn now to consideration of these deficiencies in modeling human behaviors.

Recognition of the need for greater understanding and representation of human behaviors is not new. In 2002, Vince Roske challenged the analytical community to consider a new class of problems he termed "open" systems [18]. Insertion of a human into a process is one way to change a "closed" system into an "open" system: "The presence of the human being ... produces emergent and adaptive behaviors from the system" (p. 7). He goes on to say, "In a classic command post exercise we inject human decision making into a structured system, a simulated combat environment, to generate open systems behaviors." In a response to Mr. Roske's argument, Vern Wing very clearly spelled out the shortcomings of human behavior modeling [19, pp. 26–27]:

"Traditional approaches to modeling may well be considered 'closed' representations in the sense that human interactions in model event execution have mostly been limited to rule-based control of simulation objects and a priori stipulation of plans (e.g., air tasking orders, scheme of maneuver, etc.) embedded in the model and executed at run time. As a result, our present 'closed' constructive simulations don't account for the impact of human interaction realistically—or at all. ... Our ability to represent the effects of systems within systems and human impacts on them is, at present, virtually non-existent. ... we need to devise a means to inject human-behavior-representation-in-the-loop in constructive simulations."

We would hope, given recognition of the shortcoming, that in the intervening years the industry made significant strides toward addressing the issue. Unfortunately, we find that not to be the case. In 2015, the Army Research Laboratory (ARL) completed a study identifying eleven areas of deficiencies in human modeling; specifically, the areas are identified below with a brief description from the ARL report [20]:

- Cognition: the thought process design comprised of two forms of judgment, rational analysis and intuition. (p. 4)
- Decision science: understanding of "human decision making" and the methods and tools to assist in gaining that understanding. (p. 5)
- Human physiology: the branch of biology that deals with the mechanical, physical, bioelectrical, and biochemical functions of humans in good health, their organs, and the cells of which they are composed; physiological factors include load, hydration, sleep, nutrition, personal, family factors, and unit ethical climate. (p. 6, including [21])
- Human psychology: the scientific study of mental functions and behaviors; major Soldier psychological effects resulting from combat operations are (1) psychiatric casualties suffered during combat; (2) arousal and fear; (3) the effects of close combat; (4) the effects of killing; and, (5) post-traumatic stress disorder (PTSD). (p. 8, including [22])
- Leadership: the ability to influence the actions of others through (1) having a vision about what can be accomplished, (2) making a commitment to the mission and the people you lead, (3) taking responsibility for the accomplishment of the mission and the welfare of those you lead, (4) assuming risk of loss and failure, and (5) accepting recognition for success. (p. 9, including [23])
- Morale: the capacity of people to maintain belief in an institution or a goal, or even in oneself and others; comprises six components: (1) the warrior spirit; (2) unit loyalty and pride; (3) a common shared purpose and goal; (4) trust among Soldiers of all ranks; (5) self-less service; and (6) self-sacrifice. (p. 10, including [24])
- Soldier as family member: examines military family issues associated with readiness, where military readiness is defined as a combination of a Soldier's willingness and ability to do the job during both peacetime and in combat, and the Army's ability to retain that Soldier beyond one enlistment. (pp. 11–12)
- Soldier resilience: the ability to adaptively respond to challenges and adverse events; Soldier resilience is: (1) an essential part of successful transitions in the deployment cycle; (2) critical to facilitating recovery from symptoms of combat stress; and (3) an important way to enhance the effectiveness and decrease the adverse effects of stress in all aspects of military service. More than just stress resistance, resilience is a proactive and adaptive process that emphasizes turning challenges into opportunities. (p. 13; also see http://www.realwarriors.net)

- Stress: the complex and constantly changing result of processes inside a Soldier while performing a combat-related mission, resulting in short-term behaviors that decrease a Soldier's fighting efficiency; common symptoms are fatigue, slower reaction times, indecision, disconnection from one's surroundings, and the inability to prioritize (p. 14, including [25])
- Unit as a complex adaptive system: the self-organizing properties of a unit that emerge from the complex interactions of the Soldiers within the unit and interactions of the unit with external influences, such as other units, enemy forces, the environment, etc. (p. 16)
- Unit cohesion: interpersonal bonds among unit members (social cohesion) or a shared commitment to the unit's mission (task cohesion). (p. 17, including [26])

Of these eleven areas, there were only two considered sufficiently "mature and accessible enough to support the initial prototyping and demonstration effort;" namely, human physiology, as implemented in the ARL Soldier Load Augmented Training Environment (SLATE) application, and stress, as implemented in a new application called the Effect of Stress (EoS) application "to simulate the cumulative effects of stress on the marksmanship of the individual Soldier" [20, p. viii]. Work in these areas has progressed over the past year.

There have been significant advances in the modeling of human cognition in recent years, as best exemplified in the success of products such as SOAR (see http://www. soartech.com) and ACT-R (see http://act-r.psy.cmu.edu/). Recent efforts have seen SOAR introduced into constructive simulations such as the Naval Simulation System (NSS; see http://www.metsci.com/Division/ORCA/Naval-Simulation-System-NSS-2), but such capabilities remain under evaluation for simulations such as COMBATXXI.

It is also interesting to compare the ARL findings with Mr. Wing's observations from 2002. He identified the following areas as being critical for representing human behavior: learning and competence; cognition; and adaptive behavior. Regarding the latter, he observed that humans have a unique capacity for adapting the environment rather than adapting to it [19, p. 28]:

> "The soldier who hears a round fired and ducks is adapting to his environment. The soldier who digs a foxhole, stacks sand bags, erects fortifications, seeds a minefield to limit avenues of approach, employs jamming to deny communications or surveillance, is adapting the environment. These behaviors are markedly different, and while we may be able to simulate the former, I am not convinced we have scratched the surface of the latter."

In COMBATXXI, developers had the foresight to include a software package for Human Physiology, but very little capability is implemented there at this time. The package contains Java classes for human health that currently deal with treatment of wounds, transitions from wounded to killed in the case of untreated severe wounds, suppression, and military operational protection posture (MOPP) level. The code documentation admits to the possibility of the logic dealing with other aspects concerning the health and well-being of combatants, such as fatigue, hunger, and thirst. This part of the COMBATXXI is well-suited to incorporating new models related to human physiology, and raises the possibility of creating additional packages for Human Psychology and other constructs designed to address the areas identified in the ARL study. Inquiries have begun to try to obtain the ARL software prototypes for use in investigating integration of these models in COMBATXXI, and to work closely with ARL as models of other areas become available.

5   Identifying Distinctions in Human and Unmanned Systems

As we move forward, it is necessary that we have the ability to distinguish human systems from unmanned systems in our simulations. The areas of deficiency in human modeling identified by ARL may provide a framework for consideration of the distinctions between representation of human and unmanned systems. For example, without trying to address the idea exhaustively, consider the notional contrasts/comparisons presented in Table 1.

While any of the entries in the table are open to debate (a welcomed debate), the considerations laid out in the table for humans suggest that the models of several of these factors will be difficult to develop, since several factors apparently are highly dependent on other factors and, in fact, may emerge from the complex interplay of several of the other factors. It is small wonder that such modeling has been postponed in favor of more simplified approaches in representing humans. However, there are clear distinctions in the considerations for humans and those for unmanned systems across these eleven factors that need to be addressed if we are to create effective distinctions between capabilities and performance of these systems.

When considering modeling approaches such as those embodied in products like SOAR and ACT-R, there is an interesting technical dilemma. If human cognition can be modeled in software, then that decision-making logic can be incorporated into an unmanned system (indeed, companies like SOARTech are currently doing so), in which case we have again lost or confounded the distinction between humans and unmanned systems. Clearly, there are intangible characteristics of human behaviors that must be represented in software logic in a different way to make the resulting behaviors explicitly distinguishable from unmanned system behaviors.

6   Capturing Synergies in Human-Robot Teaming

In the discussion above, we have laid out the principal difficulty in moving forward in the representation of human-robot teams. We contend that is it not enough to simply insert additional "human-like" entities into the simulations and call them "unmanned systems" possessing nearly the same behaviors implemented in nearly the same ways. Something more needs to be represented, as pointed out in the section on distinguishing humans from unmanned systems. If we can solve the problem of representing humans and unmanned systems separately, the next challenge will be in characterizing the synergies, or complications, that will be achieved in humans and robots working together to achieve mission objectives. If the first part is done well, the latter should exhibit as an emergent quality of the interaction of humans and unmanned systems. This is not how the problem is currently being addressed.

The NIST document referenced earlier [9] also identifies a variety of roles that humans will perform in human-robot interactions (HRI), to include Supervisor,

Table 1. Distinguishing characteristics of manned and unmanned systems

Factor	Considerations: humans	Considerations: unmanned systems
Cognition	Individual; highly variable and in complex interplay with other factors; attempt to enhance through training and education	Programmed; highly constrained; low to no variability by model
Decision science	Individual; highly variable and in complex interplay with other factors; attempt to regularize through training	Programmed; highly constrained; low to no variability by model
Human physiology	Individual; highly variable and in complex interplay with other factors; attempt to meet standard levels (e.g., strength, endurance, speed) through training	Mechanical/physical characteristics (e.g., reliability, fatigue, energy requirements) defined by hardware specifications; low to no variability by model (within manufactured tolerances)
Human psychology	Individual; highly variable and in complex interplay with other factors; attempt to meet standard capabilities through training	Not Applicable
Leadership	Individual; highly variable and in complex interplay with other factors; attempt to meet standard capabilities and build capacity through training	Programmed; highly constrained (e.g., as in leader-follower movement behaviors)
Morale	Individual; highly variable and in complex interplay with other factors; attempt to maintain within tolerances through training, esprit d'corps, etc.	Not applicable
Soldier as family member	Individual; highly variable and in complex interplay with other factors; attempt to maintain within tolerances through social programs	Not applicable
Soldier resilience	Individual; highly variable and in complex interplay with other factors; attempt to regulate through training	Programmed (as in agility to handle unexpected inputs); highly constrained; low to no variability by model
Stress	Individual; highly variable and in complex interplay with other factors; attempt to regulate through training	Physical/mechanical in accordance with hardware and software specifications; low to no variability by model (within manufactured tolerances)
Unit as a complex adaptive system	Individual (by unit) quality emerging from internal and external interactions (including interactions with unmanned systems); attempt to regulate through training	Some systems will have a programmed opportunity to display self-organizing or emergent behaviors based on interactions with other systems, but highly constrained by design
Unit cohesion	Individual perception of cohesion; highly variable and in complex interplay with other factors; attempt to maintain through training	Not applicable

Teammate/Wingman, Operator, Mechanic/Developer, and Bystander. In [27], the authors relate human roles (in their case, tasking user, planner, and pilot) to levels of autonomy, showing that there are differences in the way humans will perform when working with different kinds of unmanned systems. These roles and relationships raise additional questions about how the performance of human-unmanned system teams operating in various role-mission configurations will be distinguished from each other in future combat models to provide critical guidance to the formation of effective tactics, techniques, and procedures. Moreover, teaming of humans and robots raises numerous questions regarding potential changes in the psychology of the human operators compared to their command of other humans. For example, will humans be less concerned over loss of materiel when operating unmanned systems than if they were commanding humans in the field? What will be the effect on the human operator when he/she has grown dependent on employment of unmanned systems and the system is damaged or destroyed? How will the human adapt to the change in capability? How will future training cope with such issues? These are very nuanced considerations, but again, there is no foundation currently in our simulations to be able to address such questions.

7   Conclusions and Recommendations

As greater numbers of unmanned systems, in ever-increasing levels of complexity, are introduced into the military inventory, we must modernize our representations of these systems and the humans who interact with them, to begin to address a new wave of analytical questions related to future warfighting. It is not enough to simply accept the extraordinary claims made about the effects of unmanned systems on future warfare. We have come to a point in combat modeling where we can no longer be satisfied with simplistic models of human performance. We must be able to investigate the complex interplay that will occur among humans and unmanned systems. Suffice to say, we are in the early stages of a fascinating era of research and development that will bring about greater precision in our concepts and terminology relating to unmanned systems, while likely redefining our notions of manned systems as well. It is recommended that the robotics community and modeling and simulation community come together with human performance researchers to begin to address these issues, and that models like COMBATXXI be leveraged as platforms for incorporating and exploring new representations enabling analysts to begin to better understand future combat effectiveness and challenges that will emerge from the employment of unmanned systems.

Acknowledgements. The work presented here was sponsored by the Naval Postgraduate School Consortium for Robotics and Unmanned System Education and Research (CRUSER) and the Office of the Secretary of Defense Joint Ground Robotics Enterprise (JGRE). However, opinions expressed in this paper are solely those of the author and are not to be interpreted as the official position of either of those organizations.

References

1. McCaney, K.: Key tech for UAS: it's more than just flying and spying. Defense Systems, May/June (2015), pp. 16–17. https://www.scribd.com/doc/309614026/Defense-Systems-May-June. Accessed 1 July 2016
2. House of Representatives Department of Defense Appropriations Bill for 2017. House Report 114–577, Report of the Committee on Appropriations
3. Blais, C.: Representation of unmanned systems in naval analytical modeling and simulation: what are we really simulating? CRUSER Newsletter. Naval Postgraduate School, Monterey, CA. p. 6, January 2015. http://my.nps.edu/documents/105302057/105304189/CRUSER_News_2015_01.pdf/394047fa-9f16-4c12-bba4-7b8b28e201ee. Accessed 1 July 2016
4. Secretary, USAF Public Affairs (2015)
5. Fedi, F., Nasca, F.: Interoperability issues reduction in command and control for multi-robot systems. In: Hodicky, J. (ed.) Modelling and Simulation for Autonomous Systems: Second International Workshop, MESAS 2015. LNCS, vol. 9055, pp. 77–89. Springer International Publishing, Switzerland (2015)
6. Department of Defense. Unmanned Systems Integrated Roadmap FY2013-2038. Reference Number: 14-S-0553 (2013)
7. Dao, J.: Drone pilots are found to get stress disorders much as those in combat do. New York Times, 22 February 2013. http://www.nytimes.com/2013/02/23/us/drone-pilots-found-to-get-stress-disorders-much-as-those-in-combat-do.html. Accessed 1 July 2016
8. Scharre, P.: Robotics on the Battlefield Part II: The Coming Swarm. Center for a New American Security, October 2014
9. Huang, H.M.: Autonomy Levels for Unmanned Systems (ALFUS) Framework Volume I: Terminology Version 2.0. National Institute of Standards and Technology. Special Publication 1011-I-2.0, October (2008)
10. Blais, C.: What is an autonomous system? Are we talking about the same things? CRUSER Newsletter. Naval Postgraduate School, Monterey, CA, September (2015)
11. Alejo, C., Alejo, I., Rodriguez, Y., Stoilov, J., Viguria, A.: Simulation engineering tools for algorithm development and validation applied to unmanned systems. In: Hodicky, J. (ed.) MESAS 2014. LNCS, vol. 8906, pp. 281–291. Springer, Heidelberg (2014)
12. Tolk, A.: Modeling and simulation interoperability concepts for multidisciplinarity, interdisciplinarity, and transdisciplinarity – implications for computational intelligence enabling autonomous systems. In: Hodicky, J. (ed.) MESAS 2015. LNCS, vol. 9055, pp. 60–74. Springer International Publishing, Switzerland (2015)
13. Lipshitz, R., Shaul, O.B.: Schemata and mental models in recognition-primed decision making. In: Caroline, E.Z., Gary, K. (eds.) Naturalistic Decision Making, pp. 293–303. Lawrence Erlbaum Associates Publishers, Mahwah (1997)
14. Ferrati, M., Settimi, A., Pallottino, L.: ASCARI: a component based simulator for distributed mobile robot systems. In: Hodicky, J. (ed.) MESAS 2014. LNCS, vol. 8906, pp. 152–163. Springer, Heidelberg (2014)
15. Vonásek, V., Fišer, D., Košnar, K., Přeučil, L.: A light-weight robot simulator for modular robotics. In: Hodicky, J. (ed.) MESAS 2014. LNCS, vol. 8906, pp. 206–216. Springer, Heidelberg (2014)
16. Mingo Hoffman, E., Traversaro, S., Rocchi, A., Ferrati, M., Settimi, A., Romano, F., Natale, L., Bicchi, A., Nori, F., Tsagarakis, N.G.: Yarp based plugins for gazebo simulator. In: Hodicky, J. (ed.) MESAS 2014. LNCS, vol. 8906, pp. 333–346. Springer, Heidelberg (2014)

17. Hodicky, J.: HLA as an experimental backbone for autonomous system integration into operational field. In: Hodicky, J. (ed.) MESAS 2014. LNCS, vol. 8906, pp. 121–126. Springer, Heidelberg (2014)

18. Roske, V.P.: Opening up military analysis: exploring beyond the boundaries. Phalanx **35**(2), 1 (2002)

19. Wing, V.F.: Avoiding 'ready, shoot, aim': an alternate view of beyond the boundaries. Phalanx **35**(4), 26–28 (2002)

20. Fefferman, K., Diego, M., Gaughan, C., Samms, C., Borum, H., Clegg, J., McDonnell, J.S., Leach, R.: A study in the implementation of a distributed soldier representation. ARL-TR-6985. Army Research Laboratory, March 2015

21. Belenky, G.: Sleep, sleep deprivation and human performance in continuous operations. Walter Reed Army Institute of Research. United States Army Medical Research and Materiel Command, 16 March 2004

22. Grossman, D., Siddle, B.K.: Psychological Effects of Combat. Academic Press, Cambridge (2000)

23. Mills, D.Q.: The Importance of Leadership (2005)

24. Cox, A.A.: Unit Cohesion and Morale in Combat. U.S. Army School of Advanced Military Studies, 14 December 1995

25. U.S. Army Medical Department. Guide to Coping with Deployment and Combat Stress. TG320. Army Public Health Center, September 2014. https://usaphcapps.amedd.army.mil/HIOShoppingCart/viewItem.aspx?id=124. Accessed 1 July 2016

26. Evans, N.J., Dion, K.L., Gully, S.M., Devine, D.J., Whitney, D.J., MacCoun, R.J., Mullen, B., Copper, C.: Unit Cohesion and the Military Mission (1996)

27. Woolven, T., Vernall, P., Skinner, C.: Human-machine communications for autonomous systems. In: Hodicky, J. (ed.) MESAS 2014. LNCS, vol. 8906, pp. 321–332. Springer, Heidelberg (2014)

Data, Speed, and Know-How: Ethical and Philosophical Issues in Human-Autonomous Systems Cooperation in Military Contexts

Mark Coeckelbergh[✉] and Michael Funk

Department of Philosophy, University of Vienna, Vienna, Austria
{mark.coeckelbergh, michael.funk}@univie.ac.at

Abstract. Human-Autonomous Systems Cooperation raises several ethical and philosophical issues that need to be addressed not only at the stage of implementation of the system but also preferably at the stage of development. This paper identifies and discusses some of these issues, with a specific focus on human-machine cooperation problems and chances, focusing usage of these systems in military contexts. It is argued that ethical, philosophical, and technical problems include (1) data security and monitoring/management, (2) agency, distancing and speed/time, and (3) cooperation, networks and knowledge. These issues need to be taken into account not only in the application but also in processes of research and development and legal regulation.

Keywords: Human-machine cooperation · Ethics · Drones · Cyberwar · HFT · Speed · Time · Knowledge · Networks

1 Introduction

When technologies are no longer mere tools or extensions of the human, but acquire a high degree of "agency" themselves, different concepts have to be used to describe the relation between humans and machines. Systems such as autopilots or autonomous robots are no longer simply tools or even extensions of the (human) body; instead there is a relation that may be described by using the terms "cyborg" (merging of human and machine) or "cooperation" between human and non-human agents (cooperation between different agents, no merging). These new configurations raise several ethical and philosophical questions, such as: "Who is responsible for unintended damage, caused by an autonomous system?" This paper mainly focuses its discussion on cooperation problems in a military context. However, self-driving cars and traffic guidance systems, financial technologies of high speed trading (HFT = "High Frequency Trading"), as well as autopilots and drones (UAVs = "Unmanned Aerial Vehicles") will also be discussed as ethically challenging forms of autonomous systems which may lead to military applications.

© Springer International Publishing AG 2016
J. Hodicky (Ed.): MESAS 2016, LNCS 9991, pp. 17–24, 2016.
DOI: 10.1007/978-3-319-47605-6_2

2 Data Security and Monitoring/Management

A first ethical issue concerns the security of the data, given that autonomous systems are not only autonomous agents, but also smart devices – embedded into IT-networks, linked to computers, databases etc. Autonomous systems collect an enormous amount of data, which raises the question (firstly) who has access to it, or could potentially force access to it, and (secondly) what can be done with that information. Who is responsible for the interpretation of images or semantic information? E.g. in drone-operations target-profiles play a major role. Who creates such profiles and will be held responsible, if collateral damage or illegal actions are performed on the basis of deficient target-profiles? Aspects of dual use and collateral damage – even friendly fire – include a cyber-component. In military contexts there clearly is this danger. Consider for instance the case of a US-American RQ-170 Sentinel drone "hacked" down by Iranian organs in December 2011 [1]. It is important to deal with these data-vulnerabilities and risks, especially since human lives are at stake. How to protect data and defense infrastructures? The network-factor and connection of technologies (especially IT) causes strong challenges here. Should we disconnect critical infrastructure? What about care-robots or medical bots which collect a lot sensitive data (in order to function successfully)? In times of international terrorism and IT-based warfare, those "civil" structures might become targets of "military" hits as well.

Conceptual understandings of "new wars" vs. "old wars" or "symmetric warfare" vs. "asymmetric warfare" after the collapse of Soviet Union and 1990th Yugoslav Wars have been emphasized primarily in political and social terms by Kaldor [2] and Münkler [3]. But cyberwar [4, 5] once more became a new technological category of warfare and cyber can be seen as new strategic operation-sphere such as "land", "air", "water", "underwater" or "space". At the same time, "cyber" affects all classical spheres, as information technologies are used in nearly every situation. When the line between conventional and cyber warfare becomes blurred by means of these new technologies – and as even the classical categories of combatant and non-combatant become blurry as well – military organizations and politicians have to rethink how they invest and organize defense infrastructures and capacities – both in civil as well as in military situations. As one consequence of IT-developments, even the meaning of "military context", becomes questionable as well, given the use and development of IT across several domains. The application of data and information (not only semantics but also images etc.) causes new forms of actions such as more sublime forms of propaganda or blackmailing. Hackers without any classical military education could perform cyber-attacks and cause economic, psychological (especially in case of terrorism) or material damage. Where is the borderline between combatant-hackers and non-combatant-hackers? In military contexts, privacy plays another role than in civil life. But if the categories civil vs. military are changing, the limits of privacy in certain contexts of usage might also change. Ethics of data-security and information-protection in military contexts involves the problem that the values of security and safety are in tension with the values of data-security and privacy. The more secure and safe a system or society is intended to be, the more information is needed in order to ensure success. There is thus an ethical conflict between public security on the one side and data security, data privacy and information protection on the other side, e.g.:

- protect society against attacks of other nations, including espionage,
- protect society against terrorist attacks, or
- protect society against crime.

Those cases include the protection against attacks which come out of the own society (whether terroristic, criminal etc. motivated). Here we might find arguments for supporting a more strict form of surveillance of public life. But on the other hand free access to information and privacy are important moral values, which not only cause liberal political life, but also economic success and creativity (in order to create innovations).

Note that the same dilemma is characteristic for usage of data for the monitoring and management of people from one's own organization as well. Does monitoring of personnel via these technologies enhance responsible and effective behavior, or does it potentially create unworkable situations for people who are already under pressure? Putting in other words: Efficiency or Burnout? Does the flow of data enhance the safety and security of people? Or could it lead to decisions taken at a distance on the basis of data that may not correspond to the local situated and experienced knowledge of the people who use the technology? This raises knowledge problems (see below, part four). Anyway historical experiences (such as the economic collapse of GDR in 1989/90) illustrated: STASI-like surveillance diminished economic and technological efficiency. Human creativity is not such easily accessible for data-monitoring.

3 Agency, Distancing, and Speed

A second ethical issue concerns the agency of technologies and, related to that in a military context, the problem of speed. If for instance a robot is given more autonomy, technically speaking (acting on its own), decisions have to be made with regard to the degree of supervision of the robot. There are good ethical reasons to keep humans in the loop if the machine has lethal capacities (see also [6]), to ensure human judgment and human responsibility. We like to support the argument, that even so called "autonomous" systems remain means for human ends: "people kill people". However, it is a realistic scenario that if, in a military context, many autonomous systems are "employed"/applied and there might be – metaphorically speaking – an "arms race", the speed of war will increase to such a point that perhaps only non-human, autonomous systems can process what is going on and therefore make decisions. This is ethically problematic if one assumes that human judgment should be involved in actions that may have lethal consequences (for people of the own organization or for others). A ban on such systems may prevent this, but if such a ban were not very effective (which is also a realistic scenario), how can and should military organizations and societies deal with this problem?

A related problem raised by the new information technologies concerns distance as well. For instance drones seem to make the decision of lethal actions easier, but at the same time also create new forms of proximity or even intimacy that may make such actions and decisions less easy [7]. The point is that drone-operators sit thousands of kilometers away from the target, only present on a medial level with real-time images.

That might make killing easier. But on the other hand, drone-operators observe their victims a long time before starting a lethal strike. Here, the real-time pictures somehow bridge the physical distance and enable something like proximity or intimacy. There are also similar problems with technologies in civil contexts. Financial technologies [8] and high-speed treading can be seen as pre-forms or already existing forms of autonomous systems and real-time decision making under conditions that nearly exclude humans given the speed. There are paradoxical effects that have to do with the relation between speed and distance. Pre-computer and historical distance weapons (such as archery, muskets or ballistic artillery) are bound to a physical sphere where speed, time and the location as well as distance have been linked to each other: distance means a temporal delay of information, speed means higher distance of a projectile etc. But with computers and drones (again information technologies) it became possible to generate real-time images at the scale of global distance. Cyber-attacks and high frequency algorithm based counter-attacks might also be realized in real-time on a transcontinental scale. A physical link between time and space is suspended: in consequence of IT-embedded warfare, physical distance no longer means safety [9].

Again ethical problems enter the stage when it comes to decision making: automatized cyber-attacks in real time are situated in a temporal microcosm, in which the human bodily-sensory temporal mesocosm of ethical reflection or legal judgment is suspended. How can the problem of this gap between two worlds be addressed? Thus, here is an ethical conflict between the fact that the IT-basis of drones or cyber-operations enables real time decision making, but that human assessment and responsibility requires keeping temporal distance for reflection and ethical, legal or political evaluation [10]. What can be the solution? Slowing down the speed of warfare? Mechanical typewriters instead of PCs?

To further reflect on this problem concerning speed and distance, we propose to use the work of Virillo [11, 12] who offers a theory of 'dromology' (societal impacts of speed and acceleration) and also presents a paradoxical interrelation between acceleration and deceleration at the same time. Inspired by his theory, once more we want to argue that information technological networks as basis for autonomous military technologies cause an accelerated cyber-sphere (temporal microcosm) which is separated from the temporal sphere of political, ethical or juridical decision making (temporal mesocosm).

To clarify more our understanding of "temporal microcosm", we like to draw the analogy to technical mediations and visual perception. Microscopes are tools which reveal visual microworlds: e.g. perception of bacteria, cells or even smaller things. In 17th- and 18th-century sciences Antoni van Leeuwenhoek became one prominent pioneer in the field of microscopy. Even before that in the 16th- and 17th-century developments, scientists like Galileo Galilei, Johannes Kepler or Tycho Brahe started systematically using telescopes for empirical astronomic observations. Microscopes technologically reveal visual microworlds (very small), whereas telescopes enable perceptual access to visual macroworlds (very big). Glasses are examples for technologies applied in human mesocosm, because they should not translate very small worlds (microcosm) or very large worlds (macrocosm) into a human sensory scale. Instead glasses are used in order to mediate mesoworlds, which means not enhancing visual capabilities, but moreover compensate visual disabilities without leaving human sensory range of perception. Now the argument in context of time and IT-embedded warfare is that information technologies are related to very small worlds, not on the visual, but on the temporal level. The difference to microscopes here is accessibility. Whereas microscopes make invisible things visible, high frequency IT-embedded processes disable access because they do not bridge but cause a gap between speed and human capabilities of decision making.

There is also a meta-ethical issue concerning temporal forms of future and present: every ethics is linked to a concrete future as ethics always emphasizes following human actions, their consequences, conditions and values. When high-speed-wars are functionally performed in a temporal microcosm that appears to humans as "present" (we are too slowly, we cannot perceive it), what does this mean for ethics and its innate link to a concrete "future"? How is future (and past) possible in real time-actions? Future is a human-pragmatic term, which loses its meaning within real-time warfare (or high-speed trading etc.). Insofar IT-high-speed warfare could lead to the paradoxical consequence that the classical Clausewitz slogan "War is the continuation of politics by other means" [13] becomes useless, as means do not longer support a political aim, but disable political decision making in an unintended way. Three temporal logics of warfare and politics can be distinguished for illustrating this development:

- 19th-century understanding of warfare following the theoretical approach of Carl Philipp Gottlieb von Clausewitz: no nukes or ICT (bodily-mechanic temporal mesocosm, physical and physiological linking between space and time).
- 20th-century understanding of warfare including capabilities of nuclear weapons, ICBM and submarines: if nuclear strike starts, there will be enough time (minutes) for a counterstrike (still temporal mesocosm), in relation to the danger of destroying whole mankind and thereby destroying any political future on the one hand, but nuclear standoff became an element of political practice on the other hand as well.
- 21st-century ICT-related warfare: a temporal microcosm logically suspends politics as high-speed processes do not allow human decision making, fully autonomous real-time warfare might not necessarily destroy mankind as such, but "war" loses its meaning as means for political ends (political instrumental rationality is suspended) [10].

Deceleration in military contexts is often related to defensive situations (castles, partisan tactics etc.) or caused by economic benefits of "new wars" [3]. We think in consequence of the temporal microcosm deceleration becomes a legal and ethical demand as well.

4 Human-Machine Collaboration and Knowledge

A third, related and ethically relevant but also technical and philosophical issue concerns problems regarding human-machine collaboration. Even if the above mentioned problems could be addressed in a satisfactory way, decisions have to be made concerning the division of work and the distribution of knowledge (and responsibility) in hybrid human/machine systems. Such problems are analogous to those with (civil and military) airplanes. For instance, if there is an emergency, should the autonomous system be given priority, or should humans decide, even if they may be wrong? The same questions plays a crucial role in the context of self-driving cars and traffic guidance systems, where similar decisions have to be made. This raises the question what kind of knowledge autonomous systems (computing systems, robots, etc.) have, as opposed to human beings, and in which way knowledge is distributed in cooperative contexts and embedded in networks. Knowledge is needed in a situation for decision making and for acting responsibly. But how exactly do the new technologies change the knowledge configuration? Human beings interpret data, but autonomous systems also do so – based on code written by humans which enable the system to model what is going on in its environment. However, the way humans arrive at a judgment tends to be different, since humans are embodied, have emotions, and so on. They can also improvise, have a different kind of know-how. Some argue that therefore the autonomous systems should be given the final decision (to avoid emotional judgment, war crime etc.), whereas others think that humans should be given control since the kind of knowledge autonomous systems have is more limited. But what if autonomous systems have access to much more data than humans ("big data")? Or is this not the same as having knowledge? What is the difference between data, information, and knowledge?

Moreover, how universal is the way we arrive at knowledge? Does the development of autonomous systems currently take into account cultural differences? What is the knowledge-base for ethical judgments? And what kind of weapons give rise to what kind of knowledge? Compare for instance traditional Japanese or Chinese theories of war- and martial-arts with current IT-embedded warfare. Ancient sword-fights require deeply embodied knowledge, a high level of sensory skills, fast perception (into the human scale, temporal mesocosm), but also tactical knowledge. Japanese approaches of samurai sword fights [14, 15] include a strong ethos of social relations between samurai, sword, enemy, and master (something like a "feudal lord" who is the commander). Samurai sword fight theory is pretty individually oriented, because the warrior and its embodied tacit knowledge of using the sword are the conceptual epicenter of this kind of warfare. On the other hand tactical and strategic knowledge including a lot of bodily elements is integrated in the ancient Chinese approach as well [16]. But in this case not so much the individual swordfighter, but moreover the general and the way he leads troops in several situations is emphasized from a primary point of view. Again the tactical and strategic understanding of how to use geographical factors, time and rhythm of strike and counter-strike, defense and offense movements, or integration of spies is related to bodily and physiological temporal and spatial mesoworlds. The physical and bodily link between time and space remains an important axiom of those theories of warfare [10]. Insofar implicit knowledge or tacit knowledge, which needs to be generated within processes of trial and error, and is more than theoretical textbook-information, serves as the primary knowledgebase.

But what kind of knowledge is involved in (big) data analysis, computer modeling, etc.? Is this disembodied knowledge, and if so in what sense? If not, how does the embodied relation, mediated by the new technologies, differ from earlier technologically mediated ways of fighting? Also the issue of distance plays a crucial role here (see also [6, 7]). Can we wield a drone with a distance of 10.000 km such as a sword or gun in our hands? Can real-time computer pictures and joysticks in an isolated container replace both the whole-body-perception and -knowledge of a regular soldier in a battlefield? What does this mean for the attribution of responsibility and the ways we know how to detect ethical conflicts and to deal with it? Fact is that skills, emotions, intuition or sensory perceptions belong to a different domain of knowledge than computer-algorithms [17–20].

As we have seen the relations and meaning of time and space are changing. Bodily spheres of spatial-temporal knowing are replaced by cyber spheres of real-time actions. Those actions are enabled by a temporal microcosm. It is both an ethical and epistemological task to understand the structures of this new spatial-temporal form of warfare. For ethics and political philosophy applied to this problem, it might be the primary task to identify the exact ethical limits of autonomous decision-making. A gap of knowledge and a lack of time for assessment could cause inhumane consequences, collateral-damage or maybe terminator-scenarios etc. There is a need for legal regulation of new warfare and its technological structures, and for societal scenarios that explore the many ways we use and not-use those new possibilities. And, finally, these new technologies remain challenging for thinking about ethics. What is ethical decision-making, and can and should it be delegated to machines?

It may also be helpful to try to answer these questions by engaging with frameworks that are being developed in computer science and engineering. For instance, Modelling and Simulation (M&S) might help to answer the previous questions regarding knowledge involved in computer modeling. And when thinking about ethics one could look at M&S experimental frameworks build upon common vocabularies in the form of Autonomous System and M&S ontologies that aim to cover the ethical aspects [21, 22].

5 Conclusion

This paper has identified a number of ethical and philosophical problems raised by new developments in the area of autonomous systems and their actual or potential use in a military context. Particular attention has been paid to issues related to security of data flows, agency and speed/distance, and knowledge in cooperative human/autonomous system configurations. We identified ethical problems and conflicts with regard to security, speed, and cooperation, and also pointed to cultural differences with regard to knowledge in ethics and related to military technologies. It is important to take these problems into account not only when using but also when developing autonomous systems for defense/warfare. More research is needed on the (potential) impact of these systems on ethics and responsibility, and ultimately on the forms of warfare and the kinds of societies we will have in the future.

References

1. Biermann, K., Wiegold, T.: Drohnen. Chancen und Gefahren einer neuen Technik. Ch. Links Verlag, Berlin (2015)
2. Kaldor, M.: Neue und alte Kriege. Organisierte Gewalt im Zeitalter der Globalisierung. Suhrkamp, Frankfurt a.M. (2007)

3. Münkler, H.: Der Wandel des Krieges. Von der Symmetrie zur Asymmetrie. 3. Auflage. Velbrück Wissenschaft, Weilerswist (2014)
4. Gaycken, S.: Jenseits von 1984. Datenschutz und Überwachung in der fortgeschrittenen Informationsgesellschaft. Eine Versachlichung. Transcript Verlag, Bielefeld (2012)
5. Gaycken, S.: Cyberwar: Das Wettrüsten hat längst begonnen. Goldmann Verlag, München (2012)
6. Coeckelbergh, M.: Drones, morality, and vulnerability: two arguments against automated killing. In: Custers, B. (ed.) The Future of Drone Use. Qpportunities and Threats from Ethical and Legal Perspectives. T.M.C. Asser Press, Hague (2016, forthcoming)
7. Coeckelbergh, M.: Drones, information technology, and distance: mapping the moral epistemology of remote fighting. Ethics Inf. Technol. 15(2), 87–98 (2013)
8. Coeckelbergh, M.: Money Machines. Electronic Financial Technologies, Distancing, and Responsibility in Global Finance. Ashgate, Farnham (2015)
9. Funk, M.: Drohnen und sogenannte 'autonom-intelligente' Technik im Kriegseinsatz. Philosophische und ethische Fragestellungen. In: Funk, M., Leuteritz, S., Irrgang, B. (eds.) Cyberwar @ Drohnenkrieg. Neue Kriegstechnologien philosophisch betrachtet. Königshausen & Neumann, Würzburg (2016, forthcoming)
10. Funk, M.: Zeit als Element technologischer Kriegsführun. In: Funk, M., Leuteritz, S., Irrgang, B. (eds.) Cyberwar @ Drohnenkrieg. Neue Kriegstechnologien philosophisch betrachtet. Königshausen & Neumann, Würzburg (2016, forthcoming)
11. Virillo, P.: Speed and Politics: An Essay on Dromology. Semiotext(e), New York (1977/1986)
12. Virillo, P.: Negative Horizon: An Essay in Dromoscopy. Continuum, London (1989)
13. Clausewitz, C.V.: Vom Kriege. Reclam, Stuttgart (1994)
14. Musashi, M.: Fünf Ringe. Die Kunst des Samurai-Schwertweges. Trans. by Siegfried Schaarschmidt. Nikol Verlag, Hamburg (2008)
15. Yamamoto, J.: Hagakure. Ed. by Tsuramoto Tashiro. Trans. by Max Seinsch. Reclam, Stuttgart (2009)
16. Sunzi: Die Kunst des Krieges. Trans. by Dr. Hannelore Eisenhofer. Nikol Verlag, Hamburg (2011)
17. Polanyi, M.: Personal Knowledge: Towards a Post-Critical Philosophy. University of Chicago Press, Chicago (1958)
18. Dreyfus, H.: What Computers Can't Do: The Limits of Artificial Intelligence. MIT Press, New York (1972)
19. Ferguson, E.S.: Engineering and the Mind's Eye. MIT Press, New York (1992)
20. Funk, M., Coeckelbergh, M.: Is gesture knowledge? A philosophical approach to the epistemology of musical gestures. In: De Preester, H. (ed.) Moving Imagination – Explorations of Gesture and Inner Movement in the Arts, pp. 113–132. John Benjamins Publishing Company, Amsterdam (2013)
21. Hodicky, J.: HLA as an experimental backbone for autonomous system integration into operational field. In: Hodicky, J. (ed.) MESAS 2014. LNCS, vol. 8906, pp. 121–126. Springer, Heidelberg (2014)
22. Hodicky, J.: Modelling and simulation in the autonomous systems' domain-current status and way ahead. In: Hodicky, J. (ed.) MESAS 2015. LNCS, vol. 9055, pp. 17–23. Springer, Heidelberg (2015)

Human-Machine Interface for Multi-agent Systems Management Using the Descriptor Function Framework

Giovanni Franzini[✉], Stefano Aringhieri, Tommaso Fabbri, Matteo Razzanelli, Lorenzo Pollini, and Mario Innocenti

Automation, Robotics and Autonomous Systems Laboratory,
Department of Information Engineering, University of Pisa,
Largo Lucio Lazzarino 1, 56122 Pisa, Italy
{giovanni.franzini,stefano.aringhieri,tommaso.fabbri}@for.unipi.it,
matteo.razzanelli@ing.unipi.it,
{lorenzo.pollini,mario.innocenti}@unipi.it

Abstract. Human-machine interfaces for command and control of teams of autonomous agents is an enabling technology for the development of reliable multi-agent systems. Tools for proper modelling of these systems are sought in order to ease the creation of efficient interface that allow a single operator to control several agents, as well as monitor the execution state of the tasks the team is demanded to accomplish. If humans are present in the environment, the agents must sense their presence and collaborate with them toward the mission accomplishment. In this context, the descriptor function framework is a versatile tool that allows the human integration at two levels: the development of human-machine interfaces and the achievement of human-machine teaming. In this paper, we show how such results can be obtained and we propose a possible architecture for the framework implementation.

Keywords: Multi-agent system · Autonomous system · Cooperative system · Human-machine interaction · Human-autonomous system teaming

1 Introduction

Control of multi-agent systems is a challenging task that has drawn the attention of the scientific community over the last two decades, thanks to the growing interest in their potential applications in the airborne, maritime and ground domains. Teams of autonomous agents may for instance support humans in all those missions and activities that require the systematic coverage or monitoring of wide areas. Bearing in mind this type of scenarios, humans and autonomous agents should cooperate and coordinate their actions, so that the available resources are efficiently used and the mission is successfully accomplished. Hence, the study of frameworks for multi-agent system modelling and control is of primary interest, in order to achieve human-machine teaming.

J. Hodicky (Ed.): MESAS 2016, LNCS 9991, pp. 25–39, 2016.
DOI: 10.1007/978-3-319-47605-6_3

The *descriptor function framework*, developed originally at the University of Pisa and at the US Air Force Munitions Directorate since 2010 [1], is a mathematical modelling instrument that provides a simple yet effective way for describing agents capabilities and coordinate their deployment in the field. Conversely to most of the solutions proposed in literature, the descriptor function formalism can handle teams composed by *heterogeneous agents*, that is agents with different capabilities with respect to the demanded task. By means of the same formalism, it is possible to describe the desired team deployment, or, in other words, the way the team must execute the task. The benefit is twofold. First, using the same mathematical tool for both agents modelling and task description, the agents perceive the execution status of the task and the deployment of their team-mates, so that they coordinate their actions. Second, different types of tasks can be modelled within the descriptor function framework without the need of ad hoc solutions. For example, in [2] the deployment is achieved using a geometric approach; in [3] the area coverage problem was addressed using Voronoi cell decomposition of the environment; in [4] the target assignment task was solved by means of heuristic algorithms for deployment within a temporal deadline. Within the descriptor function framework, all these problems can be solved without changing the agents control strategy. The desired deployment needs only to be translated into an appropriate descriptor function.

Over the years, the descriptor function framework has proven to be a versatile instrument for the control of team of autonomous agents. However, the authors never considered the presence of humans in the field, working on the same task assigned to the agents. The aim of this paper is to show how the descriptor function framework can be extended to consider this possibility. In particular, as for the autonomous agents, we model humans by means of descriptor functions. In this way, the autonomous agents can perceive the humans and how they are contributing to the task execution. As a result, human-machine cooperation is achieved.

In addition, we also show a possible architecture for the development of a human-machine interface for command and control of the autonomous agents team. Through this interface, an operator can coordinate the agents deployed in the field, as well as monitor the execution state of the tasks assigned. Exploiting the descriptor function formalism, we also introduce the possibility of direct steering of the deployed agents. More specifically, a single operator can steer the whole team, moving all the agents at the same time. Such a capability may be useful, for example, in emergency situation where it is necessary to have a direct control of the agents movements, or can be used to move the team toward another region of interest.

The paper is organized as follows. In Sect. 2 we provide an overview of the descriptor function framework. For the sake of convenience, in the discussion we do not focus our attention on the mathematics behind the framework. The interested reader shall refer to the references provided throughout the discussion for further information about the mathematical details. In Sect. 3 we discuss how humans and their presence in the field can be introduced into the description framework, in order to achieve the human-machine cooperation. In Sect. 4 we present a possible software implementation for the framework, with reference to the *Robot Operative System* (ROS) [5] developing environment. Section 5 concludes the paper.

2   The Descriptor Function Framework

Descriptor functions are a mathematical model for describing the distribution of resources over the environment. As a matter of fact, an autonomous agent is a carrier of resources of a certain type. The task that a team of autonomous agents has to accomplish defines how these resources must be deployed in the environment. Therefore, descriptor functions are a unifying tool to model both the agents capabilities and the task we demand the team to accomplish. The use of such a modelling tool simplifies the management of large groups of agents and provide to the users a powerful yet intuitive language for handling the interactions with teams of autonomous agents.

The basis of the descriptor function framework can be found in the original works by Niccolini et al. [1,6]. The framework has been continuously improved during the years, extending its capabilities and strengthening its theoretical foundations [7,8].

2.1   Framework Overview

The descriptor function framework is based on three main definitions:

- **Agent**: the entity that operates in the environment in order to achieve the mission objectives.
- **Task**: coordination in space of the agents working on the same objective.
- **Mission**: coordination in space and time of the tasks.

Generally, mission objectives are translated into one or more tasks that the team must complete toward the mission accomplishment. Hence, a task indicates to the agents how they should deploy in the field in order to fulfil a given mission sub-objective.

Broadly speaking, teams may be composed by agents with different capabilities of executing the mission's tasks, i.e. teams may be composed by *heterogeneous* agents. In order to cope with heterogeneous teams, agent's characteristics are quantified by means of the *agent descriptor functions* (ADF). Given a point of the environment, the ADF describes the agent capability of executing a given task at that point. Hence, the ADF is a function of the agent relative position from that point. Mathematically, we define the ADF of an agent i for the task k as follows,

$$d_i^k(\boldsymbol{p}_i, \boldsymbol{q}): \mathcal{P} \times \mathcal{Q} \to \mathbb{R}^+ \tag{1}$$

where $\mathbb{R}^+ = \{x \in \mathbb{R}: x \geq 0\}$, $\mathcal{Q} \subseteq \mathbb{R}^n$, with $n = \{2,3\}$, is the domain of the environment and $\boldsymbol{p}_i \in \mathcal{P}$, with $\mathcal{P} \subseteq \mathbb{R}^m$, is the agent state vector (typically its position and orientation). For each agent, we define a number of ADFs equal to the tasks composing the missions. If the agent is unable of executing a task, the relative ADF is zero all over the environment.

Two examples of ADFs are shown in Fig. 1. Gaussian functions, like the one shown in Fig. 1(a) and (b), provide a simple tool for describing various type of omnidirectional sensors. More complex functions can be used to model sensor with limited field-of-view, see e.g. Fig. 1(c) and (d). The level curves indicates the sensor's intensity and may be a measure of the quality of the information acquired from that point. Extensive details about ADF design and their mathematical formalization can be found in [7].

As mentioned at the beginning of this section, within the descriptor function framework agents are viewed as carriers of resources. In order to execute a task,

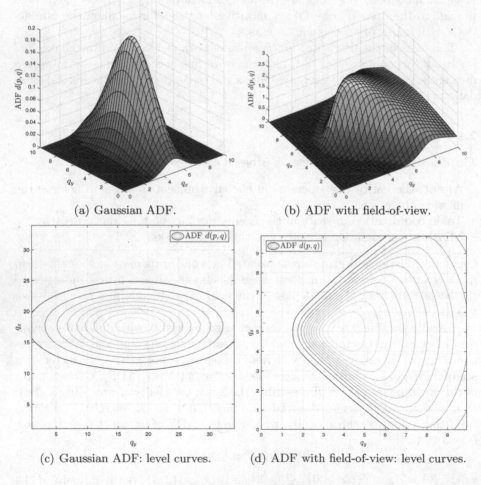

(a) Gaussian ADF.

(b) ADF with field-of-view.

(c) Gaussian ADF: level curves.

(d) ADF with field-of-view: level curves.

Fig. 1. Examples of ADFs.

we must define how these resources should be deployed in the environment. To this end, we express the desired deployment using the *task descriptor function* (TDF). The TDF relative to a task k is defined as,

$$d_*^k(t, \boldsymbol{q}) \colon \mathbb{R}^+ \times \mathcal{Q} \to \mathbb{R}^+ \tag{2}$$

Note that the TDF may change with time in case of time-varying tasks.

The current state of execution of the task is given by the *current task descriptor function* (CTDF), that is equal to the sum of all the ADFs relative to that task. The CTDF for the task k is defined as

$$d^k(\boldsymbol{p}, \boldsymbol{q}) = \sum_{i \in \mathcal{N}} d_i^k(\boldsymbol{p}_i, \boldsymbol{q}) \tag{3}$$

where $\mathcal{N}$ is the set of the agents.

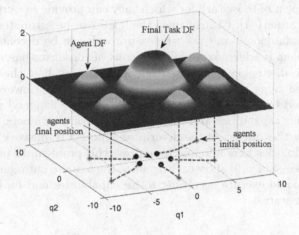

Fig. 2. Current task descriptor function and task descriptor function (taken from [6]).

Figure 2 shows an example of TDF for a *static coverage* task (see Sect. 2.3). With this type of TDF we demand the agents to cover a particular region of the environment. In this example the TDF is a two-dimensional Gaussian function, meaning that the centre of the area requires more resources than its boundaries.

The agents, in order to execute the task, must know the error of the current deployment with respect to the desired one. This information is provide by the *task error function* (TEF), which is given, for example, by the difference between the TDF and the CTDF,

$$e^k(t, \boldsymbol{p}, \boldsymbol{q}) = d_*^k(t, \boldsymbol{q}) - d^k(\boldsymbol{p}, \boldsymbol{q}) \tag{4}$$

Negative values of the TEF denote a lack of resources in the area. Conversely, positive value of the TEF indicates an excess of resources that can be redistributed over the environment.

Task execution can be formulated as an optimization problem: the agents must found the optimal deployment that minimizes a given cost function of the TEF. Using this approach, the same control strategy can be adopted by the agents for tasks execution and many different coordination problems can be handled by the framework simply by changing the TDF. In the past, control laws based on cost function gradient-descent were proposed for agents with single-integrator dynamics [1]. The use of potential field-based control was also considered [8].

The use of control laws based on TEF minimization naturally enables inter-agent cooperation. The agents will avoid regions where the error is low, i.e. areas already covered by other agents, and, as a result, they coordinate their actions during the task execution.

Therefore, the knowledge of the task current execution state, i.e. of the TEF, enables agents self-organization and adaptation. Agents coordinate their actions in order to minimize the TEF (*task-level self-organization*) and participate to the accomplishment of those task for which they can provide resources (*mission-level self-organization*) [1]. Clearly, once the TEF can be estimated, the agents can achieve full autonomy and the whole approach can be decentralized. TEF estimation problem is addressed in [6] by means of consensus-based algorithms.

In the above discussion we focused our attention on how the execution of a task is handled using the descriptor function framework. However, a mission may be composed by more than one task, that must be assigned to the agents according to their capabilities and their priority. Task assignment problem was also analysed by the authors of the descriptor function framework. Biologically inspired methodologies were adopted to address this problem. In particular, the algorithms proposed in [6,9] allow each agent of the team to autonomously decide which task it should execute according to its capabilities and its knowledge of the current task status.

2.2 Obstacle and Collision Avoidance

When moving in a structured or unstructured environment, agents must avoid collision with the obstacles (*obstacle avoidance*), as well as among themselves (*collision avoidance*). In the literature, numerous algorithms have been proposed to address these problems based, for example, on online path planning techniques, potential fields and geometric methods (see e.g. [10–12]). These methods can be readily introduced in the descriptor function framework, so that the agents can safely operate in real scenarios.

In [7] the authors adopted a potential field method to prevent inter-agent collision and obstacles avoidance by agents coordinated with the descriptor function framework.

The presence of obstacles can be also directly included in the descriptor function framework by means of *obstacles descriptor functions* (ODF). The idea is to introduce for each obstacle an ODF, such that the area occupied has no interest for the agents [13]. The TEF is then modified as follows,

$$e^k(t, \boldsymbol{p}, \boldsymbol{q}) = d_*^k(t, \boldsymbol{q}) - d^k(\boldsymbol{p}, \boldsymbol{q}) - \sum_{j \in \mathcal{O}} d_{obs,j}(\boldsymbol{p}, \boldsymbol{q}) \tag{5}$$

where $\mathcal{O}$ is the set of the obstacles in the environment and $d_{obs,j}(\boldsymbol{p}, \boldsymbol{q})$ is the ODF for the obstacle j. Note that the ODF depends on the agents positions. As the agents get closer to the obstacles, the relative ODF increases in order to reduce the TEF in that area. As a result, the agents move away from the obstacles toward regions with higher TEF value.

2.3   Tasks Examples

In this section, we present a list of tasks successfully implemented and tested using the descriptor function framework. For each task, we provide references for those readers interested in their mathematical formulations, as well as in the technical details about the implementation.

- **Uniform Deployment** [1,6]. The agents are demanded to spread over a prescribed area, so that the resources are uniformly distributed. This problem usually arises in sensors networks, where a given number of sensor must be deployed in the environment in order to cover the assigned area.
- **Static Coverage** [6,8]. Similar to the uniform deployment, the static coverage requires to deploy the agents in the environment in order to cover a given region. However, regions may have area of highest interest that should be covered first by the agents.
- **Effective Coverage** [6,7]. The effective coverage problem, originally formulated in [11], models the task of exhaustive research over a given area. The ADF here describes the efficiency of the agent in sensing the area. The task is complete when all the area of interest is explored. This could be applied to search and rescue missions.
- **Dynamic Coverage** [6,7]. This task requires the agents to continuously explore the environment, in order to keep updated their information. An example of dynamic coverage task may be the surveillance and patrolling of a sensitive area.
- **Target Assignment** [6,8]. Given K static targets and N agents, we require that at least each target is covered by an agent if $K \leq N$. Otherwise, each agent must cover one target, so that N of them are under control.

The tasks described above were tested by means of extensive simulations. Experimental tests were also conducted to understand the applicability of the framework to real mission scenarios. A test-bed composed by ground vehicles, built at University of Pisa, has been developed over the years to conduct experimental campaigns. A description of an earlier version of the test-bed is presented in [6,14]. In Fig. 3 is shown the execution of a task of effective coverage using these vehicles. The experiment was performed in July 2015 with two real agents (the two vehicles) and two virtual agents simulated by a PC. We introduced three obstacles in order to test also the agents obstacle avoidance algorithms. As can be seen in Fig. 3a, the agents successfully explored the operative space, avoiding collisions among them and with the obstacles.

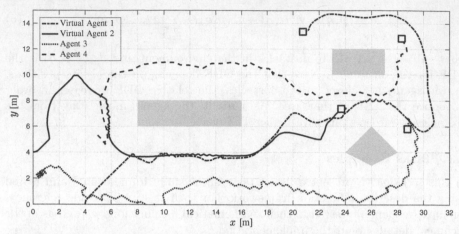

(a) Agents trajectories at the end of the effective coverage task (squares denote agents final positions).

(b) Agent 3 and 4 executing the effective coverage task.

Fig. 3. Effective coverage experimental test (July 2015).

3   Human-Machine Interaction Within the Descriptor Function Framework

3.1   Modelling the Human Presence

The descriptor function abstraction is a simple and powerful tool that confer to the framework a unique reconfigurability property. The same functions can be used to consider the presence of humans, working on the same task executed by the autonomous agents, within the framework. In the following, we will refer to them as *human agents*.

Human agents capabilities with respect to a task can be described using the same formalism adopted for the autonomous agents, i.e. through ADFs. Hence, we define the *human agent descriptor function* (HADF) for the task k,

$$d^k_{hum}(\boldsymbol{p}, \boldsymbol{q}): \mathcal{P}_{hum} \times \mathcal{Q} \to \mathbb{R}^+ \tag{6}$$

Here $\boldsymbol{p} \in \mathcal{P}_{hum}$, where $\mathcal{P}_{hum} \subseteq \mathbb{R}^{m_h}$, denotes the human agent state vector, that may be composed by its position and orientation in the environment. Since the human agents collaborate with the autonomous agents operating in the environment, the CTDF must consider their contribution to the task execution. We then modify the CTDF as follows,

$$d^k(\boldsymbol{p}, \boldsymbol{q}) = \sum_{i \in \mathcal{N}} d^k_i(\boldsymbol{p}_i, \boldsymbol{q}) + \sum_{j \in \mathcal{H}} d^k_{hum,j}(\boldsymbol{p}_j, \boldsymbol{q}) \tag{7}$$

where $\mathcal{H}$ is the set of the human agents and $\boldsymbol{p}_j$ their positions. Doing so, the TEF computation remains unchanged.

The introduction of the HADF enables the interaction between humans and autonomous agents. The latter can now sense the presence of humans through the TEF. Collision or damage to humans is prevented thanks to the collision avoidance mechanism discussed in Sect. 2.2. Furthermore, the human-machine cooperation is easily achieved. The TEF now reflects the actions taken by the human agents. Since the autonomous agents use the TEF to execute the task, coordination with the current human agents deployment naturally arises, without changing their control strategy.

In order to efficiently coordinate both the human and the autonomous agents, the same control strategy adopted by the autonomous agents can be used to suggest to the human agents how to contribute to the task. This information can be provided, for example, by means of a personal mobile devices. Doing so, the full coordination of humans and autonomous agents is achieved.

3.2 Autonomous Agents Management and Direct Steering

One of the most important features of the descriptor function framework is the possibility to perform different tasks by simply modifying the TDF. In this way, the agents control strategy does not need modifications. Hence, the framework can be used to develop human-machine interfaces that provide to an operator a simple way for monitoring and control a team of autonomous agents.

A possible architecture for the implementation of a command and control interface for team of autonomous agents based on the descriptor function framework is proposed in Fig. 4. The interaction between the operator and the team is handled via an interface that allows to monitor the team status and the task completion level. The operator can order to execute a set of tasks, i.e. assign the mission, choosing among the tasks presented in Sect. 2.3. The resulting list can be either organized by the operator, so that the tasks are executed in a given order, or can be handled by the agents, that according to their internal heuristic and the assigned task priority organize their execution (see Sect. 2.1). The interface can be also enhanced allowing the operator to define new tasks. However, TDF, ADFs and HADFs generation must be handled properly.

Using the architecture described above, we now introduce a new capability to the descriptor function framework: the direct steering of a team of autonomous

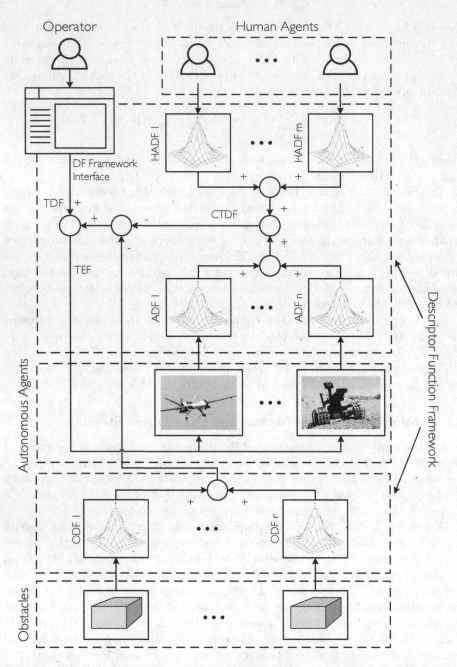

Fig. 4. Descriptor function framework architecture for command and control of team of autonomous agents.

agents. Such a capability may be useful in all that situations where the operator requires to take the direct control of the team, e.g. in response to an emergency situation or in case he needs to move the team to another geographical area. This problem was addressed by the original authors of the descriptor function framework in [14] by means of an abstraction based control in order to simplify the team steering by an operator. Some of the ideas presented in that paper inspired the creation of the descriptor function formalism.

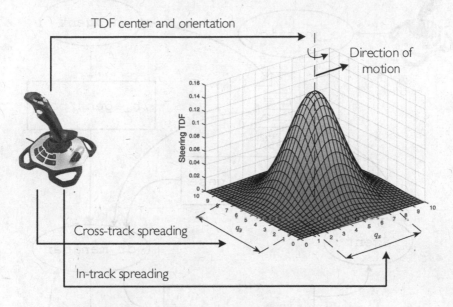

Fig. 5. TDF for autonomous agents steering.

We introduce a new TDF for team steering, which is shown in Fig. 5. The centre of this TDF, as well as its shape and dimensions, are controlled by the operator through, for example, a joystick. In this way, the operator can gather the agents and decide their spreading around the TDF centre. The TDF shown in the figure is a two-dimensional Gaussian function. Changing the standard deviations values, the operator can control the agents spreading along the in-track and cross-track directions. Since the framework integrates algorithms for obstacle and collision avoidance, during the steering the agents will not collide between them and collision with obstacles are prevented. Hence, the control of the team is significantly simplified, even in cluttered environments.

4   Implementation of the Descriptor Function Framework for Human-Machine Interaction

The descriptor function framework, with the enhancements presented in this paper, was implemented using the *Robot Operating System* (ROS) [5]. The C++

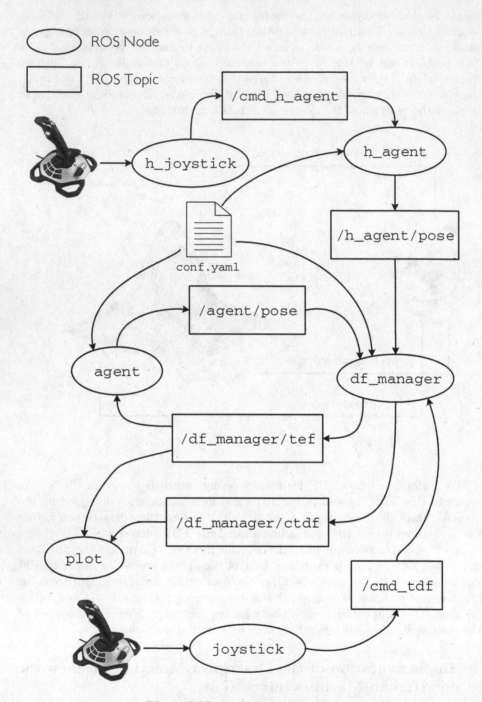

Fig. 6. ROS simulation architecture.

language was chosen for the implementation of the framework. Python was preferred for the development of viewers that help the operator in monitoring the task execution.

The architecture of the ROS implementation is shown in Fig. 6. The df_manager node computes the CTDF and the TEF using the current agents positions, their ADFs and HADFs. The autonomous agents are implemented using the agent node. The agents read the TEF from the topic /df_manager/tef, compute the control law and simulate their dynamics. The agents then write the new position into the /agent$i$/pose topic, where i is the agent's ID. Human agents are implemented using the node h_agent and their positions are published in the topic /h_agent$j$/pose, where j is the human agent's ID. The plot node is used to visualize the CTDF, as well as the TEF, in order to monitor the agents deployment and the level of completeness of the task. For the agents direct steering, we introduced the joystick node, that reads the input from a joystick and publish it into the topic /cmd_pos. The information written here are used by the df_manager in order to update the TDF during the steering. In like manner, the node h_joystick can be used to move the human agents using a joystick, in order to simulate their movements in the field.

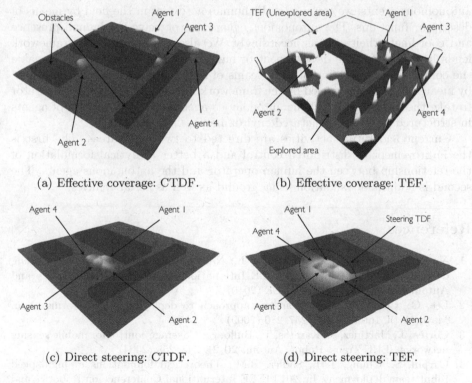

(a) Effective coverage: CTDF.

(b) Effective coverage: TEF.

(c) Direct steering: CTDF.

(d) Direct steering: TEF.

Fig. 7. Examples of task execution.

The configuration file conf.yaml, written according to the YAML standard [15], contains the simulation and the agents parameters.

Figure 7 shows some simulations performed with the framework and the developed interface. In particular, the figure shows four screenshots of the CTDF and TEF viewers provided by the plot node.

In Fig. 7(a) and (b) are shown, respectively, the CTDF and the TEF during an effective coverage task. Looking at the TEF, the operator visualize the regions of the environment not yet explored by the agents. The CTDF, instead, shows how the resources, i.e. the agents, are deployed in the field.

Figure 7(c) and (d) show the same information, this time during the direct steering of the agents. The former shows how the agents gather around the TDF controlled by the joystick. The latter figure, instead, give to the operator an idea about the joystick TDF and its dimensions, helping him during the steering of the agents.

5   Conclusions and Future Works

In this paper we discussed how human-machine teaming can be achieved within the descriptor function framework. Using the same formalism adopted for the autonomous agents, we can model the human activities in the field by means of descriptor functions. The autonomous agents can perceive the human presence and coordinate their actions accordingly. We also showed how the framework lends itself well for the development of human-machine interfaces that enable the control and monitoring of large teams of autonomous agents. Furthermore, by means of the tool provided by the framework it is possible by a single operator to take the direct control of the autonomous agents and steer a team of agents in structured as well unstructured environments.

Current and future activities are directed to two main areas. The first is the improvement of distributed control and a better analytical formulation of the relationship between the human operator and the autonomous agents. The second is additional validation using ground as well as aerial vehicles.

References

1. Niccolini, M., Innocenti, M., Pollini, L.: Near optimal swarm deployment using descriptor functions. In: 2010 IEEE International Conference on Robotics and Automation, pp. 4952–4957. IEEE (2010)
2. Lee, G., Chong, N.Y.: A geometric approach to deploying robot swarms. Ann. Math. Artif. Intell. **52**(2), 257–280 (2009)
3. Cortès, J., Martinez, S., Karatas, T., Bullo, F.: Coverage control for mobile sensing networks. IEEE Trans. Robot. Autom. **20**(2), 243–255 (2004)
4. Carpin, S., Chung, T.H., Sadler, B.M.: Theoretical foundations of high-speed robot team deployment. In: 2013 IEEE International Conference on Robotics and Automation, pp. 2033–2040. IEEE (2013)
5. Robot Operating System (ROS). http://www.ros.org/

6. Niccolini, M.: Swarm abstractions for distributed estimation and control. Ph.D. dissertation, University of Pisa (2011)
7. Braga, A.F, Innocenti, M., Pollini, L.: Multi-agent coordination with arbitrarily shaped descriptor functions. In: 2013 AIAA Guidance, Navigation, and Control Conference. AIAA (2013)
8. Niccolini, M., Pollini, L., Innocenti, M.: Cooperative control for multiple autonomous vehicles using descriptor functions. J. Sens. Actuator Netw. 3(1), 26–43 (2014)
9. Niccolini, M., Innocenti, M., Pollini, L.: Multiple UAV task assignment using descriptor functions. In: 18th IFAC Symposium on Automatic Control in Aerospace, IFAC Proceeding Volumes, vol. 43, no. 15, pp. 93–98. IFAC (2010)
10. LaValle, S.M.: Planning Algorithms. Cambridge University Press, Cambridge (2006)
11. Hussein, I.I., Stipanovich, D.: Effective coverage control for mobile sensor networks with guaranteed collision avoidance. IEEE Trans. Control Syst. Technol. 15(4), 642–657 (2007)
12. Pollini, L., Cellini, M., Mati, R., Innocenti, M.: Obstacle avoidance for unmanned ground vehicles in unstructured environments. In: 2007 AIAA Guidance, Navigation, and Control Conference. AIAA (2007)
13. Innocenti, M., Pollini, L., Franzini, G., Salvetti, A.: Swarm obstacle and collision avoidance using descriptor functions. In: 2016 IEEE Multi-Conference on System and Control. IEEE (2016)
14. Pollini, L., Niccolini, M., Rosellini, M., Innocenti, M.: Human-swarm interface for abstraction based control. In: 2009 AIAA Guidance, Navigation, and Control Conference. AIAA (2009)
15. YAML. http://yaml.org/

Autonomous Systems Operationalization Gaps Overcome by Modelling and Simulation

Jan Hodicky[✉]

NATO Modelling and Simulation Centre of Excellence, Rome, Italy
jan.hodicky@seznam.cz

Abstract. Systems with some level of Autonomy Capabilities or Semi-Autonomous Systems (SAS) are already an integral part of our life. Fully Autonomous Systems (AS) without any human in the loop are more commonly seen in the civilian sphere. However the military still needs to make a gigantic step toward to implementation of AS in the battlefield. Modeling and Simulation (M&S) and its techniques might help to understand us more quickly in the save environment the potential consequences of ASs deployment from the military perspective. The paper describes a selected set of gaps in the AS operationalization and potential solutions provided by the MS tools and techniques are discussed. The idea of the Augmented Autonomous System Reality is introduced and the way of synthetic environment description needed for the AS operationalization is described. In the end the importance of the Verification Validation and Accreditation process in the AS domain is discussed.

Keywords: Autonomous system · Modelling and simulation · Perception · Synthetic environment

1 Introduction

Systems with some level of Autonomy Capabilities or Semi-Autonomous Systems (SAS) are already an integral part of our life. Even the fully Autonomous Systems (AS) without any human in the loop are more commonly seen in the civilian sphere [1]. As another example the Google car might be taken [2]. However the military still needs to make a gigantic step toward to implementation of AS in the battlefield. Modeling and Simulation (M&S) and its techniques might help to understand more quickly the potential consequences of ASs deployment from the military perspective in the save testing environment [3]. M&S might give an extra time needed to adapt and to prepare to switch our mind set to better reflect the fact that ASs become the key components through the whole spectrum of the military operations. M&S helps us to disassociate from the reality where we as human beings are not able to see or predict all potential situation and side effects of the ASs operational use. M&S might reveal the emerging behavior of ASs deployment and to appropriately address it in the time before this commodity is at the market/battlefield; otherwise it is too risky. In the following chapters selected gaps in the ASs operationalization are described and potential solutions provided by the M&S tools and techniques are discussed. The idea of the Augmented Autonomous System Reality is introduced. The synthetic environment

© Springer International Publishing AG 2016
J. Hodicky (Ed.): MESAS 2016, LNCS 9991, pp. 40–47, 2016.
DOI: 10.1007/978-3-319-47605-6_4

description based on the layer approach is mentioned and the role of Verification, Validation and Accreditation process is discussed.

2 Human Machine Interaction

The most important role in the human interaction with systems with some level of autonomy or Autonomous System is to understand the role of the human and the way of the interaction. The critical is to understand the way to control, cooperate or collaborate between system and the operator or human companion at the battlefield. To better support these features the situational awareness of the mission is the key attribute. Situational awareness in this regard is not only the perception of ASs sensors data in the virtual environment; it is more about clear idea what the systems and human being are actually doing in the complex environment.

The way to increase the situational awareness using MS might be supported through the innovative use/reuse of existing human machine interfaces. The Augmented Reality and haptic feedbacks might be exploited to deliver the information about the battlefield in the natural way to the human in the loop or the human being as a part of deployed team. It would allow addressing the human factor- to have a feeling to be a part of the situation. However design of this approach must be driven by information management. It is useless to project all available data to the Head Mounted display (HMD) in the augmented version. The data must be processed and selected based on the type of the mission and its objective. The most important part is to define a type of information, its criticality and relation to the specific mission objective and current mission constraints. The synthetic environment might support this kind of experimentation to revel what kind of data you need to fulfill the mission from the SAS command and controlling point of view.

SAS and AS should report automatically on:

- behavior patterns that are following at the moment from the cooperation point of view
- individual/ system point of view behavior.

Therefore, even in the huge diversity of field conditions that might potentially cause the SaS and AS performance/mission failures, the human factor would allow to indicate the issues of failure detection and appropriate recovery/backup tasks.

Another important issue in the human machine interaction is performance of the human in the loop, human as a part of deployed team and the performance of ASs.

3 Training with and of ASs

Performance of the human in the loop control or the deployed human being in teaming with the AS is strongly connected to the training and education and the planning and mission rehearsal. For that we have already witnessed a few examples of the testing and experimentation and training frameworks, for example the project on Mediterranean ATM Live Exercise (MedALE) that put together the Air Traffic Controller to measure their effectiveness and different requirements when facing the issue of controlling the real aircrafts and RPAS together [4]. This experiment runs firstly in the experimentation framework in synthetic environment followed by the test cases in live-real environment.

The current challenge in these frameworks is to create a similar condition to the one you might face in the real operation. Therefore factor like stress must be modeled when controlling more SASs or SAs. Another dimension appears if the human being is teamed with the SASs or SAs in the real operation.

The operator is separated from the battlefield, that's a reality, however a factor of not being physically present in the area of deployment might cause post trauma syndrome and create conditions of not being able to adequately react like human being. So the level of an immersion is again very critical. M&S and Virtual Reality means might be very helpful when stimulating all human being senses in accordance with the situation in the battlefield and it brings the operator as close to the battlefield as possible.

When moving a task from the human to the machine we are facing a new issue. Skills related to that task are delegated to the SAS or AS and human being forgets those previously gained skills when learning a new set of skills related to that shift of task. The training method for human being and ASs should be updated but not necessarily through the whole portfolio of type of training. In the military domain generally accepted classification of training depends on the level of the MS involvement, the Fig. 1.

Therefore we speak about Training that is supported by Live, Virtual or Constructive Simulation or any combination of these. Live Simulation involves real people operating real systems in real terrain with simulated effects. Virtual Simulation involves real

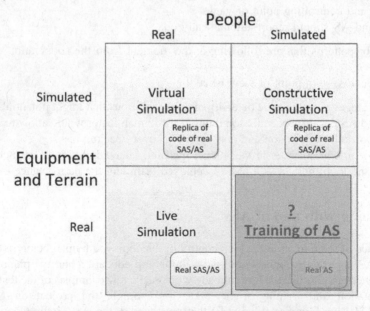

Fig. 1. M&S classification for training purposes including the AS

people operating simulated systems in simulated terrain with simulated effects. Constructive Simulation involves real operators giving orders to simulated units and/or systems in which these inputs are carried out by simulated people and simulated systems over the simulated terrain with simulated effects. There is no agreement on the naming and consequences for training related to the darker part of diagram, the right down rectangle. In this part the simulated people are working with the real equipment in the real terrain. One of the benefit of the SAS and AS design and implementation is that the code contains in the core of systems might be identically use even in the simulated environment. Thus the AS behavior is easy to implement, simply by reusing the code coming from the real systems, in the Constructive and Virtual Simulation domain.

Training related to the use of the SASs and ASs is at the Collective level, type of Computer Assisted Exercise (CAX) where the staff is trained to be operationally and procedurally ready to use capability of SASs/ASs, is covered by the Constructive Simulation. Constructive Simulation provides situational awareness to the commander with no troops on the field connection. The level of control and training is in theory exactly the same with or without the SAS. This training will not be affected, a commander control his resources no matter if human or SAS.

Individual Training is focused on the skills needed to control and cooperate with the SAS and AS and is covered by the Live and Virtual Simulation. Virtual Simulation is in general terms less expensive way to practice needed skills to control SAS/AS and to synchronize their individual tasks, even with the deployed human to fulfill the objective of the mission. Live simulation might support individual and small team training at the most realistic but the most expensive environment.

As mentioned the big question mark is the dark part in the diagram and related persisting problem of matching it with the training purposes. From the AS perspective a proposal is to use this domain for the Training of AS cooperation and collaboration and human teaming and potentially supervision of the commander if needed.

Cognitive simulation might involve the Real Operators/Commanders supervising the real systems in which the simulated people, the code replicating the human behavior, make their own decisions and give orders or released synchronization tasks based on the autonomy level to the system/systems and/or simulated human over the real terrain with simulated effects. A proposal is to called this missing part of the diagram Cognitive simulation from the AS point of view.

Education on the AS is another important objective to overcome the gap of the fear of the SAS and AS operationalization. Modelling and Simulation plays in this field important role, it offers a powerful means through an immersive environments to explain the AS operational use and potential consequences in the attractive potentially remote environment.

4   Augmented AS Reality – A Solution to Move Forward

Based on the previous chapter definition we need to create the environment that is real to the AS where people are simulated and all is happening in the real terrain. These seem to be non-logical conditions to be fulfilled but the perception of the AS might be extended to give him feeling like working with real people. The real environment for

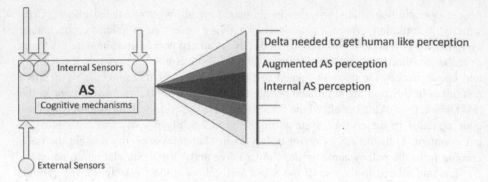

Fig. 2. AS perception and its augmentation

the autonomous system is the one reproduced based on the internal sensors. Therefore we need to create a kind of Augmented Reality for the AS in which it can safely collaborate with the simulated human under the supervision of the real operator/commander.

The most complicated is to develop this AS Augmented Reality, mainly to define a type of information we need to extra deploy to the AS, then to represent it correctly internally and externally and finally to define the required level of fidelity of this information. Figure 2 shows the augmentation of AS perception.

When SAS/AS deployed the critical questions to be answered are:

- Where is a system relatively to the word?
- What is in a system's very close environment?
- How can a system safely interact with environment?
- How can a system solve a problem that before weren't known
- Where is a system absolutely in the sense what might happened in the close future based on the real time situation?
- How can a system synchronize my mates in the reaching the global objective?
- Does a system need supervision in the moment?

To answer these questions the AS perception and difference to the human being plays important role. AS through its internal sensors and cognitive mechanism constructs its internal perception of the environment. The external sensors in this approach might enrich the situational awareness of the AS by augmenting information into AS perception. The external sensors might be understood like any source of information that is pertinent and available in the moment to help the decision making support of AS. For example it might be real time reconnaissance report from the operational area. Such approach creates the Augmented reality for AS and creates added value to the fidelity level of perceived environment by AS. Let's called Delta the difference between augmented and human being perception of the environment. It is not successfully defined at the moment. Important is to point out that Delta and required fidelity level of perceived environment might differ based on the mission objective, mission constraints and its complexity.

In the experimental framework we put the ASs in the synthetic environment that is replicating the real one. We are able to define requirements for the human being in the synthetic environment, however requirements from the AS point of view are not clearly defied yet. If it was case we could have easily transferred this requirements or description into the augmented world of AS in the real battlefield to make Delta smaller.

A proposed solution is to have more than one description of the synthetic and operation environment of for AS and human behavior cohabitation based on the levels that are mutually interconnected. M&S might help to test this approach. The proposed solution follows.

At the highest level of abstraction- operational level an operational scenario, operational objective, constrains and deployed package of AS and human team capabilities are defined and described. This layer should help to make a global recommendation/ decision of all assets deployed in the battlefield regardless its form based on the understanding of the operational context and its limitation. Details of an individual asset are not important at this level; important is the capability of the full deployed package. The terrain features are described at very high level in the form of zones/areas of responsibilities/operations. This layer uses the very high level descriptive language.

The next level is the collaboration layer. This layer contains detailed and structured information about ASs and human team members' capabilities to coordinate cooperate and collaborate. Order of Battle (ORBAT) is known at this level. Terrain features needed for teaming are incorporated, like a single assets responsibilities zones and operational coverage.

The tactical layer contains the most detailed terrain specific information needed for a single asset movement and localization and operation from a single unit point of view.

If needed, even the further layer might be incorporated based on the component or services approach. ASs might be designed and developed using components that are composed in real time to create desired functionality based on the local objective. It gives to the ASs only those features that are necessary at the moment. It is very important safety and performance feature. From that perspective the synthetic environment should only contain the features needed for a component.

Another important approach introduced here is the interconnection of all these layers. It would allow in any moment to step into the process of synthetic environment description and to use any description level – fidelity needed at the selected time to better support flexible movement from the local to the global objective of the mission and vice versa. Figure 3 describes the previous discussion.

5 Verification Validation and Accreditation in the AS Deployment

M&S in the Verification, Validation and Accreditation (VV&A) of military assets has already proven its value [5]. However the role of VV&A in the AS deployment context has a new dimension. The last example clearly showed that VV&A shouldn't be underestimated part of the design of AS when a totally failure of the SAS caused the

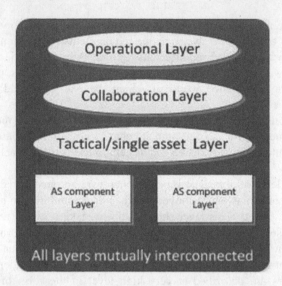

Fig. 3. Description of synthetic environment for AS operationalization

deadly casualty [6]. Therefore new ideas and techniques must be introduced into the VV&A to assure that progress of AS operationalization is not blocked by the public opinion.

To introduce the ethical factors in the AS domain is one of the critical issues in the very close future. The problem is that current VV&A techniques are not design to cover all portion of human behavior. The only method that seems to be applicable at the moment is based on the predefined set of the worst cases scenario that might happen during selected mission. This set of scenario should be standardized and to be an integral part of synthetic environment testing frameworks. In M&S experimental framework the test cases can demonstrate shared autonomy between AS and human in the loop. The level of involvement of the human in the loop is crucial, the VV&A should reflect it together with the mission objective and mission constrains.

Another aspect in VV&A is responsibilities. Who is responsible for the failure of the AS causing casualties? At the moment the shared responsibilities might be a solution. A designer, a developer, a tester and a user share responsibility based on the pre agreed possible situation. M&S can help to set up the border between individual responsibilities and prove that it is applicable concept.

6 Conclusion

In the very close future the focus in the AS operationalization should be put on reliability and robustness of the local and collaboration algorithms to be executed in the synthetic environment prior deployment. The same environment might be used as the basis for the failure detection and recovery operations from the mission/global objective point of view. The important part of the experimental framework is the synthetic environment. The paper recommended building the environment based on the inter-connected layers approaches. The experimental framework might help to define needed level of augmentation of the real environment of the AS. The way the AS perceives might be extended by the external information resources and information needed to come closer to the human behavior. Training and education is based on the level of immersion of human being. The augmentation of the AS perception might be step forward to immerse the ASs.

It is evident that the military engineering process must be updated to better incorporate the VV&A of SaS and AS. The shared responsibilities over the use of ASs must be implemented and proved through the M&S experimental frameworks.

References

1. Bruzzone, A.G., Longo, F., Agresta, M., Di Matteo, R., Maglione, G.L.: Autonomous systems for operations in critical environments. In: Proceedings of Modeling and Simulation of Complexity in Intelligent, Adaptive and Autonomous Systems 2016 (MSCIAAS 2016) and Space Simulation for Planetary Space Exploration (SPACE 2016), p. 3. Society for Computer Simulation International (2016, April)
2. Guizzo, E.: How google's self-driving car works. IEEE Spectrum Online, vol. 18, October 2011
3. Hodicky, Jan: HLA as an experimental backbone for autonomous system integration into operational field. In: Hodicky, Jan (ed.) MESAS 2014. LNCS, vol. 8906, pp. 121–126. Springer, Heidelberg (2014)
4. Pasciuto, M., Riccardi, G., Galati, P., Pusceddu, F., Nurra, P., Goiak, M., Banfi, E., Grimaccia, F., Alviani, P., Romano, M.: MedALE RTS campaign: data analysis and reporting. In: Hodicky, J. (ed.) MESAS 2015. LNCS, vol. 9055, pp. 102–127. Springer, Heidelberg (2015)
5. Collins, K., Goossens, B.: Cost effective V&V for guidance systems using enhanced ground testing (EGT). In: IEEE AUTOTESTCON, 2015, National Harbor, MD, pp. 244–250 (2015)
6. Yadron, D., Tynan, D.: Tesla driver dies in first fatal crash while using autopilot mode. The Guardian (2016). Web. 20 July 2016

To Explore or to Exploit? Learning Humans' Behaviour to Maximize Interactions with Them

Miroslav Kulich[1]([✉]), Tomáš Krajník[2], Libor Přeučil[1], and Tom Duckett[2]

[1] Czech Institute of Informatics, Robotics, and Cybernetics,
Czech Technical University in Prague, Prague, Czech Republic
{kulich,preucil}@cvut.cz
http://imr.ciirc.cvut.cz
[2] Lincoln Centre for Autonomous Systems, University of Lincoln, Lincoln, UK
{tkrajnik,tduckett}@lincoln.ac.uk
http://lcas.lincoln.ac.uk

Abstract. Assume a robot operating in a public space (e.g., a library, a museum) and serving visitors as a companion, a guide or an information stand. To do that, the robot has to interact with humans, which presumes that it actively searches for humans in order to interact with them. This paper addresses the problem how to plan robot's actions in order to maximize the number of such interactions in the case human behavior is not known in advance. We formulate this problem as the exploration/exploitation problem and design several strategies for the robot. The main contribution of the paper than lies in evaluation and comparison of the designed strategies on two datasets. The evaluation shows interesting properties of the strategies, which are discussed.

Keywords: Distant experimentation · e-Learning · Mobile robots · Robot programming

1 Introduction

With increasing level of autonomy, mobile robots are more and more deployed in domains and environments where humans operate and where cooperation between robots and humans is necessary. One of these are public spaces like libraries, museums, galleries or hospitals which are visited by many people with no or minimal knowledge of these places and which typically need some help. A robot for example can guide a human to a specific place, to direct him/her there or to provide a guided tour through a museum or gallery. In order to act effectively, the robot has to learn not only places where its help is needed but also time periods when people ask for help or interact with the robot at such places.

Imagine for example a commercial building with many offices. The best place to interact with people in the morning is near elevators as people go usually to their job and thus the highest probability of interaction is there. On the

© Springer International Publishing AG 2016
J. Hodicky (Ed.): MESAS 2016, LNCS 9991, pp. 48–63, 2016.
DOI: 10.1007/978-3-319-47605-6_5

other hand, an entrance to a canteen might be the best place around midday assuming that people go to the canteen for lunch. The problem is that the robot does not know this behavior apriori and it has to learn it. Learning of humans behavior, i.e. where and when humans ask for help, should be done in parallel with interacting with people as well as with other daily tasks of the robot, which leads to the exploration/exploitation problem.

Although the problem looks interesting and has practical applicability, it has not been addressed in the literature. One of the reasons is probably the fact methods for automated creation and maintenance of environment representations that model the world dynamics from a long-term perspective appeared just recently [19]. On the other hand, the work [19] indicates that environment models created by traditional exploration methods that neglect the naturally-occurring dynamics might still perform sufficiently well even in changing environments.

Exploration, the problem how to navigate an autonomous mobile robot in order to build a map of the surrounding environment, has been studied by the robotics community in last two decades and several strategies which can be an inspiration to solution of the exploration/exploitation problem were introduced. The earliest works [9,22,23] use a greedy motion planning strategy, which selects the least costly action, i.e. the nearest location from a set of possible goal candidates is chosen. Some authors introduce more sophisticated cost functions, which evaluate some characteristics of the goal and combine them with the distance cost, which represents the effort needed to reach the goal. For example, expected information gain computed as a change of entropy after performing the action is presented in [6], while information gain evaluated as the expected aposteriori map uncertainty is introduced in [1]. Localizability, i.e. expected improvement of robot pose estimation when performing the action is used in [18]. Particular measures are typically combined as a weighted sum. More sophisticated multi-criteria decision making approach, which reflects the fact that the measures are not independent is derived in [2,3].

All the aforementioned strategies plan only one step ahead. Tovar et al. [21], in contrast, describe an approach which selects the best tour among all possible sequences of goals of the predefined length. We extended this approach in our previous paper [15], where goal selection is defined as the Travelling Salesman Problem. The presented experiments show that the strategy which considers longer planning horizon significantly outperforms the greedy approach.

Another problem related to exploration/exploitation is robotic search which aims to find a static object of interest in shortest possible time. Sarmiento et al. [20] assume that a geometrical model of the operating space is known and formulate the problem so that the time required to find an object is a random variable induced by a choice of a search path and a uniform probability density function for the object's location. They determine a set of positions to be visited first and then find the optimal order by a greedy algorithm in a reduced search space, which computes a utility function for several steps ahead. A Bayesian network for estimating the posterior distribution of target's position is used in [8] together with a graph search to minimize the expected time needed to capture a non-adversarial (i.e. moving, but not actively avoiding searchers) object.

The variant of the problem where the model of the environment is unknown was defined in [16]. A general framework derived from frontier-based exploration was introduced and several goal-selection strategies were evaluated in several scenarios. Based on findings in [16], a goal-selection strategy was formulated as an instance of the Graph Search Problem (GSP), a generalization of the well-known Traveling Deliveryman Problem and a tailored Greedy Randomized Adaptive Search Procedure (GRASP) meta-heuristic for the GSP, which generates good quality solutions in very short computing times was introduced [17].

In this paper, we formulate the exploration/exploitation problem as a path planning problem in a graph-like environment, where the probability of an interaction with a human at a given place/node is a function of time and is not known in advance. A natural condition is to maximize the number of interactions during a defined time interval. To model probabilities at particular places, the Frequency Map Enhancement (FreMEn) [11,12] is employed, which models dynamics of interactions by their frequency spectra and is thus able to predict future interactions.

Using this model, we designed and experimentally evaluated several planning algorithms ranging from greedy exploration and exploitation strategies and their combinations to strategies planning in a finite horizon (i.e. looking for a fixed finite number of time steps ahead). For the finite horizon variant an algorithm based on depth-first search was designed and all greedy strategies were used as a gain for a single step. Moreover, both deterministic and randomized versions of the strategies, various horizons as well as resolutions of the FreMEn models were considered.

The rest of the paper is organized as follows. The problem is formally defined is Sect. 2, the method for representation and maintenance of environment dynamics is introduced in Sect. 3, while the strategies (policies) to be compared are introduced in Sect. 4. Description of the experimental setup and evaluation results on two datasets are presented in Sects. 5 and 6. Concluding remarks can be found in Sect. 7.

2   Problem Definition

To formulate the problem more formally, let $G = (V, E)$ be an undirected graph with $V = \{v_1, v_2, \ldots, v_n\}$ the set of vertices, and $E = \{e_{ij} | i, j \in \{0, 1, \ldots, n\}\}$ the set of edges. Let also c_{ij} be the cost of the edge e_{ij} representing the time needed to travel from v_i to v_j and $p_i(t)$ the probability of receiving an immediate reward at vertex v_i at time t (i.e. probability of interaction with a human at vertex v_i at time t). The aim is to find a policy $\pi : V \times T \to V$ that for a given vertex v_i and time t gives a vertex v_j to be visited at time $t + c_{ij}$, such that the received reward in the specified time interval $\langle t_0, t_T \rangle$ is maximal:

$$\pi = \arg\max_a \sum_{t=t_0}^{t_T} R_a(t),$$

where $R_a(t)$ is a reward received at time t if policy a is followed in the time interval $\langle t_0, t_T \rangle$.

We dealt with the problem when $p_i(t)$ is known in [14], where the task was defined as the Graph Searching Problem [10]. A search algorithm as a variant of branch-and-bound was proposed based on a recursive version of depth-first search with several improvements enabling to solve instances with 20 vertices in real-time.

The situation is more complicated when $p_i(t)$ is not known in advance. Instead, $p_i^*(t)$, apriori estimate of the reward, is available. In this case, a utility of visiting a vertex is twofold: (a) a reward received and (b) refinement of a probability in a vertex:

$$U_i(t) = \alpha R_i(t) + (1 - \alpha)e(p_i^*(t)),$$

where $R_i(t)$ is a reward received in v_i at time t, $e(\cdot)$ is a function evaluating refinement of the probability in a vertex, and α is a weight.

Given this formulation, the problem can be reformulated as finding a policy maximizing the utility:

$$\pi = \arg\max_a \sum_{t=t_0}^{t_T} U_a(t),$$

where $U_a(t)$ is a utility of a vertex visited at time t following the policy a.

3   Temporal Model

Frequency Map Enhancement (FreMEn) [11,12] is employed to inicialize and maintain particular probabilities $p_i^*(t)$. Unlike traditional approaches dealing with a static word, the probabilities in our case are functions of time and these are learnt through observations gathered during the mission. The FreMEn assumes that majority of environment states is influenced by humans performing their regular (hourly daily, weekly) activities. The regularity and influence of these activities on the environment states is obtained by means of frequency transforms by extracting the frequency spectra of binary functions that represent long-term observations of environment states, discards non-essential components of these spectra and uses the remaining spectral components to represent probabilities of the corresponding binary states in time. It was shown that introducing dynamics into environment models leads to more faithful representation of the world and thus to improved behaviour of the robot in robot self-localization [13], search [14] and exploration [19].

Assume now that the presence of an object in a particular node of the graph is represented by a binary function of time $s(t)$ and the uncertainty of $s(t)$ by the presence probability $p(t)$.

The key idea of the FreMEn stands in representation of a (temporal) sequence of states $s(t)$ by the most prominent components of its frequency spectrum $S(\omega)$ $= \mathcal{F}(s(t))$. The advantage of this representation is that each spectral component of $P(\omega)$ is represented by three numbers only which leads to high compression rates of the observed sequence $s(t)$.

To create the FreMEn model, the frequency spectrum $S(\omega)$ of the sequence $s(t)$ is calculated either by the traditional Fourier transform or by the incremental method described in [11]. The first spectral component a_0, that represents an average value of $s(t)$ is stored, while the remaining spectral components of $S(\omega)$ are ordered according to their absolute value and the n highest components are selected. Each component thus represents a harmonic function that is described by three parameters: amplitude a_j, phase shift φ_j and frequency ω_j. The superposition of these components, i.e.

$$p^*(t) = a_0 + \sum_{j=1}^{n} a_j cos(\omega_j t + \varphi_j), \tag{1}$$

allows to estimate the probability $p(t)$ of the state $s(t)$ for any given time t. Since t is not limited to the interval when $s(t)$ was actually measured, Eq. (1) can be used not only to interpolate, but also to predict the state of a particular model component. In our case, we use Eq. (1) to predict the chance of interaction in a particular node.

The spectral model is updated whenever a state $s(t)$ is observed at time t by the scheme described in [11] for details. This is done every time a robot visits a node v and registers an interaction in the node ($s_v(t) = 1$ in that case) or it experiences that no interaction was done ($s_v(t) = 0$).

4   Policies

Several utilities leading to different policies can be defined. These utilities are typically mixtures of exploration and exploitation gains. The exploration gain of an action expresses the benefit of performing the action to the knowledge of the environment, i.e. amount of information about the environment gathered during execution of the action. The exploitation gain then corresponds to the probability that the action immediately leads to interaction.

More specifically, the **exploitation** utility of the action a which moves the robot to the node v_i is expressed as the estimated probability of interaction at a given time:

$$U_a^{exploitation} = p_i^*(t),$$

while the **exploration** utility for the same case is expressed by entropy in the node v_i:

$$U_a^{exploration} = -p^*(t) \log_2 p^*(t) - (1 - p^*(t)) \log_2 (1 - p^*(t))$$

Figure 1(a) and (b) shows graphs for these two utilities. Note that while exploitation prefers probabilities near 1, exploration is most beneficial in nodes with highest uncertainty.

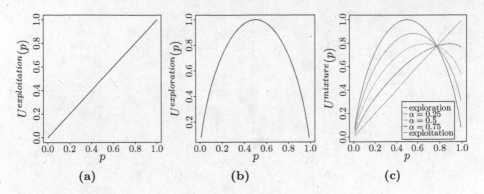

Fig. 1. Utility functions of exploration and exploitation: (a) exploitation utility, (b) exploration utility and (c) their mixture with various weights.

A linear combination of exploration and exploitation defines a new utility which is referred as **mixture** [11]. Ratio of exploration and exploitation is tuned by the parameter α (see also Fig. 1(c)):

$$U_a^{mixture} = \alpha p^*(t) + (\alpha - 1)(p^*(t) \log_2 p^*(t) + (1 - p^*(t)) \log_2(1 - p^*(t)))$$

The disadvantage of this linear combination is that the resulting function has one peak, which moves based on setting of the parameter α as can be seen in Fig. 1(c). In fact, a function which prefers (a) uncertain places, i.e. nodes with probability around 0.5 as well as (b) nodes with high probability of interaction is preferred. An example of such function is shown in Fig. 2(c). This function was formed as a combination of two functions (see Figs. 2(a) and (c)) as is expressed as

$$U^{artificial}(t) = \frac{\alpha}{1 - p^*(t)} + \frac{1}{1 + \beta(\frac{1}{2} - p^*(t))^2}$$

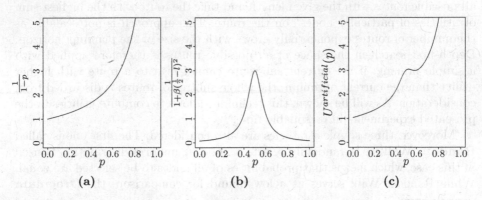

Fig. 2. Construction of the artificial utility. (a) $\frac{\alpha}{1 - p^*(t)}$ function (b) $\frac{3}{1 + 150(\frac{1}{2} - p^*(t))^2}$ and (c) their sum.

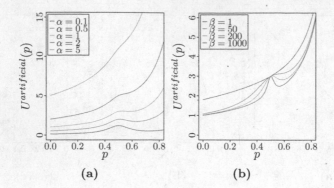

Fig. 3. Various shapes of the artificial utility with one of the parameters fixed. (a) $\beta = 100$ (b) $\alpha = 1$

A shape of the resulting **artificial** utility can be modified by tuning the parameters α and β as depicted in Fig. 3.

A randomized version based on **Monte Carlo** selection is also considered for each of the aforementioned methods. An action with the highest utility is not selected, a random action is chosen instead, but the random distribution is influenced by utilities. In other words, probability of an action to be selected directly is proportional to its utility: the higher the utility the higher chance to be selected. This process can be modeled as an "biased" roulette wheel, where an area of a particular action is equal to its utility.

Strategies using the previously described utilities are greedy in the sense that they consider only immediate off without taking into account subsequent actions. This behavior can be heavily ineffective: the greedy strategy can for example guide a robot into a remote node which can bring slightly more information than other nodes, but with a risk that no (or little) new information will be gathered on the way back. Therefore, utilities that consider some finite planning horizon are introduced. A naïve approach to compute these utilities constructs all possible routes with the given length and take the route with the highest sum of utilities of particular nodes[1] on the route. This approach is not scalable as the number of routes exponentially grows with the size of the planning horizon. Depth-first search in the space of all possible routes is therefore applied with a simple pruning: if the current sub-route cannot lead to a route with higher utility than the current optimum, the whole subtree of routes is discarded from consideration. As will be shown, this technique allows to compute utilities in the presented experiments in reasonable time.

Moreover, three simple strategies are also considered. The first one is called **Random Walk** as it randomly selects a node. A uniform distribution is used in this case, which means that probabilities of all nodes to be selected are equal. While Random Walk serves as a low bound for comparison, the **Oraculum**

---

[1] Exploration, exploitation, mixture or artificial utility can be used as the utility in a particular node.

strategy provides an upper bound. As the name suggests, using this strategy to select a node always results in an successful interaction. The Oraculum strategy is used only for comparison purposes and employs information about future interactions which is not known to other strategies.

5   Evaluation on the Aruba Dataset

The first evaluation and comparison of the strategies was performed on the Aruba dataset from the WSU CASAS datasets [4] gathered and provided by Center for Advanced Studies in Adaptive Systems at Washington State University. This dataset contains after some processing[2] data about presence and movement of a home-bound single person[3] in a large flat, see Fig. 4 in a period of 4 months. The data were measured every 60 seconds and the flat was represented by a graph with 9 nodes.

Robot behavior was simulated and its success of interactions was evaluated according to the dataset. Given a policy, the robot started in the corridor and it was navigated to the node chosen by the policy as the best every 60 seconds assuming that movement between two arbitrary nodes takes exactly 60 seconds. Every time a new node was reached, the FreMEn model of the node (initially set to constant 0.5) was updated accordingly. This was repeated for the whole dataset and for all the greedy strategies described in the previous section. Moreover, several parameter setups were considered for the Artificial strategy. As the graph is considered to be full and costs of all edges are the same, it has no sense to evaluate strategies with longer planning horizon.

The results are summarized in several graphs. First, the number of interactions, i.e. the number of time moments when the robot was present at the same node as the person was tracked, see Fig. 5. As expected Oraculum provides the best result (we will talk about SuperOraculum in the next paragraph).

Fig. 4. The Aruba environment layout.

---

[2] The original dataset [4] contains one year-long collection of measurements from 50 different sensors spread over the apartment and we filtered this data to contain information about presence of the person in particular rooms and at particular times.

[3] In fact, the person was not present in the flat occasionally or was visited by another people.

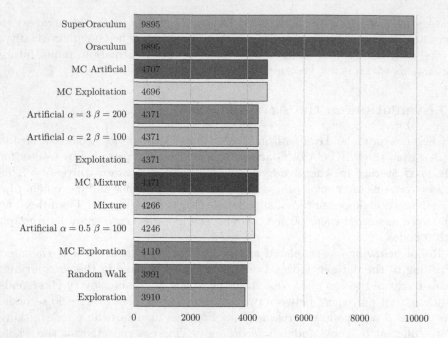

Fig. 5. The number of interactions done for the particular policies. Note that the policies in the legend are ordered according to their performance.

The randomized versions of the artificial utility (with $\alpha = 3$ and $\beta = 200$) and exploitation follow, which are by 8 % better than the other methods. The worst method is Exploration, which is even worse than Random Walk and its randomized version is then just slightly better. This is not surprising as the objective of exploration guides the robot to not yet visited areas and thus probability of interaction is small.

The graph in Fig. 6 shows another characteristics of the policies: precision of the model built by FreMEn. Given a model at some stage of exploration/exploitation, Precision is expressed as a sum of squares of differences of the real state and the state provides by FreMEn at the stage estimated over all nodes for all times:

$$error = \sum_{t=0}^{T} \sum_{i=1}^{N} (state^i(t) - p_i^*(t))^2,$$

where $state_i(t)$ is the real state of the node i, T is time of the whole exploration/exploitation process, and N is the number of nodes. First, note masterfully biggest error for the Oraculum policy. This is caused by the fact, that this policy guides the robot only to places with a person, thus FreMEn has positive samples only and it assumes that a person is present at all nodes all time. Therefore, another policy called SuperOraculum was introduced, which behaves similarly to Oraculum with one exception: it assumes that there is one person in

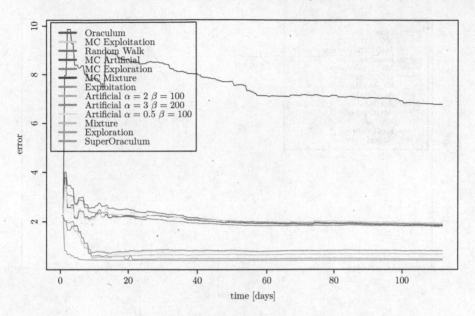

Fig. 6. Progress of FreMEn model precision.

the flat at maximum and thus probabilities of all nodes other than the currently visited are updated also. This update is done the same way the robot physically visits a node and recognizes no interaction. As can be seen, error of this policy is much smaller and serves as a lower limit. Assuming the real policies, the best one is Exploration, which is even comparable to SuperOraculum, followed by the Mixture and two Artificial policies. The other strategies provide similar results. Note also that error of the best strategies almost stabilizes (which means that the model is learned) after 14 days, while it takes longer time for the others.

Finally, the expected number of humans in the flat as assumed by the FreMEn model is depicted in Fig. 7. The number for a given FreMEn model is computed as the average number of nodes, where probability of interaction is higher than 0.5:

$$num = \frac{\sum_{t=0}^{T} \sum_{i=1}^{N} (p_i^* > 0.5)}{TN}$$

Note that the real number of humans is lower than one as the person is not always present in the flat. The results correspond to model precision. Again, the best estimates are provided by the Exploration, Mixture and Artificial policies, while the rest highly overestimates the number of humans. When comparing with the number of interactions, the results are almost reversed: the methods with a high number of interactions model the dynamics in the environment with less success than policies with a low number of interactions.

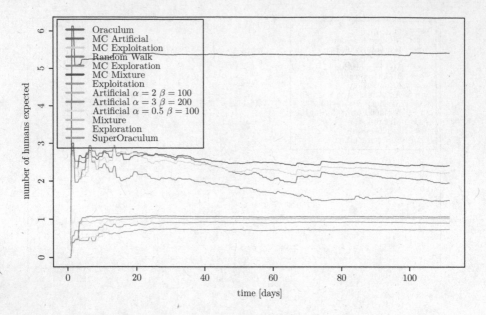

Fig. 7. The Expected number humans in the flat.

6   Deployment at a Care Site

Another evaluation was performed on the data collected within the STRANDS
project (http://strands.acin.tuwien.ac.at) during a real deployment of a mobile
robot at the "Haus der Barmherzigkeit", an elder care facility in Austria [5,7].
The robot was autonomously navigated in the environment consisting of 12
nodes (see Fig. 8) and all interactions were logged each minute during a period

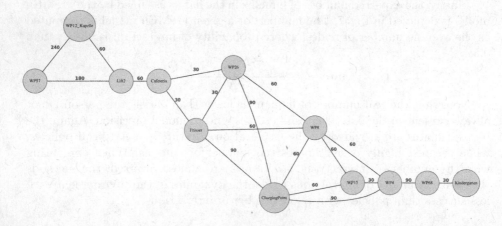

Fig. 8. The graph representing the environment in the hospital.

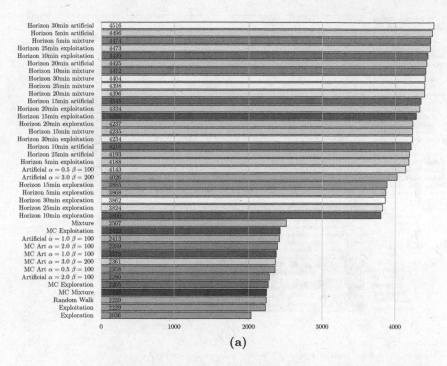

(a)

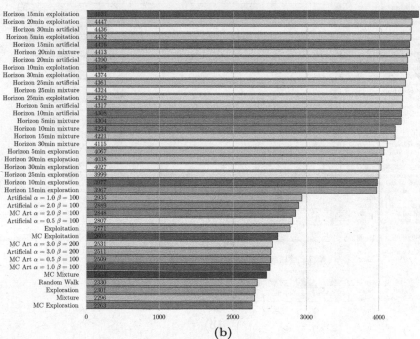

(b)

Fig. 9. The number of interactions done for FreMEn with (a) order = 0 (b) order = 1.

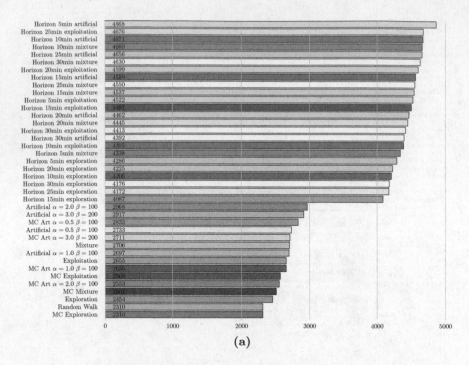

(a)

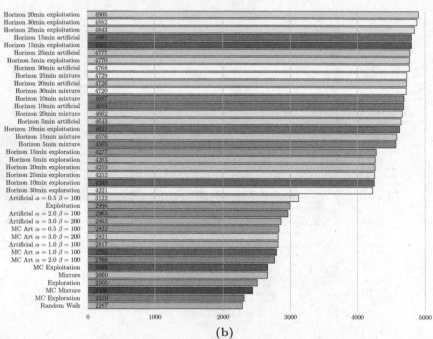

(b)

Fig. 10. The number of interactions done for FreMEn with (a) order = 2 (b) order = 4.

of one month, e.g. measurements at 40325 time moments were taken. The data can not be used directly, as information about interactions is available only for places, where the robot was present at a given time. A FreMEn model with order $= 2$ was therefore built in advance and used as ground truth to simulate interactions at all nodes and all times: interaction is detected if the model returns probability higher than 0.5. Contrary to the Aruba experiment, a number of people in the environment varies in time significantly and the time needed to move from one node to another one is not constant (the real values are drawn in Fig. 8). Strategies taking into account a planning horizon are therefore considered together with the policies evaluated in the previous section. To ensure that the robot does not stay on a single spot, we introduces an additional penalty for the current node.

The experiments were performed similarly to the Aruba case. The robot started in the *Kindergarten* node and the whole month deployment was simulated for each strategy. Experiment with each strategy was repeated several times for the order of the FreMEn model equal to 0, 1, 2, and 4. Note that the order equal to 0 means a static model, i.e. probability of interaction does not change in time.

The results are shown in Figs. 9 and 10. Generally, the policies planning several steps ahead significantly outperform the greedy ones for all assumed orders, even for the static model. The best results are obtained with the variants employing the artificial and exploitation exploitation utilities followed by mixture. Horizon planning with the exploration utility exhibits a noticeably worse behavior but still better than the greedy policies. Notice also not good performance of pure exploitation for order $= 0$, which is caused by the fact that the model is static and exploitation thus guides the robot to the same nodes regardless time of the day. It can be also seen that model order plays an important role for efficiency; the number of interactions increased between order $= 0$ and order $= 4$ by approx. 9 %. Small differences between various lengths of planning horizons can be explained by randomness of interactions and inaccuracy of the models. Interactions can be detected at times and places where they are not expected and do not occur at nodes they are expected by the model.

The proposed horizon planning can be used in real-time. Planning for twenty minutes horizon takes approx. 15 ms, while 300 ms are needed to plan for 30 min horizon, 1600 ms for 35 min horizon, 10 s for 40 min horizon, and 220 s for 50 min planning horizon.

7 Conclusion

The paper addresses the problem of concurrent exploration and exploitation in a dynamic environment and compares several policies to plan actions in order to increase exploitation, which is specified as a number of interactions with humans moving in the environment. Simulated experiments based on real data show several interesting facts:

- The policies with the highest numbers of interactions build the worst models and vice versa. Good strategies should be therefore based on exploitation rather than exploration.

- Consideration of several steps ahead in the planning process leads to significant performance improvement. The best policies with a planning horizon outperform the best greedy ones by 54–80%; the biggest improvement is for the model which assumes a static environment.
- Although FreMEn does not model dynamics in the environment exactly, it is precise enough to increase exploitation performance. The higher orders of the model lead to better results.

The next step is to employ and evaluate the best strategies in a real long-term scenario. It will be also interesting to design more sophisticated planning methods, which will be usable in large environments and for longer planning horizons.

Acknowledgments. This work has been supported by the Technology Agency of the Czech Republic under the project no. TE01020197 "Centre for Applied Cybernetics" and by the EU ICT project 600623 'STRANDS'.

References

1. Amigoni, F., Caglioti, V.: An information-based exploration strategy for environment mapping with mobile robots. Robot. Auton. Syst. **58**(5), 684–699 (2010)
2. Basilico, N., Amigoni, F.: Exploration strategies based on multi-criteria decision making for an autonomous mobile robot. In: Proceedings of 4th European Conference on Mobile Robots, pp. 259–264. KoREMA (2009)
3. Basilico, N., Amigoni, F.: Exploration strategies based on multi-criteria decision making for searching environments in rescue operations. Auton. Robot. **31**(4), 401–417 (2011)
4. Cook, D.J.: Learning setting-generalized activity models for smart spaces. IEEE Intell. Syst. **2010**(99), 1 (2010)
5. Gerling, K., Hebesberger, D., Dondrup, C., Körtner, T., Hanheide, M.: Robot deployment in long-term care. Zeitschrift für Gerontologie und Geriatrie 1–9 (2016). http://dx.doi.org/10.1007/s00391-016-1065-6
6. Gonzalez-Banos, H.H., Latombe, J.C.: Navigation strategies for exploring indoor environments. Int. J. Robot. Res. **21**(10–11), 829–848 (2002)
7. Hebesberger, D., Dondrup, C., Koertner, T., Gisinger, C., Pripfl, J.: Lessons learned from the deployment of a long-term autonomous robot as companion in physical therapy for older adults with dementia: a mixed methods study. In: 11th ACM/IEEE International Conference on Human Robot Interaction, HRI 2016, pp. 27–34. IEEE Press, Piscataway (2016). http://dl.acm.org/citation.cfm?id=2906831.2906838
8. Hollinger, G., Djugash, J., Singh, S.: Coordinated search in cluttered environments using range from multiple robots. In: Laugier, C., Siegwart, R. (eds.) Field and Service Robotics. STAR, vol. 42, pp. 433–442. Springer, Berlin Heidelberg (2008)
9. Koenig, S., Tovey, C., Halliburton, W.: Greedy mapping of terrain. In: Proceedings of IEEE International Conference on Robotics and Automation, vol. 4, pp. 3594–3599 (2001)
10. Koutsoupias, E., Papadimitriou, C., Yannakakis, M.: Searching a fixed graph. In: Meyer auf der Heide, F., Monien, B. (eds.) ICALP 1996. LNCS, vol. 1099, pp. 280–289. Springer, Heidelberg (1996). doi:10.1007/3-540-61440-0_135

11. Krajník, T., Santos, J.M., Duckett, T.: Life-long spatio-temporal exploration of dynamic environments. In: 2015 European Conference on Mobile Robots (ECMR), pp. 1–8, September 2015

12. Krajník, T., Fentanes, J.P., Cielniak, G., Dondrup, C., Duckett, T.: Spectral analysis for long-term robotic mapping. In: 2014 IEEE International Conference on Robotics and Automation (ICRA) (2014)

13. Krajník, T., Fentanes, J.P., Mozos, O.M., Duckett, T., Ekekrantz, J., Hanheide, M.: Long-term topological localization for service robots in dynamic environments using spectral maps. In: International Conference on Intelligent Robots and Systems (IROS) (2014)

14. Krajník, T., Kulich, M., Mudrová, L., Ambrus, R., Duckett, T.: Where's Waldo at time t? Using spatio-temporal models for mobile robot search. In: 2014 IEEE International Conference on Robotics and Automation (ICRA) (2015)

15. Kulich, M., Faigl, J., Přeučil, L.: On distance utility in the exploration task. In: 2011 IEEE International Conference on Robotics and Automation (ICRA), pp. 4455–4460, May 2011

16. Kulich, M., Přeučil, L., Miranda Bront, J.: Single robot search for a stationary object in an unknown environment. In: 2014 IEEE International Conference on Robotics and Automation (ICRA), pp. 5830–5835, May 2014

17. Kulich, M., Miranda-Bront, J.J., Přeučil, L.: A meta-heuristic based goal-selection strategy for mobile robot search in an unknown environment. Comput. Oper. Res. (2016). ISSN 0305-0548, http://dx.doi.org/10.1016/j.cor.2016.04.029

18. Makarenko, A.A., Williams, S.B., Bourgault, F., Durrant-Whyte, H.F.: An experiment in integrated exploration. In: IEEE/RSJ International Conference on Intelligent Robots and System, pp. 534–539. IEEE (2002)

19. Santos, J.M., Krajnik, T., Pulido Fentanes, J., Duckett, T.: Lifelong information-driven exploration to complete and refine 4D spatio-temporal maps. Robot. Autom. Lett. 1, 684–691 (2016)

20. Sarmiento, A., Murrieta-Cid, R., Hutchinson, S.: A multi-robot strategy for rapidly searching a polygonal environment. In: Lemaître, C., Reyes, C.A., González, J.A. (eds.) IBERAMIA 2004. LNCS (LNAI), vol. 3315, pp. 484–493. Springer, Heidelberg (2004)

21. Tovar, B., Muñoz-Gómez, L., Murrieta-Cid, R., Alencastre-Miranda, M., Monroy, R., Hutchinson, S.: Planning exploration strategies for simultaneous localization and mapping. Robot. Auton. Syst. 54(4), 314–331 (2006)

22. Tovey, C., Koenig, S.: Improved analysis of greedy mapping. In: 2003 Proceedings of IEEE/RSJ International Conference on Intelligent Robots and Systems, (IROS 2003), vols. 3 and 4, pp. 3251–3257, October 2003

23. Yamauchi, B.: A frontier-based approach for autonomous exploration. In: Proceedings of IEEE International Symposium on Computational Intelligence in Robotics and Automation, pp. 146–151. IEEE Computer Society Press (1997)

A Visual-Haptic Display for Human and Autonomous Systems Integration

Matteo Razzanelli[1]([✉]), Stefano Aringhieri[1], Giovanni Franzini[1],
Giulio Avanzini[2], Fabrizio Giulietti[3], Mario Innocenti[1], and Lorenzo Pollini[1]

[1] Dipartimento di Ingegneria dell'Informazione, University of Pisa, Pisa, Italy
matteo.razzanelli@ing.unipi.it
[2] Dipartimento di Ingegneria dell'Innovazione, University of Salento, Lecce, Italy
[3] Dipartimento di Ingegneria Industriale, University of Bologna, Forlì, Italy

Abstract. This paper introduces a novel concept of visual-haptic display for situational awareness improvement for crowded and low altitude airspace situations. The visual augmentation display that constitutes of Virtual Fences delimiting no-fly zones, and a specific tri-dimensional highlight graphics that enhances visibility of other remotely piloted or autonomous agents, as well as conventional manned aircraft operating in the area is presented first. Then the Shared Control paradigm and the Haptic Force generation mechanism, based on a Proportional-Derivative-like controller applied to repulsive forces generated by the Virtual Fences and other UAVs are introduced and discussed. Simulations with 26 pilots were performed in a photo-realistic synthetic environment showing that the combined use of Visual-haptic feedback outperforms the Visual Display only in helping the pilot keeping a safe distance from no-fly zones and other vehicles.

Keywords: Autonomous systems · Human and autonomous systems teaming application · Cooperative systems

1 Introduction

This paper presents a novel approach based on mixed visual and haptic aids for enhancing safety of human and autonomous systems sharing a common airspace. When tele-operating a remotely piloted vehicle (RPV) or simply managing an unmanned autonomous aerial vehicle (UAV), a human operator is physically separated from the vehicle, so he/she receives no inertial or auditory feedback from the vehicle and, at most, only partial visual cues are available. As a consequence, there is a serious risk of a reduced situation awareness.

To help the pilot focusing on the actual objective of the mission, while avoiding collisions with (moving or static) obstacles and other vehicles, and in order to effectively cooperate with other autonomous systems or remotely piloted vehicles sharing a common airspace, a combined visual and haptic display is proposed. The visual display consists of a set of graphical aids projected in an augmented

© Springer International Publishing AG 2016
J. Hodicky (Ed.): MESAS 2016, LNCS 9991, pp. 64–80, 2016.
DOI: 10.1007/978-3-319-47605-6_6

reality fashion on the on-board camera live video stream. The haptic feedback is provided using a force-feedback joystick. Detection of obstacles and other vehicles, as well as knowledge of current flight status of cooperating autonomous systems is assumed available through a sensing or a communication system. This aspect is relevant for the practical implementation of the system, but it is out of the scope of the present paper, and it will not be analyzed in the sequel.

Visual and haptic aids are generated as a function of current aircraft speed and position, with respect to nearby obstacles, and the (predicted) motion of the other cooperating autonomous systems. The visual aid is realized by means of Virtual Fences of different shape and color, where graphical features of the fence are determined in order to highlight potential collisions, safety area violations and to enhance perception of state of teaming autonomous or remotely piloted systems. The visual aid aspect (e.g. the Virtual Fences color) is updated in order to provide to the remote operator information on the distance from the forbidden zone (i.e. from the Fence itself) and the risk level in a intuitive way. At the same time, a force feedback is generated on the joystick to suggest the collision free trajectory: the haptic aid could be designed not only to warn the pilot of a possible future collision, but also to guide him to take the best corrective action (e.g. according to a precomputed avoidance trajectory) or simpler avoidance maneuvers.

In order to test the system, a sample mission involving human operators, simulated autonomous systems and remotely piloted vehicles was designed, where complex cooperative tasks such as simultaneous target acquisition and cooperative navigation in a crowded airspace at very low altitude (below buildings altitude) needs to be accomplished. Real-time simulations with human operators in the loop were performed in a 3D virtual environment. Pilot performance (minimum distance from obstacles/other vehicles and the virtual fences) were recorded when using the visual aid only, and compared with those obtained when both the haptic and the visual aid were provided to the operator(s). Preliminary results demonstrate that pilot performance is significantly improved in the latter case.

The paper is organized as follows: Sections 2 and 3 present the proposed visual aid, and haptic aid respectively; Section 4 describes the simulation environment employed in the man in the loop tests; Section 5 presents the test campaign results and Sect. 6 summarizes the conclusions of the study.

2   Visual Aids for Conflict Prevention

2.1   The Safety Fence Concept

The advantages of adopting additional visual cues in an augmented reality framework for enhancing pilot's awareness and improving precision in complex tasks has been demonstrated for a long time, e.g. by means of the so called "tunnel in the sky" [1,2]. In a recent paper [3], a novel concept was introduced in the framework of remotely operated vehicles, which was referred to as the Virtual Fence.

The Virtual Fence is a dynamic graphical representation of the admissible boundaries for safely operating the RPV. The fence is projected on the visual stream which is made available to the pilot from the onboard camera, in order to clearly highlight where he/she is allowed to fly the vehicle, with dynamic changes in shape and color that depend on the current flight condition.

More in detail, the shape of the fence takes into account

- the maximum altitude for safely operating the vehicle, according to current Civil Aviation Authorities regulations;
- the limits of those areas that cannot be trespassed under any condition;
- a safety margin which is evaluated in a worst-case scenario in the case of a loss-of-control accident.

For the latter reason the fence is bended inwards, with respect to the bounds of the admissible operational region, provided that a longer distance in free fall can be covered by the vehicle if loss-of-control occurs at higher altitude. Similarly, the safety margin is increased when the vehicle is flying at higher speed towards the limits of the admissible region, because of its higher kinetic energy that would increase the chances of violating the limits.

The availability of algorithms for predicting the future position of the aircraft as a function of its current velocity and maneuver state [4,5] allowed for implementing a dynamic variation of the fence color. The color coding can be changed, depending on the actual mission scenario. When most of the video stream background is represented by fields or trees, a bright yellow color is well visible to the pilot, and it is chosen as the standard color, when the vehicle is at a safe distance from the fence. When the trajectory prediction algorithm indicates that the pilot is approaching the fence and a violation of the bound of the operational regions is possible, the color shifts to orange. When the trajectory prediction algorithm determines that a violation of the fence is expected for the current maneuver state within a prescribed time-interval, the fence color is turned to red. The duration of the prediction time interval depends on the maneuvering performance of the vehicle, provided a reliable prediction over longer time intervals is possible for slower/heavier vehicles, whereas shorter prediction interval are available for more maneuverable vehicles, which, by the way, are more agile can also more easily be driven away from the potentially dangerous situation.

2.2   Management of Moving Vehicles

One of the original contributions of this paper is the extension of the Virtual Fence concept, which was demonstrated in [3] for fixed boundaries only, to the improvement of pilot awareness with respect to the presence of other vehicles in the same region of the airspace. This aspect is particularly relevant in actual applications, provided that other aerial or ground based agents, operating in the same area, may be difficult to detect visually from a distance using only the live camera view of the vehicle. Thus a tri-dimensional highlight graphics for all other piloted and/or autonomous agents in the area is proposed.

This is possible under the assumption that the other cooperating vehicles communicate somehow their position and flight status. As an alternative, for non-cooperative vehicles (either autonomous or piloted), it assumed that they are detected and localized with some sort of sensor (e.g. radar, transponder etc.). Anyway, a detailed discussion of this issue and possible technical implementation are outside of the scope of this paper.

The agent highlight graphics is represented by a red wire-frame sphere, which will be referred to as the Highlight Sphere, in the sequel, which is drawn around the current position of the neighboring vehicle(s). The sphere has a fixed size (10 m in our experiments) for small agents, and its size is scaled as dictated by the actual perspective view of the operational scenario, so that the sphere appears larger for closer vehicles and smaller for other ones that are far away. This aims at enhancing the pilot perception of depth and distance from the other agents. Note that larger spheres or ellipsoids could be used for larger piloted vehicles operating in the area (helicopters, large RPV's, etc.).

The synthetic environment employed in our tests allows also for emulating visual occlusions behind landmarks (building, tress etc.). This allows the pilot to visually detect other vehicles also when they are fully hidden (but the highlight sphere is not) from his view. Replication of this latter feature, display of a partially occluded Highlight Sphere, in a real augmented reality display poses non trivial problems that needs to be accurately addressed in the study. Figure 1 shows the efficacy of the superimposed highlight sphere for enhancing visual perception of nearby small flying objects.

Fig. 1. Sample onboard camera view of three nearby drones, without (above) and with (below) the superimposed highlight sphere.

3 Haptic Aid for Collision Avoidance

Usually visual cues only are used in the context of remotely operated systems, however the adoption of an artificial feel system for the stick has already been investigated as a viable approach capable of increasing the pilot/operator situational awareness, especially in terms of external disturbances, faults and environmental constraints, which degrade the vehicle maneuvering capability and the safety of the operation; this is extremely relevant for Unmanned Aerial Vehicles (UAVs) that might be operated far beyond the line of sight with relevant communication delays as well. Tactile cues have already been shown to successfully complement visual information, provided for instance by the displays of a remote Control Ground Station [6,7].

Haptic cues in support of collision avoidance have already been investigated in the past, and have been heuristically defined as repulsive forces created by objects in the environment in order to help the operator to avoid them. Research on autonomous mobile robots often presents virtual repulsive forces to avoid collisions with obstacles [6–14].

When a continuous force feedback is used, that is, forces that are strictly correlated with the action to be taken by the pilot are injected on the control stick, the haptic aid system and the pilot both contribute to the task, this constitute the so called shared control paradigm [15–19]. In addition to the use as an operational aid, shared control could also be considered as a support to training [20,21].

Unfortunately design of a haptic aid for shared control is not straightforward and much research is still needed in this field (see for example the many different approaches reviewed in [22], and the complementary techniques named Direct and Indirect Haptic aid, in short DHA and IHA, presented in [23]). The class of all Haptic aids, which produce forces and/or sensations (due to stick stiffness changes for instance) aimed at directly forcing or facilitating the pilot to take some actions instead of others is called Direct Haptic Aid (DHA). With the DHA approach, the operator must be compliant with the force felt on the stick.

A complementary use of the sense of touch is what is exploited by the Indirect Haptic Aid (IHA) class instead. The natural tendency to oppose the forces felt on the haptic device (especially by untrained pilots), is exploited to generate an haptic stimulus that requires a reaction in opposition to it, rather than compliance. This approach was proven to be able to provide equal or even better results (in terms of pilot performance improvements) with respect to a similarly designed DHA system [19,24–26].

In the present paper a DHA approach is adopted, where the choice is motivated by its positive features: a simple tuning procedure and a straightforward use by the pilots.

3.1 Generation of the Haptic Force

Among other technical aspects, two issues are particularly relevant for the generation of the haptic aid in the crowded airspace taken as sample scenario in this paper, namely:

- fusion of the contributions to the aid of each single obstacle to be avoided,
- generation of a suitable stick haptic force capable of actively communicating
  with the pilot (telling the presence of obstacles possibly hidden in his view),
  and helping him to maintain the desired separation from them.

Several approaches have been proposed in the past for generation of aid forces
in support to obstacle avoidance. Lam et al. [6] propose to generate the haptic
information by means of an artificial force field (AFF) that maps environment
constraints to repulsive forces. The generated force is proportional to the gradient
of this repulsive field. In Sangyoon et al. [14] the problem of obstacle avoidance
is addressed by generating a force that is directly proportional to the distance
from the obstacles. However, in Alaimo et al. [24] analytical and experimental
results show that a haptic force, which is simply proportional to the distance
from the obstacle, cannot stabilize the system: a relevant anticipatory effect or
phase lead is needed. We followed thus this latter approach by creating a force
field originating from all the obstacles, namely, the Virtual Fences, and all the
other UAVS present in the area and employing a Proportional-Derivative-like
(PD) force generator.

Fusion of contributions (to the aid) of each single obstacle to be avoided is
achieved by computing a global force field as the sum of repulsive force fields
generated by each single obstacle: each obstacle (another UAV or a Safety Fence)
generates a force field that pushes the vehicle away from it; the components of
the force field are summed up at the current vehicle position to form a total
repulsive force; then the total force is used to generate the haptic aid, namely
the force to be applied to the stick.

The Force fields generated by safety Fences, static or almost static UAVs
and moving UAVs have different characteristics because they represent different
threats. The force field generated by the Safety Fence is directed inward (toward
the permitted area) and is normal to the fence border (being the Safety Fence
footprint a continuous curve). The force field generated by UAVs expands with
a spherical symmetry instead (being UAVs point-like obstacles). Since a static
UAV represents a smaller threat to flight safety than a rapidly moving UAV,
the intensity of the force field of static and moving UAVs was designed to be
different. In particular, a gain function of the UAV speed was employed.

Forces are generated as a non-linear function of distance between the center
of gravity of the remotely piloted vehicle and the other fixed or moving obstacle.
This distance is computed in different ways depending on the obstacles. If the
obstacles is another UAV, the distance is computed as:

$$d_i = \sqrt{\left(x - x_i\right)^2 + \left(y - y_i\right)^2 + \left(z - z_i\right)^2}$$

where the triple (x, y, z) is the current position of the remotely piloted vehicle, and (x_i, y_i, z_i) is the position of the i-th UAV. Note that these triples are
expressed in Cartesian coordinates defined in a common Navigation Frame; these
can be easily obtained by projection from Ellipsoidal coordinates, namely Latitude, Longitude and Altitude.

The distance between the remote piloted vehicle and the fences is computed differently: each fence is defined by a list of points(vertexes) coordinates (x, y); these points are considered in groups of three adjacent points forming two side of a triangle; the point (x_H, y_H, z_H) laying on these two segments that is closest to the vehicle position (x, y, z) is computed; finally the distance from the Fence is computed as:

$$d_i = \sqrt{(x - x_H)^2 + (y - y_H)^2 + (z - z_H)^2}$$

Then each distance is used to compute a force vector; the force vector is aligned in the $[(x - x_i), (y - y_i), (z - z_i)]$ or $[(x - x_H), (y - y_H), (z - z_H)]$ direction. The force vector intensity F_i is given instead by the nonlinear function of distance d_i:

$$F_i = f(d_i) \tag{1}$$

The force was chosen for our experiments to be inversely proportional to the distance d_i.

In order to fuse the contributions of each single fence, static or moving UAV, all forces are summed up, and scaled by the weighting coefficient w_i that was selected different for the Virtual Fences, the static UAVS and the moving UAVs, to form the total force vector F_{tot}.

$$F_{tot} = \sum_{i=1}^{N} w_i F_i \tag{2}$$

where N is the number of force generating elements.

Given that the pilot is remotely controlling the vehicle using live camera feedback, and that the camera is pointed along the direction of motion of the vehicle, it is likely that his/her situational awareness (at least in terms of nearby obstacles) should be high enough for what regards what is in front of the camera, bu much lower for what is near to the borders of the camera field of view, and he/she is unaware of what lies outside of it. According to the above, we decided, for the scope of this preliminary proof of concept system evaluation, to generate an haptic feedback that considers lateral threats only. This, in addition, simplifies greatly the test scenario setup (only the lateral axis of the haptic joystick is used) and the analysis of the results (only lateral distance to obstacles is considered as performance metric).

In order to limit the haptic aid to the lateral channel only, the total force field vector F_{tot} at the current vehicle position is evaluated, but only its component along the lateral axis of the vehicle is considered.

This is achieved by rotating the F_{tot} vector, that is expressed in navigation frame, into body frame (using the vehicle Direction Cosine Matrix C_n^b), and by taking only the lateral (Y axis component):

$$F_{tot}^{lateral} = [0, 1, 0] \cdot C_n^b \cdot F_{tot}^n \tag{3}$$

Figure 2 shows an example of how repulsive forces are summed up to form F_{tot} and $F_{tot}^{lateral}$, using distances from two fences and one UAV.

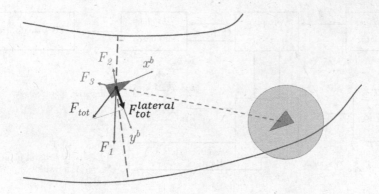

Fig. 2. Sample scheme of repulsive forces composition.

The scalar $F_{tot}^{lateral}$ is then fed to a digital Proportional-Derivative controller that generates the actual haptic force F_{haptic} to be applied at the pilot's stick. The Proportional and Derivative gains, k_p and k_d were tuned heuristically with a test pilot with the objective of providing an aiding force with the minimum necessary strength, thus providing a minimally perceivable sensation, while still providing enough support in keeping distance from obstacles.

Figure 3 shows the block diagram of the PD-like haptic force generator. Negative feedback is used to generate a stick force that pushes away from the obstacles as in the DHA paradigm.

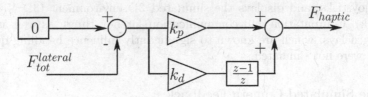

Fig. 3. Block diagram of the haptic force generator.

4   The Simulation Environment

In order to test the mixed Visual/Haptic Display described in the previous section, a simulation environment, derived from that described in [27–29] was employed. It consists of several hardware and software components: a vehicle dynamics simulator, the hardware of an actual autopilot, a virtual environment, and a ground station with two joysticks. The vehicle dynamics simulator runs in pseudo-real time on a desktop PC, and simulates the vehicle dynamics and external disturbances, emulating all the sensor readings for successive elaboration by the Guidance, Navigation, and Control system embedded in the autopilot; in addition, the simulator receives all control inputs from the autopilot, thus closing the simulation loop with the actual autopilot hardware.

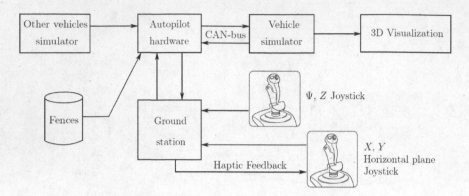

Fig. 4. Simulator's block diagram.

Just as reference, the autopilot and the simulator were interfaced using CAN-bus, and exchanged 10 CANbus packets at a rate of 100 Hz: 7 from simulator to autopilot for accelerometers, gyroscopes, magnetometers, baro-altimeter and GPS data, and 3 for autopilot commands and various debug data. The simulator timing was slaved to that of the autopilot (that was actually running in real-time) so that the CANbus datalink served both for data exchange and timebase synchronization. More details can be found in the cited references.

Figure 4 shows the block diagram of the complete simulation environment used for the man-in-the-loop experiments. The Ground station receives the aircraft status (via the autopilot), sends the pilot flight commands acquired by the two joysticks, and displays the simulated 3D environment (3D Visualization block). Computation and communication latency times, as well as video streaming delays, which are known to significantly influence handling qualities of RPVs, were not simulated.

4.1   The Simulated Camera Feedback

The proposed visual tools and haptic feedback were designed to support a pilot who is manually controlling the UAV using a live video stream from an onboard camera.

Emulation of the live video stream is achieved using a synthetic environment [27–30]. The importance of using a scenery that is representative of real places on earth, instead of imaginary non-existent places, is well known and experimental evidence can be easily found. In addition, a full immersion in a detailed scenery guarantees focus on the tasks and minimizes "distance" between performance in simulation and in the operational environment.

The simulation environment employed for the virtual experiments presented in this paper is built upon an interface between GoogleEarth and our simulator that exchange data in real-time at about 30 Hz. This refresh speed is sufficient for immersive simulation with no perception of simulator's delays.

This simulator was designed for testing the proposed pilot support techniques, but it can be regarded also as a practical tool for pilot training with the visual and haptic tools proposed in this paper. It may also serve as a briefing tool for pre-mission analysis: the intended mission may be pre-performed virtually with the simulator to discover and highlight potential issues.

Although the tests performed so far were run in simulations only, augmented reality techniques [31,32], that are becoming more and more reliable and precise, will allow in the near future a real-time implementation of the proposed visual tool within an augmented reality display where the pilot will see actual imagery coming from vehicle camera with the synthetic graphics of the safety fences as tri-dimensional geo-referenced overlay. Figures 1 and 5 were generated during use of the presented simulator.

4.2   The Haptic Stick

A large variety of commercial haptic devices exists, most of which are designed for general purpose haptic interaction with virtual worlds. These devices can be relatively cheap, but unfortunately they do not suit well the needs of shared control studies, since they have shapes, handles, and volumes of motion that are typically very different from the control devices found in vehicles [33].

Control devices that resemble closely the actual ones installed onboard vehicles or in ground control stations better suit shared control research [33]. For this reason, a novel, low cost, 2 DOFs haptic stick was designed with a configuration similar to that of a typical ground control station side stick, aiming at good accuracy, precision and contained cost. A cheap commercial off-the-shelf force-feedback enabled joystick, sold for the gaming market, was refurbished with entirely new control system to allow the degree of accuracy needed by haptic experiments.

In order to implement an haptic feedback, the joystick was designed to appear as a virtual mass-spring-damper system (usually with a critically damped transient response), the neutral point can be set dynamically (needed for implementation of IHA strategies), and it is also possible to inject external forces on the stick to implement an haptic cue (needed for the DHA strategy).

The new control system is composed of an inner motor current controller (torque, or force at the joystick tip, is linearly proportional to the motor rotor current), and an outer impedance controller that emulates the presence of a spring and a damper of given desired stiffness and damping factor. Details of the controller architecture and tuning can be found in [33].

5   Simulation Results

In order to validate and asses the performance of the proposed visual-haptic aid system, a test campaign was realized. A complex guidance task within other UAVs, fixed and moving, and with the desired path passing very close to buildings was prepared; performance of the various pilots with the two aid methods (namely with and without haptic aid) were then computed in simulated missions and analyzed to provide a critical analysis of performance.

5.1   The Operational Scenario

The area around the Coliseum, a famous landmark in the city of Rome, Italy, was selected as the area of operations. Five other UAVs that run an autonomous flight program and do not cooperate to avoid collisions are present in the same area: four of them are in hover condition, and one is moving performing a surveillance task along an approximately circular path that will cross with the piloted vehicle path one or two times during the mission. Goal of the participant is to take off, move clockwise around the Coliseum at constant speed in order to reach an easily recognizable landmark (the Roman Emperor Costantino's Arch). During exploration, the vehicle should keep distance from the other UAVs and all obstacles protected by the Virtual Fences. Two Virtual Fences were defined: one of these defines the border of the coliseum, thus protects the infrastructure; the other limits the border of the area where flight is allowed, and should not be violated since a crash due to a system fault happening when outside of the area protected by the Virtual Fence might produce a damage to persons or goods. The area is extremely crowded with lots of building and trees which create a relevant visual clutter. The flight height is below the Coliseum height, thus visual occlusions also happen with other UAVs.

Figure 5 shows a bird's eye view of the operation area. Fences are shown in yellow, the color used to communicate the absence of distance warning. Two red highlight sphere are also visible indicating the position of two other UAVs.

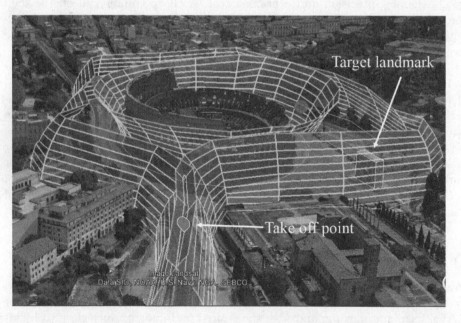

Fig. 5. Bird's eye view of the area of the scenario showing the fences and some of UAVs. (Color figure online)

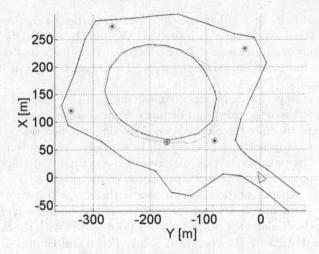

Fig. 6. Map view of the scenario showing the fences footprint (inner:red, outer:blue), hovering UAVs locations (red circles) and own position (triangle), and moving UAV trajectory (dotted gray). (Color figure online)

Figure 6 shows the map of the scenario showing the fence footprints, locations of UAVs hovering as red circles, the planned path of the moving UAV and the piloted vehicle position as a blue triangle.

5.2 Experiment Design

In order to evaluate the system performance and compare pilot behavior with the proposed Visual-Haptic Aid system, and with the Visual Aid only, a test campaign was run with a total of 26 subjects. Every pilot performed the exploration task two times: the first time with the visual aid only, the second time with the combined Visual-Haptic Aid.

The vehicle dynamics was that of a light multi-rotor. In order to simplify pilot's task the altitude controller was active and the pilot did not have to actively control altitude; in addition the altitude was the same for all subjects. The Pilot controlled the Roll and Pitch angles, thus lateral and longitudinal motion respectively, with the haptic stick. The Pitch force feedback channel of the stick was disabled, since only a lateral force was generated as explained in the previous section. In addition, the Pilot controlled the vehicle yaw rate with a second stick, similar in shape to the first one, but without any force feedback.

The Virtual Fences were set to issue the color warning at a distance of 30 m (the color code of the distance was described in Sect. 2). The distance between the two fences is below 60 m (i.e. double the Safety Fence warning Distance) in several portions of the mission path, meaning that the Visual Warning is active also at the mid point of the Virtual Fences.

Both the Safety Fence (i.e. the visual aid) and the Haptic Aid were designed with the goal of helping the pilot to keep distance from the obstacles (being them the virtual fence or another vehicle). Thus, in order to compute a performance metric, the distance from each single UAV, and the two Safety Fences was recorded; the minimum of these distances at each time instant was considered as the quantity to be maximized by the pilot. The larger the distance the better the performance.

Then, as overall performance metric in the entire flight, we scored each flight with the mean value of the minimum distance from obstacles along the path followed by the vehicle. Since the Safety Fence Warning is issued when the distance falls below 30 m, only portions of the path flown below this threshold, namely those parts of the path where the pilot received a Visual and Haptic cue, are considered in the computation of the performance metric.

Goal of this experimentation is to assess if there is a statistically relevant difference of performance (i.e. mean value of the minimum distance from obstacles and other UAVs along the path) between pilots flying with the Safety Fence Aid, and those flying with the combined Safety Fence and Haptic Aid.

5.3 Results and Discussion

A total of 26 naive subjects participated in the experiment campaign. Figure 7 shows the result of one sample subject when using the combined Visual-Haptic Aid or the Visual-Aid only. Keeping an appropriate distance (i.e. larger than the fence safety warming) from the Coliseum, that is from the inner fence, resulted quite difficult for most pilots since, for this specific mission, the Coliseum walls lied at the limit of the pilots camera field of view. As a matter of fact, the trajectory flown without the Haptic Aid passes very close to the Fence.

On the converse, the pilot of this sample flight, was able to keep a larger distance from the inner fence when using the combined Visual-Haptic Aid. Actually the pilot flew almost at the mid point of the two fences, where the haptic force nulls (left and right Safety Fences contributions cancel at the mid point). This indicates that he felt the forces and actively followed their guidance directed away from the obstacles. Figure 8 shows the time histories of the minimum distance from all obstacles (fences and UAVs) during the two missions. Distance from the obstacles is almost always larger with the Haptic Aid active, with respect to the Visual Aid only. Please note that when the distance is larger than 30 m, the Fence warning is not active.

Figure 9 shows instead all the paths flown by the 26 subjects of the test campaign. The mean value (over the path flown) of minimum of distances from obstacles for each pilot can be seen in Fig. 10, where it appears that all pilots were able to keep a larger distance from the obstacles when using the combined Visual-Haptic feedback. Finally Fig. 11 shows the average value (average over the 26 subjects) of means of minimum of distances for the two cases: combined Visual-Haptic Aid, and Visual Aid only. The vertical bars indicate the $1 - \sigma$ bounds of the distribution. It is evident that the pilots perform better when using the combined Visual-Haptic Aid. In addition, a lower dispersion of the Visual-Haptic Aid distribution can be noticed, which implies that, on average, a more precise control is achieved.

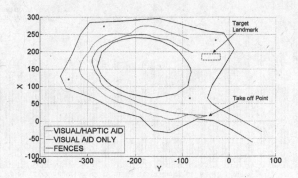

Fig. 7. Sample trajectory of one subject with and without haptic aid.

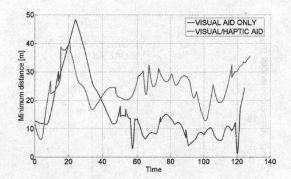

Fig. 8. Sample plots of minimum of distances of one subject with and without haptic aid.

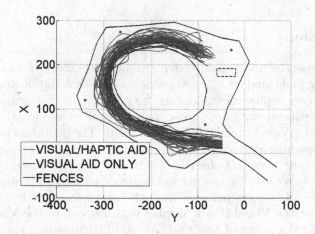

Fig. 9. Trajectories of the 26 subjects with and without haptic aid.

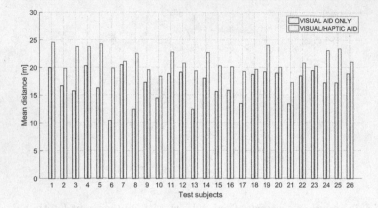

Fig. 10. Plots of mean (over the path flown) of minimum of the distances from obstacles for the 26 subjects.

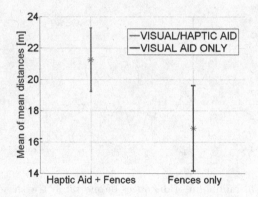

Fig. 11. Statistical analysis (mean and $1 - \sigma$ bounds) of distances for the 26 subjects set.

6   Conclusions

This paper presented and demonstrated through an extensive test campaign, using a realistic flight simulator, a novel concept of Visual-Haptic display for situational awareness improvement, designed for crowded and low altitude airspace situations. Experiments with both no fly zones (delimited by Virtual fences), static and moving UAVs were conducted with 26 pilots. The pilots had to pursue the mission goal (reaching a prescribed target) while avoiding no fly zones and other UAVs. The distance from all obstacles (virtual, static and moving), source of possible risk, was recorded. Experimental evidence has shown that pilots where able to maintain a larger separation from the obstacles, thus incurring a less risk, when using the Visual-Haptic display with respect to the Visual display only. Future developments of this work include flight testing, realization of a proper augmented reality interface, and integration of ground personnel into the augmented reality display.

References

1. Sachs, G.: Perspective predictor/flight-path display with minimum pilot compensation. J. Guid. Control Dyn. **23**(3), 420–429 (2000)
2. Mulder, M., Veldhuijzen, A.R., van Paassen, M.M., Mulder, J.A.: Integrating fly-by-wire controls with perspective flight-path displays. J. Guid. Control Dyn. **28**(6), 1263–1274 (2005)
3. Giulietti, F., Pollini, L., Avanzini, A.: Visual aids for safe operation of remotely piloted vehicles in the controlled air space. In: Proceedings of Institution of Mechanical Engineers, Part G: Journal of Aerospace Engineering, Published online before print 7 March 2016 (2016). doi:10.1177/0954410016632014
4. Innocenti, M., Pollini, L., Giulietti, F.: Visual tools for man-machine interface real time simulation. In: Proceedings of IEEE Symposium on Information Technology in Mechatronics, ITM 2001, Istanbul, Turkey, October 2001 (2001)
5. Avanzini, G.: Frenet-based algorithm for trajectory prediction. J. Guid. Control Dyn. **27**(1), 127–135 (2004)
6. Lam, T.M., Boschloo, H.W., Mulder, M., van Paassen, M.M.: Artificial force field for haptic feedback in UAV teleoperation. IEEE Trans. Syst. Man Cybern. Part A: Syst. Hum. **39**(6), 1316–1330 (2009)
7. Lam, T.M., Mulder, M., van Paassen, M.M., Mulder, J.A., van Der Helm, F.C.T.: Force-stiffness feedback in UAV tele-operation with time delay. In: AIAA Guidance, Navigation, and Control Conference, Chicago, Illinois, August 2009
8. Diolaiti, N., Melchiorri, C.: Tele-operation of a mobile robot through haptic feedback. In: IEEE International Workshop on Haptic Virtual Environments and Their Applications (HAVE 2002), Ottawa, Ontario, Canada, November (2002)
9. Barnes, D.P., Counsell, M.S.: Haptic communication for remote mobile manipulator robot operations. In: Proceedings of 8th Topical Meeting on Robotics and Remote Systems. American Nuclear Society, Pittsburgh (1999)
10. Farkhatdinov, I., Ryu, J,-H., An, J.: A preliminary experimental study on haptic teleoperation of mobile robot with variable force feedback gain. In: Haptics Symposium, 25–26 March 2010. IEEE (2010)
11. Horan, B., Crelghton, D., Nahavandi, S., Jamshidi, M., Bilateral haptic teleoperation of an articulated track mobile robot. In: IEEE International Conference on System of Systems Engineering, SoSE 2007, 16–18 April 2007 (2007)
12. Mitsou, N.C., Velanas, S.V., Tzafestas, C.S.: Visuo-haptic interface for teleoperation of mobile robot exploration tasks. In: The 15th IEEE International Symposium on Robot and Human Interactive Communication, ROMAN 2006, 6–8 September 2006, pp. 157–163 (2006)
13. Rsch, O.J., Schilling, K., Roth, H.: Haptic interfaces for the remote control of mobile robots. Control Eng. Pract. **10**(11), 1309–1313 (2002)
14. Lee, S., Sukhatme, G.S., Kim, G.J., Park, C.-M.: Haptic control of a mobile robot: a user study. In: IEEE/RSJ International Conference on Intelligent Robots and Systems, vol. 3, pp. 2867–2874 (2002)
15. De Stigter, S., Mulder, M., van Paassen, M.M.: Design and evaluation of a haptic flight director. J. Guid. Control Dyn. **30**(1), 35–46 (2007)
16. Abbink, D.A., Boer, E.R., Mulder, M.: Motivation for continuous haptic gas pedal feedback to support car following. In: Proceedings of IEEE Intelligent Vehicles Symposium, pp. 283–290 (2008)
17. Abbink, D., Mulder, M., Boer, E.R.: Haptic shared control: smoothly shifting control authority? Cogn. Technol. Work **14**(1), 19–28 (2012)

18. Goodrich, K., Schutte, P., Williams, R.: Haptic-multimodal flight control system update. In: Proceedings of 11th AIAA Aviation Technology, Integration, and Operations (ATIO) Conference, pp. 1–17 (2011)
19. Olivari, M., Nieuwenhuizen, F.M., Buelthoff, H.H., Pollini, L.: Pilot adaptation to different classes of haptic aids in tracking tasks. J. Guid. Control Dyn. **37**(6), 1741–1753 (2014)
20. Maimeri, M., Olivari, M., Buelthoff, H.H., Pollini, L.: On effects of failures in haptic and automated pilot support systems. In: Proceedings of AIAA Modeling and Simulation Technologies Conference, pp. 1–12 (2016)
21. D'Intino, G., Olivari, M., Geluardi, S., Venrooij, J., Innocenti, M., Buelthoff, H.H., Pollini, L.: Evaluation of haptic support system for training purposes in a tracking task. In: IEEE Systems, Men, and Cybernetics Society Conference (2016)
22. Petermeijer, S., Abbink, D., Mulder, M., de Winter, J.: The effect of haptic support systems on driver performance: a literature survey. IEEE Trans. Haptics **8**(4), 467–479 (2015)
23. Alaimo, S.M.C., Pollini, L., Bresciani, J.P., Blthoff, H.H.: A comparison of direct and indirect haptic aiding for remotely piloted vehicles. In: Proceedings of 19th IEEE International Symposium in Robot and Human Interactive Communication (IEEE Ro-Man 2010)
24. Alaimo, S.M.C., Pollini, L., Bresciani, J.-P., Blthoff, H.H.: Experiments of direct and indirect haptic aiding for remotely piloted vehicles with a mixed wind gust rejection/obstacle avoidance task. In: AIAA Modeling and Simulation Technologies Conference 2011 (MST-2011), Portland, Oregon (2011)
25. Profumo, L., Pollini, L., Abbink, D.A.: Direct and indirect haptic aiding for curve negotiation. In: IEEE International Conference on Systems, Man, and Cybernetics (2013)
26. Alaimo, S.M.C., Pollini, L., Innocenti, M., Bresciani, J.P., Buelthoff, H.H.: Experimental comparison of direct and indirect haptic aids in support of obstacle avoidance for remotely piloted vehicles. J. Mech. Eng. Autom. **2**(10), 2159–5275 (2012)
27. Di Corato, F., Innocenti, M., Pollini, L.: Combined vision-inertial navigation for improved robustness. In: IEEE Israel Itzhack Y. Bar-Itzhack Memorial Symposium on Estimation, Navigation, and Spacecraft Control, Haifa, Israel, 14–17 October 2012
28. Di Corato, F., Innocenti, M., Pollini, L.: Robust vision-aided inertial navigation algorithm via entropy-like relative pose estimation. Gyroscopy Navig. **4**(1), 1–13 (2013)
29. Pollini, L., Metrangolo, A.: Simulation and robust backstepping control of a quadrotor aircraft. In: AIAA Modeling and Simulation Technologies Conference, Honolulu, Hawaii (2008)
30. Pollini, L., Innocenti, M.: A synthetic environment for dynamic systems control and distributed simulation. IEEE Control Syst. Mag. **20**(2), 49–61 (2000)
31. Hutton, J., Mostafa, M.M.R.: 10 years of direct georeferencing for airborne photogrammetry. GIS Bus. (GeoBit) **11**(1), 33–41 (2005)
32. Nebiker, S., Eugster, H., Flckiger, K., Christen, M.: Planning and management of real-time geospatial UAS missions within a virtual globe environment. In: UAV-g 2011, Conference on Unmanned Aerial Vehicle in Geomatics (2011)
33. Pollini, L., Razzanelli, M., Olivari, M., Brandimarti, A., Maimeri, M., Pazzaglia, P., Pittiglio, G., Nuti, R., Innocenti, M., Buelthoff, H.H.: Design, realization and experimental evaluation of a haptic stick for shared control studies. In: The 13th IFAC/IFIP/IFORS/IEA Symposium on Analysis, Design, and Evaluation of Human-Machine Systems, Kyoto, Japan (2016)

Modelling Visual Communication with UAS

Alexander Schelle[(⊠)] and Peter Stütz

Institute of Flight Systems, University of the Bundeswehr Munich,
Neubiberg, Germany
{alexander.schelle, peter.stuetz}@unibw.de

Abstract. This work presents a communication concept for vision based interaction with airborne UAS. Unlike previous approaches, this research focuses on high level mission tasking of UAS without having to rely on radio data link. The paper provides the overall concept design and focuses on communication via gestures. A respective model describing the gestural syntax for high level commands as well as a feedback mechanism to enable bidirectional human-machine communication for different operational modes is presented in detail. First real world experiments evaluate the feasibility of the deployed sensors for the intended purpose.

Keywords: Human-Machine-Interaction · Gesture-based commanding · UAS

1 Introduction

Today's tactical unmanned aerial systems (UAS) are predominantly being used as remote sensor platforms for image intelligence purposes in low and medium altitudes. They require command and guidance information via radio link from a ground control station (GCS) for proper functionality. However a stable data connection cannot always be guaranteed due to failures on the transmission route or demand for silent operations, where the emission of radio signals is suppressed. Moreover, those systems are not able to communicate with third party persons that are not part of the guidance loop, i.e. missing persons in search and rescue missions. Alternative ways of interaction can help to overcome this hurdle by enabling a more natural link between UAS platform and human interaction partner. Here the presented approach utilizes gestures for this purpose.

Previous related work used additional sensors on ground or on the operator's body to control the primary flight controls [1–3]. Gestures were also utilized to group unmanned aerial vehicles (UAVs) by pointing at them [4]. Nagi et al. [5] made use of simple hand gestures and a face pose estimation to command a small drone indoors to fly in a specific direction. The integration of unmanned combat aerial vehicles (UCAVs) into gesture guided carrier deck operations alongside of manned aircrafts for taxiing and takeoff is a current research topic as well [1, 6]. All named approaches have in common, that they try to replace low level command and control interfaces (remote control device or ground control station) with a more natural interface to establish a unidirectional communication with the UAV.

J. Hodicky (Ed.): MESAS 2016, LNCS 9991, pp. 81–98, 2016.
DOI: 10.1007/978-3-319-47605-6_7

This concept goes one step further and focuses on the bidirectional interaction and mission relevant tasking of an airborne UAS. Therefore the focus is not on remote controlling via primary flight controls, but on the transmission of a complete commanding set, comparable to a briefing, for the execution of a complete mission task without interaction in a ground control station. To perceive relevant information, the concept of *interpersonal nonverbal communication* by using gestures to transmit information is adopted. The following chapters will describe the fundamental components for a visual communication with UAS and present implementations for different modes of operation. First experiments and their results will be covered as well, followed by a conclusion and outlook into further research topics.

2 Concept

Being able to communicate visually with UAVs enables a wide spectrum of new use cases for interaction. Intelligence, surveillance and reconnaissance (ISR) missions or even transport missions could be tasked by authorized personal on ground. Missing people could attract attention to themselves and increase the chances of being discovered. One limiting factor of current UAS is the need for a technical controlling device on ground to be able to communicate with it. Therefore the following simple use case, illustrated in Fig. 1, will be introduced to serve as an example for the description of the visual communication concept:

1. An operator on ground tasks the airborne rotary-wing UAV to detect and count persons in a given area by performing a specific set of gestures.
2. The UAV perceives those gestures and translates them into gestural command components.
3. Once the gestural command set is complete, the UAV starts its mission and flies to the commanded area to perform a person detection and counting.
4. Having completed this task, the UAV returns to the last known location of the operator and transmits its results visually (e.g. with light signals).

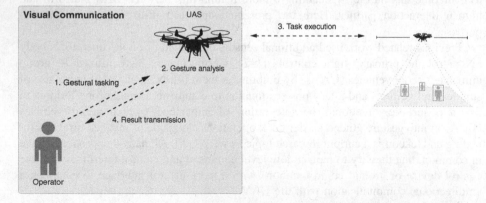

Fig. 1. Exemplary use case for visual communication between an operator and a UAV

Operational Modes and Sensor Deployment. In the given use case the process of visual communication with the human operator on ground can be divided into two operational modes: *detection* and *interaction*. The purpose of the *detection mode* is to find and track an operator on ground and spot potential interaction requests. This mode would be applicable for fixed-wing as well as for rotary-wing UAVs, as this mode requires higher flight altitudes to cover a larger field of view for the detection. Since the employment of thermal longwave infrared (LWIR) sensors for the detection of living beings is an established practice, the most suitable sensor for this mode is a thermal imager. As the spatial resolution of this type of sensors is relatively low so far, only large movements of the arms like waving and pointing can be detected as interaction requests, hence requiring a low resolution operator model for gesture recognition. The related concept of multi resolution operator models will be covered in chapter 2.3 in more detail.

The *interaction mode* on the other hand, targets the actual reception of mission related commands and therefore needs to detect more delicate and information bearing gestures. For that reason, sensors with high imaging performance have to be used to improve the sample ground distance. This involves in most cases an increase in weight due to larger lenses needed for optical magnification. Since the payload of most tactical UAVs is limited to a few kilograms, small and lightweight sensors are preferred. Another approach to improve the imaging performance is to reduce the distance to the operator. As the distance cannot be reduced arbitrary for fixed-wing aircrafts, this approach is only feasible for vehicles with a hovering ability, e.g. rotary-wing aircrafts. In this way smaller sensors can be deployed without lowering the imaging performance for the gesture recognition.

Modern gesture recognition systems utilize consumer depth sensors for efficient real-time person detection and skeletal tracking to realize natural human robot interfaces [7]. Unfortunately these depths sensors have a limited sensing range. Therefore, once an authorized human operator is found, the UAV needs to track the operator, reduce its distance and altitude and get the operator within the range of the onboard depth sensor. Table 1 shows a comparison of both modes.

Table 1. Comparison between *detection* and *interaction mode* in the given use case

	Detection mode	Interaction mode
Purpose	• Human operator detection and tracking • Recognition of interaction requests	• Recognition of gestures and translation into gestural command components
Altitude	• Higher altitude	• Close to ground
Usable human operator resolution model	• Low resolution model	• Medium or high resolution model
Recommended imaging technology	• Thermal LWIR sensor	• Depth sensor

Image Processing Requirements for Visual Communication. Vision based communication not only imposes requirements on the sensors as described in the previous chapter, but also demands the image processing pipeline to master a highly noisy environment. Apart from changing weather conditions, vibrations caused by the propulsion system and the movement of the vehicle itself, it has to deal also with inaccurate and ambiguous executions of gestures by the operator on ground. Therefore the following requirements have to be met by the implementation:

- Robust human detection and tracking with various sensor technologies (thermal, infrared, electro-optical)
- Robust skeletal tracking despite unprecise depth information
- Tolerant dealing with imprecisely performed gestures (temporally and spatially)
- Poses and gestures must be visible from the perspective of the UAV
- High processing speed for prompt feedback

2.1 The Gesture Model

Gestures can be represented in multiple ways. A common way followed in computer vision is to track the position and relations of the operator's body joints via angles or quaternions and feed a learned neural network with that data to recognize a gesture [7].

As gestures can be seen as poses changing over time, the selection of the right starting point for the measuring window is essential for the success of the method. Thinking outside the box can help to solve the problem. In the domain of linguistic and psychological sciences, the concept of spatial and temporal *gesture units* is used to describe the different phases of interpersonal interaction via gesticulation [8–10].

A gesture unit is segmented into five temporal parts: *rest position, protraction, protraction maximum, retraction* and *rest position* (Fig. 2). Obviously a rest position encloses a gesture unit and for that reason can be seen as a separator between two consecutive gestures.

To describe a rest position, the three-dimensional model for the description of gestural parts in utterances of Fricke [11] can be helpful. Here the shape features *hand configuration, orientation, position, movement* and *gravity* and the articulators *hands, feet, head* and *eyes* over time are used for description. Hence, a rest position can be described as a state with low movements and maximum gravity.

Time

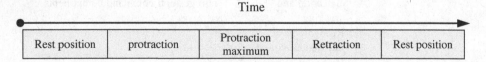

| Rest position | protraction | Protraction maximum | Retraction | Rest position |

Fig. 2. Temporal description of a gesture unit based on [10]

2.2 Syntax for a Gestural Command

Similar to the structure of a sentence with a grammatical subject, verb and object, a gestural command proposed in this work consist of at least four components: *task*

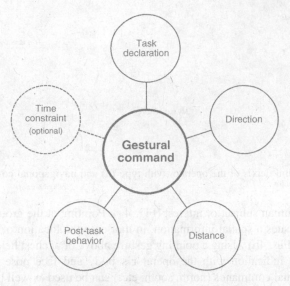

Fig. 3. Gestural command components

declaration, direction, distance and *post-task behavior*, as shown in Fig. 3. The component *time constraint* can be used optionally. In contrast to the linguistic sentence, the components of a gestural command do not have to be in a specific order.

Referring to the exemplary use case of chapter 2, the following paragraphs will describe which information each gestural command component would need to contain to transmit a complete gestural command set for the given task.

Task Declaration. The declaration needs to convey the information, which task has to be performed and if applicable, for what type of object. Table 2 gives an example.

Table 2. Example for gestural command component "task declaration"

Gestural command component	Sub-component	Information	Gestural execution
Task declaration	*Task*	"Search and count objects of type..."	Operator performs the "victory-sign" with his fingers and points them at his eyes.
	Object type	"Human"	Operator points with both hands at his body.

Direction. For the definition of the sub-component *object type* and the navigational parts *direction* and *distance* of the command set, the linguistic concept of *deixis* can be adopted. Deixis describes, how utterances are referred to persons (me, him/her), places (here, there, left, right) or to time (now, later). Research has been done on the use of deictic utterances for human-machine-interactions [12].

For instance, all poses and gestures that include arms/fingers pointing at the operators body, will somehow be related to himself and hence can be seen as a type

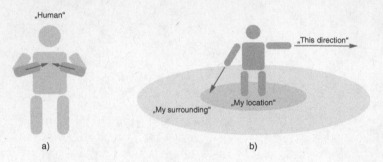

Fig. 4. Gestural deixis of the operator with type (a) and navigational commands (b)

definition for a human subject of interest (Fig. 4a). Pointing at the ground area around the operator indicates a spatial information, in that case the location of the operator or his surrounding (Fig. 4b). Using a pointing gesture above or at chest height represents a relative direction indication with the operator's body and face pose as a reference. Absolute directional commands (north, south, etc.) can be used as well by performing a specific gesture (Table 3).

Table 3. Example for gestural command component "direction"

Gestural command component	Sub-component	Information	Gestural execution
Direction	*Relative*	"Heading = 90°"	Operator points to a direction with one arm at chest height.
	Absolute	"Heading = East"	Operator performs a specific gesture that represents "east".

Distance. The command feature *distance* can be transmitted on a common way by counting with the fingers. One finger represents 100 m, two fingers 200 m and so on (Table 4). Problems occur, if distances greater than 1000 m have to be transmitted. For that case, holding the fingers horizontally counts in thousands, whereas holding the fingers vertically counts in hundreds. Since the applications of the visual communication are optimized for tactical use cases, a maximum communicable distance of 10 km is sufficient. However, this method requires a high spatial resolution of the deployed sensor to distinguish between the single fingers.

Table 4. Example for gestural command component "distance"

Gestural command component	Sub-component	Information	Gestural execution
Distance		"Distance = 500 m"	Operator holds one hand up and shows palm to UAV spreading five fingers vertically.

Post-task Behavior. As ISR missions are one of the intended application for the bidirectional visual communication, the UAS needs to know to whom it has to report the information it has acquired. This will be in most cases the operator (Table 5), but other use cases with different information receivers are imaginable. For instance, the UAS could be tasked to fly back to its home base or deliver the acquired information to the first person it finds in a specific area.

Table 5. Example for gestural command component "post-task behavior"

Gestural command component	Sub-component	Information	Gestural execution
Post-task behavior		"Return to me"	Operator points to the ground he is standing on with one arm.

Time Constraint. The gestural command component *time constraint* is an optional component that needs to be indicated, otherwise the UAS will ignore it. Thus a specific gesture has to be performed prior to the completion of the last command component, to consider the time constraint for the mission task.

Therefore the operator has to perform a specific gesture that activates the time constraint (e.g. connecting the palm of one hand with the wrist of the other), followed by the duration of the time constraint. The duration can be communicated in the same way as distances, e.g. by showing a certain number of horizontal and vertical fingers (Table 6).

Other Gestural Command Components. Besides the four mandatory and one optional component, other gesture types are required to establish a gestural communication. The *interaction request* represents the first gesture that needs to be detected. A common human way to attract attention is to wave with both arms. Monajjemi et al. [13] have demonstrated recently, that an unlearned arm-waving gesture can be detected with low computational costs and without additional learning from an airborne UAV.

To master situations that involve more than one human being within the sensor range, an *Attention!/I'm in control* gesture or pose has to be included as well to detect the operator. The so called "psi-pose" or "surrender pose" is suitable for that purpose, as this pose is often used in skeleton trackers for the estimation of the body part lengths and the initial calibration [14].

Table 6. Example of gestural command component "time constraint"

Gestural command component	Sub-component	Information	Gestural execution
Time constraint	*Activation*	"Consider time constraint"	Operator connects palm of one hand with wrist of other hand.
	Duration	"Maximum task duration = 10 min"	Operator holds both hands up and shows palms to UAV spreading all fingers vertically.

Table 7. Overview of gestural command components and sub-components with examples

Gestural command component	Sub-component	Example
Interaction request	*Gestural*	• Waving with both arms
	Non-gestural	• Flashing light with specific pattern
Attention!/I'm in command		• Both arms above the head ("surrender pose")
Neutral		• Arms hanging, close to the body
Task declaration	*Task*	• "Land…" • "Observe…" • "Fly…" • "Count…" • "Pick up item and release it at…"
	Object type	• Human • Vehicle • Area
Direction	*Relative*	• "The direction I'm pointing to"
	Absolute	• "North" • "South" • "East" • "West"
Distance	*Relative*	• "At my position"
	Absolute	• 100 m, 500 m, etc.
Post-task behavior		• "Return to me" • "Return to base" • "Observe detected object"
Time constraint	*Activation*	• Connecting palm of one hand with wrist of other hand
	Duration	• 5 min, 10 min, etc.

To complete the command set, gestures and poses that do not belong to any of the mentioned gesture types will be categorized as *neutral*. An overview of more command control components, sub-components and example gestures, is listed in the Table 7.

2.3 Multiresolution Operator Models

Due to the multi sensor approach, an implementation has to cope with different sensor performances and ground sample distances, which limit the set of detectable gestures. Figure 5 presents three models for low, medium and high resolution with corresponding 5, 10 and 14 features for pose estimation and gesture recognition.

Based on the available maximum ground sample distance, an appropriate resolution model has to be chosen to select a set of recognizable gestures for the given amount of communicable information.

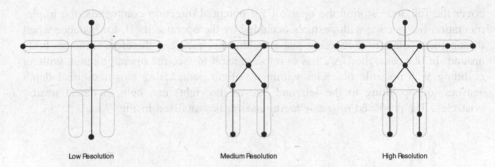

Low Resolution   Medium Resolution   High Resolution

Fig. 5. Low, medium and high resolution models of the human operator

2.4   Feedback Mechanism

In everyday interpersonal communication, two important elements can be observed. First, both interaction partners hold eye contact or at least face each other with their bodies. Second, in bidirectional conversations both participants give multimodal feedbacks, like an affirmative nod with the head or a gentle sound of agreement. Thus both elements have to be tackled. On one hand the operators face and body orientation has to be analyzed, to verify, that the operator's attention is focused on the UAV and to process only those actions that happen in that time window.

On the other hand, the UAV needs to give the operator a visible feedback for understood or unclear commands. Fixed-wing UAVs may rock their wings, as this maneuver can be spotted well from ground, whereas rotary-wing UAVs are able to fly closer to the operator and thus can make use of more information bearing communication channels like light signals and patterns. Figure 6 presents a LED based feedback approach for the interaction mode at small distances.

Pattern	Appearance	Meaning
Blinking 3x	☀ ☀ ☀ ☀ ☀	Command understood
Blinking 3x	● ● ● ● ●	Command not understood
Wiping left to right	○ ☀ ☀ ☀ ☀	Processing
Solid	● ● ● ○ ○	Number of understood commands

Fig. 6. Visual feedback approach with LED array for interaction mode

2.5   Occlusion Detection and Handling

The output of the person and face detection can be used to estimate the position of the operator and to isolate the relevant depth area for the subsequent gesture analysis. To cover the full 360° around the operator for potential direction commands, the implementation has to cope with gestures occluded by the operator itself, for instance when the operator points to a direction that is behind his back and therefore turns his body around. In that case, the UAV has to relocate itself to face the operator again, without colliding with possible obstacles within the flight path. Using two additional depth sensors (one pointing to the left and one to the right) can help to detect nearby obstacles. The proposed *operator facing maxim* is visualized in Fig. 7.

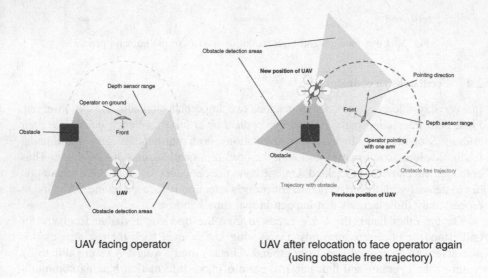

UAV facing operator   UAV after relocation to face operator again
                                       (using obstacle free trajectory)

Fig. 7. Visualization of the operator facing maxim

3   Implementation

The concept for a bidirectional visual communication with UAS has been explained in the previous chapter. The following paragraphs will describe the most promising approach for the algorithmic implementation and the selection of suitable sensors.

Operator Detection and Tracking. Performance and reliability of detection and tracking algorithms have improved constantly over the last years [15]. Despite their age, *boosted cascades of Haar-like classifiers* [16] and *Histograms of Oriented Gradients* (HOG) [17] are still promising approaches for object detection in specific domains. While the former method works best for detecting objects with bright and dark feature groups, like frontal faces, the latter is, due to the orientation analysis, more applicable for finding specific contours and shapes. Having found a potential operator on ground, a reliable tracking is important for the repositioning of the UAV to enhance its viewing conditions.

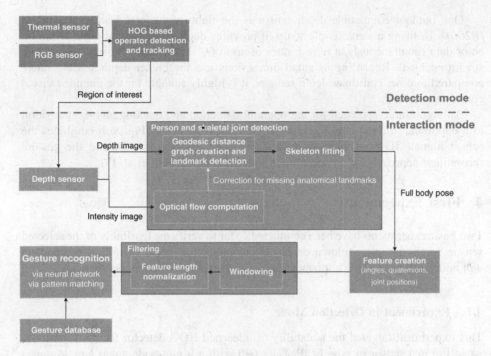

Fig. 8. Operator detection and gesture recognition approach

For that a generic, scale and rotation invariant tracker according to [18] is used. Its performant C++ implementation is part of the open source *Dlib toolkit* [19], which is available for use under the Boost Software License[1].

Gesture Detection and Recognition. The wide use of *Microsoft's Kinect* and other low cost depth sensors has created various kinds of different human detection and gesture recognition systems, including the *Open Natural Interface framework*[2] (OpenNI) and the *Natural Interaction Middleware*[3] (NiTE), which features efficient real-time depth based person detection and skeletal joint tracking capabilities, that have been used to create natural human robot interfaces [7] in the past. However, since the employed Kinect (version 1) utilizes an infrared pattern for the depth data generation, it is not suitable for outdoor use, where the infrared spectrum of the sunlight interferes with the pattern. Furthermore NiTE only supports a limited set of devices that are not state of the art.

---

[1] http://dlib.net/license.html.

[2] OpenNI framework is an open source SDK for the development of 3D sensing middleware libraries and applications, available at http://openni.ru/index.html.

[3] NiTE was a powerful middleware of PrimeSense that featured a robust user skeleton joint tracking and gesture recognition. Since its purchase by Apple Inc. in 2013, it is officially not available any more.

One outdoor compatible depth sensor is the lightweight *Intel RealSense camera (R200)*[4]. Utilizing a stereoscopic setup, it provides depth, infrared and high definition color data simultaneously at refresh rates of up to 60 Hz (up to 90 Hz with only depth stream enabled). Regarding its small dimensions and the higher depth sensing range compared to other consumer depth sensors, it is highly suitable for the intended visual communication.

An algorithmic approach for the operator detection and tracking and the transition to a depth and infrared based gesture recognition is shown in Fig. 8. It combines the robust human 3D pose estimation concept of Schwarz et al. [20] and the gesture recognition approach for natural human interfaces of Cicirelli et al. [7].

4   First Experiments

Two basic experiments have been conducted so far to verify the feasibility of the selected sensors for the data acquisition in detection and interaction mode. The following chapters will address the setup, the implementation and the result of both experiments.

4.1   Experiment in Detection Mode

This experiment targeted the suitability of a learned HOG detector for the used long-wave infrared sensor of type FLIR Tau2 640 with a 9 mm wide angle lens to detect humans and interaction requests. The sensor was integrated into a two-axis gyro-stabilized gimbal system of type DST CONTROL OTUS-L170. The drawback of this thermal sensor is the low spatial resolution of 640×512 pixels and the high distortions due to the mounted wide angle lens for the given purpose. Figure 9 shows the decreasing image quality at higher magnification settings.

Setup. The camera system has been stationary positioned at an altitude of 30 m, having a line of sight of approximately 110 m to the test subjects. The weather conditions were cloudy and two test persons have been briefed to walk along a path, stop at an arbitrary point and to start waving with both arms facing the sensor. The digital magnification has been set to a factor of 4.

Implementation. A HOG detector implementation[5] based by the version of Felzenszwalb et al. [21] has been trained with a small data set of the used thermal sensor of standing and waving persons for a specific zoom setting. In combination with a modified correlation tracker [19] a basic person detection and tracking algorithm has been realized (Fig. 10).

Results. Although the person detector has been trained on the raw data without any image quality improving pre-filtering, the person detector worked well in combination with the correlation tracker, so that acceptable true positive detection rates could be accomplished for the given setup. Figure 11 visualizes the result.

---

[4] http://click.intel.com/intel-realsense-developer-kit-r200.html.

[5] C++ HOG detector implementation included in Dlib library.

1x   2x

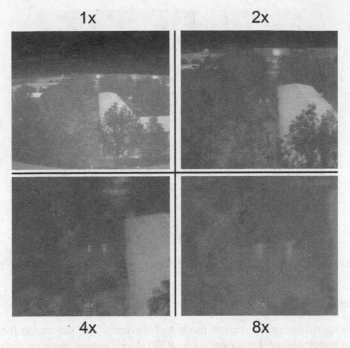

4x   8x

Fig. 9. Image quality of used thermal sensor at different zoom settings

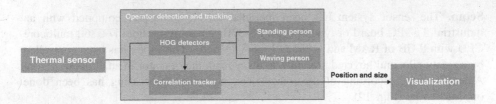

Fig. 10. Image processing chain of the first experiment in detection mode

On the other side, combining several detectors to sense motion or gestures seems not to be an expedient approach as the detector has been learned for only one phase of the gesture, in that case, when the operator stretches out both arms to the side while performing a waving motion.

Furthermore, this experiment confirms the demand for a multi resolution human operator model. Due to the low spatial resolution of the thermal sensor, only the head, both arms and the body itself can be detected, hence allowing only a limited set of recognizable gestures for the low resolution model.

Fig. 11. Result of the HOG based person detector of the first experiment in detection mode

4.2 Experiment in Interaction Mode

The second experiment in interaction mode had the agenda to determine the accuracy and range of the deployed *Intel RealSense R200* depth sensor from an airborne platform. The camera uses two infrared sensors with global shutter in a stereoscopic configuration to generate a stream of depth data and is thus qualified for an outdoor use.

Setup. The sensor system has been mounted on an octocopter equipped with an industrial 3.5" PC board of type Spectra LS-37B, featuring an Intel i7 3860 multicore CPU with 8 GB of RAM and a 512 GB mSATA SSD. The copter has been controlled by a safety pilot and hovered around 7 m away from the operator in an altitude of 3 m. Apart from the recording of the image data, no online processing has been done onboard so far (Fig. 12).

Several gestures have been performed, including the following:

- Waving with both arms
- Attention!/I'm in command
- Move left, move right
- Come closer, back up

Implementation. The implemented algorithm consists of two parts that work on different image domains. First a HOG based person detection and tracking[6] is performed on the infrared stream, similar to the approach of the first experiment. The output of this detection (Fig. 13a) is then used to select the relevant region of interest inside the depth stream, hence filtering out most of the irrelevant data and therefore

---

[6] Using the C++ HOG detector and correlation tracker implementation included in Dlib library.

Fig. 12. UAV equipped with multi sensor camera and experimental setup in interaction mode

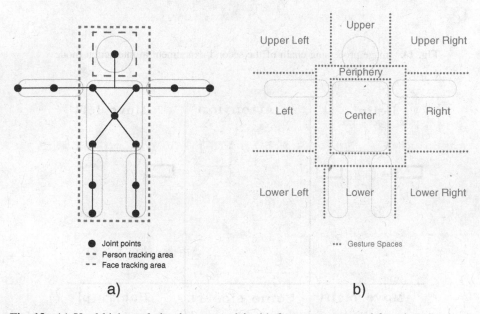

a)   b)

Fig. 13. (a) Used high resolution human model with features, person and face detection area, (b) Three-dimensional Gesture spaces around the operator's body

improving the processing speed. Next, McNeill's concept of the so called *gesture spaces* [8] comes into effect. In this implementation these gesture spaces are modelled as three-dimensional cubes that are located at specific distances around the operator's body (Fig. 13b).

When the operator performs a gesture that penetrates one or more of the gesture spaces, a trigger counter for each gesture space is incremented. If that counter exceeds a defined threshold, an activation signals is send to the gesture detection system. The duty of the gesture detection system is then to find matching activated gesture spaces that represent a gesture. Figure 14 illustrates the relevant processing steps.

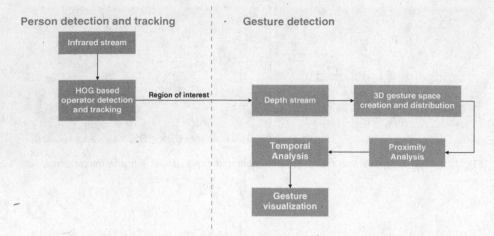

Fig. 14. Image processing chain of the second experiment in interaction mode

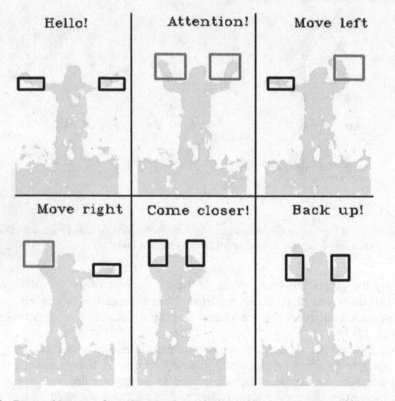

Fig. 15. Detected gestures from the experiment in interaction mode with used gesture spaces

Results. Similar to the first experiment, the HOG person detector has been trained on a small data set of the infrared camera, but delivered as well good results in combination with the correlation tracker. The maximum depth sensing range of the Intel RealSense R200 camera is with up to 10 m sufficient for the given use case, but the accuracy diminishes with increasing distance. Fluctuations of up to ± 500 mm in the depth data prevent the reliable detection of forward or backward performed gestures at this far end, like "*Come closer!*" or "*Back up!*". These gestures include hands that are outstretched behind or in front of the head, therefore the discrimination between hands and head became impossible, as both areas deliver the same noisy depth data. Filtering methods will have to be included or a reduction of the interaction distance considered to improve the accuracy to a reliable level. Otherwise backward facing gestures will have to be excluded from the gesture set. Further experiments regarding this issue are needed.

However, other two-dimensional gestures that involve movements only in the depth plane of the operator's body, like waving and pointing, can be detected reliably. Figure 15 gives an overview of the tested gestures and the involved gesture spaces.

5   Conclusion and Outlook

This work presented a concept for the high level commanding of airborne UAS by using visual communication, in particular by using gestures performed by an operator on ground. Applicable use cases and the idea of different operational modes for the multi sensor approach have been introduced as well as a new syntax for gestural commands. Exemplary gestures have been recommended that allow the transmission of the components of a gestural command without using a radio data link in between. An easy to read feedback mechanism has been suggested to enable a bidirectional human-machine interaction. One experiment in detection mode and one in interaction mode have been conducted to evaluate the feasibility of the recommended sensor technologies for the intended purpose. Further research will focus on the filtering and improvement of the sensor output to receive more reliable data for the skeletal tracking from airborne platforms. A more sophisticated gesture recognition will be implemented based on the proposed approach using point cloud data.

References

1. Venetsky, L., Tieman, J.W.: Robotic gesture recognition system, 20 October 2009
2. Pfeil, K., Koh, S.L., LaViola, J.: Exploring 3D gesture metaphors for interaction with unmanned aerial vehicles. In: Proceedings of the 2013 International Conference on Intelligent User Interfaces, pp. 257–266 (2013)
3. Wagner, P.K., Peres, S.M., Madeo, R.C.B., de Moraes Lima, C.A., de Almeida Freitas, F.: Gesture unit segmentation using spatial-temporal information and machine learning. In: FLAIRS Conference (2014)

4. Monajjemi, V.M., Wawerla, J., Vaughan, R., Mori, G.: HRI in the sky: creating and commanding teams of UAVs with a vision-mediated gestural interface. In: 2013 IEEE/RSJ International Conference on Intelligent Robots and Systems, pp. 617–623 (2013)

5. Nagi, J., Giusti, A., Di Caro, G.A., Gambardella, L.M.: HRI in the sky: controlling UAVs using face poses and hand gestures. In: HRI, pp. 252–253 (2014)

6. Vanetsky, L., Husni, M., Yager, M.: Gesture recognition for UCAV-N flight deck operations: problem definition final report, Naval Air Systems Command, January 2003

7. Cicirelli, G., Attolico, C., Guaragnella, C., D'Orazio, T.: A kinect-based gesture recognition approach for a natural human robot interface. Int. J. Adv. Robot. Syst. **12**, 22 (2015)

8. McNeill, D.: Hand and Mind: What Gestures Reveal about Thought. University of Chicago Press, Chicago (1992)

9. Bressem, J., Ladewig, S.H.: Rethinking gesture phases: articulatory features of gestural movement? Semiotica **2011**(184), 53–91 (2011)

10. Kendon, A.: Gesticulation and speech: two aspects of the process of utterance. Relatsh. Verbal Nonverbal Commun. **25**, 207–227 (1980)

11. Fricke, E.: Grammatik Multimodal: Wie Wörter und Gesten Zusammenwirken. Walter De Gruyter Incorporated, Boston (2012)

12. Kranstedt, A., Kühnlein, P., Wachsmuth, I.: Deixis in multimodal human computer interaction: an interdisciplinary approach. In: Camurri, A., Volpe, G. (eds.) GW 2003. LNCS (LNAI), vol. 2915, pp. 112–123. Springer, Heidelberg (2003)

13. Monajjemi, M., Bruce, J., Sadat, S.A., Wawerla, J., Vaughan, R.: UAV, do you see me? Establishing mutual attention between an uninstrumented human and an outdoor UAV in flight. In: 2015 IEEE/RSJ International Conference on Intelligent Robots and Systems, pp. 3614–3620 (2015)

14. Anjum, M.L., Ahmad, O., Rosa, S., Yin, J., Bona, B.: Skeleton tracking based complex human activity recognition using kinect camera. In: Beetz, M., Johnston, B., Williams, M.-A. (eds.) ICSR 2014. LNCS, vol. 8755, pp. 23–33. Springer, Heidelberg (2014)

15. Verschae, R., Ruiz-del-Solar, J.: Object detection: current and future directions. Front. Robot. AI **2**, 1475 (2015)

16. Viola, P., Jones, M.J.: Robust real-time face detection. Int. J. Comput. Vis. **57**(2), 137–154 (2004)

17. Dalal, N., Triggs, B.: Histograms of oriented gradients for human detection. In: IEEE Computer Society Conference on Computer Vision and Pattern Recognition, pp. 886–893 (2005)

18. Danelljan, M., Häger, G., Shahbaz Khan, F., Felsberg, M.: Accurate scale estimation for robust visual tracking. In: British Machine Vision Conference, p. 65.1 (2014)

19. King, D.E.: Dlib-ml: a machine learning toolkit. J. Mach. Learn. Res. **10**, 1755–1758 (2009)

20. Schwarz, L.A., Mkhitaryan, A., Mateus, D., Navab, N.: Estimating human 3D pose from time-of-flight images based on geodesic distances and optical flow. In: 2011 IEEE International Conference on Automatic Face and Gesture Recognition and Workshops, pp. 700–706 (2011)

21. Felzenszwalb, P.F., Girshick, R.B., McAllester, D., Ramanan, D.: Object detection with discriminatively trained part-based models. IEEE Trans. Pattern Anal. Mach. Intell. **32**(9), 1627–1645 (2010)

Autonomous Systems and MS Frameworks and Architectures

Using AUTOSAR High-Level Specifications for the Synthesis of Security Components in Automotive Systems

Cinzia Bernardeschi[1(✉)], Gabriele Del Vigna[1], Marco Di Natale[2],
Gianluca Dini[1], and Dario Varano[1]

[1] Department of Information Engineering,
University of Pisa, Largo L. Lazzarino 1, 56122 Pisa, Italy
{cinzia.bernardeschi,gianluca.dini}@ing.unipi.it,
g.delvigna88@gmail.com, dario.varano@gmail.com
[2] Scuola Superiore Sant'Anna, Piazza Martiri della Libertà 33, 56127 Pisa, Italy
marco.dinatale@sssup.it

Abstract. The increasing complexity and autonomy of modern automotive systems, together with the safety-sensitive nature of many vehicle information flows require a careful analysis of the security requirements and adequate mechanisms for ensuring integrity and confidentiality of data. This is especially true for (semi-)autonomous vehicle systems, in which user intervention is limited or absent, and information must be trusted. This paper provides a proposal for the representation of high-level security properties in the specification of application components according to the AUTOSAR standard (AUTomotive Open System ARchitecture). An automatic generation of security components from security-annotated AUTOSAR specifications is also proposed. It provides for the automatic selection of the adequate security mechanisms based on a high-level specification, thus avoiding complex and error-prone manual encodings by the designer. These concepts and tools are applied to a paradigmatic example in order to show their simplicity and efficacy.

Keywords: Security · Modelling · AUTOSAR

1 Introduction

Robots, unmanned aerial vehicles (UAVs) [1], self-driving cars, and unmanned underwater vehicles (UUVs) [2] are examples of complex networks of autonomous systems that were considered just fiction a few decades ago [3]. They share the common technological denominator of being a networked embedded and control system composed of many sensors, actuators and embedded computers [4]. As with many of these complex networked systems, external intruders can intentionally compromise the proper operation and functionality of these systems.

Modern cars are not exempt from these threats. Currently, automotive systems integrate an increasing number of features aiming at providing active safety

© Springer International Publishing AG 2016
J. Hodicky (Ed.): MESAS 2016, LNCS 9991, pp. 101–117, 2016.
DOI: 10.1007/978-3-319-47605-6_8

and then full autonomy [5,6]. These functions execute on a distributed architecture of embedded computers, or *Electronic Control Units* (ECUs), with the final objective of controlling the vehicle actuation systems, such as steering, braking, acceleration, lights. ECUs are interconnected by wired networks such as the Controller Area Network (CAN) and Ethernet with the integration of wireless capability, e.g., keyless entry and diagnostic, entertainment systems. This increased connectivity leads to an increasing number of access points and potential cyber security threats. Koscher et al. [7] demonstrate that an attacker who is able to infiltrate any Electronic Control Unit (ECU) can leverage this ability to completely circumvent a broad array of safety-critical systems. Furthermore, Stephen Checkoway et al. [8] demonstrate that remote exploitation is feasible via a broad range of attack vectors including CD players and Bluetooth sub-system. The impact of these cyber security threats is getting more and more relevant as cars are getting more and more autonomous and interconnected. It follows that cyber security is a requirement that has to be addressed since the early stages of the project.

In this paper, we provide a set of *modelling extensions* to address cybersecurity requirements at design stage in the AUTOSAR (AUTomotive Open System ARchitecture), an open industry standard for automotive software architectures [9]. AUTOSAR provides a component-based system design and a development approach based on a three-layered architecture: the Application layer, that contains the Application Software Components providing system specific functionality; the Run Time Environment layer, an auto-generated layer providing for the implementation of application functions in concurrent threads and the implementation of communication; and, finally, the Basic software layer, that contains standardised operating system, IO and other services, including libraries and communication services [10].

In AUTOSAR, safety and security services are being standardised with respect to the set of basic services that may be required by the application, such as the basic cryptographic functionalities provided by the Crypto Service Manager (CSM) or the definition of integrity-related message authentication codes (MACs) in messages (SecOC component) [11,12].

With reference to the AUTOSAR component-based methodology, we show how:

(i) to *annotate* a component diagram by means of cyber security concepts during the modelling phase; and,

(ii) to automatically synthesize AUTOSAR-compliant *security components* from such an annotated component diagram.

This introduces the following advantages. First, this allows designers to take into account security aspects in the early phases of system design. In-vehicle communications among components over the internal buses can be protected from cyber threats such as eavesdropping, integrity and spoofing. Next, the automated synthesis of security components allows a designer to handle cyber security concepts at a high level without being an expert of security and so avoiding errors and inaccurate selections of methods and algorithms. Finally, the synthesized security components are AUTOSAR-compliant and thus they can readily be plugged into an AUTOSAR application.

With respect to the modelling extensions, we define two sets of elements aimed at the specification of: the *trust level* of a functional component, which gives an indication of the effort required to compromise the component; and, the *security requirements* of a communication between components, which specifies the demand in terms of confidentiality and authenticity on such a communication.

As an example showing the result of the application of our methodology, models and tools, we discuss a set of application components as a typical representative of active safety or autonomous driving subsystems, with communications that are characterized by integrity and/or confidentiality requirements.

Our work can be placed in the research thread about enriching modelling formalisms with security requirements and constraints. Relevant examples are those based on UML such as UMLSec, MDS and MARTE [13–17]. These proposals tend to address general application domains, i.e., distributed applications or embedded, real-time applications. In contrast, our proposal has been conceived for the automotive domain and to extend the AUTOSAR modelling and development methodology.

The rest of the paper is organised as follows. Section 2 summarizes the AUTOSAR concepts of interest for this work. Section 3 presents the modelling extensions that are required for the specification of application-level security requirements. Section 4 presents our synthesis tool. Section 5 illustrates the application of our methodology, models and tools to an autonomous driving subsystem, a typical representative of active safety which requires integrity and confidentiality of communications. Finally, Sect. 6 draws final conclusions and illustrates future works.

2   AUTOSAR in a Nutshell

The objective of the AUTOSAR consortium and standard (www.autosar.org) is to create an open and standardised software architecture for automotive systems allowing for the exchange and integration of software components on a standardised platform. AUTOSAR provides a set of specifications that apply to the software architecture, including the definition of port-based component interfaces and a methodology for the development process.

A fundamental concept in AUTOSAR is the separation between application and infrastructure. With reference to Fig. 1, AUTOSAR *Software Components* (SW-Cs) encapsulate application functionalities that run on the AUTOSAR infrastructure. Each software component is represented by a model that consists of a structural representation of the component interfaces, described by ports for data-oriented or client-service interoperability. Each port is typed by a data or operation interface and defines the points of access for the component. In addition, the behaviour description of each component includes the component

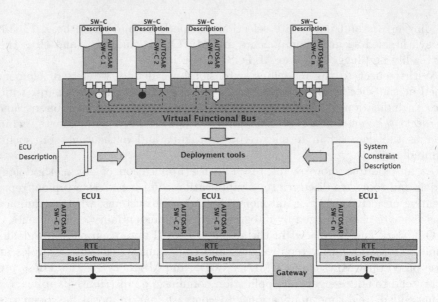

Fig. 1. AUTOSAR architecture

functions (or runnables) and the set of events that trigger the execution of those functions. The *Virtual Functional Bus* (VFB) is the set of all the connections that the designer defines between the components' ports to specify the interoperability of components in an automotive system. These connections are defined in AUTOSAR at an abstract level.

From an architectural standpoint, AUTOSAR consists of three layers (see Fig. 2): the Application layer, the Runtime Environment (RTE) layer, and the Basic Software (BSW) layer. The Application Layer contains the application implementation in terms of software components. The RTE layer is a middleware that provides for the implementation of components' behaviour (executing the runnables by threads and the related scheduling configuration) and the implementation of the communication among components. Finally, the Basic Software provides basic services and software modules on each ECU, i.e., including the operating system, the communication stack and all drivers. Approximately eighty BSW modules are defined and grouped into service modules, such as System services, Memory Services, Communication Services, and so on. According to the AUTOSAR methodology, software components can access BSW modules only through the RTE. So, thanks to the RTE abstraction layer, software components can be developed independently of the underlying hardware, which means that they have the transferability and reusability property.

In order to provide the actual implementation of software components and their VFB communications over a network of ECUs, AUTOSAR requires the designer to specify the execution platform in terms of network topology and configuration of the ECUs (see *ECU Description* and *System Constraints Description* in Fig. 1) as well as the mapping of software components to ECUs. Each

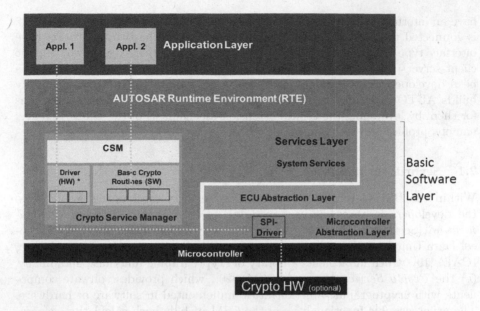

Fig. 2. AUTOSAR layers

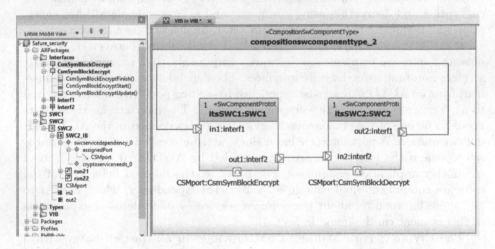

Fig. 3. Sender-receiver application in Rhapsody

instance of a software component is statically assigned to one ECU. Then, based on the platform description and mapping, a set of synthesis tools generate the appropriate RTE and provide for the configuration of the *Basic Software* (BSW) modules on each ECU.

Figure 3 shows an example of sender-receiver application which comprises two interconnected software components, SWC1 and SWC2. The input data port in1 of SWC1 is connected to output data port out2 of SWC2. The two data ports have an interface type `interface1`. In addition, the input data port `in2` of `SWC2` is connected to the output data port `out1` of `SWC1`. The two data ports have interface type `interface2`. The two software components have also two `CSMport` client-server ports that we introduce in the next section. The application has been developed using Rational Rhapsody, a modelling tool by IBM. Rhapsody builds AUTOSAR concepts on top of UML and allows us to define extensions for them by leveraging the typical extension mechanisms of the UML language, namely, profiles and stereotypes.

2.1   Security as a Service

Within the BSW layer, AUTOSAR makes security mechanisms available to the developers in three different modules: (a) the *Secure On-board Communication* (SecOC) module [18], which routes IPDUs (Interaction layer Protocol Data Units) with security requirements; (b) the *Crypto Abstraction Library* (CAL) [19], which implements a library of cryptographic functions; and, finally, (c) the *Crypto Service Manager* (CSM) [20], which provides software components with cryptographic functionalities implemented in software or hardware. The cryptographic functionalities of the CSM include hash calculation, generation and verification of message authentication code, random number generation, encryption and decryption using symmetric and asymmetric algorithms, generation and verification of digital signature, and, finally, key management.

In AUTOSAR, *services* can be seen as an hybrid concept between BSW modules and software components. Software components that require AUTOSAR services use standardised service interfaces. The dependency of a software component from an AUTOSAR service is modelled by adding ports (hereinafter referred to as "service ports") to the software component. The interface for these ports needs to be one of the standardised service interfaces defined in the AUTOSAR documentation. A port interface has a single attribute called `isService`, that is set to true if the interface is actually provided by AUTOSAR services instead of another application component. Furthermore, the internal behaviour of the software component shall contain a `SwcServiceDependency`, which is used to add more information about the required service (a more detailed explanation of this element can be found in Sect. 4).

The Crypto Service Manager CSM provides an abstraction layer, with a standardised interface of cryptographic functionalities to higher software layers. The services offered by the CSM can be used locally only: it is not possible to access them from a different ECU.

In Fig. 3, the software components `SWC1` and `SWC2` include two service ports of type `CsmSymBlockEncrypt` and `CsmSymBlockDecrypt`, respectively, to use the encryption/decryption service of the CSM respectively.

As shown on panel in the left hand-side of the figure, the functions available at the interface are, respectively, functions `SymBlockEncryptStart()`, `SymBlockEncryptUpdate()` and `SymBlockEncryptFinish()` for `CsmSymBlockEncrypt`, and functions `SymBlockDecryptStart()`, `SymBlock`

`DecryptUpdate() SymBlockDecryptFinish()` for `CsmSymBlockDecrypt`. Furthermore, the description of each software component includes the `SwServiceDependency` on `CryptoServiceNeeds` (left hand side of the figure).

This is the typical use of CSM functions by application components according to AUTOSAR. However, there are two drawbacks to this approach. Component developers are responsible for the selection and use of the right cryptographic functions for guaranteeing an adequate level of integrity and confidentiality to the data they exchange. In addition, the AUTOSAR model does not show on which component communication(s) the encrypted information is supposed to be used. This information is hidden inside the component implementation and disappears completely from the model.

3   Extending AUTOSAR for Security

In terms of security, AUTOSAR models focus on the mechanisms that should be implemented as part of the BSW layers and are therefore to be considered as architecture patterns. However, AUTOSAR mostly disregards the application level, that is, for instance, how the designer of an application with security issues should specify that its communications need to be suitably protected.

We define a possible extension to AUTOSAR consisting of two types of modelling elements, defined in Rhapsody by means of stereotypes:

- the trust specification of a functional component and
- the security requirement specification of a communication between components.

3.1   Trust Specification of Functional Components

A functional component, either a software component or a port, may be associated to a *Trust Specification* which specifies to what extent the element can be trusted to provide the expected function, or service, with respect to attacks targeted to compromise the functionality of the element (a metamodel view of the extensions is shown in Fig. 4).

A trust specification consists of:

- a *trust specification identifier* (`trustSpecID`), which identifies the specification, and
- a *trust level* (`trustLevel`) which provides an indication of the extent to which the element can be trusted. The `trustLevel` is an attribute of type `trustLevelType` that corresponds to an integer in the range 1 to 5, being 1 the highest trust level and 5 the basic one.

It follows that a trust specification is formally defined as:

```
TrustSpecification = ⟨ trustSpecID: String,
                       trustLevel: trustLevelType ⟩
```

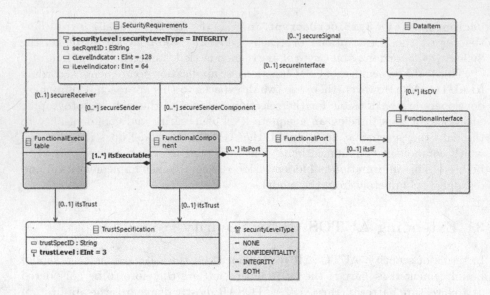

Fig. 4. The metamodel with the proposed AUTOSAR extensions

The trust specification is a measure of the effort required to create and carry out attacks to the element. An high trust level corresponds to a low probability of successful attack. The notion of trust specification is similar to *attack potential* in [21].

The trust level attribute is intended to be used in the mapping phase, upon defining the allocation of software components to ECUs. Components with high trust level should be assigned to high secure ECUs. As the mapping of software components to ECUs is outside the scope of this paper we are not going to refer to trust specification any further.

3.2   Security Requirement Specification of Communications

With reference to Fig. 5, a security specification on a communication consists of four attributes:

– a *security requirement identifier* (`secRqmtID`), which uniquely identifies the requirement;
– a *security level* (`securityLevel`), which specifies the desired secure communication options. It is of type `securityLevelType`, an enumerated that contains four self-explicative values that codify: no security, confidentiality, integrity, and, both confidentiality and integrity;
– a *confidentiality level indicator* (`cLevelIndicator`) and
– an *integrity level indicator* (`iLevelIndicator`).

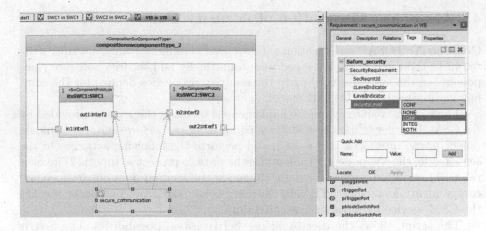

Fig. 5. Secure communication.

A security requirement is formally defined as:

```
SecurityRequirement = ⟨ secRqmtID: String,
                        securityLevel: securityLevelType,
                        cLevelIndicator: EInt,
                        iLevelIndicator: EInt ⟩
```

where

```
securityLevelType = { CONF,INTEGR, BOTH, NONE }
cLevelIndicator = { 128, ....}
iLevelIndicator = { 64, .... }
```

The attributes *confidentiality level indicator* and *integrity level indicator* provide a quantitative indication of confidentiality and integrity, respectively, of communication. A confidentiality level indicator `cLevelIndicator` equal to 128 means that the computation complexity necessary to break the communication confidentiality should not smaller than $\mathcal{O}(2^{128})$. This requirement can be fulfilled by using the AES-128 cipher, for example. Analogously, an integrity level indicator `iLevelIndicator` equal to 64 means that the computation complexity necessary to break the communication integrity (i.e., to find a collision) should not be smaller than $\mathcal{O}(2^{64})$. According to AUTOSAR Secure On-Board Communication, this requirement can be fulfilled by using a 64-bit Message Authentication Code (MAC), or larger.

The definitions in the metamodel of Fig. 4 allow for a security requirement to be applicable to any of the following.

- Selected data items exchanged between two ports by two components.
- All the data items exchanged between a specified pair of sender and receiver runnables.
- All the data produced by a component.
- All the data belonging to a given interface specification.

4   Automatic Generation of Security Components

Given an AUTOSAR specification with secured communications, a script, written in Python, has been developed to automatically add security software components to the system according to the security properties defined for the communication in the AUTOSAR model.

The security requirements are implemented by using the services provided by the CSM. In order to use these services, components must have suitable elements (client ports, interfaces, and so on), and perform the following actions. On the sender side, the component: (1) identifies the data to protect as input; (2) invokes the CSM service to secure the data; (3) sends the secured data on the specified communication channel/RTE call. On the receiver side, the component invokes the CSM service to extract the secured data.

The script allows the user to choose between two possibilities. The first is to extend the already existing sender or receiver components of the secured communication. Alternatively, new components can be added, acting as filters.

Technically, this procedure has been implemented in the model, by extending the AUTOSAR description field of the ports involved in the communication (tag `desc`) by two additional tags: the tag `SecurityNeeds`, which specifies the security level (none, confidentiality, integrity or both), and the tag `NewComponent`, which indicates if a new (filter) software component must be added.

The standardised format for exchanging data between different AUTOSAR compliant tools is AUTOSAR XML (ARXML). The input parameters of the script are the name of the input ARXML file and, optionally, a name for the output file. If no name is specified for the output file, the script use a default name for it.

Suppose that we are interested in confidentiality. Therefore, a message should be encrypted by the sender and decrypted by the receiver. For this purpose, the CSM offers the Symmetrical Block Encryption (and Decryption) service, which guarantees confidentiality of the received data, under the condition that the key used for computation is not compromised by an external entity.

The steps in order to specify that a software component wants to use the Encryption/Decryption service, are the following:

- The software component that wants to use the Encryption/Decryption service needs to have a client port.
- The interface of such a port has to be named (all the names of all the interfaces provided by the CSM are defined by the AUTOSAR standard):
    - `CsmSymBlockEncrypt` if the software component is a sender, or
    - `CsmSymBlockDecrypt` if, otherwise, it is a receiver.
- `isService`, a flag of the port interface, specifies whether communication occurs between a software component and an AUTOSAR service (true) or not (false).
- `serviceKind`, an attribute of the port interface, provides further details about the nature of the applied service. In our case it must be set to `criptoServiceManager`.

– The internal behaviour element of the software component must contain a SwcServiceDependency, which makes it possible to associate ports defined for a software component to a given AUTOSAR service.

– SwcServiceDependency must contain both the required AUTOSAR service (cryptoServiceNeeds) and one or more RoleBasedPortAssignment, which is a container for references to the service client ports of the software component (defined at the first point).

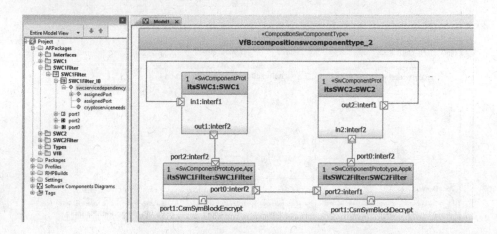

Fig. 6. Model with security components.

If we specify SecurityNeeds=CONF and NewComponent=TRUE for both the sender and the receiver of the secured communication in Fig. 5, then executing the script on the ARXML representing the system in Fig. 3 results in the system shown in Fig. 6. Notice that the modified ARXML file is AUTOSAR-compliant and so can be imported in Rhapsody. Thus all the elements added by the script are visible in the graphical representation of the system. As it turns out, the script generated two components (SWC1Filter and SWC2Filter). On the sender side, the filter component SWC1Filter takes the data produced by the sender component SWC1, encrypts and sends them out to the filter component SWC2Filter. On the receiver side, this component receives the encrypted data, decrypts and sends them to the receiver component SWC2.

5   A Simple Example

There are many instances of AUTOSAR communications that are sensitive to security issues and require support for guaranteeing the confidentiality and integrity of the exchanged information.

Many active safety and autonomous driving applications make use of information coming from sensory input devices, such as lidars, radars and cameras in order to sense the surrounding environment and detect the roadmarks and objects (vehicles, pedestrians) on and around the street.

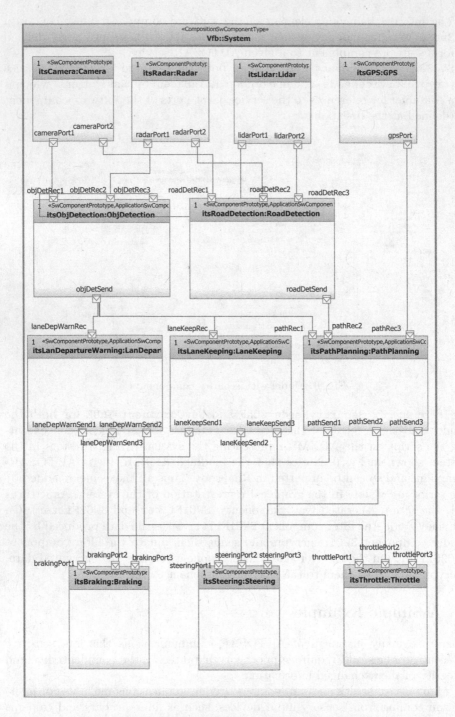

Fig. 7. AUTOSAR specification of the sample model.

To improve the precision in the detection of the vehicle position and to assist in the navigation, these data are typically integrated with information coming from the GPS system. GPS information can also be considered as not only characterized by integrity, but also confidentiality requirements.

Position information coming from the GPS, together with object and road position information coming from sensors are typically forwarded to several navigation and active safety functions, including, for example, Path planning, Lane keeping and Lane Departure warning. These functions, in turn, produce commands for the actuation systems (steering, throttle and brakes) for which integrity must be preserved. The low-level control systems for throttle, brakes and steering proceed to arbitrate among these incoming requests and determine the final actuation commands that go to the low-level control software.

The corresponding AUTOSAR model with sensors and actuators as `SensorActuatorsSwComponentType` and `ApplicationSwComponentType` elements is shown in Fig. 7.

Confidentiality and integrity requirements are added to the communications between the `GPS` and the `PathPlanning` components, and between the latter and all the actuators. Other communications are only characterized by integrity requirements. The security tag has been added to the `desc` tag of the corresponding ports before exporting the ARXML file.

After the system is modelled using Rhapsody, we export the ARXML file. The file is processed by our generation script, which provides for the synthesis of the security mechanisms and the generation of a new ARXML file. Figure 8 shows the part of the model related to the GPS software component and its communication with other components obtained as a result of this step.

The figure shows the original elements and the newly generated ones. The generated filters components have client ports to call the CSM functions for integrity (MAC) and confidentiality (symmetric block encryption).

The automatic generation of the security components allows the developers to work at a high level of abstraction in a completely transparent way, without requiring knowledge of the details of the CSM and the cryptographic routines in it. In addition to filters, our script also generates the RTE calls for reading and writing over sender/receiver ports. The RTE calls for the `PathPlanningFilter` software component are shown below.

```
#if (!defined RTE_PathPlanningFilter_H)
#define RTE_PathPlanningFilter_H
#include <Std_types.h>
#ifdef __cplusplus
extern"C" {
#endif /* __cplusplus */
;
Std_ReturnType Rte_Read_port0_data(int data);
;
Std_ReturnType Rte_Write_port9_data(int data);
;
```

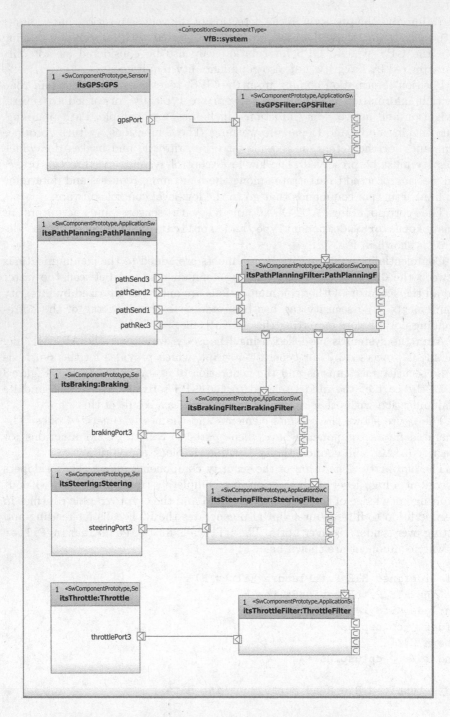

Fig. 8. Part of the sample model with security components.

```
Std_ReturnType Rte_Read_port10_data(int data);
;
Std_ReturnType Rte_Read_port11_data(int data);
;
Std_ReturnType Rte_Write_port8_data(int data);
;
Std_ReturnType Rte_Write_port12_data(int data);
;
Std_ReturnType Rte_Write_port7_data(int data);
;
Std_ReturnType Rte_Write_port8_data(int data);
;
Std_ReturnType Rte_Call_port3_CsmMacGenerateFinish();
Std_ReturnType Rte_Call_port3_CsmMacGenerateStart();
Std_ReturnType Rte_Call_port3_CsmMacGenerateUpdate();
Std_ReturnType Rte_Call_port4_CsmMacVerifyFinish();
Std_ReturnType Rte_Call_port4_CsmMacVerifyStart();
Std_ReturnType Rte_Call_port4_CsmMacVerifyUpdate();
Std_ReturnType Rte_Call_port5_SymBlockEncryptFinish();
Std_ReturnType Rte_Call_port5_SymBlockEncryptStart();
Std_ReturnType Rte_Call_port5_SymBlockEncryptUpdate();
Std_ReturnType Rte_Call_port6_SymBlockDecryptFinish();
Std_ReturnType Rte_Call_port6_SymBlockDecryptStart();
Std_ReturnType Rte_Call_port6_SymBlockDecryptUpdate();
#ifdef __cplusplus
} /* extern "C" */
#endif /* __cplusplus */
#endif
```

The names of the RTE functions have a standard format. For each port, the call for the RTE is composed by four parts. The first part is the return type, which is Std_ReturnType. The second one is defined by the port's interface. In case of a SenderReceiver interface, it is Rte_Write for sender ports and Rte_Read for receiver ones. In case of a ClientServer interface it is Rte_Call. The third part is the name of the port. Finally, the fourth one is defined again by the interface. In case of SenderReceiver interface, it is the name of the data related to the interface, whereas in the case of ClientServer interface it is the name of the operation related to the interface.

6   Conclusions

This paper advocates the modelling of security issues in the early phases of system design. Extensions to AUTOSAR for expressing the trust level of components and the security requirement of communications has been introduced. A tool has been implemented that automatically generates filters that implement the security issue on communications by using the CSM services. The tool is intended to be used to ease the work of system designers and to avoid oversight caused by the complexity of the AUTOSAR standard.

This paper is focused on security requirements specification, leaving verification of achievement of security goals to further work.

More in general, modeling should be not limited to just the communication aspect. Rather, modeling should address security as much as possible. For instance, well-known security engineering best-practices make it possible to harden the software components. These include, for example, using safe string libraries, diligent input validation, and checking function "contracts" at module boundaries. Modeling should allow the designer to require the employment of these practices. For instance, a class diagram, possibly extended by means of proper stereotypes, may mandate the use of a `SecureString` class instead of a customary `String` library.

In a similar fashion, modeling should address other aspects of the system. According to the "defence in depth" principle, just hardening the software components is in general not sufficient. Another design countermeasure consists in reducing the attack surface. Consider the Bluetooth vulnerability documented by Checkoway et al. [8], for example. Using a safe `strcpy` library function would certainly harden the Bluetooth implementation component. However, further security improvements could derive from requiring that, in contrast to current procedures, the Bluetooth component will respond to pairing requests only after user interaction.

Acknowledgement. This work has been developed under the framework of the European project SAFURE (Safety And Security By Design For Interconnected Mixed-Critical Cyber-Physical Systems) under grant agreement No. 644080.

References

1. Martini, S., Di Baccio, D., Romero, F.A., Jiménez, A.V., Pallottino, L., Dini, G., Ollero, A.: Distributed motion misbehavior detection in teams of heterogeneous aerial robots. Robot. Auton. Syst. **74**, 30–39 (2015)
2. Caiti, A., Calabro, V., Dini, G., Duca, A.L., Munafo, A.: Secure cooperation of autonomous mobile sensors using an underwater acoustic network. Sensors **12**(2), 1967–1989 (2012)
3. Wyglinski, A.M., Huang, X., Padir, T., Lai, L., Eisenbarth, T.R., Venkatasubramanian, K.: Security of autonomous systems employing embedded computing, sensors. IEEE Micro **33**(1), 80–86 (2013)
4. Sangiovanni-Vincentelli, A., Di Natale, M.: Embedded system design for automotive applications. Computer **10**, 42–51 (2007)
5. Guizzo, E.: How Google's self-driving car works. IEEE Spectr. Online **18** (2011)
6. Barari, A.: GM Promises Autonomus Vehicles by End of Decade, 17 October 2011. http://www.motorward.com/2011/10/gm-promisesautonomous-vehicles-by-end-of-decade

7. Koscher, K., Czeskis, A., Roesner, F., Patel, S., Kohno, T., Checkoway, S., McCoy, D., Kantor, B., Anderson, D., Shacham, H., et al.: Experimental security analysis of a modern automobile. In: 2010 IEEE Symposium on Security and Privacy (SP), pp. 447–462. IEEE (2010)
8. Checkoway, S., McCoy, D., Kantor, B., Anderson, D., Shacham, H., Savage, S., Koscher, K., Czeskis, A., Roesner, F., Kohno, T., et al.: Comprehensive experimental analyses of automotive attack surfaces. In: USENIX Security Symposium, San Francisco (2011)
9. AUTOSAR. (http://www.autosar.org/)
10. Di Natale, M., Sangiovanni-Vincentelli, A.: Moving from federated to integrated architectures in automotive: the role of standards, methods and tools. Proc. IEEE 98(4), 603–620 (2010)
11. AUTOSAR. Specification of Safety Extensions: AUTOSAR Release 4.2.1
12. AUTOSAR. Specification of Security Extensions: AUTOSAR Release 4.2.1
13. Jürjens, J.: UMLsec: extending UML for secure systems development. In: Jézéquel, J.-M., Hussmann, H., Cook, S. (eds.) UML 2002. LNCS, vol. 2460, pp. 412–425. Springer, Heidelberg (2002)
14. Jürjens, J.: Towards development of secure systems using UMLsec. In: Hussmann, H. (ed.) FASE 2001. LNCS, vol. 2029, pp. 187–200. Springer, Heidelberg (2001)
15. Basin, D., Doser, J., Lodderstedt, T.: Model driven security for process-oriented systems. In: Proceedings of the Eighth ACM Symposium on Access Control Models and Technologies, pp. 100–109. ACM (2003)
16. Saadatmand, M., Cicchetti, A., Sjödin, M.: On the need for extending marte with security concepts. In: International Workshop on Model Based Engineering for Embedded Systems Design (M-BED 2011) (2011)
17. UML MARTE – The UML Profile for MARTE: Modeling and Analysis of Real-Time and Embedded Systems. http://www.omgmarte.org/
18. AUTOSAR. AUTOSAR Specification of Module Secure Onboard Communication: AUTOSAR Release 4.2.2
19. AUTOSAR. AUTOSAR Specification of Crypto Abstraction Library: AUTOSAR Release 4.2.2
20. AUTOSAR. AUTOSAR Specification of Crypto Service Manager: AUTOSAR Release 4.2.2
21. EVITA. Deliverable D2.3: Security requirements for automotive on-board networks based on dark-side scenarios. EU FP7 Project No. 224275, E-safety vehicle intrusion protected applications (2009). www.evita-project.org

Modelling & Simulation Architecture Supporting NATO Counter Unmanned Autonomous System Concept Development

Marco Biagini and Fabio Corona[(⊠)]

NATO Modelling & Simulation Centre of Excellence, Rome, Italy
{mscoe.cd01,mscoe.cd04}@smd.difesa.it

Abstract. The North Atlantic Treaty Organization (NATO) is dealing with possible future threats, which can be envisioned for the operational scenarios in the next twenty years. Allied Command for Transformation (ACT) is in charge to conduct Concept Development & Experimentation (CD&E) cycle for NATO, and a project named Counter Unmanned Autonomous Systems – (C)UAxS was initiated with the aim to deliver to the NATO Military Authorities a concept that provides taxonomy matrix, threats analysis and future capability implementation recommendations for countermeasures against UAxS in all operational domains, such as air, land, sea and cyberspace.

The NATO Modelling & Simulation Centre of Excellence (M&S CoE) received a Request For Support from ACT to collaborate with the CUAxS concept development process. The M&S CoE has previously started an initiatives regarding UAxS systems called Simulated Interactive Robotics Initiative (SIRI). In addition collaborating with several Science and Technology Organization panels working groups, focusing its efforts on interoperability between simulation environment and Command and Control (C2) systems, languages and data model (i.e., National Information Exchange Model). In this framework, the M&S CoE developed an M&S architectural model, exploiting also the Modelling & Simulation as a Service (MSaaS) paradigm, suitable to provide an initial idea of possible tools could be adopted and customized to support the CUAxS project, as in the Concept Development Assessment Game (CDAG) execution, through the verification and validation of Multi-domains UAxS and their countermeasures.

Keywords: Counter autonomous systems · SIRI · NIEM · MSaaS

1 Introduction

The continuous evolution of unmanned systems with autonomous or semi-autonomous functionalities, in civilian and military fields (dual use), urged the North Atlantic Treaty Organization (NATO) to deal with possible future threats, which can be envisioned for the operational scenarios in the next twenty years.

The Allied Command for Transformation (ACT) is in charge to conduct Concept Development & Experimentation (CD&E) cycle for NATO. The project named Counter Unmanned Autonomous Systems – (C)UAxS was initiated with the aim to

© Springer International Publishing AG 2016
J. Hodicky (Ed.): MESAS 2016, LNCS 9991, pp. 118–127, 2016.
DOI: 10.1007/978-3-319-47605-6_9

deliver to the NATO Military Authorities an operational concept. Furthermore providing taxonomy matrix, threats analysis and future capability implementation recommendations for countermeasures against UAxS in all operational domains, such as air, land, sea and cyberspace.

The NATO Modelling & Simulation Centre of Excellence (M&S CoE) received a Request For Support from ACT to collaborate with this concept development process. Therefore the Centre hosted and participated in the 3rd CUAxS project workshop. Moreover, the M&S CoE worked on robotics with initiatives like Simulated Interactive Robotics Initiative (SIRI), in collaboration with the US Joint Staff J6 Division. This initiative is focused on the interoperability between Multi-robots Systems and Command and Control (C2) systems using National Information Exchange Model (NIEM) Data Model. Regarding this particular interoperability issue, the M&S CoE is participating to the 145 working group of the NATO Modelling and Simulation Group, a panel of the Science and Technology Organization (STO), contributing to the development and standardization of the C2SIM language extension for autonomous systems.

This paper will outline the main aspects of the ACT CUAxS project, it will briefly illustrate the initiatives of the M&S CoE in the robotic field and its interoperability issues. In addition introducing the development of a M&S architecture aimed to support the CD&E activities related to the CUAxS project. Results of this approach will be illustrated as example of experimentation performed using the M&S architecture envisioned.

2   Counter Autonomous Systems (C)UAxS Project

The CUAxS is a NATO ACT led CD&E project [1] whose aim is to deliver a capstone concept to define the requirements for NATO capability development addressing possible countermeasures against unmanned autonomous systems in the four dimensions (Air, Ground, Sea and C3IS - Command, Control, Communication & Information Systems) in whatever mission (armed or unarmed, combat or reconnaissance, etc.) and the protection of own UAxS.

The need for such countermeasures was born from a military perspective regarding UAxS and their increasing opportunities to be used in joint operations. In addition the level of autonomy of these systems will evolve quickly together with the technology. UAxS have the potential to be used across the whole spectrum of operational functions in low or high intensity conflicts, and by state and non-state actors in a defensive or offensive way.

The implementation of this concept is expected to contribute to the improvement of the overall situational awareness and defence capability. Moreover integrating the existing capabilities like counter-air, anti-surface and anti-submarine and ground defence. Therefore the project purposes are: to update the situational awareness about UAxS in the four dimensions, defining clearly the understanding of "autonomy" and the "level of human interaction" aspect; to identify the various threats to better determine the countermeasures and provide a better assessment about their implementation; to address a future possible CUAxS capability development according to the full DOTMLPFI spectrum (Doctrine, Organization, Training, Materiel, Leadership, Personnel, Facilities and Interoperability).

These goals are expected to be achieved through the following actions:

– Providing a commonly agreed definition of autonomous systems;
– Providing a stratification matrix based on criteria allowing to define the level of autonomy of a system;
– Determining the threats that UAxS may represent;
– Addressing the impact of the concept across the DOTMLPFI spectrum;
– Providing some suggestions to facilitate the legal/ethical acceptance of the utilization of AxS countermeasures based on the stratification matrix;
– Suggesting a way ahead for a possible future implementation of a CUAxS capability.

The main deliverable of the CUAxS project will be the production of the concept document, moreover an experimentation phase is envisioned, comprehending a Disruptive Technology Assessment Game – DTAG [2] and a Concept Development Assessment Game – CDAG [3].

Both Assessment Games use vignettes within an overall military scenario. DTAG is used to assess the impact of technology on recognizable situations and CDAG is a qualitative analytical method for assessing concepts or conceptual documents. It can be used at various stages in the concept development process. During DTAG potential technologies or focus areas are identified, which are intended for the generation of Idea of Systems (IoS) cards. An IoS card is a card with the description of a potential new

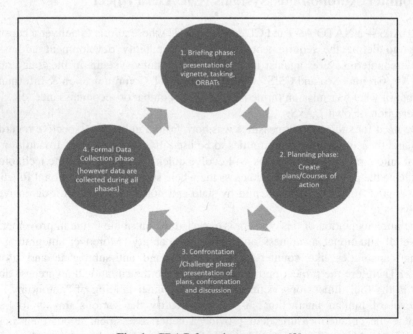

Fig. 1. CDAG four phase process [3]

military system or capability. These IoS cards are then made available to players during a table-top based war game. This game aims are to explore how the conduct of operations may change as a result of introduction of new technologies and unmanned autonomous systems. Furthermore investigating about the importance of relevant counter-measures to the IoS cards used in the game.

Likewise, the CDAG is an open table-top analytical war game played by concept developers and end users to assess concepts or elements of concept in an operational context. In the framework of the CUAxS project, CDAG is played to proof the concept using technology cards to simulate the future technologies or scenarios where countermeasures against UAxS are applied. The CDAG is executed in a four phase process as illustrated in Fig. 1.

3 M&S CoE Initiatives on UAxS

Before dealing with the involvement of the M&S CoE in the CUAxS project, a brief overview of the initiatives of the CoE on M&S and Robotics are here illustrated.

3.1 Simulated Interactive Robotics Initiative (SIRI)

Simulated Interactive Robotics Initiative (SIRI) is a cooperative project between the M&S CoE and the US Joint Staff J6, in collaboration with an Italian MoD contractor, the SSI company. It is focused on interoperability issues for integrating a Multi-robot System (MRS) in a Multinational Coalition Scenario [4]. In particular, the initiative is focused on exploring the use of National Information Exchange Model (NIEM) MilOps domain, an eXtensible Markup Language (XML)-based data model for message exchange in an unmanned systems environment.

NIEM seeks to enhance operational effectiveness and promote interoperability by allowing many organizations to access and utilize data and information. NIEM is a standardized format for eXtensible Markup Language (XML)-based data exchanges that serves as a model for information transmission between entities. The model provides a framework with consistent naming and design rules and a standard process for developing data exchanges, and is structured with a core containing common elements and several domains that can inherit elements and modify attributes to accommodate the specific needs of various communities. There are 16 existing domains, each managed by a domain steward who provides training, resolves technical issues, keeps the domain harmonized with the NIEM core and recommends new core components and processes. Information Exchange Packages and Documentation (IEPDs) containing XML schemas are stored in repositories at the domain and core levels and made available for future data interface development. IEPDs can be partially or fully reused, simplifying the development process and reducing the time and resources required for implementation [5].

Going into details, the reference operational scenario was called the Cooperative Multi-robot Information Exchange Demonstrator (COMIED), made of a swarm of Unmanned Ground Vehicles (UGVs), both virtual and real, a planning station and a

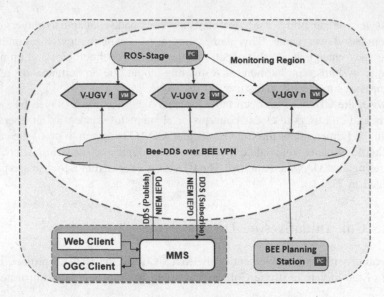

Fig. 2. SIRI overall architecture [4]

Mission Management Station (MMS). The UGVs were capable of coordinating their activities to explore the environment in a safe, efficient and effective way during the detection, identification, classification and neutralization of threats. The V-UGVs were developed based on the ROS/Stage [6] simulation environment. A customized version of the Data Distribution Service Standard (DDS), the BEE-DDS, was developed by the M&S CoE's contractor, to connect the various distributed nodes. Figure 2 shows this architecture.

A demonstration was conducted from April 2014 to April 2015 with a collaborative evaluation and effort between the NATO M&S CoE and the US Joint Staff J6, supported by the Georgia Tech Research Institute in Atlanta and the SSI company in Rome [7]. The Multi-robot System (MRS) was located in Rome (Italy) and was composed by a swarm of 4 networked Virtual UGVs and a real prototype. The MMS, based on the FalconView tool, was remotely connected from US via Virtual Private Network (VPN) over Internet. The event involved exchanging NIEM-conformant XML messaging messages between UGVs and the MMS, as well as sending NIEM-conformant XML messaging command messages from the MMS to the UGVs.

3.2 NATO STO IST 136 - Security Challenges for Multi-domain Autonomous and Unmanned C4ISR Systems

M&S CoE participated to the meeting of the 136 Specialist Team of the Information System Technology (IST), another STO panel [8]. The meeting took place at NATO Center for Maritime Research and Experimentation (CMRE) in La Spezia, Italy, in March 2016. It brought together experts and practitioners from NATO Nations, military agencies, industry and academy. During the event they were presented and discussed the state-of-the-art developments and security challenges for multi-domain unmanned and autonomous Command, Control, Communications, Computers, Intelligence, Surveillance and Reconnaissance (C4ISR) systems. During the meeting a variety of topics and activities involving emerging models of synchronized operations, unmanned, autonomous and semi-autonomous systems UAxS's, with types of missions and C4ISR functions being performed, were explored.

Such venue had the ambition to combine the vision of the operational communities (ACT and NATO Headquarters), the strategic foresight of NATO bodies (CMRE and NATO Communications and Information Agency – NCIA), the technical insight of STO Panels, such as IST and NATO Modelling and Simulation Group (NMSG). Furthermore in order to start to address the security requirements and challenges regarding multi-domain UAxS's.

3.3   STO CSO NMSG 145 – Operationalization of Standardized C2-Simulation Interoperability

The M&S CoE participates to the NMSG 145 Research Task Group [9]. It has the aim to operationalize the Command and Control – Simulation environments (C2SIM) interoperability standards and technologies. In particular, the group is developing extensions to the unified C2SIM (Mission Scenario Development Language – MSDL/Coalition Battle Management Language   C BML) core Data Model for specific functional areas (e.g., Autonomous systems). They publicize also the standards development process and motivate suppliers to develop products, other than educate the community of practice on C2SIM technology. A final goal is to make recommendations for formalizing the C2SIM standard with a STANAG. The M&S CoE is part of the subgroup is in charge to develop of the C2SIM extension for UAxS.

4   NATO ACT CUAxS CD&E Workshop

The M&S CoE hosted and participated at the 3rd workshop of the CUAxS project. The workshop goal was to make tangible progress on the concept development of the CUAxS. The outcomes of the experimentation phase of DTAG, which took place in Norfolk, VA (USA) in January 2016, were considered. Regarding the UAxS capability envisioned during the DTAG, were taken into account the functionalities of the UAxS and their "level of autonomy." In particular, the autonomy concept was defined on the interaction basis with humans, independently from the technology level. Furthermore on the premises of the previous 2013–2014 Multinational Capability Development Campaign (MCDC) cycle [10]. This interaction, based on the operational scenario, comprehends both control and data link. In order to introduce a concise classification, this "level of autonomy" is characterized by a number in the range 0 to 6, from a fully controlled system to a totally independent one.

Another important element developed to support the CUAxS concept is the "Stratification matrix". This matrix put in relationship the level of autonomy with the type of operations (the NATO Campaign themes) and the operational functional areas, as defined in the Allied Joint Doctrine [11], or type of unit (i.e., combat, combat support, combat service support). Each row of this matrix refers to an operational scenario and it reports the suitable levels of autonomy depending on the kinds of operational unit, as reported in the columns.

Finally, the countermeasures development process advanced with the definition of the UAxS functionalities, in order to identify the possible vulnerabilities of these systems and, therefore, the countermeasures to exploit these weaknesses. In this framework, M&S CoE proposed to design an architectural concept based on M&S tools suitable to support the CUAxS concept development and experimentation activities and the implementation of these tools to support the Concept Development Assessment Game (CDAG) wargame [3].

5   Modelling & Simulation Architecture Supporting (C)UAxS CD&E Activity

In order to fully support ACT CD&E process, the M&S CoE is developing an M&S architectural model, in collaboration with other NATO and US bodies, industry and academia. The approach followed under the Modelling & Simulation as a Service (MSaaS) paradigm [12], as being developed by the MSG-136 research task group [13], is here exposed. The architectural model is following the recommendation for M&S experimental frameworks for Autonomous Systems [14, 15]. The main goals are the implementation of the following main capabilities:

– Interoperability between Robotic Operating System (ROS)-based UAxS and Standard\National\NATO C2\C4ISR systems, through the message exchange using NIEM Data Model and C2SIM language;
– Synthetic–Based Environment (SBE), implemented with a federation of systems, like Robot Scenario Generator and Animator (R-SGA), Networks and Communications Simulator (Cyberspace Arena), C2 systems and real Robot prototypes.

The SBE concept originates from the implementation and customization of an ongoing National (Italian) Military Research Program (PNRM), the Cyber Security Simulation Environment (CSSE). It arises from the need to study, through the use of advanced simulation systems, problems related to cyber threats facing the communications networks (tactical or infrastructured) of military units may be subjected engaged in.

In details, the architecture of the SBE is designed to integrate a federation of simulators and a real/virtual robotic environment, both interacting with real C2 systems. The simulation federation is based on an HLA Run-Time Infrastructure (RTI) and it is composed by: a Robot Scenario Generator and Animator (RSGA), responsible for the scenario management, including the terrain generation, entity and event interaction, and virtual robot representations in the scenario; a behavior generator for (C)UAxS, responsible for implementing the cooperative behavior of the autonomous systems; a Networks and Communications Simulator (Cyberspace Arena), such as a network simulator with the added capability to be stimulated by pretending cyber-attacks; virtual robots, built on ROS and implemented in virtual machines (VMs); real robots,

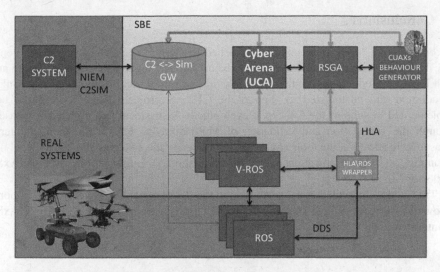

Fig. 3. Conceptual architecture of M&S tools to support the CUAxS project

which can be prototypes or commercial-of-the shelf (COTS) products; an HLA/ROS wrapper, integrated in the VMs or as a separate component, which allows the federation of the robotic platforms, real or virtual, to the HLA RTI; real C2 systems, for the integration between the real and synthetic worlds; one or more gateways for communication and interoperability between C2 systems and the HLA federation. This environment will be integrated in a cloud infrastructure for providing and consuming M&S services under the MSaaS paradigm, as depicted in Fig. 3.

The acquired expertise on NIEM MilOps and C2Sim through previous experimental initiatives (SIRI) and participation to the MSG-145 will be exploited to use these languages for message exchange between C2 systems and UAxS. The aim is to realize mission control and feedback during a simulation involving UAxS, using standard languages and data models which can be used in the military and civilian worlds. In addition high level languages that are as close as possible to the human natural language in which standard military orders are issued.

This simulation environment is suitable to support the CDAG implementation and some of the execution phases introduced in the Sect. 2. With the effort to maintain the some level of the flexibility offered by the CDAG, the scenarios and the Orders of Battle (ORBATs) will be pre-set, using on-demand services like terrain generation and Computer Force Generated (CFG) service, through a Web interface.

The Concept and Technical Cards could be digitalized or substituted by simulation routines and added to the scenario of the vignette to be played. So, the planning phase of the CDAG can be performed with the simulation aid and the confrontation phase can be anticipated by the planned course of action run on the simulation environment. This will add automation at the CDAG execution, speeding the process and standardized way to record and analyze the results of the planned actions.

6   Conclusions

In conclusion, a M&S architecture is modelled to support the CD&E process in general. This architectural model is suitable to be used to run a gap analysis, performing an high level risk reduction and, finally, to provide an initial idea of possible tools could be adopted and customized to support the CUAxS project. These tools could be implemented to support the Concept Development Assessment Game (CDAG) phase, through the verification and validation of Multi-domains UAxS and their countermeasures. In addition, the tools could be used to verify the conceptual maturity level of autonomy and the stratification matrix (mission threats), outputs from ACT CUAxS workshop.

This study is intended as a contribution to the development of M&S tool to support innovative ideas for future capability implementations and recommendations for UAxS countermeasures.

References

1. NATO ACT CEI CAPDEV: Autonomous Systems Countermeasures (2016). http://innovationhub-act.org/AxSCountermeasures. Accessed May 2016
2. NATO STO SAS 082: Disruptive Technology Assessment Game - Evaluation and Validation (2012). http://www.cso.nato.int/activities.aspx?pg=2&RestrictPanel=6&FMMod=0&OrderBy=0&OrderWay=2. Accessed May 2016
3. NATO STO SAS 086: Maritime Situational Awareness: Concept Development Assessment Game (CDAG) (2010). http://www.cso.nato.int/activities.aspx?pg=3&RestrictPanel=6&FMMod=0&OrderBy=0&OrderWay=2. Accessed May 2016
4. SSI Finmeccanica Company: SIRI Operational Scenario, Taranto (2015)
5. NIEM: National Information Exchange Model (2016). https://www.niem.gov/Pages/default.aspx. Accessed May 2016
6. ROS: Robotic Operating System (ROS) Documentation (2016). http://wiki.ros.org/. Accessed May 2016
7. Litwiller, S., Weber, M., Klucznik, F.: Improving robotic and autonomous system information interoperability: standardizing data exchange with XML. In: Hodicky, J. (ed.) MESAS 2015. LNCS, vol. 9055, pp. 24–39. Springer, Rome (2015)
8. Byrum, F., Sidoran, J.: IST 136 Roadmap - Security Challenges for Multi-domain Autonomous and Unmanned C4ISR Systems (Draft - unpublished), STO CSO (2016)
9. NATO STO NMSG 145: Operationalization of Standardized C2-Simulation Interoperability. STO CSO - STO activities (2016). http://www.cso.nato.int/activities.aspx?RestrictPanel=5. Accessed May 2016
10. MCDC: Policy Guidance - Autonomy in Defence Systems (2014). http://innovationhub-act.org/sites/default/files/u4/Policy%2520Guidance%2520Autonomy%2520in%2520Defence%2520Systems%2520MCDC%25202013-2014%2520final.pdf. Accessed May 2016
11. NATO Standardization Agency: Allied Joint Doctrine - AJP 1.0 (D). NATO document, Brussels (2010)
12. Siegfried, R., Van den Berg, T., Cramp, A., Huiskamp, W.: M&S as a service: expectations and challenges. In: Fall Simulation Interoperability Workshop, Orlando, FL, USA, pp. 248–257 (2014)

13. NATO STO MSG 136: Modelling and Simulation as a Service. STO CSO - STO activities (2016). http://www.cso.nato.int/activities.aspx?RestrictPanel=5. Accessed May 2016
14. Hodicky, J.: Modelling and simulation in the autonomous systems' domain - current status and way ahead. In: Hodicky, J. (ed.) MESAS 2015. LNCS, vol. 9055, pp. 17–23. Springer, Heidelberg (2015)
15. Hodicky, J.: HLA as an experimental backbone for autonomous system integration into operational field. In: Hodicky, J. (ed.) MESAS 2014. LNCS, vol. 8906, pp. 121–126. Springer, Heidelberg (2014)

HLA Interoperability for ROS-Based Autonomous Systems

Arnau Carrera[1]([⊠]), Alberto Tremori[1], Pilar Caamaño[1], Robert Been[1],
Diego Crespo Pereira[2], and Agostino G. Bruzzone[3]

[1] NATO STO CMRE, La Spezia, Italy
{arnau.carrera, alberto.tremori, pilar.caamano,
robert.been}@cmre.nato.int
[2] Universidade de Coruña, Coruña, Spain
diego.crespo@udc.es
[3] University of Genoa, Genoa, Italy
agostino@itim.unige.it

Abstract. The requirements for autonomous systems (of systems) have started to include the cooperation between heterogeneous assets in order to accomplish complex missions. Therefore, interoperability – both at the conceptual and technical level – between different types of systems and domains is essential. In the M&S community HLA is the reference standard to design, develop and test interoperable systems of systems. In this article, a HLA-based link between simulation and an autonomous system using the ROS middleware is presented. The integration of an Autonomous Underwater Vehicle (AUV), more specifically the SPARUS II, in a HLA federation using the proposed link has been tested for a harbour protection mission. For this scenario, the hardware and software of the AUV has been included in a federation together with a virtual simulator. The link allows easy inclusion of ROS-based assets in HLA federations, thereby enriching both the M&S and robotic communities which will benefit from this approach which allows the development of more complex and realistic simulated scenarios with hardware- and software-in-the-loop.

Keywords: High level architecture (HLA) · Robot operating system (ROS) · Interoperability · Autonomous underwater vehicle (AUV) · Autonomous systems · Hardware in the loop (HIL) · Software in the loop (SIL)

1 Introduction

The development of autonomous systems requires the construction of complex hardware and software systems. To simplify the software development, several robotics frameworks have been developed in the last years. The aim of the majority of these frameworks is to provide hardware abstraction, low-level device control, implementation of commonly-used functionality, and message passing. The best known frameworks are ROS [1], MOOS [2], Player [3], YARP [4], and OROCOS [5]. One of the most widely used is the Robotic Operating System (ROS).

Developments in the area of robotics are commonly expensive and lengthy. After the first stages of design, the hardware (HW) and software (SW) are tested through

© Springer International Publishing AG 2016
J. Hodicky (Ed.): MESAS 2016, LNCS 9991, pp. 128–138, 2016.
DOI: 10.1007/978-3-319-47605-6_10

several (re-)defined phases until the final system is deployed. In these phases, the use of simulation is desired and is widely diffused in the robotic community with simulated events injected directly in the operating system of the robot. Nevertheless the use of an approach closer to the M&S community, with the "immersion" of the system in a simulated scenario by HLA is still not very diffused. By *cross-communities* this approach of validation and verification (V&V) of both the SW and HW can be carried out in more realistic environments prior to their implementation and deployment, thereby increasing the reliability and robustness of the final systems. Also, new applications for an existing robotic platform would ideally need to go through a similar V&V process. Moreover, the use of simulators with synthetic environments is a complementary approach to the standard simulation used in robotics and will improve the quality of testing systems, reducing both time and resources for V&V [6].

The use of Modelling and Simulation (M&S) techniques could really benefit robotics developers. In order to optimize this process, and to promote interoperability, the developers are advised to follow standards, which for M&S is the High Level Architecture (HLA) [7] (IEEE standard). The use of HLA allows the creation of heterogeneous and complex experimental frameworks, even mixed simulated and real systems simultaneously increasing the richness of the simulations [8]. Two examples of complex simulations where M&S and HLA are extensively used are NASA [9] and ESA [10] agencies, but HLA is also the reference standard for the defence sector and in particular by NATO (STANAG 4603).

The authors of this paper have proposed a new approach to bridge the Robotic and M&S communities by designing and developing a wrapper to grant HLA-based interoperability to autonomous systems using the ROS Framework. The main purpose of developing the connection between HLA and ROS is to minimize the effort of including existing autonomous 'ROS systems' in complex, interoperable and standards-based simulated scenarios.

To test the proposed wrapper between the M&S standard and the robotic middle-ware, a HLA federation has been developed including hardware and software in the loop. The included hardware consisted of an Autonomous Underwater Vehicle (AUV) called SPARUS II, together with its control architecture COLA2. A maritime simulator was used, for the representation of a complex maritime scenario in a 3D realistic environment.

The paper is organized as follows. Section 2 introduced previous cases of HLA in the robotics field. Section 3 compares the communication system used in ROS and HLA and it presents the designed middleware. Section 4 explains the use case and the different elements composing it. Section 5 summarizes the contributions of this paper and presents the future work.

2 Background

To the best of the author's knowledge, there is no previous work published with the purpose of connecting the ROS framework with HLA-based federations. There have been other developments related to the robotics field and interoperability using HLA; below, we have highlighted three different examples of HLA and robotics:

- In 2001, Lane et al. [11] proposed an architecture for Unmanned Underwater Vehicle (UUV) based on HLA. The team divided the robot in subsystems according to functionalities and made them interoperable using HLA. This architecture allows inclusion or replacement of subsystems. Furthermore, they use HLA to perform fast simulations with simulated sensors. However, they conclude that the effort to maintain and develop UUV subsystems in this structure requires a lot of extra effort. Moreover, they doubt that the proposed fast simulation of some sensors was valid for long term simulations.
- In 2005, Joyeux et al. [12] proposed inclusion of simulation capabilities in an existent robotic architecture called LAAS. The aim of this work was to enable the use of the same code in simulation and in real environments, and the combination of simulated and real elements. In this case, the control architecture was modified replacing the message passing between elements of the HLA standard.
- In 2011, Nebot et al. [13] presented a new architecture for controlling a group of heterogeneous robots cooperating to achieve a global goal. In this case the HLA allows the data distribution and implicit communication among the parts of the systems, this also allows operation of simulated and real systems simultaneously. In this case, the sensors and complete vehicles are HLA compliant. A layered control architecture was proposed where the Player robotics framework controls the low level modules, HLA distributes the communication and the JADE [14] software coordinates the cooperation of the robots.

In the literature sub-set mentioned above, the authors have detected as a common goal the possibility to connect simulated and real systems using a standardized architecture. The first article considered an overhead to maintain HLA compatibility in the low levels, whereas others have integrated HLA in the abstracted layers of the hardware. The mentioned cases have developed a new architecture model based on HLA standards.

The aim of our proposal is to preserve the existent control architecture and its framework in the system, and to only add a layer to enable interoperability of the desired parts of the (system of) systems, at software and/or hardware level. This approach will avoid re-designing the entire system and maintains the manufacturers' software 'as is', i.e. without modifications.

3   ROS-HLA Wrapper

A ROS-HLA wrapper has been developed to guarantee technical and conceptual interoperability between the robotic system (HW and SW) and the simulated environment. This wrapper is installed in the ROS system and is able to centralize the different communications in the autonomous system and to exchange the desired information with the HLA federation.

In order to design the wrapper, it was necessary to perform a study of the different types of communications of both standards to find the most suitable adaptation. Section 3.1 summarizes the principal similarities in ROS and HLA. This study points out the required elements and a unique intermediary module linking the HLA and ROS in order to respect the requirements of both communications protocols. The details of the design and implementation are presented in the Sect. 3.2.

3.1 Comparison of the Communication Protocols in ROS and HLA

To understand the communications it is necessary to remember the aim of the two frameworks. HLA is designed in order to standardize the exchange of information between different simulators distributed over a heterogeneous network. ROS, however, offers support for passing messages between processes mainly in the same system or over a local network. The aim of this functionality is to share information of sensors, actuators and algorithms to control the behaviour of a system.

To facilitate the comprehension it is worth to mention the organization of HLA and ROS. HLA is organized in a *federation* which is formed by *federates*. A *federate* is a simulator composed by an *ambassador* and multiple processes; the *ambassador* is responsible to share the information. ROS is organized in a more modular form where each process is called *node* and is responsible to share the information. A *master* is required only to stablish the connection between nodes.

These different characteristics imply some design differences which are explained in the following:

Network Topology/Structure. The first important difference is the network topology, HLA uses a centralized network (bus) in order to increase efficiency and to provide certain functionalities (e.g., time management). This bus of communication is called runtime infrastructure (RTI). On the other side, ROS uses a decentralized structure (peer-to-peer), to be more robust against failures and to increase scalability. To resolve this difference the wrapper will have to centralize all the different ROS communications in one node and transmit them to the HLA Federation.

Definition of the Shared Information. Both systems share the requirement to define a document with the structured data shared between the elements. In HLA this document is called Federation Object Module (FOM), it has to be shared by all the systems in the federation. It specifies all the information related with the data sharing. ROS uses separate documents for each type of shared information, which only need to be known by the processes that use this data. These documents are called *messages* and are created using a simple interface definition language (IDL) which only defines the type and name of the data contained. The proposed wrapper defines a FOM which includes the information of the *message* and extends it to fulfil the requirements of HLA.

Communication Style. HLA and ROS systems use two types of communications: synchronous and asynchronous.

Asynchronous Style. In HLA each kind of data (*Object*) is composed of two parts: the *Class* and the *Instance*. For example: *federate A* declares in the *federation* that it will include *Object_1* when the RTI finds some other, say, *federate B* which has an *Instance* of the *Object_1*; it will then create a new *Instance* to receive the information in *federate A*. The instance in *B* is *posting* the information and the instance in *A* is *reflecting* it. On the other hand, in ROS, each *node* declares the information to be sent (*publish*) and to be received (*subscribed*) assigning them a name (*topic*) and type (*message*). In this case, when the *node* is connected to the *master* at initialization time, it gives this information to it. The *master* creates the connection (*pipes*) between the different *nodes* according to *publishers* and *subscribers*.

Synchronous Style. In HLA this communication is called *Interactions*, and the same class can perform the function to receive and send interactions through the *ambassador*. The ROS approaches this communication style, calling it *Services*, where each node can declare service *servers* (receivers) or *clients* (senders) which are defined by name (*topic*) and type (*message*).

The wrapper is situated between the two communication protocols, so when it receives information from one framework it has to send it on the other. The wrapper can create different *Objects* and *Instances* according to a configuration file. The *Instances* have been modified to include ROS functionalities, when it *posts* it is due to the reception of a ROS *message* (*subscription* callback) and when it *reflects* it is *publishing* a ROS *message*. The synchronous communications is limited by the ROS part being only possible to receive or send interactions, not in a bidirectional manner like in HLA. So when it receives an HLA *Interaction* it *calls* a ROS server, and when it receives a ROS *call* it sends an HLA *Interaction*.

3.2 ROS-HLA Wrapper

The authors adopted the strategy of developing a ROS *node* which converts the information from ROS to HLA, and vice versa. Only one *node* will be required in each ROS system and it centralizes all the exchange information between the autonomous system and the *federation*. This approach isolated the HLA code in one process avoiding modification of the control architecture existing in the autonomous system.

To adapt the node to different autonomous systems and federations it is necessary to identify the required information to be exchanged adapting the FOM and developing the HLA *Objects* and *Interactions* together with the ROS *messages* and *services* (see Fig. 1). So for each kind of data exchanged, the user implements the required *Class*, *Instance*, and *Interaction* which besides the HLA structure includes the ROS functionalities. Figure 2 shows a standard HLA implementation used in all *federates*. The wrapper is a ROS node which creates the necessary HLA Classes, Instances, and Interactions according to the configuration file. This file defines the exchange of information and the direction of the communication in order to define the correct ROS initializations. Figure 1 illustrates the description of the wrapper with an object diagram.

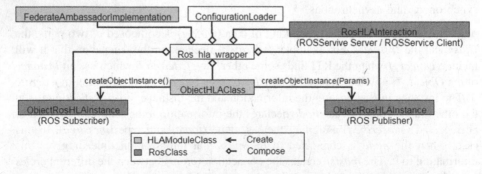

Fig. 1. Object diagram of the ROS HLA middleware or wrapper implemented.

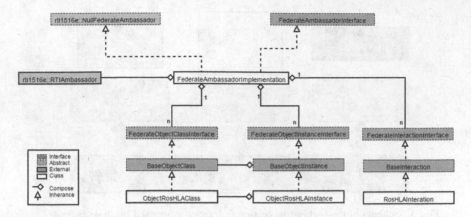

Fig. 2. Class diagram of the HLA architecture implemented by the HLA system developed in this work.

4 Experimental Use Case

The ROS-HLA wrapper presented in this paper has been developed at the NATO STO's Centre for Maritime Research and Experimentation (CMRE) in the context of the Persistent Autonomous Reconfigurable Capability (PARC) project. The aim of the PARC project is to address the technology and engineering requirements of future unmanned systems of systems in the maritime domain. It is focused on increasing the persistence, interoperability and scalability of such systems whilst addressing standardization, information assurance and cost aspects.

Taking into account the environment and the expertise of the CMRE, the chosen use case is a harbour inspection scenario, where an AUV has to patrol a harbour area, visiting several strategic (inspection) points. The harbour has been represented using a virtual simulator of a maritime scenario and the autonomous system used is the SPARUS II AUV [15] and COLA2 [16] control architecture, which is ROS based. Moreover, the control architecture has been divided in two parts: the *back-seat* controlling the high-level decision and the *front-seat* at the low-level (i.e. sensors and actuators). Therefore, the federation designed is composed by three federates (see Fig. 3): the simulator, the front seat, and the back seat of the SPARUS II AUV. The Run Time Infrastructure used is the product PitchRTI distributed by Pitch; experimentations based on MAK RTI are also planned.

The following sections introduce a brief description of the SPARUS II AUV and the COLA2. We also present the new division in COLA2 to split the front seat and back seat in different systems and the addition of the dynamic simulation.

4.1 Sparus II AUV

The SPARUS II AUV is a lightweight AUV developed by the University of Girona (UdG) which is controlled using the Component Oriented Layer-based Architecture for

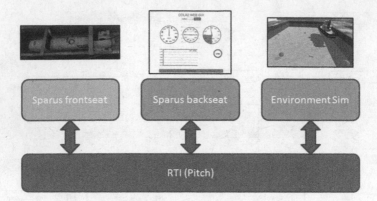

Fig. 3. Schema of the harbour protection federation composed by three federates.

Autonomy (COLA2). The COLA2 is a ROS-based control architecture, hence all the different elements are organized as independent *nodes* which interact using a *publish/subscribe* method (or *service* calls). The COLA2 has been organized in four different groups/layers: backseat, front seat, SPARUS simulator and the SPARUS real hardware. This new semantic separation allows us to organize the COLA2 in a more usual structure for AUVs. Moreover, it makes it easier to execute the modules independently on different machines or federates.

Figure 4 shows the four modules which can be executed on different machines using the ROS-HLA wrapper to send the information through the RTI. In addition, the shared information by the HLA and ROS is highlighted in green. Below, we explain each module and the kind of information which has been selected as input and output.

COLA2 *Back-Seat*. This group contains all the behaviours of high-level decision making. In the use case presented in this paper, the SPARUS II AUV is performing either way-point navigation or navigates according to the commands given by a human operator. The inputs of this layer are desired positions; trajectory (formed by several way-points) and navigation information (position and velocity of the AUV). This information or the Human interaction commands are used to generate the output which consists of position and velocity commands for the AUV.

COLA2 *Front-Seat*. This group contains the low-level controls; it is able to mix all the information received by the sensor and estimate the current position and velocity of the AUV. On the other hand, it generates the proper commands for the AUV to reach the desired position or speed. Moreover, there are safety procedures which are enabled if some error appears in the sensor data. Therefore, the inputs are the position or velocity commands from the COLA2 backseat and the IMU (acceleration and orientation), GPS (global position in surface), DVL (velocity of the AUV), and Pressure (to estimate the depth); the outputs are the estimated position and velocity of the AUV, desired position generated from safety node and thruster set-point.

Simulator and Real Hardware. Depending on the specific application, the vehicle can be completely simulated, partially simulated or not simulated by using just the real

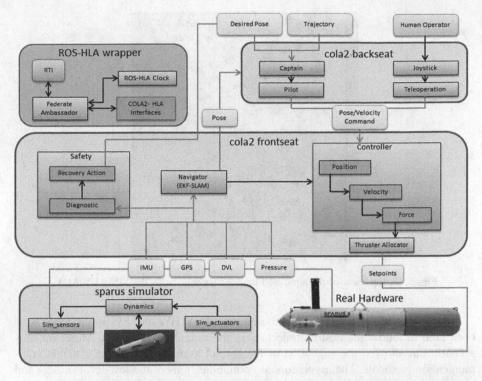

Fig. 4. Schema of COLA2 architecture organized in four different groups.

hardware. When the real hardware is used, the COLA2 front seat is running on the system the HLA communication is skipped, using the real hardware connections. When the vehicle is simulated, the dynamics and sensors simulation can be executed on a different system than the COLA2 front seat. To simulate the AUV, the node receives the Set-point of the thrusters, which are then converted to forces applied to the vehicle; then, using a model of the vehicle, the new position and velocity are estimated. Finally, the new position and velocity are used to generate the simulated navigation sensors.

4.2 Validation Scenario

In the scenario used for the validation of the ROS-HLA wrapper, the SPARUS II AUV was put in a water tank and executing the COLA2 front seat. Outside the vehicle, there are two other systems: the back seat and the environment simulator. The navigation sensors of the AUV are simulated in the external simulator and sent through HLA to the COLA2 front seat. The front seat then estimates the position of the vehicle and according to the commands of the backseat generates the commands for the actuator. In this scenario the commands are shared between the real hardware and the simulator. The harbour mission consists of following a trajectory and visiting a set of inspection points, where the AUV carries out simple operations (search for threats and communication through gateways), see Fig. 5.

Fig. 5. A top view of the simulated harbour scenario with the SPARUS AUV.

In this scenario configuration, both systems (AUV HW and SW in the loop) have been able to follow the desired trajectory in the virtual environment. Moreover, this scenario has allowed the validation of the correct exchange of all the different communication protocols. The asynchronous communications of the low-level sensors and actuators, shared between the COLA2 front seat and the SPARUS II simulator, and the high-level communications represented by navigation information and position and velocity commands, shared between the COLA2 backseat and the COLA2 front seat. The synchronous communications have been tested sending command to start and stop trajectories and define points to be visited by the AUV using the simulator.

5   Conclusions

This article presented the first steps towards the creation of a HLA-based environment to connect ROS-based robotic systems. This environment may be used for testing (V&V), but also for a broader area of applications such as the simulation of a heterogeneous vehicle/sensor network over the internet. The authors explained the approach to develop a wrapper connecting the ROS framework with the HLA standard, which has been designed and implemented with the objective of easily connecting autonomous systems (hardware- and/or software) to realistic modelling and simulation HLA- based environments. The proposed wrapper maintains the existing control architecture, and can be adapted to the user's requirements. It has been successfully tested using a SPARUS II AUV in a simulated harbour inspection scenario. The hardware and software of the AUV have been included in the loop of the simulation and the different types of communications have been tested.

Future developments of the federation presented will include a more complex environmental simulator and a simulator for the underwater/radio frequency communications between the different assets in the scenario. New missions will for example include a two AUV scenario, i.e. both a real one at sea and a virtual AUV in a simulated representation of the real environment. On the other hand, will be investigated the integration of Command and Control (C2) systems in the Federation, in order to enrich the simulation with the possibility to evaluate the scenario and command the virtual and real assets.

In this context we envision a continuous effort to improve and expand the M&S capability to support autonomous systems S&T by contributing in a more consistent way to all three main areas related to the life cycle of new systems and processes (Engineering-CD & E-Training), for example by exploring new areas in the future such as the application of synthetic environments for supporting Human Machine Interface innovation in scenarios involving autonomous and manned assets in the maritime framework.

References

1. Quigley, M., Conley, K., Gerkey, B.P., Faus, J., Foote, T., Leibs, J., Wheeler, R., Ng, A.Y.: ROS: and open-source Robot Operating System. In: International Conference on Robotics and Automation (ICRA) Workshop on Open Source Software, Kobe, Japan (2009)
2. Newman, P.: MOOS: Mission Oriented Operating Suite. In: Oxford Mobile Robitcs Group (2001)
3. Gerkey, B., Vaughan, R.T., Howard, A.: The player/stage project: tools for multi-robot and distributed sensor systems. In: Proceedings of the 11th International Conference on Advanced Robotics (ICAR 2003), Coimbra, Portugal (2003)
4. Metta, G., Fitzpatrick, P., Natale, L.: YARP: yet another robot platform. Int. J. Adv. Robot. Syst. 3(1), 43–48 (2006)
5. OROCOS Project, Open Robot Control Software (2003). http://www.orocos.org/
6. Hodicky, J.: Modelling and simulation in the autonomous systems' domain - current status and way ahead. In: Hodicky, J. (ed.) MESAS 2015. LNCS, vol. 9055, pp. 17–23. Springer, Heidelberg (2015)
7. IEEE Standard for Modeling and Simulation (M&S) High Level Architecture (HLA) Framework and Rules. In: IEEE Std. 1516-2010 (Revision of IEEE Std. 1516-2000), pp. 1–38 (2010)
8. Hodicky, J.: HLA as an experimental backbone for Autonomous System integration into operational field. In: Hodicky, J. (ed.) MESAS 2014. LNCS, vol. 8906, pp. 121–126. Springer, Heidelberg (2014)
9. Reid, M.R., Powers, E.I.: An evaluation of the high level architecture (HLA) as a framework for NASA modeling and simulation. In: Proceedings of the 25th NASA Software Engineering Workshop, Greenbelt, MD, USA (2000)
10. Arguello, L., Miró, J.: Distributed interactive simulation for space projects. In: ESA Bulletin, pp. 125–130 (2000)
11. Lane, D.M., Falconer, G.J., Randall, G., Edwards, I.: Interoperability and synchronisation of distributed hardware-in-the-loop simulation for underwater robot development: issues and experiments. In: Proceedings of International Conference on Robitics & Automation (ICRA), Seul, Korea (2001)

12. Joyeux, S., Alami, R., Lacroix, S., Lampe, A.: Simulation in the LAAS architecture. In: Proceedings of the International Conference on Robotics and Automation Workshop on Software Development in Robotics, Barcelona, Spain (2005)
13. Nebot, P., Torres-Sospedra, J., Martínez, R.J.: A new HLA-based distributed control architecture for agriculture teams of robots in hybrid applications with real and simulated devices or environments. Sensors 11(4), 4385–4400 (2011)
14. Bellifemine, F., Poggi, A., Rimassa, G.: JADE-A FIPA-compliant agent framework. In: Proceedings of PAAM, London, UK (1999)
15. Carreras, M., Candela, C., Ribas, D., Mallios, A., Magí, L., Vidal, E., Palomeras, N., Ridao, P.: Sparus II, design of a lightweight hovering AUV. In: Proceedings fo the 5th International Workshop on Marine Technology, Martech 2013, Girona, Spain (2013)
16. Palomeras, N., El-Fakdi, A., Carreras, M.: COLA2: a control architecture for AUVs. IEEE J. Ocean. Eng. 4, 37 (2012)

APRICOT: Aerospace PRototypIng COntrol Toolbox. A Modeling and Simulation Environment for Aircraft Control Design

Andrea Ferrarelli[1], Danilo Caporale[2], Alessandro Settimi[2,3]($\boxtimes$), and Lucia Pallottino[2]

[1] Vehicle Engineering, Università di Pisa,
Largo Lucio Lazzarino 1, 56122 Pisa, Italy
[2] Centro di ricerca "E. Piaggio", Università di Pisa,
Largo Lucio Lazzarino 1, 56122 Pisa, Italy
alessandro.settimi@for.unipi.it
[3] Department of Advanced Robotics, Istituto Italiano di Tecnologia,
via Morego, 30, 16163 Genova, Italy

Abstract. A novel MATLAB/Simulink based modeling and simulation environment for the design and rapid prototyping of state-of-the-art aircraft control systems is proposed. The toolbox, named APRICOT, is able to simulate the longitudinal and laterodirectional dynamics of an aircraft separately, as well as the complete 6 degrees of freedom dynamics. All details of the dynamics can be easily customized in the toolbox, some examples are shown in the paper. Moreover, different aircraft models can be easily integrated. The main goal of APRICOT is to provide a simulation environment to test and validate different control laws with different aircraft models. Hence, the proposed toolbox has applicability both for educational purposes and control rapid prototyping. With respect to similar software packages, APRICOT is customizable in all its aspects, and has been released as open source software. An interface with Flightgear Simulator allows for online visualization of the flight. Examples of control design with simulation experiments are reported and commented.

Keywords: Aircraft control design · Aircraft dynamics simulation · Linear and nonlinear control

1 Introduction

Aircraft planning and control design requires a simulation environment that is highly configurable based on specific aircraft characteristics or mission objectives. Simulation environments are also necessary to design control systems and validate flight planning strategies. There are several solutions available as commercial or open source software packages. Among these, most are coded in programming languages as Java or C++ and focus on the simulation of specific vehicles as multirotor aircrafts or on generic aircrafts, see [1,2], while others are

© Springer International Publishing AG 2016
J. Hodicky (Ed.): MESAS 2016, LNCS 9991, pp. 139–157, 2016.
DOI: 10.1007/978-3-319-47605-6_11

user interfaces for auto-pilot control systems, see [3,4]. In this sense, an easy to use tool for control design is missing. Other simulators are available with a commercial licence or closed source, see e.g., [5–7]. Our aim with APRICOT (Aerospace PRototypIng COntrol Toolbox) is to provide a simulator environment with a focus on control system design, which is multi-platform, highly customizable and open source[1]. For code, videos and details on APRICOT please refer to [8]. Moreover, being based on MATLAB/Simulink, it can be easily used for education purposes or by control system designer for rapid control prototyping in industry.

The 6 degrees of freedom nonlinear aircraft dynamics can be simulated with a preferred degree of accuracy, meaning that aerodynamic coefficients, stability derivatives [9], actuators and sensor dynamics, disturbances in measurements, wind gusts, control limits and other characteristics can be enabled separately and with different models by simply changing related MATLAB functions or Simulink diagrams. Moreover, custom atmospheric models can be used; by default the International Standard Atmosphere model [10] is implemented. A manual input interface has also been implemented to perturb the aircraft on-line during the simulation through an external gamepad to validate the effectiveness of the implemented control laws in response to various disturbances.

The possibility to visualize the simulation in a detailed 3D environment is obtained thanks to an interface with the open-source flight simulator FlightGear [11–13], as shown in Fig. 1. Both the toolbox and the flight simulator support multiple platforms (MacOS, Linux, Windows). Also, different aircraft models can be easily loaded from various sources like XML files, DATCOM files and even custom formats can be easily supported.

Fig. 1. APRICOT simulation animated in Flightgear.

---

[1] APRICOT Software available at http://aferrarelli.github.io/APRICOT/.

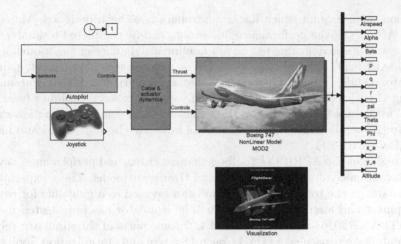

Fig. 2. APRICOT Simulink scheme

The whole system is organized so that it is highly usable and reconfigurable, in that any detail of the simulation can be easily customized from the aircraft model to the used control law. In particular, the main features of APRICOT are the possibility to easily customize the geometric and physical characteristics of an aircraft for what concerns the model and the environmental disturbances. In particular, different unmanned aerial vehicle (UAV) models can be included and simulated in APRICOT such as quadrotors and fixed wings UAVs. As for the control design, control laws can be implemented with Simulink blocks and MATLAB functions; several control laws are already provided in the toolbox. The APRICOT Simulink scheme is reported in Fig. 2.

Another major difference with other simulation environments, where a control law is typically tested on the subsystem for which it has been designed (e.g. a longitudinal controller is tested on the longitudinal subsystem), APRICOT allows multiple controllers to run simultaneously on a subsystem or on the full system dynamics. In other words, with APRICOT a more realistic behavior can be reproduced and tested with separated and/or redundant controllers, providing the control designer with an easy assessment of robustness in presence of failures.

Other than robustness with respect to failure, control laws can be tested to track a given flight trajectory. An optimization based planning is used to steer the system between desired configurations while minimizing fuel consumption and actuation effort and verifying state constraints. A feed-forward control, based on the obtained trajectory, can be used jointly with a feedback controller.

For both robustness and tracking purposes, various classical and modern control techniques, as those reported in [14–16], are available in APRICOT to control both longitudinal and lateral dynamics. Linear controllers have been implemented in the toolbox to test the system even while working far from the operation point around which linear controllers have been designed. Moreover, within APRICOT the performance assessment can be conducted to analyze the whole system behaviour due to the full nonlinear dynamics of the model.

The APRICOT control laws are based on pole-placement, Linear Quadratic Regulator (LQR), Linear Quadratic Gaussian (LQG) and Linear Parameter-Varying (LPV) techniques and nonlinear Lyapunov based techniques (see, e.g., [17–19] for detailed discussions on these methods and similar application examples). In [20] we illustrate how these control laws have been designed and implemented in APRICOT.

To highlight the APRICOT toolbox characteristics and performance, several tests have been conducted with a Boeing 747 aircraft model. These experiments are available in the toolbox as demos and can be used as a guideline for control development and aircraft customization. The simulator has been tested mainly on MATLAB R2016a and FlightGear 3.4.0. Some parts of the simulator rely on the Simulink Aerospace, MATLAB Control System and Optimization Toolboxes.

The paper is organized as follows. In Sect. 2 we illustrate the simulation model used in APRICOT. The usage and the customization features of the environment are shown in Sect. 3. Simulation results and performance are reported in Sect. 4.

2   Modeling and Simulation Environment

This section is dedicated to the description of the aircraft dynamics and the world model necessary to understand and use APRICOT simulator. For a more formal description and equations please refer to [20].

2.1   Dynamic Equations

The aircraft model considered in this work is based on the full nonlinear 6 DoF dynamics. This is a classical model available in literature, see, e.g., [14,15], and can be used as a starting point to customize any aspect of the simulation.

The system has 6 dynamic states x_d and 6 kinematic states x_k:

$$x_d = \begin{bmatrix} V \alpha \beta p q r \end{bmatrix}^T \quad x_k = \begin{bmatrix} x_G y_G z_G \phi \theta \psi \end{bmatrix}^T$$

where, referring to Fig. 3, $V = V_T$ is the airspeed, α is the angle of attack, β is the sideslip angle. p, q, r are roll pitch and yaw angular rates in body coordinates, respectively, x_G, y_G, z_G are center of mass coordinates of the aircraft and ϕ, θ, ψ are the Euler angles, in fixed frame.

The whole state vector is defined as $x^T := [x_d^T, x_k^T]$. The input vector is $u = [\delta_{th}, \delta_e, \delta_a, \delta_r]^T$, namely the thrust, elevator, aileron and tail rudder commands. The dynamics of x_d depends on the forces and moments acting on the system (*i.e.*, aerodynamic forces, engine thrust and gravitational forces) and it is expressed in body coordinates.

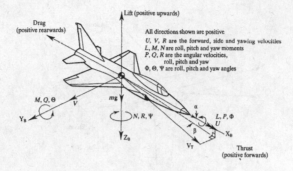

Fig. 3. Aircraft coordinated system, from [21].

2.2   Aerodynamic Forces and Moments

The aerodynamic drag D, lateral Y_A and lift L forces and moments, $\mathscr{L}$, $\mathscr{M}$ and $\mathscr{N}$, depend on the aircraft geometry, aerodynamic coefficients and dynamic pressure. They are given in wind axis coordinate frame by

$$\begin{cases} D = C_D\, q_{dyn}\, S \\ Y_A = C_Y\, q_{dyn}\, S \\ L = C_L\, q_{dyn}\, S \end{cases}$$

$$\begin{cases} \mathscr{L} = C_l\, q_{dyn}\, S\, b \\ \mathscr{M} = C_m\, q_{dyn}\, S\, \bar{c} \\ \mathscr{N} = C_n\, q_{dyn}\, S\, b \end{cases}$$

where the parameters S, $\bar{c}$ and b are aircraft geometric characteristics, see Fig. 4, and they correspond to the wing area, the mean chord of the wings and the wing length. The variable q_{dyn} is the dynamic pressure, C_D, C_Y, C_L are drag, lateral and lift aerodynamic coefficients, C_l, C_m, C_n are aerodynamic moment coefficients.

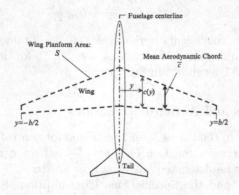

Fig. 4. Geometry of the aircraft, from [22].

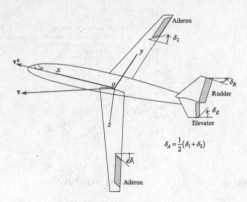

Fig. 5. Surface controls of the aircraft, from [22].

The dynamic pressure is computed as $q_{dyn} = \frac{1}{2}\rho V^2$ where the air density ρ is altitude dependent. For this reason an atmospheric model is required, such as the ISA (International Atmospheric Model) [10] used in this work.

The aerodynamic coefficients depend on the system states and on the control surfaces (elevator, aileron, rudder) and can be computed around an equilibrium configuration, see Fig. 5 as described next.

The longitudinal aerodynamic coefficients are

$$\begin{cases} C_D(\alpha, M) = C_D + C_{D_\alpha}\alpha + C_{D_M}\Delta M \\ C_L(\alpha, q, \dot{\alpha}, M, \delta_e) = C_L + C_{L_\alpha}\alpha + C_{L_q}\frac{q\bar{c}}{2V} + C_{L_{\dot{\alpha}}}\frac{\dot{\alpha}\bar{c}}{2V} + C_{L_M}\Delta M + C_{L_{\delta_e}}\delta_e \\ C_m(\alpha, q, \dot{\alpha}, M, \delta_e) = C_{m_\alpha}\alpha + C_{m_q}\frac{q\bar{c}}{2V} + C_{m_{\dot{\alpha}}}\frac{\dot{\alpha}\bar{c}}{2V} + C_{m_M}\Delta M + C_{m_{\delta_e}}\delta_e \end{cases}$$

where $\Delta M = (M - M_0)$, M is the Mach number and M_0 is the corresponding trimmed value.

On the other hand the laterodirectional aerodynamic coefficients are

$$\begin{cases} C_Y(\beta, \delta_r) = C_{Y_\beta}\beta + C_{Y_{\delta_r}}\delta_r \\ C_l(\beta, p, r, \delta_a, \delta_r) = C_{l_\beta}\beta + C_{l_p}\frac{pb}{2V} + C_{l_r}\frac{rb}{2V} + C_{l_{\delta_a}}\delta_a + C_{l_{\delta_r}}\delta_r \\ C_n(\beta, p, r, \delta_a, \delta_r) = C_{n_\beta}\beta + C_{n_p}\frac{pb}{2V} + C_{n_r}\frac{rb}{2V} + C_{n_{\delta_a}}\delta_a + C_{n_{\delta_r}}\delta_r \end{cases}$$

The aerodynamic coefficients derivatives can be obtained from the literature for different equilibrium configurations, see [20,23] for details. They can be modified in APRICOT as shown in Sect. 3.

2.3   Other Forces and Actuator Dynamics

The engine response to the thrust lever is modeled for control purposes as a first order system with transfer function $G(s) = \frac{\tau}{s+\tau}$, where $\tau > 0$. More detailed models can be easily implemented based on user needs.

The peak thrust and the Specific Fuel Consumption (SFC) of the engine are not constant but depend on the altitude and the Mach number as shown

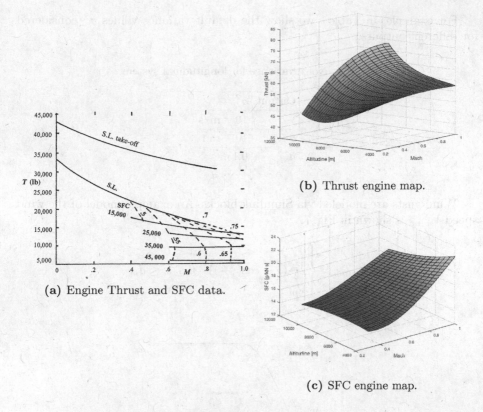

(a) Engine Thrust and SFC data.

(b) Thrust engine map.

(c) SFC engine map.

Fig. 6. Engine characteristics.

in Fig. 6a. Considering the engine curves and the equilibrium point, 3D engine maps are generated as in Fig. 6b and c via least squares polynomial fitting.

In the model are also included the actuator dynamics, rise limit and saturation of the control surfaces.

Finally the forces acting on the center of mass of the aircraft, expressed in body coordinates, are:

$$\begin{cases} X = -\cos\alpha\, D + \sin\alpha\, L - mg\sin\theta + X_T \\ Y = Y_A + mg\cos\theta\sin\phi \\ Z = -\sin\alpha\, D - \cos\alpha\, L + mg\cos\theta\cos\phi \end{cases}$$

where X_T is the engine thrust.

2.4   Sensor Noise and Wind Gusts

By default, all sensors are affected with a zero mean gaussian noise with a variance that depends on the output type, therefore on the sensor type. Noise models for sensors can be customized in APRICOT.

For example, in Table 1 we show the default variance values σ^2 considered for different outputs.

Table 1. Noise variance for longitudinal system.

Output	σ^2
V	10^{-2} m/s
θ	10^{-5} rad
h	0.1 m

Wind gusts are modeled via Simulink blocks. An example model of the wind speed V_{wind} is shown in Fig. 7.

$$V_{wind} = \begin{cases} 0 & x < 0 \\ \frac{V_m}{2}(1 - \cos(\frac{\pi x}{d_m})) & 0 \leq x \leq d_m \\ V_m & x > d_m \end{cases}$$

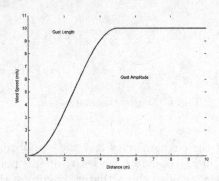

Fig. 7. Wind velocity with respect to the travelled distance.

3   APRICOT Environment

In this section we illustrate the main features available to the user to fully customize APRICOT environment. Indeed, it has been organized as a collection of MATLAB scripts, functions and Simulink blocks that can be singularly modified and tested creating several possible combinations.

First of all, APRICOT initialization process consists of running several scripts to load information on the aircraft and the world and to configure the control laws and the flight plan to be tested.

The main steps in the initialization process are represented in Fig. 8. Each step has associated MATLAB scripts that the user can edit to configure the simulation environment.

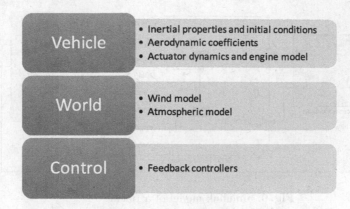

Fig. 8. Initialization of the toolbox.

Initialization of the Vehicle. The first script in the initialization process, named `init_aircraft.m` and reported below, regards the vehicle parameters and characteristics. The inertial properties and the initial conditions are loaded into the 6 DoF Simulink Block, reported in Fig. 9, that contains the dynamic equations.

Initialization of the vehicle - init_aircraft.m

```
1  %Mass of the vehicle
2  mass = 288772; % kg
3  %Inertia tensor for the nonlinear simulink model
4  Inertia = diag([24675560  44876980  67383260]);
5  Inertia(1, 3) = 1315126;
6  Inertia(3, 1) = 1315126;
7
8  %Initial position in inertial axes [Xe, Ye, Ze]
9  Init_pos = [0, 0, -6096];
10 %Initial velocity in body axes [u, v, w]
11 Init_vel = [252.98, 0, 0];
12 %Initial Euler orientation [roll, pitch, yaw]
13 Init_ang = [0, 0, 0];
14 %Initial body rotation rates [p, q, r]
15 Init_rot = [0, 0, 0];
```

The aerodynamic coefficients can be loaded as MAT files into the MAT-LAB function `init_aero_coefficients.m`. Forces and moments are computed in `Aircraft_Forces.m` by using the derivatives of the aerodynamic coefficients with respect to each state variable, as shown in Sect. 2.2. This is the output of the Forces & Moments block of Fig. 9, and the input of the vehicle model.

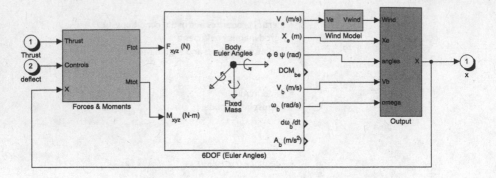

Fig. 9. Simulink model of a Boeing 747.

An example of aerodynamic coefficients matrix format

```
1  global CAeroMatrix
2  CAeroMatrix = [CD0 CDa CDap CDq CDM CDde 0 0 0 0 0;...
3                 0 0 0 0 0 0 Cyb Cyp Cyr Cyda Cydr;...
4                 CL0 CLa CLap CLq CLM CLde 0 0 0 0 0;...
5                 0 0 0 0 0 0 Clb Clp Clr Clda Cldr;...
6                 Cm0 Cma Cmap Cmq CmM Cmde 0 0 0 0 0;...
7                 0 0 0 0 0 0 Cnb Cnp Cnr Cnda Cndr];
8
9  save('CAeroMatrix')
```

The data shown here can be loaded from file, so that the end user does not need to manually edit this configuration scripts by itself. This can be done by selecting the path of external files in the MATLAB function `Aircraft_Forces.m`.

The dynamics of the actuators and the engine model are loaded in the Simulink Block represented in Fig. 10. Here the user can consider the nonlinearities in the engine. If a different actuator model is available, e.g. obtained

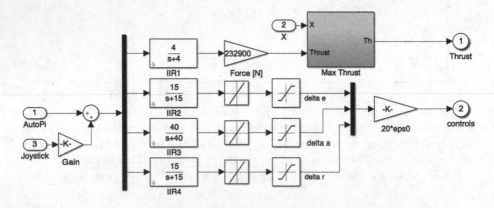

Fig. 10. Actuators dynamics and engine model.

by identification on a dataset, it can be used to replace the default dynamics, provided that the control interface is the same, *i.e.*, thrust (normalized as [0, 1] for null to full thrust), elevator, aileron and rudder (normalized in the interval [−0.5, 0.5]) as input signals and the effective thrust and angles of the control surfaces as outputs.

The experienced user can nonetheles choose to edit, replace or improve the provided MATLAB functions and Simulink schemes to customize the default behavior of any part of the simulator, exception made for the basic rigid-body equations.

Some key parameters, such as the control law and the disturbance characteristics, can be chosen directly from the control GUI, as shown in Sect. 3.

Initialization of the World. From `Aircraft_Forces.m`, APRICOT uses an atmosphere model to compute aerodynamic forces and moments. For example, the ISA model [10] parameters definition is shown below.

Atmosphere model

```
1  % Atmospheric model
2  alt = abs(h);
3  gamma = 1.4;
4  T0 = 288.15; p0 = 101325; M0 = 0.800488;
5  R = 287.053;
6  T = T0 - 6.5*alt/1000;               %Temperature in K
7  press = p0*(1 - 0.0065*alt/T0)^5.2561; %Pressure in Pa
8  rho = press/(R*T);                   %Density in kg/m^3
9  a = (gamma*R*T)^0.5;                 %Speed of sound in m/s
10 qdyn = 0.5*rho*V^2;                  %Dynamic pressure
```

The wind model is thus loaded in the Simulink Block reported in Fig. 11.

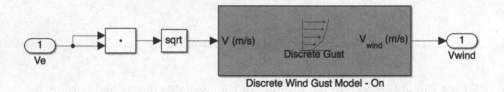

Fig. 11. Wind model.

Initialization and User Interface for the Control Design. Control laws setup in APRICOT follows the scheme in Fig. 12.

The user can choose to interact with the aircraft control system by means of a GUI (see Fig. 13) where default or user defined controllers can be loaded either on the full dynamics model or on the reduced longitudinal or lateral dynamics models. The GUI is organized in different panels to modify different aspects of the control laws acting on the aircraft.

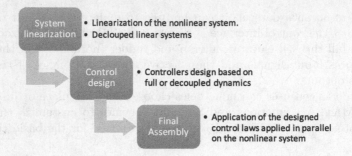

Fig. 12. Control walkthrough.

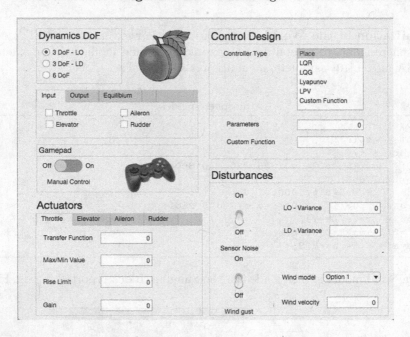

Fig. 13. The APRICOT control GUI.

User can also choose to use a subset of the available inputs and outputs for a given controller, enabling in this way fail-safe tests in different conditions of actuation or sensing. The same applies for disturbances, whose entity or models can be varied to assess the system performances in various conditions. This is particularly useful when designing a control law. By default the user can choose between the full nonlinear dynamics to be controlled, or between the longitudinal and laterodirectional subsystems. The longitudinal subsystem state vector is taken as $x_{LO} = [V, \alpha, q, \theta, h]^T$, with inputs $u_{LO} = [\delta_{th}, \delta_e]^T$. The laterodirectional subsystem state vector is taken as $x_{LD} = [r, \beta, p, \phi, \psi, y]^T$, with inputs $u_{LD} = [\delta_a, \delta_r]^T$.

In [20] the reader can find a more detailed description of the control laws implemented by default in APRICOT. These are the classical LQR, LQG, LPV and Lyapunov based nonlinear controllers and can be chosen in the Control Design panel, reported in Fig. 13.

Input control from an external pad can be enabled in the Gamepad panel, and the user can choose which commands are related to which control inputs from the Joystick block, see Fig. 2. The gamepad can be configured to provide disturbances on the auto-pilot control signals, or to control the airplane manually.

The actuator models described in Sect. 3 can be customized in the Actuators panel shown in Fig. 13. Moreover, from the Disturbances panel the user can test its controls under different conditions, as illustrated in Sect. 2.4.

Flight Planning. Flight planning is a critical task as the aircraft is subject to constraints in actuation, energy consumption and compliance with air traffic control specifications, in order to avoid midair collisions. Besides, control authority should be minimized whenever possible to extend the life of actuation surfaces and components. It is then essential to consider these aspects in order to generate reference trajectories to be used as feed-forward control inputs, and to validate the generated plans via simulation.

In APRICOT, this is achieved through optimization-based techniques. It is possible to consider constraints on the system dynamics, states and inputs, or to obtain plans for unconstrained problems. As shown in Fig. 14, the flight planning process is divided into three main steps.

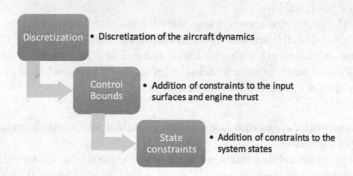

Fig. 14. Flight planning process.

As discussed in Sect. 2.3, the fuel consumption of the aircraft is described through SFC and thrust engine maps. The fuel flow is computed as the product of SFC times the thrust X_T of the engines

$$\dot{m}_{fuel} = SFC\ X_T.$$

A simplifying assumption in the planning setup can be made considering a constant SFC equal to its trimmed value, while the thrust X_T is taken as an optimization variable. It is worth noting that in APRICOT the complete computation of the fuel flow is used, see Fig. 6, and can also be customized.

Examples of flight plans are given and commented in Sect. 4. The MAT-LAB functions LOoptfun.m and LDoptfun.m implementing the flight planning algorithm take as input the following parameters:

- initial conditions,
- final conditions,
- initial time,
- final time,
- discretization period.

4 Simulations

In this section simulation results are reported for different simulated flights with different controllers among those illustrated in the previous sections, and given as example demos in APRICOT. The details of the implemented control laws are provided in [20].

Nonlinear and LQR Controls: First, we compare the performance of a Lyapunov based controller with an LQR controller on the nonlinear longitudinal dynamics in ideal conditions, *i.e.*, with no disturbances, but considering the actuator nonlinearities.

In Fig. 15 results are shown when initial condition is $x_0 = [V, \alpha, q, \theta]^T = [262.98, 0.2, -0.2, 0.1]^T$ around the trim condition $\bar{x} = [252.98, 0, 0, 0]^T$.

The system controlled with the linear control law has higher variations of angular velocities, angle of attack and sideslip angle with respect to the behaviour obtained with the Lyapunov based control.

Flight Planning: An example setup for longitudinal and laterodirectional planning is now illustrated.

For the longitudinal dynamics, we want to compute a plan to steer the system from the initial configurations $x_0 = [V, \alpha, \theta, q, h]^T = [252.98, 0, 0, 0, 6096]^T$ to the final configurations $x_f = [V, \alpha, \theta, q, h]^T = [252.98, 0, 0, 0, 7096]^T$, subject to saturations of the control variable as $-0.5 \leq \delta_e \leq 0.5$ and $0 \leq \delta_{th} - \delta_{th,0} \leq 1$, with a thrust control at the equilibrim $\delta_{th,0} = 0.7972$. The altitude overshoot is limited to 10 %.

In a similar way the laterodirectional planning is executed considering the following constraints on the ailerons and the tail rudder, corresponding to a maximum excursion of $\pm 20°$, and given as $-0.5 \leq \delta_a \leq 0.5$, $-0.5 \geq \delta_r \leq 0.5$.

In this way it is possible to compute trajectories to steer the system between several waypoints to obtain a complicated path, as that in Fig. 16a whose first $100s$ are the result of the aforementioned planning problem.

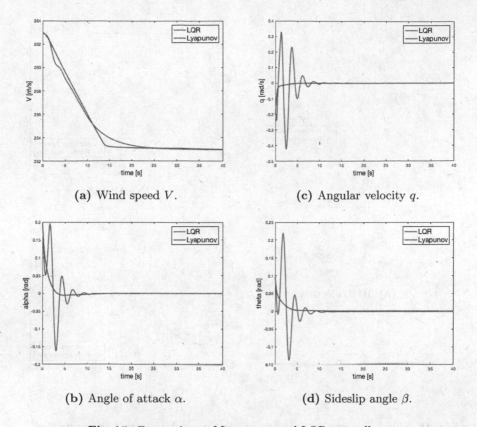

(a) Wind speed V.

(c) Angular velocity q.

(b) Angle of attack α.

(d) Sideslip angle β.

Fig. 15. Comparison of Lyapunov and LQR controllers

LQR and LQG Controllers: In the case of LQR and LQG control laws, in Fig. 16 we assess the performance of the simulator and the flight planner comparing the ideal aircraft trajectory with the simulated one considering the complete nonlinear model affected by disturbances. Note that for each waypoint reported in Fig. 16a different aircraft orientations are required and correctly tracked. The planned and executed trajectories are very close. To better appreciate the system evolution, videos of experiments are visible on APRICOT website [8].

In Fig. 17 the improvement in the LQG control system performance with respect to the LQR case in presence of disturbances can be appreciated. This is due to the disturbance rejection capabilities of the LQG controller, that translates in reduced oscillations of the aircraft and a more comfortable flight for the passengers.

LPV Controller: Finally we consider the quadratic cost index

$$J(t) = \int_0^t x(\tau)^T Q x(\tau) + u(\tau)^T R u(\tau) \, d\tau$$

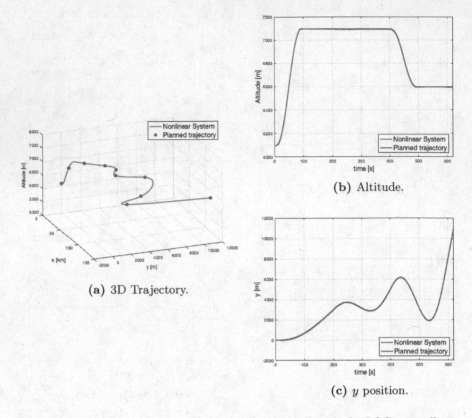

(a) 3D Trajectory.

(b) Altitude.

(c) y position.

Fig. 16. Simulation results on the flight plan tracked with the LQG controller.

with diagonal matrices Q and R, obtained for the laterodirectional dynamics when the aircraft recovers from a severely perturbed initial state with $\theta = 0.2$ and $\phi = 0.2$, comparing the performance of an LQR and an LPV control law. In this example, the LPV control law has been obtained with multiple LQR controllers designed for different values of θ. The longitudinal dynamics is controlled with a single LQR controller. Simulation results are reported in Fig. 18. The LPV controller improves the trajectory tracking and energy efficiency performance of the aircraft with respect to the LQR controller, which is optimized for a single operating point and performs worse far from it.

4.1   Simulator Performances

A comparison with existing toolboxes has not been possible, mainly due to the fact that, to the best of authors knowledge, there is currently no other open source toolbox that has the functionalities of APRICOT. Despite that, we show some performance indicators obtained for different use cases.

Regarding the flight planning phase, to solve the constrained optimization problem illustrated in the simulation section we registered an execution time of

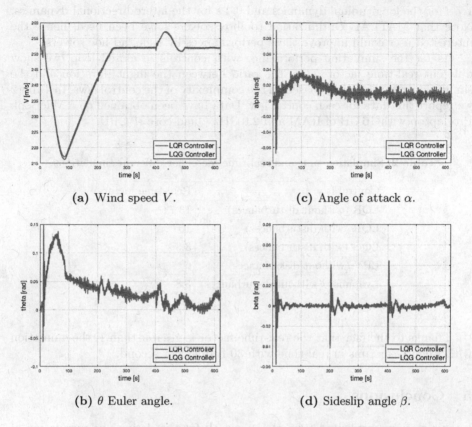

(a) Wind speed V.

(c) Angle of attack α.

(b) θ Euler angle.

(d) Sideslip angle β.

Fig. 17. Comparison of LQR and LQG controllers with noise and wind gust.

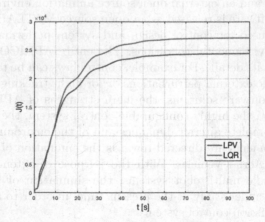

Fig. 18. Comparison between LPV and LQR performance.

1.7 s for the longitudinal dynamics and 0.4 s for the laterodirectional dynamics. Note that MATLAB Optimization toolbox solvers have been used, hence the interested user could improve these performances by using ad hoc solvers.

As for the simulation performance with controls in closed loop, we show different real-time factors (*i.e.,* the ratio between the flight duration and the simulation execution time) based on the complexity of the control laws. In Table 2 we report this data for each control law. Data have been obtained on a MacBook Pro laptop with 16 GB of RAM and 2.0 GHz Quad-core i7 CPU.

Table 2. Simulation time and real-time factor for different simulations.

Control law	Real-time factor
LQR (without disturbances)	13.7
LQR (with disturbances)	10
LQG (with disturbances)	3.3
LPV (without disturbances)	6
Lyapunov (without disturbances)	5.8

Thanks to the fact that the real-time factor is greater than 1, the animation with FlightGear runs in real time with 30 frames per second.

5   Conclusions

In this work we presented a novel framework for the design and simulation of flight planning and aircraft control systems. The toolbox, named APRICOT, is highly versatile, customizable and provided with user interfaces such as a GUI, a gamepad interface and an external open source animation environment, namely Flightgear. The software is released as an open source MATLAB/Simulink toolbox[2] and can be used for control design and system performance evaluations under different environmental conditions. The entire APRICOT framework is customizable in all its details. For example, control laws can be tested for robustness with respect to external perturbations or for flight tracking purposes. With respect to other software solutions, the main strengths of APRICOT are: the open source nature, the highly configurable control system, the ease of use, the availability of a complete aircraft dynamics and of the environmental model.

Future developments are directed towards the simulation of quadrotors and other Unmanned Aerial Vehicles. With the purpose of extending APRICOT simulation to handle multi-robot systems, the simulation of both aerial and ground vehicles is under study at the present time, in order to allow the design of coordination/mission control systems.

---

[2] APRICOT Software available at http://aferrarelli.github.io/APRICOT/.

References

1. JSBSim. http://jsbsim.sourceforge.net/
2. jMAVSim. https://github.com/PX4/jMAVSim
3. Ardupilot. http://ardupilot.org/
4. PX4. http://px4.io/
5. Bittar, A., Figuereido, H.V., Guimaraes, P.A., Mendes, A.C.: Guidance software-in-the-loop simulation using X-plane and simulink for UAVs. In: 2014 International Conference on Unmanned Aircraft Systems (ICUAS), pp. 993–1002. IEEE (2014)
6. Jenie, Y.I., Indriyanto, T.: X-plane-simulink simulation of a pitch-holding automatic controlsystem for boeing 747. In: Indonesian-Taiwan Workshop, Bandung, Indonesia (2006)
7. Aircraft control toolbox. Princeton Satellite Systems. http://www.psatellite.com/act/index.php
8. APRICOT. https://github.com/aferrarelli/APRICOT/
9. Heffley, R.K., Jewell, W.F.: Aircraft Handling Qualities Data (1972)
10. Cavcar, M.: The international standard atmosphere (ISA). Anadolu Univ. Turkey **30** (2000)
11. Ondriš, D., Andoga, R.: Aircraft modeling using MATLAB/FlightGear interface. Acta Avionica **15**(27) (2013)
12. Nusyirwan, I.F.: Engineering flight simulator using MATLAB, Python and FlightGear. In: SimTecT, Melbourne, Australia (2011)
13. Moness, M., Mostafa, A.M., Abdel-Fadeel, M.A., Aly, A.I., Al-Shamandy, A.: Automatic control education using FlightGear and MATLAB based virtual lab. In: 8th International Conference on Electrical Engineering, pp. 1157–1160 (2012)
14. Stevens, B.L., Lewis, F.L., Johnson, E.N.: Aircraft Control and Simulation: Dynamics, Controls Design, and Autonomous Systems. Wiley, Hoboken (2015)
15. Cook, M.V.: Flight Dynamics Principles: A Linear Systems Approach to Aircraft Stability and Control. Butterworth-Heinemann, Oxford (2012)
16. Tewari, A.: Advanced Control of Aircraft, Spacecraft and Rockets, vol. 37. Wiley, Hoboken (2011)
17. Chrif, L., Kadda, Z.M.: Aircraft control system using LQG and LQR controller with optimal estimation-Kalman filter design. Procedia Eng. **80**, 245–257 (2014)
18. Marcos, A., Balas, G.J.: Development of linear-parameter-varying models for aircraft. J. Guidance Control Dyn. **27**(2), 218–228 (2004)
19. Härkegård, O., Glad, T.: Flight Control Design Using Backstepping. Linköping University Electronic Press, Linköping (2000)
20. Ferrarelli, A., Caporale, D., Settimi, A., Pallottino, L.: Apricot: aerospace prototyping control toolbox. Dynamics and control details (2016). https://github.com/aferrarelli/APRICOT/blob/master/APRICOTExtended.pdf
21. Donald, M.: Automatic Flight Control System. Prentice Hall, Upper Saddle River (1990)
22. Tewari, A.: Automatic Control of Atmospheric and Space Flight Vehicles: Design and Analysis with MATLAB® and Simulink®. Springer Science & Business Media, Heidelberg (2011)
23. Caughey, D.A.: Introduction to aircraft stability and control. In: Lecture Notes. Cornell University (2011)

Human Driven Robot Grasping: An Interactive Framework

Hamal Marino[1]([✉]), Alessandro Settimi[1,2], and Marco Gabiccini[1,2,3]

[1] Centro di ricerca "E. Piaggio", Largo Lucio Lazzarino 1, 56122 Pisa, Italy
hamal.marino@centropiaggio.unipi.it
[2] Department of Advanced Robotics, Istituto Italiano di Tecnologia,
via Morego, 30, 16163 Genova, Italy
[3] DICI, University of Pisa, 56122 Pisa, Italy

Abstract. One main problem in the field of robotic grasping is to teach a robot how to grasp a particular object; in fact, this depends not only on the object geometry, but also on the end-effector properties. Different methods to generate grasp trajectories (way-points made by end-effector positions and its joint values) have been investigated such as kinaesthetic teaching, grasp recording using motion capture systems, and others. Although these method could potentially lead to a good trajectory, usually they are only able to give a good initial guess for a successful grasp: in fact, obtained trajectories seldom transfer well to the robot without further processing. In this work, we propose a ROS/Gazebo based interactive framework to create and modify grasping trajectories for different robotic end-effectors. This tool allows to shape the various way-points of a considered trajectory, and test it in a simulated environment, leading to a trial-and-error procedure and eventually to the real hardware application.

Keywords: Object grasping and manipulation · Grasp synthesis · Grasp planning · Grasp simulation · Human in the loop

1 Introduction

In the field of robotic grasping, there are various methods for how to teach a robot to grasp a certain object (see [1] for a recent survey). Different hypotheses can be made by such methods, e.g. knowing the object, or at least its class (such an object is thus called "familiar"), in advance rather than having no a priori information, and they lead to substantially different approaches. In many of these approaches, successful examples are needed beforehand in order to repeat them, or generalize them to the actual scenario.

For such methods requiring good prior data, many ways exist to generate data to be then used by the robot; kinaesthetic teaching is one of those, but

This work is supported by the grant No. 645599 "SoMa" – Soft-bodied intelligence for Manipulation – within the H2020-ICT-2014-1 program.

© Springer International Publishing AG 2016
J. Hodicky (Ed.): MESAS 2016, LNCS 9991, pp. 158–167, 2016.
DOI: 10.1007/978-3-319-47605-6_12

it is worth noticing that it is not always possible to use it when dealing with under-sensorized robotic hands. Another way to obtain a grasp trajectory is to use motion capture systems, having both the hand position and configuration, as well as the object pose, tracked by the cameras: this has the disadvantages to be possibly very expensive, and rely on very precise markers positioning.

These, and possibly other methods, will give a good starting point to look for a successful grasp, but may need further refinement in order to achieve good performances: such trajectories will often transfer poorly if used with no processing.

Here, we present a framework based on ROS [2] which can be used to create and/or modify grasping trajectories for a variety of robotic end-effectors, exploiting human intuitiveness to refine grasps which can then fulfill their purpose.

The framework can be used in a trial-and-error fashion, shaping the trajectory way-points (WPs) via a graphical user interface (GUI) in Rviz [3], and simulating, using Gazebo [4], the hand motion and interaction with the object and environment to validate the grasp. The URDF-based nature of the framework permits to work easily with different robotic end-effectors. The GUI is designed to let the user modify each actuated joint, as well as the hand-object relative pose, at each WP of the trajectory.

Resulting grasp performance can be evaluated in simulation before transferring to the real robot, reducing the time needed for refinement. Moreover, using simulation it is possible to extract useful features such as, for example, contact points, even for under-sensorized set-ups. This information can then be used as exemplary data for training purposes in programming by demonstration or machine learning algorithms.

While a very comprehensive tool for grasp planning has been developed in recent years [5], which includes many features such as computing various grasp metrics for evaluating grasp properties, it has the disadvantage of using its own robot model format and simulation engine (a necessity at the time in which its development started). Nevertheless, under-actuated hands (e.g. [6]), which are recently becoming widespread, can not be simulated in such quasi-static simulation environment. We thus decided to use a dynamic simulator that could handle those, and relied on Gazebo and URDF, which also are now *de facto* standards in robotics research.

2   The Interactive Grasp Generation Framework

The proposed framework consists of four principal components:

- a grasp generation system,
- a GUI based on RViz, namely Grasp Modification Utility (GMU), used to create/modify grasp trajectories,
- a dynamic simulation environment, namely Gazebo Simple Grasp Utility (GSGU), used to simulate the grasp trajectories in the Gazebo simulator,
- a robot, where to finally validate the grasps through use.

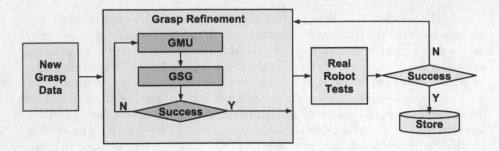

Fig. 1. Work-flow block diagram

2.1 Work-Flow Description

A possible work-flow is depicted in Fig. 1. After acquiring or creating new grasp data, a refinement process can be started, involving iteration of checking and modifying the way-points in the GMU and testing the resulting grasp trajectory in the GSGU. After a good result is obtained, real tests can be performed: the process can end if the validation is successful, otherwise a new refinement procedure starts.

New Grasp Data. Generating new grasping data is the first step needed to obtain a successful grasp trajectory. Although the first version of this data does not need to be perfect, as it will be possible to adjust it later on, having a good initial guess is a step closer to achieving the desired behavior.

To this end, when the necessary hardware is available, a possibility to obtain a good starting point is to record a grasp in, e.g., a motion capture system, then down-sampling the trajectory at need to obtain a manageable number of way-points.

In Fig. 2, a few instants during a grasp trajectory recording using an optical motion capture system (Phase Space, San Leandro, CA –, USA) are shown: the trajectory is originally recorded at 480 Hz, then down-sampled to 15 Hz to have a manageable amount of data to post-process.

It is worth noticing that, even when such hardware is not accessible, it is still possible to create a completely new trajectory using the GMU software, as can be seen in the GMU GUI on the right of Fig. 6.

Grasp Refinement. The core component presented in this work is then the iterative grasp refinement capability of the work-flow, as shown in the central block of Fig. 1.

Via visual inspection in the GMU, the way-points hand pose and actuated joints configuration can be manually changed using Rviz interactive markers: this can be seen in Fig. 3.

The resulting trajectory can then be tested in the GSGU: an example of this is depicted in Fig. 4.

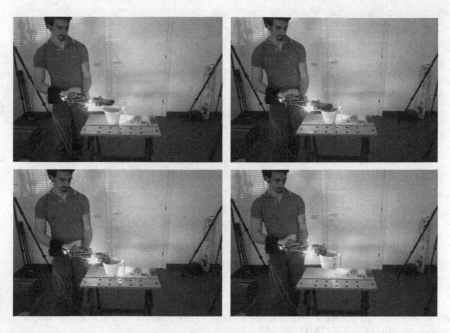

Fig. 2. Recording the grasp of a pitcher performed by a human wearing the SoftHand with handle, using the Phase Space motion capture system.

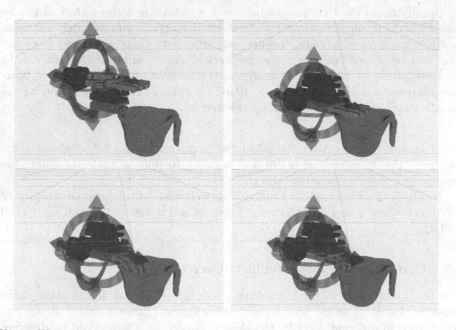

Fig. 3. Way-points of the trajectory for a SoftHand grasping a pitcher: each of them can be refined by an expert before proceeding to the simulation via GSGU, or after some weaknesses have been found during the iterative refinement-testing procedure.

Fig. 4. Simulation screen-shots obtained from GSGU when using a grasp trajectory previously refined using GMU.

Specifying on the ROS parameter server which trajectories to test, it is possible to perform single testing of a specific trajectory, as well as batch testing of multiple trajectories at once. Results, stored as both Gazebo log and ROS bag files, can be played back for visual inspection, and desired information can be obtained either at run-time or analysing the recorded files. To facilitate post-hoc analysis, a Gazebo plug-in is included for taking timed screen-shots of the simulation, which can then be easily checked by the user.

Real Robot Tests. After the simulated performance has achieved a satisfying level, real tests can be performed in order to fully validate, or define the weaknesses, of each grasp trajectory.

In Fig. 5, the Vito robot in Centro Piaggio is used to validate the grasping of an object whose grasp trajectory has been refined iterating through GMU and GSGU.

2.2   Core Database and Graphical User Interface

The basic component of the framework is a database, storing information about considered objects to be grasped and end-effectors. Since a single object can be grasped in different ways by the same end-effector, there would be different entries in the database corresponding to different cases. As an example, consider the simplified database extract shown in Tables 1, 2, and 3, where a single object

Fig. 5. Vito robot grasping a pitcher after the corresponding trajectory has been refined using the procedure illustrated in this paper.

Table 1. Database entries, "Objects" table

ObjectID	3D views	ObjectName
o1	PointCloud files	Cylinder

Table 2. Database entries, "End-Effectors" table

End-EffectorID	End-EffectorType	Name
e1	RightSoftHand	right_hand
e2	LeftSoftHand	left_hand

Table 3. Database entries, "Grasp" table

GraspID	ObjectID	End-EffectorID	GraspName
g1	o1	e1	cylinder_top_right_hand
g2	o1	e1	cylinder_bottom_right_hand
g3	o1	e1	cylinder_side_right_hand
g4	o1	e2	cylinder_top_left_hand
g5	o1	e2	cylinder_bottom_left_hand
g6	o1	e2	cylinder_side_left_hand

(namely a cylinder), two end-effectors (a right and a left robotic hand), and a few possible grasps (three per end-effector) are considered.

Using this database, the user can load a single grasp to visualize it in the GMU. Then, using the GUI and RViz both reported in Fig. 6, the user can add

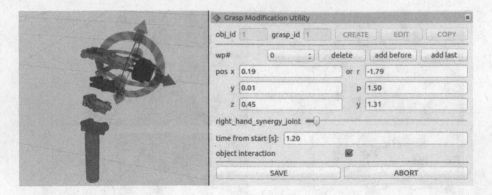

Fig. 6. On the left, RViz 3D rendering is used to visualize the various way-points position with respect to the considered object (the green cylinder). On the right, the interactive GUI that allows to modify/create new grasps and add/modify/remove way-points for a single grasp. WPs shade from blue to red as the hand approaches the object. (Color figure online)

WPs to the grasp and modify the relative position between the end-effector and the object together with the joint values in each WP. For the sake of clarity, each way-point has the following listed properties:

1. pose with respect to the object
2. joint values
3. time of execution with the respect to the grasping procedure starting time.

3   Applications

This framework has been used in various projects involving grasping, being validated through different experiments.

3.1   Multi-robot Object Handling

One important application was [7], in which the problem of moving objects using multiple robots and support surfaces has been addressed. An object recognition system localized the object to be moved and then various grasp trajectories were executed to perform the task. These grasp trajectories have been generated using the work-flow described in Sect. 2.1 and validated in different experiments, as shown in Fig. 7.

3.2   Learning New Grasps Using Successful Examples

Many algorithms exist which are capable of learning successful grasps from examples of which enough information is available. Examples of such algorithms can

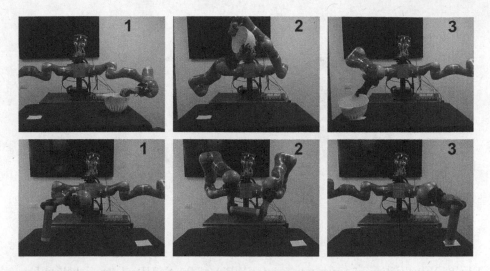

Fig. 7. Handoff experiments with a colander (on the top) and a cylinder (on the bottom).

be found in [1], while a very recent example is represented by [8], and they mostly rely on the full hand and object shape, as well as the internal hand configuration during the trajectory.

While in some cases this information is obtainable, in some others (e.g., cases in which under-sensorized robotic hands are involved, or an object tracking system is not available) attaining it is not trivial, and simulated data could come in handy for generating exemplary data for learning purposes. Using a full-fledged, multi-body physics simulator makes it possible to provide a full history of contact points, as well as object motion, and internal hand configuration.

This latter aspect is especially important for under-actuated hands as the SoftHand, used in the provided examples, for which the sensorization is a problem of ongoing research [9].

Environmental Constraints Exploitation. A special case in which using the Gazebo Simple Grasp Utility can be considered very useful is when a close interaction with the external environment is required, as in the study of Environmental Constraints Exploitation: strategies can be tested in simulation prior to move to reality, including considerations on the relative force levels to which different approaches can lead.

In Fig. 8, two way-points of the grasp trajectory for a shallow box, which will exploit the planar surface on which the box is, are depicted when generated inside the GMU. The execution of the trajectory using the GSGU is instead shown in Fig. 9, where contacts are highlighted via blue spheres and normal contact forces via green lines to show that there are both hand-environment and hand-object contacts during the grasping action.

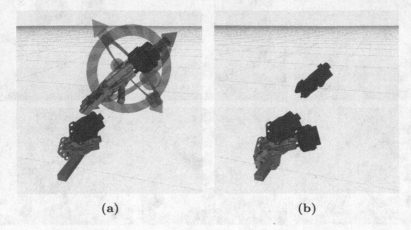

(a)   (b)

Fig. 8. Visualization of grasp way-points (WPs) of the SoftHand for a shallow box using GMU. Highlighted are initial configuration at pre-grasp (a) and a WP closer to the object to be grasped (b). (Color figure online)

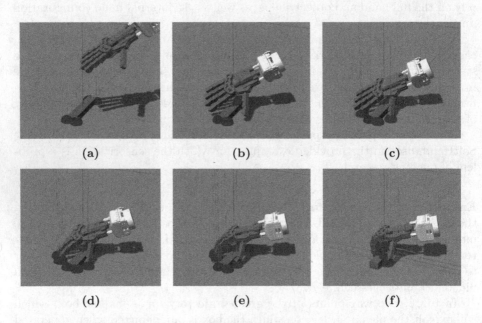

(a)   (b)   (c)

(d)   (e)   (f)

Fig. 9. Grasping a shallow box using the SoftHand inside the Gazebo simulator using GSGU. Contacts among hand, object, and environment are highlighted via blue spheres, while contact normal forces are shown using green lines. (Color figure online)

4   Conclusions

In this work, a framework for facilitating the creation and refinement of robotic grasp trajectories has been illustrated. This framework, based on ROS/Gazebo, allows to visualize in a highly interactive environment the trajectory which will then be executed by the robot, and to exploit human skills in order to fine-tune the sequence of way-points, also visualizing what a simulated execution of the grasp will look like.

Grasps generated and refined using these tools have been successfully used on real robots, while ongoing research involves the use of the simulator outputs as data for learning grasps on novel objects, eventually exploiting interactions with the external environment.

The code for this framework is available at https://bitbucket.org/hamalMari no/gazebo_simple_grasp_utility.

References

1. Bohg, J., Morales, A., Asfour, T., Kragic, D.: Data-driven grasp synthesisa survey. IEEE Trans. Robot. **30**(2), 289–309 (2014)
2. Quigley, M., Conley, K., Gerkey, B., Faust, J., Foote, T., Leibs, J., Wheeler, R., Ng, A.Y.: ROS: an open-source robot operating system. In: ICRA Workshop on Open Source Software, vol. 3, p. 5 (2009)
3. Rviz - 3d visualization tool for ROS. http://wiki.ros.org/rviz
4. Koenig, N., Howard, A.: Design and use paradigms for Gazebo, an open-source multi-robot simulator. In: Proceedings of 2004 IEEE/RSJ International Conference on Intelligent Robots and Systems (IROS 2004), vol. 3, pp. 2149–2154. IEEE (2004)
5. Miller, A.T., Allen, P.K.: GraspIt! a versatile simulator for robotic grasping. IEEE Robot. Autom. Mag. **11**(4), 110–122 (2004)
6. Catalano, M.G., Grioli, G., Farnioli, E., Serio, A., Piazza, C., Bicchi, A.: Adaptive synergies for the design and control of the Pisa/IIT SoftHand. Int. J. Robot. Res. **33**(5), 768–782 (2014)
7. Marino, H., Ferrati, M., Settimi, A., Rosales, C., Gabiccini, M.: On the problem of moving objects with autonomous robots: a unifying high-level planning approach. IEEE Robot. Autom. Lett. **1**, 469–476 (2016)
8. Kopicki, M., Detry, R., Adjigble, M., Leonardis, A., Wyatt, J.L.: One shot learning and generation of dexterous grasps for novel objects. Int. J. Robot. Res. **35**(8), 959–976 (2016)
9. Santaera, G., Luberto, E., Serio, A., Gabiccini, M., Bicchi, A.: Low-cost, fast and accurate reconstruction of robotic and human postures via IMU measurements. In: 2015 IEEE International Conference on Robotics and Automation (ICRA). IEEE (2015)

The Unmanned Autonomous Systems Cyberspace Arena (UCA). A M&S Architecture and Relevant Tools for Security Issues Analysis of Autonomous System Networks

Marco Biagini[1], Sonia Forconi[1(✉)], Fabio Corona[1], Agatino Mursia[2],
Lucio Ganga[2], and Ferdinando Battiati[3]

[1] NATO Modelling & Simulation Centre of Excellence, Rome, Italy
{mscoe.cd01,mscoe.cde02,mscoe.cd04}@smd.difesa.it
[2] LEONARDO Finmeccanica, Rome, Italy
{agatino.mursia,lucio.ganga}@leonardocompany.com
[3] Scuola delle Trasmissioni e Informatica, Rome, Italy
ferdinando.battiati@esercito.difesa.it

Abstract. In the framework of the modern tactical scenarios and the increasing employment of Unmanned Autonomous Systems (UAxS) in multi-battlespace domains (land, naval, air and cyberspace), the threats to the communications and networks available among the units on the battlefield are becoming ever more challenging. It thus becomes crucial to protect communications and networking of these systems from possible hostile actions aimed at jeopardizing mission execution in the Cyberspace. This paper is focused on the required properties and capabilities of a UAxS Cyberspace Arena (UCA), a simulation-based communication and networking environment where it will be possible to evaluate UAxS tactical communication solutions as well as the related countermeasures in case of cyber-attacks and in terms of their resilience and reactivity to the considered security threats.

The UCA is developed as an emerging concept to support UAxS Concept Development and Experimentation phases and its overarching architecture and related M&S tools are described, focusing on a Networks and Communications Simulator (Cyber Arena), within a Modelling and Simulation as a Services approach. In conclusion, the UCA architecture aims to demonstrate how it will be possible, in such an environment, to evaluate UAxS Security issues and challenges related to tactical communication and networking solutions in case of cyber-attacks, both in term of their resilience and reactivity to the considered security threats.

Keywords: Unmanned autonomous systems · Cyberspace · CSSE · Cyber defence

© Springer International Publishing AG 2016
J. Hodicky (Ed.): MESAS 2016, LNCS 9991, pp. 168–175, 2016.
DOI: 10.1007/978-3-319-47605-6_13

1 Introduction

In the context of modern strategies for combat and patrol operations, tactical scenarios pose demanding challenges to the communication and networking infrastructure available among the units on the battlefield. Furthermore, during these operations the use of Unmanned Autonomous Systems (UAxS) in multi-battlespace domains such as the land, naval, air and space is becoming actual and challenging. Military decision making support systems at all levels depends essentially on the communication networks and in the case of failure might negatively influence the mission execution [14]. In the case of communication failure, the technique of Modelling and Simulation might be implemented to overcome it for a defined time [15]. It is crucial to protect communications and networking of these systems from possible hostile actions aimed at jeopardizing mission execution in the Cyberspace. Considering the Cyberspace a virtual transversal domain to the battlespace domains, this paper describes the required properties and capabilities of a UAxS Cyberspace Arena (UCA).

The UCA is being developed as an emerging concept to support UAxS Concept Development and Experimentation phases. It originates from the implementation and customization of an ongoing National (Italian) Military Research Program (PNRM), the Cyber Security Simulation Environment (CSSE). The UCA aims to provide a simulation-based communication and networking environment where it will be possible to evaluate UAxS tactical communication solutions as well as the related countermeasures in case of cyber-attacks and in terms of their resilience and reactivity to the considered security threats.

Therefore, the first section of this paper briefly illustrates main initiatives of the NATO Modelling and Simulation Centre of Excellence (M&S CoE) in the field of multi-robots simulation environment. Then the CSSE Program is introduced in the next section, in order to present its objectives and how it contributes in the international context to the studies about the problems related to cyber threats facing the communications networks (tactical or infrastructured) of military units.

In the following section the central topic of the paper is addressed. The requirements for the development of a UCA and the related modelling and simulation (M&S) tools, in terms of properties and capabilities, are described aiming at the delivery of an environment capable at investigating cyber security issues in such tactical context. The UCA concept is based on an integrated simulation environment allowing to model UAxS communication networks, the security threats typical of scenarios where they operate, as well as the related countermeasures. As result, the section illustrates the UCA overarching architecture and related M&S tools, focusing on a Networks and Communications Simulator (Cyber Arena). This architecture is developed as a possible federation of systems, like a Robot Scenario Generator and Animator (RSGA), possibly a C2 system, real and virtual Robots, exploiting heterogeneous technologies, such as Robotic Operating System (ROS), Systems in the loop (SITL) and High Level Architecture (HLA) Run-Time Infrastructure (RTI), gateways between different communication protocols within a Modelling and Simulation as a Services approach.

In the conclusions, it is stressed that the UCA architecture aims to demonstrate how it will be possible, in such an environment, to evaluate UAxS Security issues and challenges related to tactical communication and networking solutions in case of cyber-attacks, both in term of their resilience and reactivity to the considered security threats.

2 NATO M&S Activities Supporting UAxS Concept Development and the UCA Architectural Design

The NATO M&S CoE has being involved in several initiatives regarding the UAxS concept Development and Experimentation. Following a brief overview of these initiatives to introduce the Cyber Space Arena Concept.

The Simulated Interactive Robotics Initiative (SIRI). It was a cooperative project between the M&S CoE and the US Joint Staff J6, in collaboration with a former Finmeccanica company. It was focused on interoperability issues for integrating a Multi-Robot System (MRS) in a Multinational Coalition Scenario [4]. In particular, the initiative was focused on exploring the use of National Information Exchange Model (NIEM) MilOps domain. It is an eXtensible Markup Language (XML)-based data model for message exchange in an unmanned systems environment [5]. The MRS was based on Unmanned Ground Vehicles (UGVs) and their Artificial Intelligence was based on the ROS [6]. MRS were remotely controlled by US [7].

The M&S CoE has then hosted and participated at the 3rd workshop of the CUAxS project. The workshop goal was to make tangible progress on the concept development of the CUAxS. The outcomes of this workshop were:

- the "Stratification matrix". This matrix put in relationship the level of autonomy with the type of operations (the NATO Campaign themes) and the operational functional areas, as defined in the Allied Joint Doctrine [11], or type of unit (i.e., combat, combat support, combat service support)
- the definition of the UAxS functionalities, in order to identify the possible vulnerabilities of these systems and, therefore, the countermeasures to exploit these weaknesses.

In this framework, M&S CoE proposed to design an architectural concept based on M&S tools suitable to support the CUAxS concept development and experimentation activities and the implementation of these tools to support the Concept Development Assessment Game (CDAG) wargame [3].

Following the M&S CoE participated to the meeting of the 136 Specialist Team of the Information System Technology (IST), another STO panel regarding Security Challenges for Multi-domain Autonomous and Unmanned C4ISR Systems [8]. During the workshop was given by the CoE representative the contributes to the team regarding the SIRI experience and in that occasion were put the basis for a M&S based tool to support the countering UAxS Concept Development.

In addition the M&S CoE participates to the NMSG 145 Research Task Group with a permanent representative [9]. This Tak group has the aim to operationalize the Command and Control – Simulation environments (C2SIM) interoperability standards and technologies. In particular, the M&S CoE is contributing to the development of the recommendations for formalizing the C2SIM standard with a STANAG. The CoE involvement is as part of the subgroup who is in charge to develop the C2SIM extension for UAxS.

3　Cyber Security Simulation Environment (CSSE)

The Unmanned Autonomous Systems Cyberspace Arena project originates from the implementation and customization of an ongoing National (Italian) Military Research Program (PNRM), the Cyber Security Simulation Environment (CSSE). It arises from the need to study, through the use of advanced simulation systems, problems related to cyber threats facing the communications networks (tactical or infrastructured) of military units may be subjected engaged in. CSSE has been transposed the directions provided by the working groups (current and old) in the International arena such as:

- NATO SAS-065 (NATO C2 Maturity Model),
- SAS-085(C2 Agility)
- MSG-117 (M&S in support of Cyber Defense).

The CSSE demonstrator is an open and non-classified environment, its configurability and the ability to create and/or modify equipment models, protocols, threats and countermeasures entirely new make it a versatile tool for the institutional activities of the Italian Army School of Transmission and Computing (SCUTI).

The CSSE project objectives are:

- analyze the state of art in the fields of Modelling and Simulation and Cyber Security with a detailed focus on military networks and cyber threats;
- define and describe operational scenarios, making also reference to the outcome of NATO SAS-065 and NATO SAS-085 activities, in which operate military tactical networks subject to cyber attacks;
- define and develop a simulation architecture that will allow for building a test bed environment (demonstrator) in which attackers and defenders can exercise the scenarios, cyber threats and related countermeasures previously identified without disturbing the real operational network;
- evaluate, on the demonstrator, different situations, building a repository of reference scenarios to be used for cyber operators training;
- disseminate the results obtained from the campaign of experiments

The demonstrator architecture is open experimenting cyber issues not only on tactical networks but in general on communication networks and the Live - Constructive simulation techniques is used to evaluate state-of-the-art cyber threats and countermeasure.

The demonstrator can also be seen as one component of a future integrated system (Cyber Trainer) in which exercises are performed by several groups that operate in Red versus Blue Forces type scenarios.

4   Cyber Arena: "Communication and Networking Simulation"

Modelling and Simulation (M&S) is a key tool in supporting Unmanned Autonomous Systems (UAxS) CD&E activities and addressing associated security challenges focussing on the communications and networking protection of these systems from possible hostile actions aimed at jeopardizing mission execution in a virtual domain namely Cyberspace Arena.

4.1   Unmanned Autonomous Systems Cyberspace Arena

The Unmanned Autonomous Systems Cyberspace Arena (UCA) is an emerging concept developed to support the Unmanned Autonomous Systems (UAxS) Concept Development and Experimentation (CD&E) phases. The UCA concept is based on an integrated simulation environment to provide a simulation-based communication and networking environment to evaluate UAxS tactical communication network, the security threats typical of scenarios where they operate, the related countermeasures in case of cyber-attacks and in terms of their resilience and reactivity to the considered security threats.

In the UAxS conceptual architecture, illustrated in Fig. 1, the UCA element provides the robots communication and network simulation capability. The M&S of Communication and Networking components plays a relevant role in all simulation architecture oriented to test net-centric architectures. Performances of communication and networking component in some scenarios (i.e. in the mobile and tactical scenarios) are often unpredictable due to:

- Effects of the land orography
- Low bandwidth available
- Presence of noise (environment or intentional jamming)
- Communication and networking devices probability failure
- Low availability of communication infrastructures

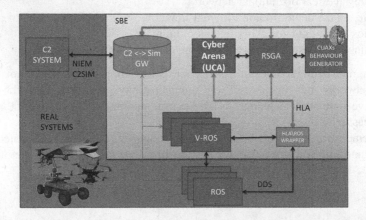

Fig. 1. Conceptual architecture of M&S tools to support the UAxS CD&E phases

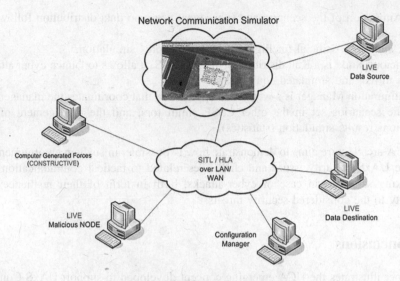

Fig. 2. The UCA components

The UCA components, illustrated in Fig. 2, are:

- Data source and Data destination represents the start point and the end point of the information exchange that will suffer the cyber attack
- Network Communication Simulator tool to provide to NATO modelling and simulation tools (OPNET) to develop, design, analyze and to verify and validate (V&V) network and communication architectures and solutions applying NATO standards (NAF)
- System-in-the-Loop (SITL) capability allows for establishing a connection "Live-Constructive" through which the real hardware and the simulation environment interact as a single unified system. This allows for:
  - Analyze effects of a simulated network on a real application
  - Utilize simulation as a traffic generator to load real network
  - Conduct stress tests on real equipment/application in an environment that simulate operational conditions
- HLA (High Level Architecture) is an architecture of "general purpose" type defined for the simulation reuse and interoperability. HLA supports the data exchange, with or without "Time Synchronization", so as other synchronization type, rescue/recovery operations, information distribution and dissemination. HLA is a IEEE international open standard that is evolving through international processes. This connectivity assures that HLA based experimental frameworks should be plug and play connected to UCA [16].
- Computer Generated Forces (CGF) is a tool with the following functions:
  - Creating and managing libraries of object (platform, sensor, weapon, etc.)
  - Scenario composition, defining the geographical location, kinematic and events.
  - Application of tools to the Mission Planning support

- Animation of the scenario and subsequent scenario data distribution follow the standard
- Using AI (Artificial Intelligent) tool for complex simulation.
- Malicious Node is a Kali distribution of Linux OS, it allows to launch cyber attacks both to real and simulated equipments.
- Configuration Manager is a web based application that coordinates the management of the scenarios set in the other CSSE simulators, and the management of the sessions results simulation (statistics).

The UCA architecture aims to demonstrate how is possible, in such an environment, to evaluate UAxS Security issues and challenges related to tactical communication and networking solutions in case of cyber-attacks, both in term of their resilience and reactivity to the considered security threats.

5 Conclusions

The paper illustrates the UCA emerging concept developed to support UAxS Concept Development and Experimentation phases and the possibility to evaluate UAxS tactical communication solutions as well as the related countermeasures in case of cyber-attacks. The UCA overarching architecture and related M&S tools presented is focusing on the relevant role plays by the M&S of Communication and Networking components. Also relevant aspects in the UCA field are the robots communication payload models, the robotic cyber attack models and the real systems to simulated environment interaction. The UCA architecture demonstrate how it is possible to evaluate UAxS Security issues and challenges related to tactical communication and networking solutions in case of cyber-attacks.

References

1. NATO ACT CEI CAPDEV: Autonomous Systems Countermeasures (2016). http://innovationhub-act.org/AxSCountermeasures. Accessed May 2016
2. NATO STO SAS 082: Disruptive Technology Assessment Game - Evaluation and Validation (2012). http://www.cso.nato.int/activities.aspx?pg=2&RestrictPanel=6&FMMod=0&OrderBy=0&OrderWay=2. Accessed May 2016
3. NATO STO SAS 086: Maritime Situational Awareness: Concept Development Assessment Game (CDAG) (2010). http://www.cso.nato.int/activities.aspx?pg=3&RestrictPanel=6&FMMod=0&OrderBy=0&OrderWay=2. Accessed May 2016
4. SSI Finmeccanica Company: SIRI Operational Scenario, Taranto (2015)
5. NIEM: National Information Exchange Model (2016). https://www.niem.gov/Pages/default.aspx. Accessed May 2016
6. ROS: Robotic Operating System (ROS) Documentation (2016). http://wiki.ros.org/. Accessed May 2016
7. Litwiller, S., Weber, M., Klucznik, F.: Improving robotic and autonomous system information interoperability: standardizing data exchange with XML. In: Hodicky, J. (ed.) MESAS 2014. LNCS, vol. 9055, pp. 24–39. Springer, Heidelberg (2015)

8. Byrum, F., Sidoran, J.: IST 136 Roadmap - Security Challenges for Multi-Domain Autonomous and Unmanned C4ISR Systems (Draft - unpublished). STO CSO (2016)
9. NATO STO NMSG 145: Operationalization of Standardized C2-Simulation Interoperability. STO CSO – STO activities (2016). http://www.cso.nato.int/activities.aspx?RestrictPanel=5. Accessed May 2016
10. MCDC: Policy Guidance – Autonomy in Defence Systems (2014). http://innovationhub-act. org/sites/default/files/u4/Policy%2520Guidance%2520Autonomy%2520in%2520Defence% 2520Systems%2520MCDC%25202013-2014%2520final.pdf. Accessed May 2016
11. NATO Standardization Agency: Allied Joint Doctrine – AJP 1.0. NATO document, Brussels (2010)
12. Siegfried, R., Van den Berg, T., Cramp, A., Huiskamp, W.: M&S as a service: expectations and challenges. In: Fall Simulation Interoperability Workshop, Orlando, FL (USA), pp. 248–257 (2014)
13. NATO STO MSG 136: Modelling and Simulation as a Service. STO CSO – STO Activities (2016). http://www.cso.nato.int/activities.aspx?RestrictPanel=5. Accessed May 2016
14. Hodicky, J., Frantis, P.: Decision support system for a commander at the operational level. In: Dietz, J.L.G. (ed.) KEOD 2009 – Proceedings of International Conference on Knowledge Engineering and Ontology Development, Funchal – Madeira, October 2009, pp. 359–362. INSTICC Press (2009). ISBN 978-989-674-012-2
15. Hodicky, J., Frantis, P.: Using simulation for prediction of units movements in case of communication failure. World Acad. Sci. Eng. Technol. Int. J. Electr. Comput. Energ. Electr. Commun. Eng. 5(7), 796–798 (2011)
16. Hodicky, J.: HLA as an Experimental Backbone for Autonomous System Integration into Operational Field. In: Hodicky, J. (ed.) MESAS 2014. LNCS, vol. 8906, pp. 121–126. Springer, Heidelberg (2014)

NoStop: An Open Source Framework for Design and Test of Coordination Protocol for Asymmetric Threats Protection in Marine Environment

Simone Nardi$^{(\boxtimes)}$ and Lucia Pallottino

Research Center "E. Piaggio", Università di Pisa, Pisa, Italy
nardi@mail.dm.unipi.it, lucia.pallottino@unipi.it

Abstract. *NoStop* is an open source simulator dedicated to distributed and cooperative mobile robotics systems. It has been designed as a framework to design and test multi–agent collaborative algorithms in terms of performance and robustness. The particular application scenario of a team of autonomous guards that coordinate to protect an area from asymmetric threat is considered. *NoStop* system is an integrated tool able to both evaluate the coordination protocol performance and to design the team of guards involved in the asymmetric threat protection. Moreover, *NoStop* is designed to validate robustness of coordination protocol through the use of a remote pilot that control the intruder motion to escape from the guards that monitor the area and accomplish its mission. The project core is a simulation server with a dynamic engine and a synchronization facility. Different coordination protocol can be designed and easily integrated in *NoStop*. The framework is fully integrated with the Robot Operating System (ROS) and it is completed by a control station where the remote pilot moves the intruder following the guards evolution in a $3D$ viewer.

Keywords: Asymmetric threat · Multi-agent · Simulation · Game theory · Distributed algorithm

1 Introduction

The problem of detecting and accordingly reacting to an asymmetric threat in marine environments is a challenge both from research and technological point of view [1]. The surveillance sensors currently available on naval platforms are sufficient to identify and classify asymmetric threats, in time for the gradual appropriate response to the threat, in nominal working conditions. Indeed, it is well known that adverse weather conditions lead to degradation of sensors performance. As a consequence, the time available for a possible reaction after the detection, identification and classification procedures [2] can be drastically decreased in such conditions [3]. The short time–to–reaction may increase the

© Springer International Publishing AG 2016
J. Hodicky (Ed.): MESAS 2016, LNCS 9991, pp. 176–185, 2016.
DOI: 10.1007/978-3-319-47605-6_14

Fig. 1. Example of an asymmetric threat detected by a team of marine autonomous robots. The team of robots must efficiently monitors the area around the ship

possibility of human errors especially in stressful situations (e.g. an incorrect assessment of the necessary reaction).

The goal of innovative surveillance systems is hence to guarantee an adequate supervised area in any working conditions.

In this work, the area monitoring problem considered assumes that every region of the environment can not be under the robot sensor footprint (i.e. monitor) at every time instant. Moreover, it is supposed that the decision process of intruders is unknown to the team of robots (i.e., *guards*). For this reason, it is necessary to test the robustness of each coordination protocol to determine the applicability in real world scenario. To prove the robustness of coordination protocol we developed a novel simulator, *NoStop*, dedicated to the evaluation of coordination protocols of unmanned vehicles involved in asymmetric threats protection. *NoStop* is designed to be a generic framework for implementing and testing multi–robot collaborative algorithms in distributed frameworks. Moreover the *NoStop* framework is suitable for the performance evaluation of algorithms based on different specifications of both monitoring robots (or guards) and intruders such as velocity, probability of detection and available sensors.

The project is fully integrated with the well-known Robot Operating System (ROS) [4], and it is composed by five different modules:

1. a core engine, which manages the interaction between the world, the team of guards and the intruder;
2. a monitoring module, which manages all sensors dedicated to the detection of the intruder;
3. an agent module, which automatically handles everything a vehicle needs to be integrated in the framework, except the robot control laws that must be customized based on the considered scenario;
4. a ground control station, which allows an operator to move the intruder in the scenario and, moreover, shows the current results of the coordination protocol of the team;
5. an evaluation module, which computes performance of the selected coordination protocol.

Main characteristics of the *NoStop* simulator are that it is an open source software[1] and that it can be used to test the robustness and efficiency of designed coordination protocols through an operator that maneuvers the intruder trying evade from monitoring autonomous agents. Another particularly relevant aspect is the fact that for the implementation of a custom agent, a developer receives all the sensors and control actuators as an abstraction layer from the hardware. Such abstraction layer quickly enables the developer to apply the tested control law in a real robot hardware, accordingly changing only the drivers.

The *NoStop* framework has been tested and evaluated with four different known coordination protocols based on game theoretic algorithms [5–7]. Based on the *NoStop* tests results of such approaches a novel distributed coordination protocol [8,9] has been proposed. Moreover, through the *NoStop* framework potentiality and improvements of the proposed protocols have been validated.

The paper is organized as follows: in Sect. 2 the requirements which our framework was designed for, are described. The software architecture is reported in Sect. 3. The hardware integration is addressed in Sect. 4. The application and validity of the *NoStop* framework are described in Sect. 5. Finally Sect. 6 presents some conclusive remarks and the planned future work.

2   Design Requirements

NoStop has been developed with a set of requirements that were identified as main features from state of art simulators. One of the mayor features of our framework is the possibility to use the same code for both simulated and real agents. The only changes required should be the input/output drivers, not the control law or its implementation. Such features are achieved by the fully integration of the developed system with the Robot Operating System (ROS) and the dynamic simulator Gazebo. Moreover, the simulator has not hard–coded assumptions on the evaluated system, such that new modules with new features can be easily integrated into the framework. *NoStop* has been designed as modular as possible, following the Gazebo example that fully represents this approach by using interfaces and plugins. The developed system support multi–process applications where each robot controller runs in its own process or computer, while the simulation handles dynamic integration and model collisions. Such representation leads us to use hardware in the loop during the test of each protocol.

NoStop framework has been designed with the purpose to test and validate coordination protocols of team involved in asymmetric threat protection. In such scenario, an intruder must be detected and tracked by a team of coordinated autonomous guards based on local information on the surrounding (sensed) environment or information exchanged with neighbouring guards. To validate the coordination protocol a double level evaluation process is performed. The first level tests the performance of the coordination protocol with a statistical approach computing the minimum number of coordinated guards required to

---

[1] The entire code can be downloaded from https://github.com/SimoneNardi/nostop.

protect a given area. The second level tests robustness of the proposed solution thanks to a remote pilot that may control the intruder movements through a joystick.

In the *NoStop* system the coordination protocol is considered as an high level control loop and it is independent from control laws implemented on each agent. To separate high level control from vehicles dynamics, an abstraction layer has been developed to get information from each agents once they have reached the position assigned by the high level control loop.

3   Software Architecture

In this section, some of the main *NoStop* software components are described, focusing on the design choices. From an high level point of view, *NoStop* has a server that acts as the world (*Simulator*), a set of agents (*Clients*), a remote pilot control station (*Visualizer*) and an evaluation module (*Analysis*). The most relevant sub–modules of each component are shown in Fig. 2.

The *simulator* basic loop sends the environmental information to the agents, receives new actuator controls from them, integrates the dynamic, executes the detection update function, based on the agent communication network it sends detection information (e.g., presence of intruders in the area), and starts again.

The *client* control loop handles sensors and actuators, providing the data to the customized low level control loop of each agent. It has access to each agent state and to the inter–agent communication device (with possibly limited area) that allows the development of distributed algorithms. The low level control loop receives the environmental information from the simulator, it executes the coordination protocol under evaluation, and sends the resulting commands to the simulator. Each client has a communication area which is used by a communication filter module to filter all the messages outside the area to simulate a

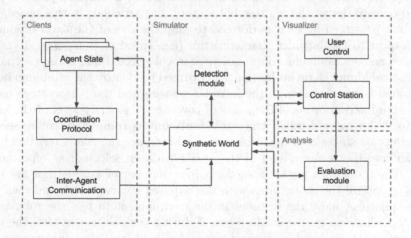

Fig. 2. The *NoStop* software architecture

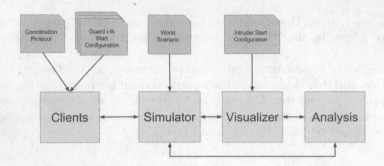

Fig. 3. The *NoStop* configuration files

local communication among agents. Similarly, each client has sensor area which is used to detect the presence of intruders in the area in the detection module.

The *analysis* component computes performance indexes of the chosen coordination protocol based on the agents' states.

The *visualizer* component shows results of the simulations in terms of performance indexes of the coordination protocol and it allows a remote pilot to control the intruder movements in order to test the robustness of the coordination protocol.

The framework parses a configuration file containing description of the world, the agents (both guards and intruder) and the coordination protocol. Such configuration files are used by each component to initialize each control loop, as shown in Fig. 3.

The work–flow of the framework is composed by two phases:

1. Statistical Evaluation phase;
2. Robustness Validation phase.

Once the scenario has been defined, the Statistical Evaluation phase is performed once to design the multi–robot system. In particular, in this phase, the procedure presented in [8] is performed to map the size of the team of guards with respect to the intruder characteristics (e.g. speed or dynamics), intruder detection sensors available, coordination protocol selected and chosen scenario. A statistical Monte Carlo evaluation is performed to identify the minimum number of guards as a function of the intruder velocity and the performance index of the coordination protocol (i.e., rate of coverage or security level of the area, refer to [8] for more details). Once this procedure is completed, robustness of the performed statistical evaluation can be tested once the characteristic of the intruder and the security level of the area have been selected, as reported in Fig. 4. The framework instantiates the correct number of guards that are necessary to control the chosen area with the required security level, and then the remote pilot can move the intruder in the environment to test the robustness of the coordination protocol. Moreover, if during the robustness test, the performance of the protocol is below a given threshold, the minimum number of guards is increased to guarantee the selected security level of the area.

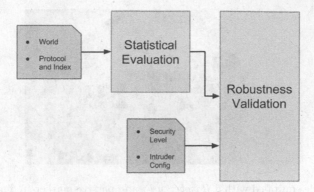

Fig. 4. The *NoStop* flowchart

Once both phases have been performed a validated tool to design the guards team for a given scenario, coordination protocol and intruder characteristic is provided.

3.1 Coordination Protocol Design

Coordination protocols consists of two main features: a local steering function and global performance index. Based on local information available (through a detection sensor or communication with neighbouring robots) each guard computes, with the local steering function, its target configuration. On the other hand, the global performance index is computed by the evaluation module (in the Analysis component) of the *NoStop* framework and it uses information from the whole environment. New coordination protocols can be integrated into the *NoStop* framework using configuration files or by implementing an abstract layer representing a generic coordination protocol. Such abstract layer helps/constraints the user in the design of new coordination protocols. In general, each coordination protocol is composed by three steps:

1. local steering computation;
2. selection of next target configuration;
3. movement towards target;

First information from the detection module is used to evaluate the next target configuration and the motion to reach it. In the end, guards perform the motion towards target configurations based on their own control laws. Once each guard has reached the target configuration, the *NoStop* framework computes the global performance index, and the protocol loop is repeated.

4 Hardware Integration

All the code written in *NoStop* can be reused on the real hardware thanks to the communication facility provided by ROS. When in the configuration file an agent

Fig. 5. A vehicle equipped with a *Raspberry Pi* and passive marker (red and blue ball) for localization (Color figure online)

has been declared as not simulated commands are sent via a serial communication directly to the hardware. This is done through a serial communication block that fully complies with the standard messages that the client/server exchanges during the simulation. With this approach only a serial bus device is necessary on the hardware to receive and execute the actuation commands. The commands for the robots currently used are *linear velocity* and *angular velocity*. The hardware used to test the coordination protocols in the laboratory, before performing experiments with marine autonomous vehicles, is shown in Fig. 5.

For the experiments, the localization framework developed in [10] has been used due to the high performance reached in the position and orientation accuracy. In the vehicle there is a *Raspberry Pi*, which is the main core of the robot. On board there are a wireless key to communicate with the other agents and a Linux OS on which the various algorithms run. Plugged to it via a serial bus there is the actuators which receive the actuation commands from the *Raspberry Pi* and sends them to the motors.

One advantage to have this architecture is that we can work with real and simulated robot simultaneously simply by selecting the appropriate type of the robots in the configuration file.

5   *NoStop* Evaluation

Thanks to *NoStop* framework, many different coordination protocols have been verified and developed, both on the software and on the hardware side. In particular, in case of asymmetric threat protection, tested coordination protocols come from the field of game theoretic algorithms.

One protocol tested with the *NoStop* framework is the one proposed in [11], where team reaches correlated equilibria. Another one verified in simulation is the one proposed in [12] where pareto equilibria are reached by the guards. Moreover, the protocols prosed in [6] and in [7] have been verified to converge to Nash equilibria. All those protocols have been designed for static scenarios, where the intruder is not supposed to move, i.e., it is a fixed threat. In case of asymmetric threats the intruder moves in the environment toward its target hence, the algorithms reported in [8] (*DHSL*) and [9] (*T-DHSL*) have been extended to cope with dynamic scenarios and thus tested and evaluated with the *NoStop* framework. As mentioned above, for each protocol, the *NoStop* simulation computes a map between the minimum number of robots, the intruder velocity and the security level of the selected area.

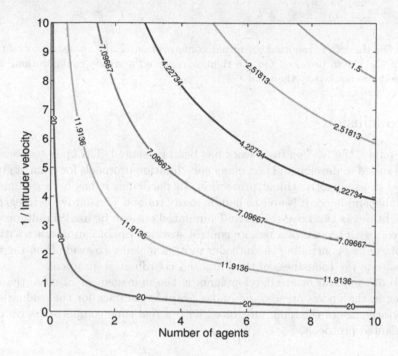

Fig. 6. Tool for design the size of the team of robots: the minimal number of robots is identified with the maximum intruder velocity and the maximal security index of the area

Indeed, in case of open sea scenario (with no close islands or land) the statistical evaluation of the *DHSL* protocol, computes the tool reported in Fig. 6. In this case, the robustness validation phase uses this tool to determine the size of the team: if the remote pilot controls an intruder with maximum velocity equals to 5 and desired security level of 7, the *NoStop* framework, proposes a team composed by 5 vehicles. In Fig. 7 are reported some snapshots from the robustness evaluation phase of the *DHSL* protocol. The figure on the left reports an initial configuration, where the intruder is located in the middle of the scenario and a team of 5 guards are randomly deployed in the environment. The figure on the right reports a *steady* configuration where the intruder is successfully tracked by the team.

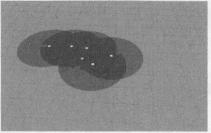

Fig. 7. On the left is reported an initial configuration of the robustness evaluation phase of the *DHSL* protocol. On the right is reported a steady configuration, where the intruder is tracked by the team

6 Conclusion

In this paper, the *NoStop* framework has been presented. The open source simulator is suited to develop and test many coordination protocols for team of guards involved in asymmetric threat protection. In particular it has been designed to be scalable and hence it is able to handle many robots. The hardware integration is straightforward and real robots and simulated one can be used simultaneously. Moreover, with the use of a remote control station, a pilot can interact with the team of guards, controlling the intruder motion in order to evade from the team and evaluate the robustness of the proposed coordination protocol.

One of the main future developments is the management of more than one intruder in the operation scenario and a graphic interface for the evaluation of the performance of the team integrated with a real time comparison with other implemented protocols.

References

1. Blank, S.J.: Rethinking asymmetric threats. Technical report, DTIC Document (2003)
2. Sutton, D.J.: Maritime force protection operations analysis methodology development. In: International Maritime Protection Symposium, USA, pp. 12–14, December 2005
3. Kessel, R.T., Strode, C., Hollett, R.D.: Nonlethal weapons for port protection: scenarios and methodology. In: 5th European Symposium on Non-lethal Weapons (2009)
4. Quigley, M., Conley, K., Gerkey, B., Faust, J., Foote, T., Leibs, J., Wheeler, R., Ng, A.Y.: Ros: an open-source robot operating system. In: ICRA Workshop on Open Source Software, vol. 3, p. 5 (2009)
5. Marden, J.R.: Selecting efficient correlated equilibria through distributed learning. In: American Control Conference (ACC), pp. 4048–4053. IEEE (2015)
6. Goto, T., Hatanaka, T., Fujita, M.: Payoff-based inhomogeneous partially irrational play for potential game theoretic cooperative control: convergence analysis. In: American Control Conference (ACC), pp. 2380–2387. IEEE (2012)

7. Zhu, M., Martínez, S.: Distributed coverage games for energy-aware mobile sensor networks. SIAM J. Control Optim. **51**(1), 1–27 (2013)

8. Nardi, S., Santina, C.D., Meucci, D., Pallottino, L.: Coordination of unmanned marine vehicles for asymmetric threats protection. In: OCEANS 2015-Genova, pp. 1–7. IEEE (2015)

9. Nardi, S., Fabbri, T., Caiti, A., Pallottino, L.: A game theoretic approach for antagonistic-task coordination of underwater autonomous robots in asymmetric threats scenarios. In: OCEANS 2016-Monterey. IEEE (2016)

10. Faralli, A., Niko, G., Nardi, S., Pallottino, L.: Indoor real-time localisation for multiple autonomous vehicles fusing vision, odometry and IMU data. In: Hodicky, J. (ed.) MESAS 2016. LNCS, vol. 9991, pp. 288–297. Springer, Heidelberg (2016)

11. Borowski, H.P., Marden, J.R., Shamma, J.S.: Learning efficient correlated equilibria. In: 2014 IEEE 53rd Annual Conference on Decision and Control (CDC), pp. 6836–6841. IEEE (2014)

12. Jason, R.M., Young, H.P., Pao, L.Y.: Achieving pareto optimality through distributed learning. SIAM J. Control Optim. **52**(5), 2753–2770 (2014)

Autonomous Systems Principles and Algorithms

Advancement in Multi-body Physics Modeling for 3D Graphical Robot Simulators

Gianluca Bardaro[✉], Luca Bascetta, Francesco Casella, and Matteo Matteucci

Politecnico di Milano, Dipartimento di Elettronica, Informazione e Bioingegneria,
Piazza Leonardo da Vinci 32, 20133 Milano, Italy
{gianluca.bardaro,luca.bascetta,
francesco.casella,matteo.matteucci}@polimi.it

Abstract. In this paper we present an interface to develop a communication between two different simulators: Gazebo, aiming at scene realism, and OpenModelica, focused on accurate dynamic simulation. This communication allows us to create a cooperative simulation loop, having a single shared simulated environment, and exploiting the best characteristics of each simulation.

Keywords: Multi-body simulation · 3D simulation · Gazebo · OpenModelica

1 Introduction

Modeling and simulation are important tools in many different application domains. The variety of applications implies that different aims exist which drive the development of models and simulation environments/tools. Let's consider, for instance, autonomous vehicles or, more in general, autonomous robots, one could be interested in studying the dynamic behavior of the corresponding multi-body system for design purposes or to assess the stability/performance of a controller. On the other hand, another researcher could be focused on accurate modeling of the environment and the robot sensory system to develop and test perception algorithms. In the former case, a multi-body dynamic simulator should be chosen, in the latter a robotic simulator including world simulation will be preferred. Unfortunately, no single size fits them all; modeling sensors and environment in a multi-body simulator is a hard task, conversely, 3D robotic simulators aims at scene realism, but they do not ensure an accurate and physically-consistent simulation. At the end of the day, for the development of an autonomous vehicle, or a mobile manipulator, two different models and two different software environments are required.

This work aims at combining the best of the two worlds, integrating sensors and world simulation provided by most of 3D robotic simulators with the detailed modeling capability of multi-body simulators. Our approach is based on the cooperation between two simulators, and the corresponding modeling languages, which are the most popular in their respective fields. Gazebo and the Simulation

© Springer International Publishing AG 2016
J. Hodicky (Ed.): MESAS 2016, LNCS 9991, pp. 189–195, 2016.
DOI: 10.1007/978-3-319-47605-6_15

Description Language (SDF) from the robotic world, and OpenModelica and the Modelica language for the family of multi-body simulators. Although SDF provides a simple way to describe the environment and the sensors, it lacks the tools to accurately specify the dynamic behavior of the robot. The proposed solution uses SDF to provide a general description of the world and the robot, and enhance it by integrating the required constructs of Modelica code. This combined model can be used by the two simulators, Gazebo and OpenModelica, working in the same execution loop on different elements of the simulation.

2   Gazebo and OpenModelica Simulators

Gazebo [2] is the 3D graphical robot simulator most commonly used when working with ROS[1], the Robot Operating System. It consists in two different parts: a server, executing the simulation, and a client, which implements both visualization and a GUI to interact with the simulation. This structure, coupled with the open source nature of Gazebo, provides great flexibility.

Like most of robot simulators, Gazebo strives to provide a real-time simulation using physics engines inherited from the video-game world, which trade execution time for accuracy. The default engine in Gazebo is ODE (Open Dynamic Simulator)[2] which is a popular choice for robotics simulation applications, but has some known drawbacks [1], like the method used to approximate friction, and a poor support for joint-damping.

One of the strongest feature of Gazebo is the simplicity in describing the simulated environment, including all onboard sensors. The scene is detailed using SDF[3] an extensible XML format capable of describing all aspects of robots, static and dynamic objects, lighting, terrain, and physics. Gazebo is often chosen for its native integration with ROS.

OpenModelica[4] is an open-source modeling and simulation environment created to support the development of models and simulators based on the Modelica language. Modelica[5] is a non-proprietary, object-oriented, equation based language to model complex and multi-domain physical systems including mechanical, electrical, electronic, hydraulic, thermal, control, electric power or process-oriented sub-components. For this reason, Modelica is particularly suitable to model complex multi-body systems, like robotic arms and mobile manipulators, together with their actuation and control systems. On the other hand, a realistic simulation of the environment and of the exteroceptive sensors, like cameras and laser scanners, is out of its scope.

---

[1] Robot Operating System (ROS). http://www.ros.org.
[2] Open Dynamics Engine (ODE). http://www.ode.org.
[3] SDF format. http://sdformat.org.
[4] OpenModelica. https://openmodelica.org.
[5] Modelica. https://www.modelica.org.

3   The Cooperative Simulation Loop

Even with their respective different characteristics both Gazebo and OpenModelica are full-fledged simulators, therefore some of their features overlap. For this reason, it is necessary to specifically define which part of the simulation will be managed by each simulator. Trying to exploit the best features of each world, in this first implementation, we decided to divide the tasks as it follows.

OpenModelica manages all the dynamics of the simulation, keeps track of the simulation time and calculate the new pose of each object at each simulation step, before and after collisions. The Modelica model describes the result of interaction between all different classes of objects in the world as well. Moreover OpenModelica sets the pace of the entire cooperative simulation by triggering the Gazebo simulation step inside its own simulation loop.

Gazebo manages the world and the interaction between the objects. The scene is created in Gazebo and includes all the simulation elements, but only with a kinematic description, to avoid conflicts between the two simulators. Other elements, like for example sensors or static objects, exist only in the Gazebo representation, since they do not have any dynamic behavior.

To achieve the cooperation between the two simulators we implemented the following communication interface. On the Gazebo side we exploited the fact that the simulator can be used as a library, therefore we embedded the simulation loop in a standard C++ program. At each execution of the program a step of the Gazebo simulation is executed, and between each step it is possible to modify any element of the scene, giving us a complete control over the execution flow.

For the Modelica model we took advantage of two specific features: external functions and external objects. External functions allow to include C code to interface the model simulation with an external executable. Additionally, if a persistent state is required between the external program and the internal Modelica model, an external object can be defined and transferred between function calls. External objects are defined as pointers to a specific memory area, they contain any type of C variable, e.g., structures, and they can be included in the parameters of an external function to remain persistent between the two execution environments (i.e., the internal Modelica model and the external C library).

Listing 1.1 shows the implementation of the external function inside the Modelica code. OpenModelica provides as inputs information about the objects in the form of coordinates for position and orientation and receives form Gazebo details about possible collisions between the objects. Since a variable, and possibly greater than one, number of contact points may exist, the external function return an array. Listing 1.2 show the corresponding prototype for the C function.

The execution loop of each simulator is kept independent to preserve all the simulator features and ensure a correct execution of the two environments, therefore two different executable are active at each time, one for Gazebo and one for OpenModelica. They are synchronized using a combination of external functions and Unix domain sockets (see Fig. 1).

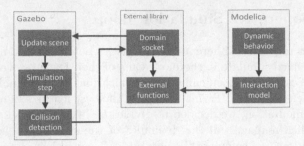

Fig. 1. Structure of the interface and workflow of the cooperative simulation loop

The Modelica model leads the execution. At first, the dynamic behavior of all the elements in the simulation is computed by the Modelica simulator, and before the end of the simulation step external functions are called, one for each possible interaction between two elements of the scene. The input parameters of the functions are the unique IDs of the elements and their absolute positions, the implementation of the function in the external library opens a domain socket to connect with the running instance of Gazebo and transfers the parameters. Gazebo, currently in stand-by waiting for a connection, receives the parameters and updates the position of all the elements in the scene. Now that the position of the simulated objects are synchronized between the two simulator, Gazebo executes a simulation step and detects possible collisions between elements in the scene. Using the unique IDs provided by the external function the correct collisions are picked and sent back to the domain socket, the external library then will return the value through the function parameters closing the communication loop. The values provided by Gazebo are the contact points, the depth of the collision and the direction of the forces. Depending on the result obtained from Gazebo, OpenModelica can now compute the correct interaction between all the colliding elements and complete the cooperative simulation loop. Then a new interaction begins, going on back and forth between the two simulators until the simulation is stopped.

```
function collisionDetection
    input ExternalInterfaces.GazeboInterface gI;
    input Integer maxContacts;
    input Real r_a[3];
    input Frames.Quaternions.Orientation Q_a;
    input Real r_b[3];
    input Frames.Quaternions.Orientation Q_b;
    output Real numberOfContactPoints;
    output Real cp_a[maxContacts, 3];
    output Real cp_b[maxContacts, 3];
    output Real depth_a[maxContacts];
    output Real depth_b[maxContacts];
    output Real n_a[maxContacts, 3];
```

```
output  Real  n_b[maxContacts,  3];
external  ''C''
     annotation(Library  =  ''Gazebo'',
     Include  =  ''#include \''gazebo_interface.h\'''');
end  collisionDetection;
```

Listing 1.1. External function interface on the Modelica side

```
void collisionDetection(void *gI, int maxContacts,
     double *r_a, size_t r_a_dim, double *Q_a,
     double *r_b, size_t r_b_dim, double *Q_b,
     double *numberOfContactPoints,
     double *cp_a, size_t cp_a_dim1, size_t cp_a_dim2,
     double *cp_b, size_t cp_b_dim1, size_t cp_b_dim2,
     double *depth_a, size_t depth_a_dim,
     double *depth_b, size_t depth_b_dim,
     double *n_a, size_t n_a_dim1, size_t n_a_dim2,
     double *n_b, size_t n_b_dim1, size_t n_b_dim2)
```

Listing 1.2. External function interface on the C side

4   An Essential Use Case

In this section we describe an essential use case aimed to show how the interface and the cooperation between the two simulators work.

The scene is composed by a fixed plane, used to describe the ground, and three spheres, with different mechanical properties, falling from a different height.

4.1   Model Description

The description of the simulated environment starts form the Gazebo definition of the scene. Using SDF as a starting point is the most reasonable course of action, as in more complex simulations some elements of the scene will be present only in the Gazebo environment. Being an XML format the scene is described in a strict hierarchical way, as shown in the following piece of code, describing one of the spheres.

```
<model name='sphere1'>
  <link name='sphere1_1'>
    <kinematic>1</kinematic>
    <pose>0 0 10 0 0 0</pose>
    <collision name='sphere1_1_collision'>
      <geometry><sphere><radius>.1</radius></sphere></geometry>
    </collision>
```

```
    <visual name='sphere1_1_visual'>
      <geometry><sphere><radius>.1</radius></sphere></geometry>
    </visual>
  </link>
</model>
```

For each element of the scene we have to define its visual representation for visualization and its collider for collision detection. It is fundamental to specify any element as kinematic (or static) to avoid conflicts between the physics engine, which has to consider only collisions, and OpenModelica. In the SDF model each element is associated with a name, which has to be unique, that will be used as an ID to identify elements during the communication between the two simulators.

For each dynamic element in the SDF file we add an object in the Modelica model using the same characteristics of shape and position used in Gazebo. Now each object have to be completed with its mechanical properties, for example weight and inertia. For each couple of objects that may have an interaction we have to instantiate an interaction model, this instance also includes the external function and the external object to communicate with Gazebo. The external object in each instance of the interaction model is initialized with the ID of the two objects involved in the interaction, this unique couple of IDs is used as an identifier during the communications between the two simulators.

4.2   Simulation

First, the wrapper for the Gazebo simulation loop is executed so as to load the scene and setup the Gazebo server. After the initialization the server waits for connections. The OpenModelica simulation can be now started, simulating the model derived from the same scene loaded in Gazebo. It activates the communication with Gazebo and starts the cooperative simulation loop. At any time, the Gazebo client can be executed to have a 3D graphical representation of the simulated environment.

In the presented use case, when the simulation starts, the spheres are immediately affected by gravity and fall down. Even if there are no possible collisions at this moment, the two simulators keep exchanging information, until the spheres reach the plane. At this point Gazebo detects a collision and informs OpenModelica about direction and depth, and according to the specific interaction model for the sphere and the plane the Modelica model computes the new position of the sphere with an accuracy that is not achievable with Gazebo alone.

4.3   Conclusions

In this work we implemented an interface between two different simulators: Gazebo and OpenModelica. The aim was to provide a single simulation loop shared between two normally separated environments in an effort to exploit the feature available in each one. This arrangement is really useful in some important fields of robotics, like autonomous vehicles, where the fidelity of a multi-body simulation is required for safety reasons, but the interaction with the external world, in the form of sensors and software interfaces, provided by robotic simulator is fundamental.

Our implementation pave the way for more complex interactions between the simulators. First of all, making the cooperative simulation loop able to interact flawlessly with ROS, this is achieved by correctly synchronizing the simulation time in both simulators. Other extensions are in the direction of a co-simulated environment, where only some element of the simulation (i.e. the robot) are described in OpenModelica and Gazebo manages the rest of the scene. Lastly, it is possible to explore the use of OpenModelica as a physic engine integrated inside Gazebo.

References

1. Drumwright, E., Hsu, J., Koenig, N., Shell, D.: Extending open dynamics engine for robotics simulation. In: Balakirsky, S., Hemker, T., Reggiani, M., Stryk, O., Ando, N. (eds.) SIMPAR 2010. LNCS, vol. 6472, pp. 38–50. Springer, Heidelberg (2010)
2. Koenig, N., Howard, A.: Design and use paradigms for gazebo, an open-source multi-robot simulator. In: IEEE/RSJ International Conference on Intelligent Robots and Systems, Sendai, Japan, pp. 2149–2154, September 2004

Robust Place Recognition with Combined Image Descriptors

Martin Dörfler[1(✉)] and Libor Přeučil[2]

[1] Department of Cybernetics, Faculty of Electrical Engineering,
Czech Technical University in Prague, Prague, Czech Republic
martin.dorfler@fel.cvut.cz
[2] Czech Institute of Informatics, Robotics and Cybernetics,
Czech Technical University in Prague, Prague, Czech Republic
libor.preucil@ciirc.cvut.cz

Abstract. In this paper, a method of place recognition is presented. The method is generally classified under the bag-of-visual-words approach. Information from several global image descriptors is incorporated. The data fusion is performed at the feature level.

The efficacy of the combined descriptor is investigated on the dataset recorded from a real robot. To measure the composition effect, all component descriptors are compared along with their combinations. Information on computational complexity of the method is also detailed, although the algorithms used did not undergo a big amount of optimization. The combined descriptor exhibits greater discriminative power, at the cost of increased computational time.

Keywords: Visual place recognition · Robust image features · Bag of visual words

1 Introduction

In the task of visual navigation of mobile robots, the first problem encountered is often the initialization. Determining the initial location of the robot in the environment is necessary precondition for further navigation, as well as a possible recovery method in cases where the navigation experiences a failure. For the robot equipped with a camera, a possible approach consists of calculating a similarity of observed environment appearance with the appearance of known locations, and selecting the closest match as a probable robot location. This task is called place recognition.

In preceding years, good results were obtained using robust features detected in the image. Variety of image features were investigated in the literature. The

L. Přeučil—The presented research was supported by the Czech Technical University in Prague under grant SGS16/160/OHK3/2T/13, by the Technology Agency of the Czech Republic under the project No. TE01020197 Centre for Applied Cybernetics, and by Horizon 2020 program under the project No. 688117 "Safe human-robot interaction in logistic applications for highly flexible warehouses".

© Springer International Publishing AG 2016
J. Hodicky (Ed.): MESAS 2016, LNCS 9991, pp. 196–203, 2016.
DOI: 10.1007/978-3-319-47605-6_16

different types of local image features contain different information. By employing complemental image features, robustness of the place recognition algorithm can be increased and uneven density of features in the environment compensated.

Furthermore, in a feature-starved or highly self-similar environment, the presence of local features is insufficient to distinguish the locations from one another. A global descriptor might be able to characterize high-level differences not present at the level of singular details.

One possible approach would be switching descriptors used in the case of lower localization quality. A possible problem is that an abrupt switching of localizing method would introduce discontinuities in the localization result. Instead, we decided to use a combined descriptor, containing a BoW (bag of visual words) representation and global image descriptors. A distance in the combined descriptor space is used as a similarity measure.

As a work in progress, this paper presents the combined descriptor approach. Several global features were investigated, and effects of their inclusion experimentally evaluated. The approach was compared to plain BoW visual place recognition. Comparisons were performed on outdoor data collected by a real robot.

2   Previous Work

The topic of appearance-based localization has been extensively studied and much work on this topic is available. Many results have been obtained by using local image features. These approaches identify salient regions of the image that can be identified despite changes in illumination, scale and point of view. Furthermore, given their locality, such methods are not thwarted by occlusion of the part of the image, as the local features in the remaining part are not disturbed.

There are many variants of local image descriptor. SIFT [1], SURF [2] and similar methods [3] detect salient points as a peak in the image gradient. Works [4] or [5] detect image regions stable to change in the scale.

A common weakness of the local image features is their quantity. With several hundred features per image, matching against large image sets gets prohibitively expensive. Bag-of-words techniques (BoW) circumvent this problem by building a vocabulary of common image features [6]. Presence or absence of these features is a descriptor of the image. While this descriptor is of a global character, advantageous properties of local descriptors (such as invariance, or resistance to occlusion) are partially preserved.

A successful example of such approach is the method FabMap, presented in [7]. In addition to the use of a visual dictionary, it achieves additional performance gains by modeling feature probability by Chow-Liu tree. Realtime recognition is reported even on large datasets [8].

Another approach for appearance-based localization consists of method to characterize the whole image. The so-called *global descriptors* use features such as lies, edges, or gradient of image function to make a compressed representation of the image frame. Various properties of the image have been used for this task. For example, in [9] the balance of color components of the image is used.

A GIST method proposed in [10] divides the frame in 16 parts and extracts prevailing gradient direction in each by applying Gabor filters. The approach was later refined in [11] by using PCA to reduce the dimensionality of the descriptor, as well as in [12] by exchanging the gradient direction by BRIEF descriptor.

Some of these methods are of deeper relevance to this paper. These are covered in more detail in the Sect. 3.1 and following.

There have been previous attempts to combine local and global descriptors. Most cited employ a multi-step approach, using one method to pre-select likely candidates for further processing by a more computationally costly steps. For example, in [13] a global color descriptor was used to select candidates for subsequent matching based on line features described by their line support regions. The authors of [14] use saliency measure to select interest regions of the image to save the costly computation of the gist descriptors.

In the following section, our approach employing combination of local and global features is presented.

3   Proposed Approach

To perform a place recognition in locations where local image features may be scarce, a different kind of information needs to be incorporated in the decision-making. Our aim is to extract such information in form of global image descriptors, and integrate it seamlessly into the place recognition algorithm. The objective is to perform the fusion at the earliest possible point in the pipeline. This way, it is possible to take advantage of later parts of the pipeline which handle the dependency between the features. Also, fitting in the common framework means the proposed method can be without much difficulty meaningfully compared to its predecessor.

For this reason, we propose using a pipeline similar to the one used in the place recognition by a bag-of-words approach. In the first steps of image processing, the local image features are extracted. During the training, a set of commonly appearing features are selected. Their presence or absence will henceforth be used as features identifying respective image frames. During the recognition, a vector identifying the presence of all the relevant features is passed to the algorithm and the most similar of the learned images is selected. Optionally, some weighting or feature distribution model is used to balance the fact that the presence of features is not independent event and some normalization can improve the results.

To extend this model, more features are introduced in the descriptor. In the image processing stage, a set of global image descriptors is extracted from the image. These descriptors are converted in a vector of features, which are then included in the descriptor constructed in the bag-of-words calculating stage. Proper normalization is performed to maintain similar range of values for all parts of the descriptor.

One advantage of so constructed descriptor: the use is straightforward. The distance in the combined descriptor space can be used as a (dis)similarity measure for the purposes of place recognition.

Furthermore, when considering the combined descriptor, the additional members play a very similar role to the already existing ones. They are simply another features, describing the scene. It is thus equally straightforward to integrate the combined descriptor into any system based on a set of features. In this paper, such approach was demonstrated with FabMAP [7,8].

In the original implementation, FabMAP is using a bag-of-visual-words approach to place recognition. Improvements are obtained by modeling the conditional dependence of the features in the descriptor, which correspond to the prevalence of vocabulary landmarks in the target scene. This approach can also be applied to the global features, when properly normalized.

Following sections detail the global image descriptors selected for making the combination descriptor. At this stage, the main criteria of selection were the diversity of underlying principle, ease of implementation, and sensitivity to the rotation. As stated previously, many global image descriptors are influenced by the precise position and orientation of the robot at the time of taking the picture. Only a minority exhibits rotational invariance. As this property is desirable and possible with the rest of the algorithm, global descriptors were selected that can provide it also.

3.1 Color Histogram

One of the first global image descriptors in use is a color histogram [9]. It describes the image by its most straightforward characteristic - the pixel values.

A simple variant of the color histogram shows the relative prevalence of the three color components, quantized to the fixed scale. A more involved approach consists of expanding beyond the RGB color space. HSL model is a natural candidate here. It's components are meaningful for perceiving humans, and the transformation between RGB and HSL is nonlinear, thus beyond abilities of linear model to learn. Including these values thus brings new information in the recognition task.

The resulting descriptor size is determined by the number of the color channels, and the size of histogram bins. The number of the bins is usually kept low for better generalization. Otherwise, filtering the resultant histogram may be necessary to prevent the effects of the noise.

3.2 Edge Histogram Descriptor

Another way of characterizing the image is by describing its texture. The methods, collectively called *texture descriptors*, attempt to describe the image in the terms of patterns and their prevalence in the different parts of the image.

For this work, a method called Edge Histogram Descriptor [15] was chosen. It performs the task by cataloguing the prevailing direction of the edges present in the image. This is done by processing the image by a bank of convolution filters and looking for the highest response at each pixel. The distributions of the responses are summarized in the histogram. Depending on the implementation, the descriptor is formed by the histogram of the whole image, several histograms of various subregions of the image, or some combination.

To maintain the rotational invariance, only the whole image histogram is usable in this case. Relaxing this limitation to the invariance to rotation along the z axis (panning), it is possible to employ subregions that are horizontal slices of the image.

4   Experiments

To investigate the benefits of extended descriptors, their efficacy was tested on the data recorded with the real robot. A place recognition was performed, first using the unmodified BoW descriptor (i.e. running FABMAP2 algorithm as implemented in the openFABMAP [8] project), color histogram descriptor, edge histogram descriptor, and possible combinations.

Computing this additional information increases the processing time necessary for each frame, as well as the computational complexity of the matching process. This cost is fairly straightforward, time to process each frame is increased by the amount needed for each descriptor calculation. Please note that the algorithms used are generally not optimized, and these values serve only for relative comparison, not as a definitive statement on the method efficacy. For that reason, relative time requirements are shown side-by-side with the actual values in the Table 1. As we can see, the increase in the processing time is modest, between 5 % and 7 %.

As the first step, the properties of extended descriptor as a dissimilarity measure were investigated. The descriptor was constructed according to the Sect. 3. The relation between distance in the real world and the distance in the descriptor space is shown on the Fig. 1. The inclusion of additional information has changed the shape of graph, making the two variables more dependent. Thus, the utility of the descriptor has increased and it is better representative of real world differences.

Table 1. Computation time to construct descriptors

Descriptor	Computation time [s]	Relative computation time
BoW	0.834	1.0
Color histogram	0.014	0.016
Edge density histogram	0.037	0.044
BoW + color histogram	0.879	1.054
BoW + edge histogram	0.880	1.055
Full descriptor	0.894	1.071

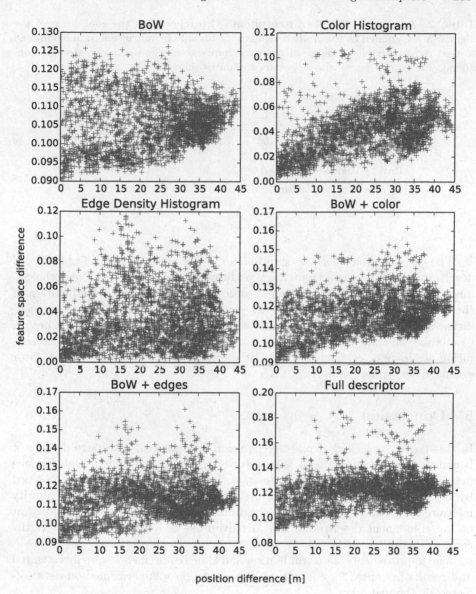

Fig. 1. The real-world position difference plotted against distance in the feature space. The feature space distance is an abstract measure without direct physical interpretation.

The effectiveness of the combined descriptor in a complete place recognition pipeline was tested in the next step. From the descriptors of target locations, a map was built and consequently used to identify the most similar place for each frame in the experiment. As in the previous step, the descriptors and their combinations have been investigated separately.

Table 2. Accuracy of the place recognition. Also reported is the confidence of the algorithm, calculated as the median relative likelihood of the true solution, compared to next most probable candidate. High value imply greater measure of certainty. Confidence 1.0 indicates case where several candidates share the first position.

Descriptor type	Recognition accuracy	Confidence
BoW	0.515	555.7
Color histogram	0.330	1.0
Edge density histogram	0.208	1.0
BoW + color histogram	0.689	719.78
BoW + edge histogram	0.679	719.6
Full descriptor	0.689	719.78

The Table 2 show that the stand-alone performance of the selected global descriptors is not very good under the conditions of the experiment. Nevertheless, incorporating each of them provides considerable benefits. The combination of the BoW descriptor with any of the two global descriptors exhibits greater recognition accuracy. The results obtained with color histogram are slightly better. Combining all three descriptors does not provide further increases in the recognition accuracy or confidence. Hence, it seems advisable to use BoW descriptor extended by a color histogram.

5   Conclusion

In this paper, a method of place recognition is presented. An image descriptor is constructed by combining a bag-of-words approach and several global image descriptors. The probability dependency of the descriptor components is modeled by a Chow-Liu tree. We have found such descriptor to be a good similarity measure for place recognition. Its discriminative powers are greater than that of the component descriptors. The disadvantage is a modest increase in the computing time.

The improvements in discrimination and time requirements were investigated and results presented for comparison. Investigation was performed on data collected by the real robot.

The result show that introducing additional features in the place descriptor increases the discriminative power. There is a trade-of in accuracy and computational complexity, but the gains clearly outweigh the costs, at least in the investigated conditions. The selection of particular descriptors and their efficacy specifically in such difficult conditions will need to be a subject of further investigation. Also, the combined descriptor does not preclude the use of the component descriptors individually, to speed up the recognition in the uncomplicated cases. Efficacy of such setup is yet to be evaluated.

References

1. Lowe, D.G.: Distinctive image features from scale-invariant keypoints. Int. J. Comput. Vis. **60**, 91–110 (2004)
2. Bay, H., Ess, A., Tuytelaars, T., Van Gool, L., Gool, L.V., Baya, H., Essa, A., Tuytelaarsb, T., Van Goola, L.: Speeded-up robust features (SURF). Comput. Vis. Image Underst. **110**, 346–359 (2008)
3. Agrawal, M., Konolige, K., Blas, M.R.: CenSurE: center surround extremas for realtime feature detection and matching. In: ECCV 2008, IV, pp. 102–115 (2008)
4. Matas, J., Chum, O., Urban, M., Pajdla, T.: Robust wide baseline stereo from maximaly stable estreal regions. In: Proceeding of the Britsh Machine Vision Conference, pp. 384–393 (2002)
5. Chung, J., Kim, T., Nam Chae, Y., Yang, H.S.: Unsupervised constellation model learning algorithm based on voting weight control for accurate face localization. Pattern Recogn. **42**, 322–333 (2009)
6. Sivic, J., Zisserman, A.: Video Google: a text retrieval approach to object matching in videos. In: 2003 Proceedings of Ninth IEEE International Conference on Computer Vision, vol. 2, pp. 1470–1477 (2003)
7. Cummins, M., Newman, P.: Fab-map: probabilistic localization and mapping in the space of appearance. Int. J. Robot. Res. **27**, 647–665 (2008)
8. Cummins, M., Newman, P.: Appearance-only slam at large scale with FAB-MAP 2.0. Int. J. Robot. Res. **30**, 1100–1123 (2011)
9. Ulrich, I., Nourbakhsh, I.: Appearance-based place recognition for topological localization. In: Proceedings 2000 ICRA. Millennium Conference. IEEE International Conference on Robotics and Automation. Symposia Proceedings (Cat. No.00CH37065), vol. 2, pp. 1023–1029 (2000)
10. Oliva, A., Torralba, A.: Modeling the shape of the scene: a holistic representation of the spatial envelope. Int. J. Comput. Vis. **42**, 145–175 (2001)
11. Liu, Y., Zhang, H.: Visual loop closure detection with a compact image descriptor. In: 2012 IEEE/RSJ International Conference on Intelligent Robots and Systems, pp. 1051–1056 (2012)
12. Snderhauf, N., Protzel, P.: Brief-gist - closing the loop by simple means. In: 2011 IEEE/RSJ International Conference on Intelligent Robots and Systems, pp. 1234–1241 (2011)
13. Murillo, A.C., Guerrero, J.J., Sagues, C.: Surf features for efficient robot localization with omnidirectional images. In: Proceedings of 2007 IEEE International Conference on Robotics and Automation, pp. 3901–3907 (2007)
14. Siagian, C., Itti, L.: Biologically inspired mobile robot vision localization. IEEE Trans. Robot. **25**, 861–873 (2009)
15. Park, D.K., Jeon, Y.S., Won, C.S.: Efficient use of local edge histogram descriptor. In: Proceedings of the 2000 ACM Workshops on Multimedia, MULTIMEDIA 2000, pp. 51–54. ACM, New York (2000)

Assessing the Potential of Autonomous Multi-agent Surveillance in Asset Protection from Underwater Threats

Tommaso Fabbri[1,2,3(✉)], Simone Nardi[1,2,3], Luca Isgró[4], Lucia Pallottino[1,2,3], and Andrea Caiti[1,2,3]

[1] Interuniversity Center of Integrated Systems for Marine Environment (ISME), Genova, Italy
[2] Department of Information Engineering, University of Pisa, Pisa, Italy
tommaso.fabbri@for.unipi.it
[3] Interdepartmental Research Center E. Piaggio, University of Pisa, Pisa, Italy
[4] IBR Sistemi s.r.l., Genova, Italy
luca@ibrsistemi.com

Abstract. A Serious Game (SG) system for the assessment of the potential of the multi-vehicle surveillance is presented. The SG system is applied to the problem of protection of strategic assets from underwater asymmetric threats. The SG platform integrates the active sonar performance evaluator able to estimate the real performance on the basis of the environmental conditions. The final goal is to provide new technology tools to realize a Decision Support System (DDS) to support the design phase of a naval unit. The SG system is developed in the framework of the ProDifCon project supported by the (DLTM) (Italy).

Keywords: Serious-game · Asymmetric threat · Active sonar system · Surveillance system

1 Introduction

Nowadays, *Serious Game (SG)* is an emerging technology able to take advantage of the power of computer games to engage users for a specific purpose. Thanks to its ability of combining entertainment in games and seriousness in education, SG is applied to skill training [1], education health care [2], military exercise [3] and various other areas. A gaming system allows scenarios to be played and replayed several times by modifying key-variables to test changes in components or outcomes. Furthermore, a SG system can accumulate learning from user experience, and incorporate the gained knowledge into subsequent rounds. In like manner, starting from the acquired knowledge and the user experience, it is possible to use Serious Games to assist during the design phase but also improve/optimize product requirements. In this context, this paper presents a SG system developed during the Integrated Design Control and Defense of Military Ship (ProDifCon) project to face the problem of asymmetric threats in maritime environment in order to develop and test innovative surveillance systems.

© Springer International Publishing AG 2016
J. Hodicky (Ed.): MESAS 2016, LNCS 9991, pp. 204–213, 2016.
DOI: 10.1007/978-3-319-47605-6_17

The ProDifCon project has been designed with the main aim of developing new technology tools in order to realize a Decision Support System (DDS) implementing the idea of Whole Warship (WW): the ship represents a complete complex system composed of the resources of the naval unit, the Platform, and the Combat System (CS). In such framework, an important goal is the identification of a collection of possible countermeasures against asymmetric threats and the determination of the impact of such countermeasures during the project of the ship platform. The available surveillance sensors have reached high level of performance if operating in nominal conditions: these sensors (radar, electro-optic devices, Diver Detection Sonar (DDS) ...) are able to detect and classify asymmetric threats in time to perform deterrence through the proper escalation of forces [4]. However, unfavourable meteorological oceanographic conditions can cause the deterioration of the sensor performance and therefore the reduction of the time required for the proper escalation of forces that may increase the possibility of human errors, especially in stressful conditions [5,6]. In order to overcome the limitations of current surveillance systems and guarantee an adequate supervised area in any working conditions, the Interuniversity Center of Integrated Systems for Marine Environment (ISME) [12] identified as new surveillance systems those obtained by coordinating a heterogeneous network of remotely operated or autonomous vehicles equipped with standard surveillance sensors. The introduction of the innovative surveillance system involves the analysis of new tasks like: how to coordinate the vehicles to guarantee a proper level of coverage? Which kind of vehicles and which on-board sensors to use? ... Furthermore, the innovative surveillance system has direct impact during the design phase of a new ship, e.g. required lodging space for a sufficient number of vehicles, deployment facilities and ship equipment.

To find answers of these open problems, this paper presents a SG system able to test the effectiveness of the new surveillance system proposed within the ProDifCon project. The SG system developed by I.B.R. Sistemi s.r.l. [11] integrates the functionalities provided by the ISME performance evaluator of active sonar systems (e.g. DDS, Side-Scan Sonar (SSS)) able to predict the real performance of sonar system with respect to the environmental variables considered.

The paper is organized as follows. The operating scenario is described in Sect. 2; Sect. 3 presents the SG system and its main components. Section 4 illustrates the active sonar subsystem developed. Finally, Sect. 5 summarizes the work and draws the main conclusions anticipating the next applications.

2   Scenario

As described in Sect. 1 the actual surveillance system is effective for the threat protection if operating at nominal conditions. The deterioration of environmental conditions, and/or the particular tactical situation, can degrade the performance of surveillance systems. The disposition of the heterogeneous network of mobile sensors in the perimeter area of the naval platform may extend the coverage and, as a result, increase the time available for deterrence procedures.

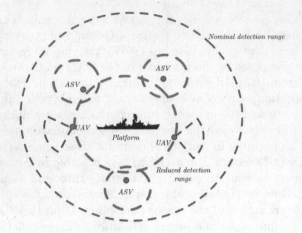

Fig. 1. Typical operative scenario of the proposed surveillance system

As an example, Fig. 1 illustrates the selected operational scenario where the reduced coverage of the on board surveillance system of the mother platform is partially counterbalanced by the use of autonomous or remotely operated vehicles arranged on the perimeter area of the mother platform. The proposed surveillance systems is composed by vehicles operating above the sea-surface, e.g. Autonomous Surface Vehicle (ASV), Unmanned Aerial Vehicle (UAV) and vehicles operating below the sea-surface like Autonomous Underwater Vehicles (AUV). In order to arrange the sensors carriers in perimeter areas of the mother platform, it is necessary to characterize the performance of the sensors used, depending on the environmental conditions. In this family of scenarios, the advantages over real-world exercise are plenty like the ability to include high-density traffic area, with no disruption to port or industrial facilities or the ability to embed new technologies. SG scenarios contribute important elements that real-world exercise has to avoid for economic or safety reasons.

3   Testbed

The partner I.B.R. Sistemi s.r.l. [11] is an Italian software house specialized in virtual reality in the marine simulation domain. As project partner, IBR Sistemi provided a custom version of its Joint Tactical Theatre Simulator (JTTS) [13], an advanced naval scenario simulator, developed for military and civilian maritime industry and research. The JTTS allows wide range of applications ranging from desktop trainer to cooperative full mission bridge simulator. Figure 2 shows an example of a civilian maritime simulation scenario.

The JTTS is characterized by a distributed architecture which components can be summarized as follows and schematically in Fig. 3:

– **Sea Manager** responsible for the management of the simulated scenario. Its components include environmental data (**Environment**) and the entities (component **Entity**), controllable or not involved in the scenario.

Fig. 2. Example of simulation scenario from the JTTS

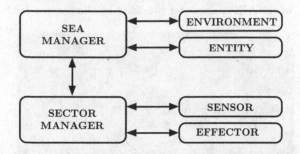

Fig. 3. Distribute software architecture of the JTTS

– **Sector Manager** responsible for the data flow and management between the environment and the controllable units: **Sensors** providing situation awareness by detecting and classifying hostile activities; **Effectors** able to apply stopping force (lethal or non-lethal).

The JTTS provides wide variety of sensors and effectors ranging from radars, binocular, laser range finder to rocket launcher and small arms and naval mines. Given the experience and background grained from the partner I.B.R. Sistemi s.r.l. in the field of naval simulation systems, the sensors deployed above the sea-surface are simulated in realistic way. These sensors, defined *Like Real*, are able to accurately reproduce the real dynamics under varying environmental conditions.

The Automatic Radar Plotting Aid (ARPA) simulator is able to generate the data flow as a real antenna emulating the propagation of the signal and providing as output high fidelity images. The simulator is able to provide different output under varying environmental conditions: e.g. different sea-state levels produce output images characterized by noise and clutter. Figure 4 shows the interface of the radar ARPA simulator.

The Electro Optic Device (EOD) is able to simulate the common electro-optic devices used during surveillance operations, with functionalities of detection and classification of possible threats. The interface EOD is able to

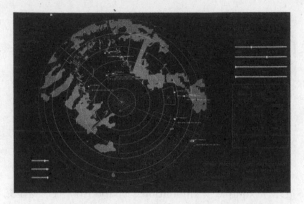

Fig. 4. Interface of the ARPA simulator provided by the partner I.B.R. Sistemi s.r.l.

Fig. 5. Interface of the EOD simulator provided by the partner I.B.R. Sistemi s.r.l.

generate images from the simulated environment. The performance of this family of devices change in particular working-conditions like fog, rain and different time of the day (e.g. daylight and night-time). The system enables the direct interpretation of the data by the human operator or by automated image processing algorithms. As an example, Fig. 5 shows an example of the output generated by the EOD interface. The JTTS platform is used for preliminary exercise of new concepts and evaluate the impact of the proposed surveillance system during the project of the ship platform and the effectiveness of the surveillance coordination algorithms for asymmetric threats protection.

4   Active Sonar Subsystem

Sonar systems represent by far the most reliable platform in the underwater coverage applications. As matter of fact, sound waves present low attenuation and long propagation distance compared to other sensing technologies (e.g. light,

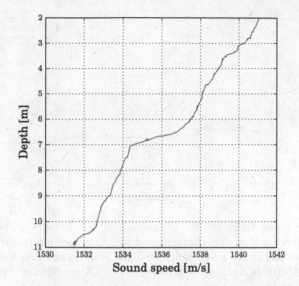

Fig. 6. Sound speed profile from data collected by a CTD during sea-trials in the Gulf of La Spezia (Italy) during July 2015.

magnetism, ...). The leading technology for detecting and tracking underwater intruders is active, monostatic sonar using principles of beam forming in its signal processing [9]. Environmental conditions and/or the particular tactical situation can significantly degrade the performance of sonar systems. The deterioration of performance due to environmental characteristics are mainly a result of meteorological and sea-morphological conditions: presence and variation of the thermocline and the morphology of seabed may reduce the operational range. In the same manner, the tactical choice of positioning components of the surveillance system along a particular route can interfere with performance of other sensors. As an illustration of the environmental variables involved in the computation of the sensor performances, Fig. 6 shows the sound speed profile from data collected by a CTD sensor during sea-trials in the Gulf of La Spezia (Italy).

Under these circumstances, it is necessary to determine the real operative performances of active sonar systems in function of the particular environmental/tactical situation. As matter of fact, Fig. 7 shows the comparison of the Signal to Noise Ratio (SNR) in function of the distance from the emitting source for an acoustic sensor characterized by a transmitting frequency of 70 KHz and source level of 220 dB. Considering a constant sound speed profile of 1500 m/s (green line) the SNR presents a decreasing trend until 70 m from the source and after that an approximately steady trend with a value of 20 dB at the distance of 400 m from the emitting source. On the contrary, considering the sound speed profile illustrated in Fig. 6, the SNR (blue line) is characterized by a decreasing

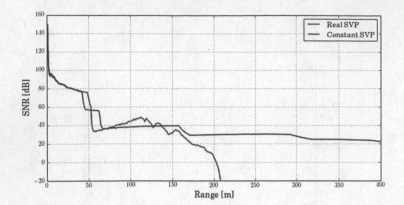

Fig. 7. Signal to Noise Ratio (SNR) in function of the distance from the emitting source, for an active sonar system characterized by a transmitting frequency of 70 KHz and source level of 220 dB. In green is depicted the SNR considering a constant sound speed profile of 1500 m/s. In blue is depicted the SNR considering the sound speed profile illustrated in Fig. 6.

trend similar to the other until 150 m from the emitting source; after that, the SNR continues to decrease reaching a value of -20 dB at the distance of 200 m from the emitting source.

The *active sonar subsystem* is responsible for the generation of joint probability maps of detection in the neighbourhood of the sensor units. This map expresses the probability of detecting an intruder belonging to a given class as a function of the spatial position of the intruder with respect to the sensor. To calculate the real capabilities of the sensor units, the subsystem implements acoustic mathematical models. Starting from the hardware specifications of the sensor units and the environmental information provided by the simulated scenario, the mathematical models are able to evaluate the sensor performance. The active sonar subsystem requires five types of environmental information: *sea state* - describing the general condition of wind waves and swell; *ambient noise* or traffic level; *rainfall intensity* - the amount of precipitations over a set period of time; *sound velocity profiles* - the speed of sound in seawater at different vertical levels and finally *seabed type* - the morphological characteristics of the seabed. The active sonar subsystem requires the operative specifications of the sensor unit including vertical and horizontal transmitter beam width, detection range, bandwidth, frequency and others.

Within the simulation scenario is possible to configure and place a variable number of active sonar systems also characterized by various hardware specifications, in order to define the anti-intrusion system. As shown in Fig. 1, such sonar systems can represent on-board equipment of a moving unit, like ships and AUV, or placed on a fixed position. The developed active sonar subsystem is able to simulate the behaviour of the most common underwater surveillance sensors like: Forward Looking Sonar (FLS), SSS and DDS. Figure 8 shows an example of the probability map of detection computed for a common DDS placed at 5 m

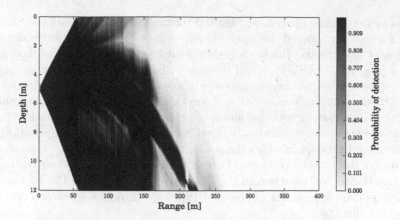

Fig. 8. Probability of detection computed by the active sonar subsystem for a DDS placed at 5 m depth. The environmental information (sound velocity profile, ambient noise ...) considered in the computation are data shown in Fig. 6 collected by real sensors in the Gulf of La Spezia (Italy).

depth considering the environmental information coming from data collected by real sensors in the Gulf of La Spezia (Italy). The sensor unit is characterized by transmitting frequency 70 KHz, source level 220.0 dB, bandwidth 20 KHz and vertical beam width 11°, maximum detection range 500 m (the other sensor specifications are omitted). As shown in figure, the unfavourable environmental conditions produce a reduced detection range from the maximum declared of 500 m to 200 m. This test proves the importance of modelling the performance of sonar system to evaluate the real one.

Recalling the software architecture of Sect. 3, the new component active sonar subsystem has been developed as *plug-in* of Sensor type integrated into the JTTS. The component, starting from the data provided by the Environment (though Sea Manager) builds the performance map as shown in Fig. 8. Furthermore, the new integrated software component is able to generate alarms if new threats are detected.

5   Conclusions and Future Works

A new SG platform to assist the design phase of a new military ship has been presented. The evaluation of the real performance of the on-board sensor starting from environmental conditions and sensor specifications allow to assess the weaknesses and strengths of the actual surveillance system. As an example, active sonar subsystem has been integrated in a custom version of JTTS demonstrating a significant divergence between the nominal and the estimated real performance. To overcome the limitations of the actual surveillance system the deployment of a distributed multi-vehicle surveillance system may restore the operative conditions to detect and classify possible asymmetric threats and apply the proper deterrence procedure. Starting from a mature SG platform, the next step is focused on prove if the available surveillance algorithms are really effective against asymmetric threats together with the determination of the type of vehicles (e.g. AUV, ASV ...) and sensors to be used during operative scenarios. By means of game theory, passivity theory and Monte Carlo simulations, in [14–16] the authors conducted a theoretical analysis of the performance of the surveillance system with autonomous or remotely operated vehicles. In this context, the surveillance mission is faced as dynamic coverage application in a structured environment in which the goal is to maximize a coverage metric of the area around the mother platform. Future works will be focused on testing the above-mentioned contributions in the SG platform to estimate the best surveillance configuration in terms of size and typology during asset protection from underwater threats.

Acknowledgements. This work has been supported by the Ligurian Cluster on Marine Technologies (DLTM), project ProDifCon.

References

1. Andersen, B., Fradinho, M., Lefrere, P., Niitamo, V.: The coming revolution incompetence development: using serious games to improve cross-cultural skills. In: Third International Conference Online Communities and Social Computing, San Diego, USA, July 19–24 (2009)
2. Papastergio, M.: Exploring the potential of computer and video games for health and physical education: a literature review. Comput. Educ. **53**(3), 603–622 (2009)
3. Yildirim, S.: Serious game design for military training. In: Games: Design and Research Conference, Volda University College, 3–4 June (2010)
4. Darren, D., Sutton, J.: Maritime force protection operations analysis methodology development. In: International Maritime Protection Symposium, USA, December 2005
5. Kessel, R.T., Strode, C., Hollett, R.D.: Non-lethal weapons for port protection: scenarios and methodology. In: 5th European Symposium on Non-lethal Weapons (2009)
6. Caiti, A., Munafò, A., Vettori, G.: A geographical information system (gis)-based simulation tool to asses civilian harbor protection. IEEE J. Oceanic Eng. **37**, 85–102 (2012)
7. Caiti, A., Fabbri, T., Fenucci, D., Munafò, A.: Potential games and AUVs cooperation: first results from the THESAURUS project. In: OCEANS, Bergen. MTS/IEEE, Bergen (2013)
8. Howard, A., Mataricć, M.J., Sukhatme, G.S.: Mobile sensor network deployment using potential fields: a distributed, scalable solution to the area coverage problem. In: Asama, H., Arai, T., Fukuda, T., Hasegawa, T. (eds.) Distributed Autonomous Robotic Systems 5, pp. 299–308. Springer, Heidelberg (2002)
9. Kessel, R.T., Hollett, R.D.: Underwater intruder detection sonar for harbour protection: state of the art review and implications. In: 2nd IEEE International Conference on Technologies for Homeland Security and Safety, Istanbul, Turkey, October (2006)

10. Kessel, R.T.: NATO Harbour Protection Table-Top Exercise (HPT2E): Final report, CMRE-RE 2013–004. La Spezia, Italy (2013)
11. IBR Sistemi s.r.l. http://www.ibrsistemi.com
12. Interuniversity Center of Integrated Systems for Marine Environment (ISME). http://www.isme.unige.it
13. Joint Tactical Theatre Simulator. http://www.ibrsistemi.com/#!maritime/f0ky5
14. Nardi, S., Della Santina, C., Meucci, D., Pallottino, L.: Coordination of unmanned marine vehicles for asymmetric threats protection. In: OCEANS Genova. IEEE (2015)
15. Nardi, S., Fabbri, T., Caiti, A., Pallottino, L.: A game theoretic approach for the coordination of underwater autonomous vehicles against asymmetric threats. Submitted to OCEANS Monterey. IEEE (2016)
16. Fabiani, F., Fenucci, D., Fabbri, T., Caiti, A.: A distributed, passivity-based control of autonomous mobile sensors in an underwater acoustic network. In: 10th IFAC Conference on Control Applications in Marine Systems (2016)

Rendering of 3D Maps with Additional Information for Operator of a Coal Mine Mobile Robot

Tomáš Kot[(⊠)], Petr Novák, Jan Babjak, and Petr Olivka

Department of Robotics, Faculty of Mechanical Engineering,
VŠB-Technical University Ostrava,
17. listopadu 15, 708 33 Ostrava, Czech Republic
{tomas.kot,petr.novak,jan.babjak,petr.olivka}@vsb.cz

Abstract. The paper focuses on visualization of point clouds made by a 3D scanner mounted on a mobile robot Telerescuer designed for reconnaissance of coal mines affected by a disaster. Briefly are described some algorithms used for point cloud pre-processing – voxelization for data reduction, outliers removing for filtering of erroneous data and smoothing for additional filtering of noise data. These algorithms are implemented in C++ using the Point Cloud Library.

The next parts focus on the rendering engine created for this application, with more detailed information about drawing individual points with specific size and using the point colours to support better representation of shapes in the map by shading/lighting and additional colouring based on orientation of normal vectors. Mentioned are also some crucial optimizations of rendering and processing performance build on a simple custom system similar to Octree.

The final part presents some methods of adding additional information to the map, including sensor readings (temperature, gas concentration, wind speed etc.) and distance measurements (exact numeric measuring, rough dimension estimation by colour coding, corridor cross-section etc.). Integration of these data and the advanced rendering techniques not typically used for point cloud visualization are the innovative approaches described in this paper.

Keywords: Visualization · 3D map · 3D scanning · Point cloud · Mobile robot · PCL

1 Introduction

Underground coal mines are very dangerous places and accidents there are often very grave and lethal. One of the most typical causes of catastrophes is underground explosion caused by dangerous concentrations of coal dust or methane. Typically the area of the mine affected by an explosion is sealed by a thick dam with a service hole and human rescuers are not allowed to enter the zone until the monitored parameters drop below critical limits. This means a lot of wasted time which could be already devoted to exploration and rescuing operations.

A logical solution is to use mobile robots, which could be applied much earlier, because a machine is immune to many hazards. Mobile robots can perform

© Springer International Publishing AG 2016
J. Hodicky (Ed.): MESAS 2016, LNCS 9991, pp. 214–225, 2016.
DOI: 10.1007/978-3-319-47605-6_18

reconnaissance of the tunnels – provide information about physical state of walls and ceilings, report damaged places, measure temperatures and concentrations of gases and other dangerous substances. The research in this area has been already running for many years, for example [1, 2]. A new research project "System for virtual TELEportation of RESCUER for inspecting coal mine areas affected by catastrophic events (TeleRescuer)" has started in 2014 in the framework of an EU programme Coal and Steel under the grant agreement No. RFCR-CT-2014-00002. The goal of this project is to develop a mobile robot possessing all useful tools and features for this task in one body and – which is unique – to get the important certifications for deployment in coal mines without risks of causing additional damage (explosion safety etc.) [3–5].

2   3D Map in the Form of a Point Cloud

The mobile robot Telerescuer is equipped with a huge variety of sensors, including a 3D scanning device consisting of the Sick LMS111 2D laser range finder mounted on a turning platform providing the third dimension (Fig. 1). The point of this sensor is to make 3D maps of the inspected coal mine by combining individual 3D scans performed in discrete locations, typically few meters far from each other [6].

With smaller distances between the scans, the resulting map has higher resolution and contains more details, but the data size increases dramatically, which requires more processing power and communication bandwidth when the data are transferred to the operator of the mobile robot.

The resulting 3D map of the mine is made in the typical form of a point cloud [7–9]. The goal of the Telerescuer project is to provide "virtual teleportation" of a human rescuer (operator) into the sealed coal mine affected by an accident. Because of this, the point cloud has to be rendered on the operator screen in a clear, interactive and illustrative manner, so that the operator can inspect all important properties in real time, including especially sensor readings and dimensions – that means all parameters not clearly visible on camera pictures. The operator needs to be able to watch the actual surroundings of the robot to be able to properly drive the robot in the complex

Fig. 1. Model of the 3D scanning device

environment, and also to freely check all shafts and tunnels already inspected by the robot. These specific requirements led to creation of a custom point cloud rendering graphical engine with specific features and optimizations.

2.1 Point Cloud Filtering

Before additional analysis and processing can be done on the point cloud data, it is very important to perform some filtering. One of the typical problems of point clouds acquired by 3D scanning is noise caused by measurement errors. This can lead to presence of sparse points that do not represent real physical shapes. These false points typically lay out of larger clusters of points and this fact can be used to detect and remove them.

The algorithm can be implemented for example using the *Point Cloud Library (PCL)* – a library containing a lot of very useful tools for point cloud processing [10]. In this library, the algorithm is called *Statistical Outlier Removal* [11] and works by performing statistical analysis on neighbouring points of each point. Removed are points that do not pass a test on specific criteria.

Another big problem here is the fact that the point cloud was made as a combination of multiple individual 3D scans performed in discrete locations. The scanner Sick LMS111 has a working range of 20 m, so each 3D scan can contain points located within a sphere with 40 m diameter. However, with increasing distance from the scanner the accuracy and density of measured points lower, so the scans must be made much more often than just every 20 m – ideal value is between 2 and 5 m. This increases the details of the point cloud, but also the number of points (complexity, data size), because the scans overlap and every object in the tunnel is scanned multiple times. Many points are completely redundant, because they occupy almost the same coordinates as other points.

This problem can be solved by performing a *Voxelization filter* on the point cloud. In *PCL*, the algorithm is called *Voxel Grid* [12] and works by projecting a 3D grid over the point cloud. All points lying in each cell of the grid are replaced by a single point with coordinates calculated as average of the replaced points. The general use of this filter is so called down-sampling (reduction of complexity while preserving the overall shape). In our case the grid was chosen quite small (10 mm), so that no important details are lost and the filter mostly removes just duplicate points (Fig. 2).

Another very explicit negative effect of noise in the point cloud data caused by measurement errors is when what should be a smooth surface is actually represented as rough. This can be dealt with by smoothing, for example using the *PCL* algorithm *Moving Least Squares* surface reconstruction method [13]. An important configurable

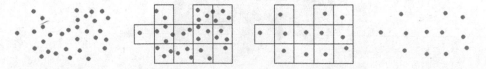

Fig. 2. Principle of the Voxel Grid filter

Fig. 3. Impact of the search radius parameter of the Moving Least Squares filter

value for this algorithm is search radius – too high values can erase also important details. In our case the ideal value was 100 mm (Fig. 3).

3 Graphical Engine

The main goals of the graphical engine for this application are:

- Draw the point cloud fast enough for real-time inspection with quick reactions.
- Clearly and intuitively illustrate the shape of the tunnels, obstacles etc.
- Clearly and intuitively integrate important sensor readings and similar data into the point cloud.

Especially the last two points are problematic if some existing generic point cloud visualization software is used. The best solution was to create a custom graphical engine tailored to the needs of this project. The engine is implemented in C++ and uses the Direct3D 9.0c graphical API for hardware graphic acceleration of many complex calculations related to rendering.

3.1 Definition and Rendering of Individual Points

Every point in the point cloud stored in a special *PCL* array contains the following parameters:

- Position vector $\mathbf{p} = (p_x, p_y, p_z)$.
- Normal vector $\mathbf{n} = (n_x, n_y, n_z)$.
- Colour vector $\mathbf{c} = (r, g, b, a)$.

Position vector is mandatory, because each point must have its position in the 3D space. Normal vector of a discrete point seems to be illogical, because normals are typically related to surfaces. But mathematically also a single point can have a normal vector tied to it and the only question is how to calculate the normal and what does it represent. Fortunately, the *PCL* smoothing algorithm *Moving Least Squares* mentioned earlier has the side effect of generating a normal vector for every point based on the imaginary surfaces detected in the point cloud data during the smoothing process. The last parameter – colour – has a straightforward way of presentation and the meaning of the colour can vary (this will be discussed later).

The points with the mentioned parameters (total of 3×4 B + 3×4 B + 4×1 B = 28 B per point) represent *vertices* in Direct3D and are stored in a *vertex buffer* rendered as the *point list* primitive type, which means that every vertex is drawn on the screen as exactly one pixel. During the rendering process of Direct3D, every vertex is processed by a *vertex shader*, which primarily transforms 3D coordinates to 2D screen coordinates, and by a *pixel shader*, which can modify the colour of the resulting pixel. Both *shaders* are fully programmable and are used for a variety of special effects.

3.2   Perspective Foreshortening – Size of Points

For good visual impression it is necessary to draw the point cloud with perspective projection, which is easily achieved in Direct3D by using a *4 × 4 perspective projection matrix* in the *vertex shader* stage. Objects further from the camera appear to be smaller, which is how the human brain expects it; any other projection (for example orthogonal) would be confusing.

A problem is with the points – when rendered as a Direct3D *point list*, every point occupies exactly one pixel on the screen, regardless its distance from the camera. Distances between points are affected by perspective foreshortening but size of the points is not, which makes large gaps between points close to the camera and the operator loses the impression of being close to a wall – this can be very dangerous for direct control of the robot (Fig. 4).

The points could be drawn as spheres, boxes or just squares always facing the camera (so called *"billboarding"*) with their physical size affected by the perspective projection, but this unacceptably increases the overall number of vertices calculated by Direct3D (4 vertices per each point for billboards; 8 vertices for boxes and even more for spheres) and requires also rendering of surface polygons (triangles) unlike with just mere pixels.

Fig. 4. Impression of being close to a wall – without and with perspective foreshortening applied on individual points

One possible solution of this problem is to use the output parameter *PSIZE* of *vertex shader*. This parameter is then used by the *GPU (Graphics Processing Unit)* as the size of the point drawn on the screen (in pixels). This way it is possible to get points drawn bigger than just 1×1 pixels with almost no additional cost. The value of *PSIZE* can be set individually for every vertex and is calculated in the *vertex shader* as the reciprocal value of the point's distance from the camera in 3D space.

3.3   Improving Shape Representation by Lighting and Colouring

The colour used to drawn each point on the screen can be used in many ways. The most obvious use is to map real colours from cameras onto points in the corresponding locations. In the case of a dark and dirty coalmine, this is not really useful, because even when properly lit by powerful lights, most surfaces are grey or black (Fig. 5).

Much more useful is to encode additional information for example from sensors (will be discussed in the following chapters) and another possibility is to use colours for better visual impression, which can greatly help the operator to orientate in the point cloud representation of the real coal mine.

We can use two main characteristics of a colour – hue and brightness. The resulting pixel colour of each point in this software is calculated as a combination of the following parameters:

- c_h – colour vector (r_h, g_h, b_h) based on the absolute height of the corresponding point in the 3D space (its p_z coordinate). The colours generated by this algorithm create a linear gradient with key colours (from lowest p_z to highest): green – yellow – purple – blue – azure. The colours were chosen based on natural habit that ground is green (grass) and sky is blue.

Fig. 5. Rendering with no point colours (all points are white)

- c_n – colour vector (r_n, g_n, b_n) based on the normal vector of the corresponding point. This colour is a gradient between red, green and blue key colours (red when the normal is aligned with the x axis of the global coordinate system, green for the y axis and blue for the z axis).
- a – ambient lighting scalar factor. Ambient light is constant in the whole scene and brightens up all points for better visibility.
- d – diffuse lighting scalar factor. Diffuse light depends on the angle between the normal vector of the point and the vector of light rays hitting the point.
- s – specular lighting scalar factor. Specular light depends also on the vector from the point to the virtual camera used to watch the 3D scene from and creates bright "reflections" of the light source.

The final colour vector is then calculated as:

$$c = (0.7 \cdot c_h + 0.3 \cdot c_n) \cdot (a + d + s), \tag{1}$$

which means that the biggest impact (70 %) on the final colour hue has the c_h component (Fig. 6) and the brightness is given by lighting ($a + d + s$). Lighting calculations require not only the normal vectors, but also a light source – this can be for example a virtual directional light characterized only by a vector of light rays (all rays are parallel – simulation of a light source located infinitely far away). Lighting greatly helps to visualize shapes of objects by simulating light interaction with the (imaginary) surfaces (Fig. 7).

Fig. 6. Rendering with point colours generated from height and normal (Color figure online)

Fig. 7. Rendering with point colours and lighting (Color figure online)

3.4 Efficiency of Rendering

The point cloud of a full 3D map of a coal mine scanned by the robot can contain hundreds of millions of points. Such high amount of graphical objects cannot be drawn on a standard hardware with acceptable frame rate without additional optimizations.

The graphical engine created for this application uses the Octree system [14] to divide points into box nodes. Before actual rendering, the Octree is used to detect nodes (and thus points lying in the nodes) which are not visible by the virtual camera. These points are not rendered, which in typical situations saves even around 70 % of points, because typical view is from inside the mine shafts looking towards one section of the mine. The test of node visibility for the camera is performed as a very fast frustum-box intersection test (the frustum is defined by the camera aspect ratio and field of view).

The view frustum test is not very efficient when the operator is looking in the direction of a very long corridor with large parts of the mine behind it. It was important to implement another optimization – level of detail. Distance of every visible Octree node from the virtual camera is calculated and the further the node is from the camera, the less points corresponding to the node is then rendered. This optimization has huge impact on drawing efficiency and is completely invisible for the operator (points far from the camera blend together anyway).

4   Adding Additional Information to the 3D Map

Besides the clear and illustrative view of the 3D map, integration of additional information directly into the 3D map is the most important innovation of this project in the field of 3D map visualization.

4.1   Sensor Readings

Values acquired by sensors (gas concentrations, wind speed, temperature etc.) can be easily visualized by colour gradients (green – yellow – orange – red) applied on points around the locations where measurements were performed (Fig. 8). For least amount of confusion, the colour vector c_s generated from sensor value completely replaces c_h and c_n, so the final colour is calculated as:

$$c = c_s \cdot (a + d + s), \tag{2}$$

The operator can freely switch freely between individual sensors and the default mode with no sensor visualized.

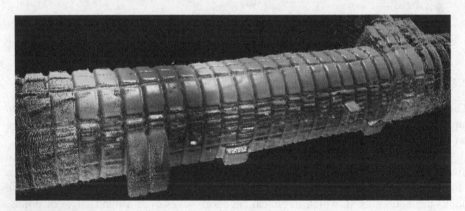

Fig. 8.   Using colour gradient to visualize temperatures in a tunnel (Color figure online)

4.2   Distance Measuring

The ability to accurately ascertain physical distances in the 3D map is very important for the operator – especially to be able to decide how far an obstacle is from the robot and whether a particular corridor is wide enough to move through.

The operator can click on any point in the 3D map visualization and the application will show exact distance to that point. Alternatively, the operator can click on two points, the points are then connected by a line and the length of this line is displayed (Fig. 9).

Fig. 9. Measuring distance between two arbitrary points

Fig. 10. Distance measuring matrix (Color figure online)

For quick overview of size of the tunnel and general distances, the application also provides a special mode "distance measuring matrix". When activated, the point cloud is overlaid with a matrix of alternating dark/light strips with 1 m width and a red strip every 10 m (Fig. 10). The initial colour vector from this matrix (c_m) is used in combination with standard colours and lighting:

$$c = (0.7 \cdot c_h + 0.3 \cdot c_n) \cdot (a + d + s) \cdot 0.5 + 0.5 \cdot c_m, \tag{3}$$

4.3 Cross-Section

Shape of a tunnel can be clearly visualized by turning on the cross-section functionality of the rendering engine. This mode works by calculating a plane (by default parallel to the view direction, but with the ability to rotate and move it freely) and checking intersection of this plane with the point cloud. All points with distance from the plane below a specific threshold are highlighted in plain light red colour (Fig. 11).

Fig. 11. Shape information about the tunnel in the form of cross-section (Color figure online)

5 Conclusion

Although the project is still in progress and the point cloud visualization application is not finished yet, all the algorithms described in the paper have been already implemented and are currently being tested and improved. The reference point cloud used to generate images in the paper was made in a real coal mine from 3D scans created in 2 m distances in the total length of 22 m of a tunnel. The overall number of points after filtering is over 2.1 million and thanks to the optimizations, the rendering speed does not drop below 250 frames per second on the testing configuration (Intel Core i5-3330, 8 GB RAM, Nvidia GeForce 750 GTX). This leaves a lot of power reserve for even many-times larger point clouds.

The system is applicable as a general point cloud visualization and renderer, although it was designed primarily for coal mines with their special properties. Unique features of this system are: free walking or orbit camera, advanced rendering engine with illustrative colouring and lighting, sensor data integration, distance measurements and visualization and interactive cross-sectioning.

Additional work will be devoted for example to merging the point cloud with an existing 2D or 3D map of the mine (when available).

Acknowledgment. The project has been carried out in a framework of an EU programme of the Research fund for Coal and Steel under the grant agreement No. RFCR-CT-2014-00002.

References

1. Ray, D.N., Majumder, S., Maity, A., Roy, B., Karmakar, S.: Design and development of a mobile robot for environment monitoring in underground coal mines. In: Proceedings of the 2015 Conference on Advances in Robotics (2015). ISBN: 978-1-4503-3356-6
2. Gomathi, V., Sowmeya, S., Avudaiammal, P.S.: Design of an adaptive coal mine rescue robot using wireless sensor networks. Int. J. Comput. Appl. **2015**(2), 8–11 (2015)
3. Novák, P., Babjak, J., Kot, T., Olivka, P., Moczulski, W.: Exploration mobile robot for coal mines. In: Hodicky, J. (ed.) MESAS 2015. LNCS, vol. 9055, pp. 209–215. Springer, Heidelberg (2015). doi:10.1007/978-3-319-22383-4_16
4. Novák, P., Babjak, J., Kot, T., Moczulski, W.: Control system of the mobile robot TELERESCUER. Appl. Mech. Mater. **772**, 466–470 (2015)
5. Moczulski, W., Cyran, K., Novak, P., Rodriguez, A., Januszka, M.: TeleRescuer - a concept of a system for teleimmersion of a rescuer to areas of coal mines affected by catastrophes. VI. Międzynarodowa Konferencja Systemy Mechatroniczne Pojazdów i Maszyn Roboczych 2014 (2014)
6. Olivka, P., Mihola, M., Novák, P., Kot, T., Babjak, J.: The 3D laser range finder design for the navigation and mapping for the coal mine robot. In: Proceedings of the 2016 17th International Carpathian Control Conference ICCC (2016). ISBN 978-1-47-993528-4
7. Blanco, J.L.: Efficiently rendering point clouds of millions of points. http://www.mrpt.org/tutorials/programming/gui-windows-and-3d-opengl-graphics/efficiently_rendering_point_clouds_of_millions_of_points/
8. Rusu, R.B., Willow, G., Park, M.: 3D is here: Point Cloud Library (PCL). In: IEEE International Conference on Robotics and Automation (ICRA), pp. 1–4 (2011). ISBN 978-1-61284-386-5
9. Universität Karlsruhe. Point Cloud Representation. http://geom.ivd.kit.edu/downloads/pubs/pub-linsen_2001.pdf
10. PCL – Point Cloud Library. http://pointclouds.org/
11. Removing outliers using a Statistical Outlier Removal filter. http://pointclouds.org/documentation/tutorials/statistical_outlier.php
12. Downsampling a PointCloud using a VoxelGrid filter. http://pointclouds.org/documentation/tutorials/voxel_grid.php
13. Smoothing and normal estimation based on polynomial reconstruction. http://pointclouds.org/documentation/tutorials/resampling.php
14. Octree. https://en.wikipedia.org/wiki/Octree

Geographical Data and Algorithms Usable for Decision-Making Process

Dana Kristalova[✉], Martin Vogel, Jan Mazal, Petra Dohnalova,
Tomas Parik, Adam Macurak, and Katerina Fialova

University of Defence, Brno, Czech Republic
{dana.kristalova,martin.vogel,jan.mazal,
petra.dohnalova,tomas.parik,adam.macurak,
katerina.fialova}@unob.cz

Abstract. The traffic-ability of military vehicles in the terrain outside of communication is not trivial matter. The article deals with the application of different types of geographic data sources within the decision-making process. The Commanders of the military or rescue units are participated in this decision-making process especially in the field. The key role is offered for the use of geographic information systems and application of geographical-tactical analyses, the methods of mathematical modelling, simulation and optimization for the purpose of scheduling the appropriate routes of movements of military vehicles in the operating environment. The special algorithms for searching of optimal path have to satisfy the criteria that are set of for solution of tactical tasks in autonomous systems. It is possible the time and speed limits and safety of peoples to determine. The geographical conditions, tactical conditions and types of vehicles are the most important factors for estimation of time of movement in the different types of terrain. Lots of experiments in military area in the Czech Republic have been performed and unmanned ground vehicle TAROS for gathering of the data was used and method of laser-scanning was tested. The measurement has been evaluated by mathematical statistics and computer sciences. Solution of these tests it is possible to use also in crisis management for emergency systems in case of natural disasters such as floods, fires etc.

Keywords: Geographical data · Geographic factors · Movement of vehicles · Pass ability of an area · Cross-country movement · Movement in terrain · Decision-making process · Crisis management · Unmanned ground vehicle

1 Introduction

Analogue map products are the primary basis for the decision-making process in the selection of the optimal variants of the route. Choosing the right documents, selection of the appropriate methodology for the evaluation of the different geographical factors in a cartographical measurement and a research and also a creation of suitable algorithms to determine of the final route of movement is necessary for a successful decision. Last but not least the influence of tactical factors and a consideration of the possibility of the vehicles due to their tactical-technical data are important. The use of

© Springer International Publishing AG 2016
J. Hodicky (Ed.): MESAS 2016, LNCS 9991, pp. 226–241, 2016.
DOI: 10.1007/978-3-319-47605-6_19

this evaluated data must conform to the manners of the military units according to the doctrine, due to the preferred tactics and due to identify of HVT (High Value Target - it is the means or ability, that the enemy needs to complete the task).

Simultaneously, the evaluation of terrain that is suitable for further activity is controlled by the STANAGs (Standardization Agreement) – see [1]. See Fig. 1. An analysis of geographic products is thus one of the steps within the IPB, and generally it is given by the publications [2]. The methodology is united for all states of NATO (North Atlantic Treaty Organization), however, the article deals with the possibilities of analogue geographic documents available in the Czech Republic - both the military and civilian resources.

A decision making process can be understood, in civil (managerial) terms, as a process of solving decision-making problems, i.e. problems with more (at least two) solution options where a manager achieves a desired state by means of that decision. Whether it involves strategic or operational decision making, its quality has an influence on efficiency and effectiveness of follow-up operations. It is necessary to consider a fact that a majority of decisions is related to problem solving. Managerial (or commanding) decisions may concern common, reoccurring problems as well as unusual and complicated ones. In relation to a subject of work we can talk about decision making of specific character, as a rule, requiring a creative approach, great knowledge and experience, often even intuition, which, in its nature, deals with ill-structured problems.

However, there is a potential here, that by means of appropriate development in technological computing apparatus, along with gradual integration into a current way of decision making, the decision-making activities will gradually acquire character of well-structured problems in the future. Nowadays, when the world is dramatically changing, the ability to find, correctly identify and effectively solve a problem is becoming really critical. The role of managers (commanders) is, in relation to problems, irreplaceable since they remove obstacles on the way to better results [3].

The decision-making process within a military field is related to a fairly specified area, which is not, by its fundamental aspects, too different from a concept applied in a

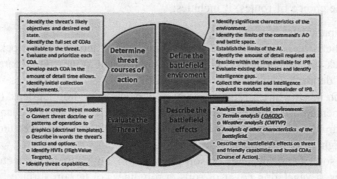

Fig. 1. The diagram shows several steps to the evaluation of the intelligence preparation of battlefield (IPB). This schema is relevant to the decision-making process of commander. The second step describes the effect of the terrain and weather conditions on military units. The success of this analysis corresponds to the amount and quality of input geographical information.

civil environment. However, its specific environment, where the decision-making process is executed, is especially typical for a degree of a risk that can be brought about by a wrong decision. When making military decisions there are factors, coming to the fore much more explicitly than in a civil sphere, such as time (decision-making speed), issues of available resources (material, human), unknown areas (terrain, enemy, population), a degree of uncertainty, and especially a factor of possible losses of personnel and materiel. We cannot omit a factor of the operational environment and requirements for speed and quality of decision making [4, 14].

Under combat conditions a commander is usually forced to decide explicitly without delay, having a lack of relevant (needed) information. The decision-making results in pronouncing a decision in terms of a commander's combat order or directly an order or fire task that is unambiguously obligatory for all subordinates. Therefore it is necessary to pay utmost attention to this process because wrong decisions may have fatal consequences, even at the lowest command levels, which is the feature highlighting or properly distinguishing the decision making in the military practice [3]. The lack of information or failure of the communication means might be overcome by the use of simulation techniques [15, 16].

2 Cross-Country Movement

The issue of capability of the terrain (Cross-Country Movement, Traffic Ability of a Terrain) is still a current topic, despite the fact that for a long time the new approaches are developed. These approaches could contribute to optimizing the search paths [5]. Finding of the relevant algorithms is not a trivial matter, because the selection of the most appropriate routes and the estimate of the time that is needed for the move is a function of the quantity various factors: geographical, tactical, technical and the influences that are predetermined by the human manners.

Analysis of the Cross-Country Movement (abr. CCM) means the assessment of several geographical and tactical factors together, i.e. that it is complex multi-field analysis [6–8]. Apart from these geographical factors (abr. GF) and their parameters that affect the choice of routes, it includes:

- Relief (a parameter is a gradient).
- Micro-relief – i.e. embankments, excavations, holes, terrain steps, rock cliffs, terraces, rock groups, boulders, stone fields or rows of stones, etc. (parameters are height or depth, length, slope gradient, width).
- Vegetation – structure of partial forests, vineyards or hop-gardens (dimension, shape, orientation), structure and specific characteristic of woody plants (spacing between trunks, thickness of trunks measured at height 1.3 m over terrain, vegetation height, sort of plants).
- Soils – a sort of soil (depends on soil granulation), a type of soil at factual weather conditions, a vegetation cover of soils, a roughness of terrain surface.
- Waters – rivers, streams, lakes, dams, etc. (their parameters are width, depth, water flow rate and flow speed, characteristics of banks and of bottom, overall covering of terrain by drainage and mutual position of drainage and other subjects).

- Weather conditions – precipitation, fogs, temperatures, humidity, speed of wind, light conditions.
- Settlements – built-up of given territory by settlements, location, structure, shape and orientation in regard of troop movement, construction material, height of buildings, (in)flammability of buildings.
- Communications - railways (number of tracks, traction – the kind of drive, track gauge, transportation significance) and roads (width or number of traffic lanes, quality of roadway wear course, transportation significance).

The impact of all factors should be expressed by "Coefficient of the deceleration" (abr. CoD). The value of the coefficient of the slowdown (C_i, $C_i \in \langle 0, 1 \rangle$ or ($C_i \in \langle 100\%, 0\% \rangle$)) is assigned to each geographical factor Fi, which is located in the section of the ground, and that affects the speed of the vehicle. The value of this coefficient indicates how many times (how much percent) the factor to slow down the vehicle. The coefficients of the slowdown (according to the Table 1) define the degree of Cross-Country movement.

Table 1. Determination of the levels of Cross-Country Movement (Pass-ability of the Terrain)

Pass-ability of the section	C_i
NO GO section	0
SLOW GO section	0,5
GO section	1
Section without information	1

The common impact of GF on the deceleration of vehicle movement at given section of route can be expressed by the following algorithm [7, 8]:

$$v_j = f(v_{max}, c_1, c_2, \ldots c_n) \qquad (1)$$

where:

v_j = vehicle speed at j-section of vehicle path,

v_{max} = maximum road speed,

c_i = i-coefficient of deceleration due to geographical factor F_i computed for j-section with invariable values c_i,

n = number of geographical factors effecting at given section of the terrain,

k = number of section on vehicle path.

The total CoD depends on the partial CoD of the different GF and is given by this formula [7, 8]:

$$C = \prod_{i=1}^{8} c_i \qquad (2)$$

where, C = total CoD, c_i = partial CoD (C_1 is CoD of the relief, C_2 CoD of the soils, C_3 CoD of the vegetation,..).

These basic algorithms were particularized by a huge number of measurements, data processing and calculations. The authors tried to depict all the important links of the GF. A large number of field tests were realized, and thus, it was possible to include real (not only laboratory or theoretical) measurement.

The resulting effect of all the geographic factors on the deceleration of the vehicle in a given section of track shall be expressed in the following formula:

$$v_j = v_{max} * \prod_{i=1}^{n} C_i, \quad i = 1 \ldots n, \ j = 1 \ldots k \tag{3}$$

where:

v_j [km/h] ... is the speed of the vehicle in the j-th section of track vehicles,
v_{max} [km/h] ...is the maximum speed of the vehicle for communication,
C_i ...is the i-th coefficient of a slowdown,
n ...is the number of geographic factors operating in the given section of the terrain,
k ...is the number of sections of the vehicle on the track.

These factors and their parameters determine 3 levels of Cross-Country Movement – GO, SLOW GO and NO GO. The level called "GO" means the movement without a loss of speed the level "SLOW GO" means partial deceleration of the speed of the movement and the last level "NO GO" signifies that the movement is not possible. These terms are given in [6–8]. But the purpose of the analysis is very important.

The analysis is different according to the type of military (or civilian) unit and the meteorological conditions.

From the point of view of means of transport (used for movement) following basic types of terrain are determined: terrain passable for full track vehicles, terrain passable for wheeled vehicles, terrain passable for other means of transport, terrain passable for infantry troops only.

3   Analogue and Digital Geographical Data

The scheduling of movement routes may take place in an office, often far from the real battlefield. At this point we can use all the available sources as maps, plans, aerial photos, scenes (obtained by RS – Remote sensing of Earth). The overview of existing digital data and GIS used in the Army of the Czech Republic and their possible use in tactical-geographic analysis is described in [9].

In real time the soldier often has only an analogue map or evaluation of the supporting documents, which due to the devastating effects of war need not be current. The determining of the correct routes of a movement or suitable visible or hidden areas may not be easy.

That is why it is calculated with the introduction of the "System of the 21th century Soldier" or some similar system in the future. This system is developing, verifying and applying in similar versions in many advanced armies all over the world. If the soldier will have the appropriate analogue or digital data, its decision-making process will be easier and faster. Commonly available sources are topographic maps and aerial photos, very good source would be the forestry maps and, in particular, their conversion into digital format. The new, highly current and accurate source of data is the acquisition of the field by the method of laser scanning, which can currently assess the most appropriate route for the movement of the vehicle.

3.1 Topographical Maps

Topographic maps (abr. TM) are designed for a security of defence of the Czech Republic and primarily for an orientation in the terrain and for a study of geographical factors. On topographic maps, important positional and altitude elements of terrain are recorded (greatly in detail).

Topographic maps allow you to evaluate the spatial relationships, evaluate the visibility between objects, determine the coordinates, determine the altitude and the azimuths and determine the slopes of the terrain. The contents of the maps are divided into the planimetry and altimetry. Another division according to the character of the objects: points, line, aerial. This is one way how to convert selected analogue data to the digital form and these digitalized data it is possible use to simulation of movement of vehicles in terrain (Fig. 2).

Fig. 2. The mirror of the map displays the cartographic projection of a terrain, its shapes and objects. Frame data include geodetic coordinates and its division, rectangular coordinate network UTM, Point "P" to determination of the direction of magnetic north and lots of labels. Out of frame data include different type of the map scale, the name of the map sheet, marking a series of maps, the issue number and marking sheet maps, data about geodetic and altitude system, interval of recta-angle network, contour interval and units for altitude, data about grivation and meridian convergence, magnetic azimuth and bearing, diagram of the administrative division, overview of neighbour map sheets, military designation of the map sheet, codename maps, legend and abbreviations, diagram of the UTM and diagram of elevation guide.

3.2 Forestry Maps

Forestry maps are very interesting source of data on the vegetation and paths. For each analogue or digital map there is a digital file. In this file there are the following: 8 classes according to the age of the trees, a species of trees, the approximate height of the trees according to the tables of speed of growth, and other information about the type of forest. Further maps contain detailed drawings of paved and unpaved paths, trails and footpaths, the boundaries of the individual areas, protected areas and a large number of map markers for the various landmarks (e.g. high seat, apiary, waste dump, the cottage, bushes). These points are very useful and can help with orientation in difficult conditions and the subsequent decision-making process.

Unfortunately, these maps are not publicly accessible. The above mentioned data in topographic maps are missing, or are not recorded in such detail. However, when comparing the topographic maps and forestry maps, it was found a large amount of new information. A unit of soldiers, which had detailed information source about paths and landmarks, was guided much better, than a unit only having topographic maps.

3.3   Aerial Surveying Photos

Aerial photos are the common product, which is easily accessible from public sources. Due to the fact that the majority of the movements of military reconnaissance units takes place in the woods and on the slide, there are not many paths through the forest cover can be seen, the aerial imageries are used only as a suitable complement of topographical or forest maps.

3.4   New Sources

Given the above positives and drawbacks of basic data sources, and given the trend to use new means, methods and simulation technology this year the experimental measurements with robotic means TAROS v2 hold in military area Libavá (in the Czech Republic). TAROS v2, which develops the national company VOP CZ in cooperation with the University of Defence, is an autonomous unmanned ground vehicle designed primarily for combat support units and reconnaissance purposes. It is a way to get the digital current data about the surrounding area and take advantage of the laser scanning method.

4   The Applied Methods

Thanks to the joint consideration of these factors and their standards indicating the degree of continuity, it would be possible to determine the correct route transfers and calculate the time estimates for the movements of various military or ambulance units. Speeds are relevant not only to the type of terrain, but also the type of (military) equipment. To devise a methodology for estimating the speed of movement of the influence of the terrain surface is necessary to establish a method of obtaining the relevant data (inclination of slopes, the frequency of the micro-relief shapes, types of surface soil conditions, terrain and weather conditions), to analyze data, identify ways to evaluate the data and build the algorithms for the calculation of time limits movements. It would be possible to modify the algorithms and other aspects (in terms of security, economic, or the shortest distance).

The use of environmental variability and the typical characteristics of each type of terrain with regard to the availability of these spaces as well as on the available types of military vehicles is most important when testing the polygons are drawn. Straight and sloping spaces, flat and rough were tested. The surfaces of a grassy, rocky, sandy, clay, asphalt and snowy were investigated. For the preparation and implementation of these tests a large number of calls with the appropriate personnel is necessary and ensuring these areas is not easy. It is possible to use different methods for obtaining and evaluating these data, it is the right to choose the most practical.

5 The Calculations and Results

Several methodologies (in particular assessing the impact of geographical factors on the movement) were created at the Department of Military geography and Meteorology in the course of carrying out the tasks relevant to the specific research [10, 11]. Several effects, which had a majority influence on the ride of vehicles in the terrain, and which were still relatively neglected were evaluated during the research. Influence of micro-relief on the movement of military vehicles was the first [6], the influence of human reactions and of the surrounding environment was the second. New approaches for a comprehensive evaluation of the operating factors and their parameters, it has also been described in some articles [12].

The result of the research, which takes place in the present, should be used to design a digital interface for collecting, managing, and redistribution of geographic data relevant to a given issue. Documents containing database tactical-technical data of vehicles and their traction diagrams (on whose basis it is possible to define the maximum possible speed attainable on exit or descent of the concrete slopes), detailed geographic data, algorithms for the determination of the coefficient of the slowdown on the basis of the frequency and the size of the micro-relief shapes, the coefficients of a deceleration defined on the basis of adhesive factors for the main types of surfaces and the coefficients of deceleration determined on the basis of meteorological characteristics would have been necessary for the new information system. These coefficients slowdown associated with each field types, however, interact and, therefore, it is not easy to quantify the impact of elementary.

One way for calculating of the total CoD depends on the partial CoD of the different GF and is given by formulas (1–3) and [4–6] and an overview of the models for determining the speed of the vehicles is given below.

5.1 The Summary of the Various Models of Paths Optimization

The algorithms of the route optimization (for communication and outside of them) may not be intended only for the war purposes because finding optimal routes outside the communication may be relevant also in civilian crisis situations, or the provision of assistance when natural disasters such as floods, fires, storms etc.

The Model of the Micro-relief. Micro-relief is a neglected factor in optimizing route. There are several reasons:

- The absence of country-wide mapping of this factor (the maps, which provided the input data, are TM in scale 1:10 000, these maps are not in using today (the date of editing was between years 1958–1964!). Unfortunately, other map resources for these measurements were not available at the time of the creation of models. Today, it is possible to use civilian product ZABAGED in scale 1:10 000 or one of the products of ALS (aerial laser scanning), especially DSM 1G (Digital Surface Model the 1st Generation).
- The apparent "small size" of these shapes, and thus, in the context of generalization of maps, totally inaccurate data on maps.

The input data were obtained by the map measurement research (the length of the micro-relief shapes, their numbers in the squares of 10 by 10 km and the average height of these shapes). The route optimization model due to micro-relief can be solved by different ways. The model was created and the values of the average length, numbers and height of the micro-relief shapes were accepted.

Model "Matlab". The coefficients of the vehicle deceleration due to one obstacle and due to the influence of a probable number of obstacles in real morpho-metric type of total length of a route have been obtained by calculation of many simulations transits. The average elongation of route, then the average size of an obstacle and the fact that a driver sees the obstacle in distance d/2 and bypasses it by angle 45° is accepted and the probability that the obstacle is met in ¼ of size is accepted too, for one obstacle it is given by coefficient $\rho = 1.0155$ (see [6], p. 68).

Model "3D Terrain". The composition and calculation of this model of routes optimization of the vehicle in the field is based on the data and equations and application of the programming language C++. The table that was created from the values of the map measurement research has been accepted as input values for a model of the micro-relief. For the calculation of the elongation of the route it is appropriate to consider, for which vehicle the simulation is created. It is assumed that ambulances or other operational vehicles are equipped with GPS devices. The total elongation for a vehicle equipped with GPS devices searching the direct route is about 5–8 % (depending on the morpho-metric type). See Fig. 3. This model can be optimized by

Fig. 3. There is a type of terrain that is created based on the values of the map measurement research on the left, on the right this is the evaluation of the 1000 transits by the terrain (The lengthening is 119 m to 1 km.) These models and algorithms are built in C++ programming language.

modifying the algorithm, where the route leads only over the apexes of the obstacles that occur on the route. The vehicle is still oriented by using GPS to the target point. Here the value of the elongation of the route is 1–1.4 %, compared to 5–8 %.

Unfortunately, not all vehicles have a GPS or other navigation instruments. The crew knows only the coordinates of the starting and destination point and a bypassing of obstacles leads to change of the azimuth to the target point. Here the average value of the elongation of the route is 12–15 %.

Model "Real Map". Input data for the next models of optimization were gathered using digitalization of layers of micro-relief, waters and railways from the TM 1:10 000. The obstacles were selected carefully, the limits for CCM were considered. The first simulation model was for influence of micro-relief only but the second was for an influence of micro-relief, waters and railways together. The values of elongation of routes for micro-relief only were 7.4 % for non optimized route and 1.2 % for optimized route, for joint model it was 14.9 % and 3.8 %.

Model of the Optimization of Routes. This model offers a solution to the optimization of routes generally valid for any terrain or for influence of any geographical factor. Some of other ideas, how to optimize routes are quoted from [5–8]. The general solution for this issue (optimizing routes for communication or outside of them) can be expressed as two processing stage:

- To construct a graph, the emphasis is on the correct determination of values of weight coefficients for links of individual nodes. The starting model is represented by a mathematical chart of a traffic network, which represents initiatory data model for solving given tasks. During the solution, the initial data model is being gradually modified based on influence of individual elements and their anticipated (calculated) path, where the time of appearance in individual (calculated) segments of optimum path is extrapolated.
- **To implement the algorithm** for searching of the shortest, fastest, safest or cheapest route. Another separate part is effective searching for optimum path of individual element. The key element in this part is effectiveness of the algorithm finding optimum (usually the shortest) path in a large not-oriented weighted chart (millions of nodes and dozens of millions of links). A searching has to be quickly enough to enable the solution "in the real time" for a large number of moving elements. A solution for each element depends on previous calculation of the optimum path (for the previous element).

Solution of both problems has the same basic principles, but with different data models and process of its construction. More detailed information on this issue you can see in this publication [8].

5.2 Model "Variation of the Function"

For the evaluation of the dependency of the shape of the surface and the driving speed math function "variation feature" (variations) has been selected. A numerical expression of the influence of the micro-shapes could be characterised by other features, used in the engineering fields and for determining the roughness of surfaces. See [6].

The calculation of the curve that defines the estimate this dependency can be divided into three steps:

- How to calculate the "roughness of routes" (x axis)? See Fig. 4 (on the left).
- How to calculate vehicle speed (y values)? The measured values of speed relevant to the types of surfaces have been used and a comprehensive table of speed from the huge number of rides in terrain was drawn up.
- How to establish a curve? An example of the calculation of the variation is based on the use of tabular data relevant to the length of elementary sections and elevation coordinates of the beginning and end of the connecting line See Fig. 4 (on the right).

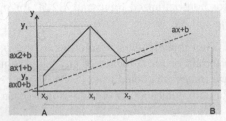 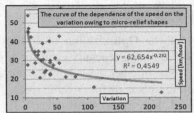

Fig. 4. On the left there is the principle of variation of function is the expression of the roughness of the terrain on the basis of the summaries of the products of the values of the tangents directives and the lengths of elementary sections. The absolute value of the tangent (this is the quotient of the differences of heights or elevation differences of extreme points to the horizontal length of the section) is multiplied by the length of a section (also in absolute value) and by the summarization of these products the value of the variations of the function between the starting and final point is calculated. It was not very precise, therefore variations were converted to the reference "zero" level, i.e. to a linear trend-line (broken line). The dependence curve of the speed on the variation (it is conditional on the roughness of the terrain) is on the right.

5.3 Regression Model

One of the way, how to evaluate the speed of vehicles in terrain, is the use of mathematical-statistical calculations in a form of a regression model. [6]. The Program "R" (the sophistic software for regression analysis) was used to evaluate the speed of vehicles depending on many factors. A simple regression model was built, which describes the dependence of the speed of the drive based on the numerical representation of categorical variables. The input data was compiled into a table about 1872 records with 13 parameters (type of vehicle, driver experience, the practice of the use of the vehicle, type of surface – grass, silt, mud…, lit by the sun, etc.) and then the regression equation, which approximately describes the real speed of the vehicles, was established. On the basis of the carried out calculations the equation of regression was established.

The regression equation has the form:

$$Speed\ of\ vehicle = 5.9170 + 1.2999^*vehicle + 4.8573^*driver + 4.9551^*primary\ vehicle +$$
$$1.1451^*surface + 2.7789^*ride\ category - 0.1066^*variation\ of\ micro-relief\ shape -$$
$$0.0270^*slope\ variation - 0.2917^*slope + 0.9476^*meteorological\ condition - 5.4804$$
$$^*sunshine$$

$$(4)$$

5.4 Evaluation of the Influence of the Surface Using a Programming Environment in the Language "C++" in Vector Format

Model simulating the ride vehicles in the field has been created in the programming language C++ [6, 13]. Input data are defined by the curve of terrain profile and were obtained by two methods – by terrestrial laser scanning (measurement of the coordinates of the profile was targeted with step 10 cm) and by total station Leica (characteristic fracture points of terrain shapes in the same profile were targeted on the basis of a subjective selection of surveyor). Length and height coordinates were used. Several algorithms have been built. Their purpose was: to retrieve data, to display the off-road curve, refining the methodology of the rolling wheel after the terrain and the final output was the determination of the value of the time needed to complete the profile. Other input data were maximum vehicle speed, wheel diameter, the maximum speed of the vibrations the wheels – always relevant to a given type of vehicle. These data were calculated in models at the software ADAMS.

The author recommends use this model in particular in conjunction with the air laser scanning and use of UAV (Unmanned Aerial Vehicle).

5.5 Unmanned Ground Vehicle TAROS

Research of the autonomous movement of the vehicle in the real terrain takes place in the context of development. The measurement was focused on the acquisition, training, validation, and processing data in the framework of the development of the model of optimal manoeuvre the robotic device on the battlefield in the area of operations. Data was gathered from sensory systems, and on the basis of these data the vehicle reconstructs the surrounding space (Fig. 5).

Fig. 5. Unmanned Ground Vehicle TAROS v2. The scanned data is used as a starting basis for the calculation of throughput analysis in complex terrain.

It consists of:

- The 3D laser scanner (LIDAR);
- The differential GPS device for the localization of the device to the nearest hundredths metres;
- The inertial unit for determining angles of rotation of the vehicle in the space.

The optimal model of manoeuvre which is a part of the long-term research decision support for ACR Commander on the University of Defence is built on a complex mathematical model. The basic entry to this model there are the data about vehicle surroundings that are getting by the laser scanner and from the information about the current position, and the rotation of the vehicle in the area. The obtained data are used as input to the Simulator. The Simulator is a key element of the verification of the correctness of the design and operation of the model. Verification takes the form of mathematical simulation, in which the proposed model is verified as in the experiment. The next stage of the verification is verification of the model in the real environment, which is the next stage in the planned project. When measuring 6 independent experiments were carried out. Each experiment was focused on a separate key area, which was necessary to verify.

These are the following areas:

- The movement of vehicle on the road.
- The movement of vehicle outside of the communication with a significant change of elevation of the terrain.
- The movement of the vehicle around the near negative obstacle.
- The movement of the resource in the area with higher grass and shrubs.
- The movement of the resource in the tunnel.
- The endurance test of the engine when the vehicle is moving in difficult terrain.

From each experiment a comprehensive set of data was obtained. It was subjected to a thorough analysis, on the basis that the proposed model has been verified. The results of the analysis are also used for adjusting the input parameters of the model. A total of more than 6 GB of data was obtained in the context of all the experiments and stored. This data will be analyzed in the context of the other phases of the research component of the project.

6 Map Outcomes

The potential graphic outputs should be maps of optimal paths from the start to the final points (with a time calculation for the move), secondary data could be used for the creation of the current flow maps of the terrain, which would have been over existing products as well as from the standpoint of the methodology of determining how the terrain, so from the standpoint of data bases (especially during the use of products produced by the method of laser scanning) (Fig. 6).

Aspect of the database data bases were open to question, however, is given to the development of methods and means for the collection of data, it is assumed that in the future the current ignorance of the field will not be a problem.

 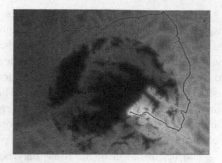

Fig. 6. On the left there is the scanner records the "point cloud" as a result of the 3D measurement. Concentrated points show a shape characterising the barrier (figures people are back - this is a simple example, but the multi-objective analysis is required to assess more complex shapes). Robotic device using laser scanner detects obstacles while trying to optimize the manoeuvre. It is looking for the best route through the space in such a way that the manoeuvre to satisfy certain criteria in terms of fluidity, speed, options of device, etc. (on the right).

7 Conclusion

The available analogue data documents are the primary source for the evaluation of the situation on the battlefield. Topographic maps produced by the VGHMÚř Dobruška (Military Geography and Meteorology Service Department), forestry maps ("map of growing forest units") and images of the terrain (whether the air surveying the slides or the slides from Web browsers) and the older topographic maps of micro-relief units were included among these data documents. All of these products have their advantage and disadvantage and it is appropriate, in the context of the decision-making process and optimization-use these facts. It is possible to get a very detailed idea of the area by combining the information from the particular products. The current topographic maps contain unfortunately much less data than maps created from the previous mark guide. In these maps the basic information about the forest units (e.g. fraction, which expresses the height of trees, their spacing and thickness of the tribes–including the type of crop) are not mentioned, or are mentioned only sporadically. Missing data can be found in the above mentioned forest maps and similarly, so data that are not in the current topographic maps must be obtained from other analogue map resources.

On the basis of the products mentioned above, the dates of the individual elements (which have an impact on the potential route of movement of military units) were obtained by methods of cartographic metric investigation. The movement of military units is a basic tactical activity and the process of planning and decision-making is usually subject to just map the elements, whether analogue or digital. Cartographic investigation methods help obtain data so that at first glance may not be obvious, and the evaluated data are used as input data for the optimization algorithms.

That is why it is calculated with the introduction of the "System of the 21th century Soldier" in the future. This system is developing, verifying and applying in similar versions in many advanced armies all over the world.

The decision-making process has its own rules however it is conditional on the explanatory value of up-to-date geographic data. This data is becoming an essential part of the decision-making process when planning of a successful movement (for peace and for war) is one of the fundamental questions. For its creation it is necessary to know the impact of geographical factors on the manoeuvre, and if it is possible to use algorithms to find optimal routes. "The optimization of the routes" means not only finding the shortest route, but also to ensuring the safety of movement, or at least limitation of risk factors and so the compliance with time limits or acceptance of the economic aspects of the movement can play an important role.

The optimization of the route may be useful for ambulances or other operational vehicles for a solution of crises or natural disasters. These vehicles are equipped with GPS devices, which can maintain the direction to the target point in the current time and the issue of optimization of a movement can be calculated and used for a movement over the communication or outside of them. Here is a great space for the use of the UGV and new methods, therefore the vehicle TAROS was tested.

Another solution is the use of math-static models and model based on simulations of rides in terrain. The database, which is used for calculations, is created from the vast amount of data measured in the field. Capture the dependencies between individual factors is not a trivial matter, and therefore, the implementation of field tests is very beneficial. The scientific team is gradually getting to still more specific conclusions.

Acknowledgements. The work presented in this paper has been supported by the Ministry of Education (project of specific research SV15-FVL-K110-10-KRI) and by the Ministry of Defence the Czech Republic (research project DZRO K-110).

References

1. NATO Standardization Agency: AJP 2 (A) SD1, Allied Joint Doctrine for Intelligence; Counter Intelligence and Security. Edition A Version 1 Ratification Draft, Brussel (2013)
2. Headquarters Departement of the US Army, FM 2-01.3, Inteligence Preparation of the Battlefield/Battlespace. Washington, DC (2009)
3. Košťan, P., Bělohlávek, F., Šuleř, O.: Management. Business Books (Computer Press). Computer Press, Brno (c2006). ISBN 80-251-0396-X. Bělohlávek, F.: Decision-Making Process, Incomia, Praha (2006)
4. Mokrá, I.: A model approach to the decision-making process. In: Conference Proceedings 3, Applied Technical Sciences and Advanced Military Technologies, vol. 3, no. 1, pp. 278–281 (2012). ISSN: 1843-6722
5. Mazal, J.: Real time maneuver optimization in general environment. In: Brezina, T., Jablonski, R. (eds.) Recent Advances in Mechatronics, pp. 191–196. Springer, Heidelberg (2010). ISBN 978-3-642-05021-3
6. Kristalova, D.: Vliv povrchu terénu na pohyb vojenských vozidel (The Effect of the Terrain Cover on the Movement of Military Vehicles), The Ph.D. thesis (in Czech). The Univerzity of Defence, Brno, The Czech Republic, 318 p. (2013)
7. Rybanský, M.: Cross-Country Movement - The Impact and Evaluation of Geographical Factors, The Czech Republic, Brno, 114 p. (2009). ISBN: 978-80-7204-661-4

8. Zelinková, D.: Analýza získávání a využitelnosti informací pro vyhodnocení průchodnosti území (The Analyse of Collecting and Applicability of Information for the Cross-Country Movement), The Diploma thesis (in Czech). VA Brno, The Czech Republic, Brno, 118 p. (2002)

9. Kristalova, D.: The overview of existing digital data and GIS used in the army of the Czech Republic and their possible use in tactical-geographic analysis. In: The Conference Paper, MMK 2011, The Czech Republic. 8 p. (2011). ISBN: 978-80-904877-7-2

10. Rybansky, M., Zikmund, J., Kristalova, D., Rydel, M.: Metodika vyhodnocování vlivu mikroreliéfu a terénních překážek na průchodnost vojenských vozidel – kolová vozidla (The Metodologhy of the Evaluation of the Micro-Relief and the Terrain Obstacles on the Movement of the Military Wheeled Vehicles), Identification Number J-4-720/74, The Czech Republic, Vyškov, 30 p. (2010)

11. Rybansky, M., Zikmund, J., Kristalova, D.: Metodika určování vlivu povrchu terénu na pohyb vojenských kolových vozidel dle AVTP-1/01-80 a FMS-33 (The Metodologhy of the Determination of the Effect of the Terrain Cover on the Movement of the Military Wheeled Vehicles), Identification Number J-4-720/75, The Czech Republic, Vyškov, 45 p. (2011)

12. Křišťálová, D.: Nové datové trendy pro stanovení průchodnosti území (The New Data Trends for the Determination of the Levels of Cross-Country Movement). The Conference Paper, The Czech Republic, Taktika 2012, 8 p. (2012). (in Czech). ISBN 978-80-7231-887-2

13. Kristalova, D.: An effect of sandy soils on the movement in the terrain. In: Hodicky, J. (ed.) MESAS 2014. LNCS, vol. 8906, pp. 262–273. Springer, Heidelberg (2014). ISBN 978-3-319-13823-7

14. Hodicky, J., Frantis, P.: Decision support system for a commander at the operational level. In: Dietz, J.L.G. (ed.) Proceedings of the International Conference on Knowledge Engineering and Ontology Development, KEOD 2009, October 2009, Funchal, Madeira, pp. 359–362. INSTICC Press (2009). ISBN: 978-989-674-012-2

15. Hodicky, J., Frantis, P.: Online versus offline critical geographic information system. In: Proceedings of the Informatics, Wireless Applications and Computing and Telecommunications, Networks and Systems 2011. Part of the IADIS Multi Conference on Computer Science and Information Systems 2011, July 2011, Roma, pp. 127–131. IADIS Press (2011). ISBN: 978-972-8939-39-7

16. Hodicky, J., Frantis, P.: Using simulation for prediction of units movements in case of communication failure. World Acad. Sci. Eng. Technol, Int. J. Electr. Comput. Energ. Electron. Commun. Eng. 5(7), 796–798 (2011)

Fusion of Monocular Visual-Inertial Measurements for Three Dimensional Pose Estimation

Gonzalo Perez-Paina[1]([✉]), Claudio Paz[1], Miroslav Kulich[2], Martin Saska[3], and Gastón Araguás[1]

[1] Center for IT Research, National Technological University, Córdoba, Argentina
{gperez,cpaz,garaguas}@frc.utn.edu.ar
[2] Czech Institute of Informatics, Robotics, and Cybernetics, Czech Technical University in Prague, Prague, Czech Republic
kulich@ciirc.cvut.cz
[3] Department of Cybernetics, Faculty of Electrical Engineering, Czech Technical University in Prague, Prague, Czech Republic
saska@labe.felk.cvut.cz

Abstract. This work describes a novel fusion schema to estimate the pose of a UAV using inertial sensors and a monocular camera. The visual motion algorithm is based on the plane induced homography using so called spectral features. The algorithm is able to operate with images presenting small amount of corner-like features, which gives more robustness to the state estimation. The key contribution of the paper is the use of this visual algorithm in a fusion schema with inertial sensors, exploiting the complementary properties of these two sensors. Results are presented in simulation with six degrees of freedom motion that satisfies dynamic constraints of a quadcopter. Virtual views are generated from this simulated motion cropped from a real floor image. Simulation results show that the presented algorithm would have enough precision to be used in an on-board algorithm to control the UAV in hovering operations.

Keywords: Sensor fusion · Visual odometry · Inertial sensors · Pose estimation · UAV · Kalman filter

1 Introduction

Reduced size Unmanned Aerial Vehicles (UAV), also known as Micro-aerial Vehicles (MAV), have gained popularity in the last years. This is due mainly to their low cost and ability to operate either in outdoor and indoor environments. For the case of multicopters [8], they have the additional ability to fly in a hovering mode, which is useful for inspection tasks.

This work was partially founded by the project "Multi-Robot Autonomous System", MINCyT ARC/13/13 & MEYS 7AMB14AR015, and the project "Mobile Robot Localization using Metric and Semantic information", UTN-PID 2173.

© Springer International Publishing AG 2016
J. Hodicky (Ed.): MESAS 2016, LNCS 9991, pp. 242–260, 2016.
DOI: 10.1007/978-3-319-47605-6_20

The state estimation [17] is the problem of determining a set of different variables of interest from measurements of on-board sensors, which presents varying uncertainties and noise. Particularly, for state estimation in UAVs, these interesting variables are usually those that describe the UAV position and orientation in a three dimensional space. Due to this, the state estimation is usually solved robustly integrating or fusing information from different sensors, such as inertial units (accelerometers and gyroscopes), magnetic compasses, altimeters (barometers or sonars), cameras, GPS receivers, etc. Different sensors have their own advantages and disadvantages, depending on the flying conditions, like flight altitude, indoor/outdoor operation, etc. On the other hand, given the limited payload of MAVs which constraints the available computational power, one of typical setups for state estimation is to use inertial sensors (mainly accelerometers and gyroscopes) together with a monocular camera. Moreover, this result is useful for UAV application in GPS-denied areas, like indoor environments, urban canyons, etc.

Even though there are different algorithms for sensor fusion, the most widely used are those based on the Kalman filter and its variants. Recently, the algorithms based on graph-based optimization are gaining popularity. From the camera point of view there are also a variety of algorithms which can be used to compute the six degrees of freedom (6DOF) motion parameters. These are divided into two main categories, those that use image features (like corners, lines, etc.) or those that do not (optical flow, photometry error minimization, or frequency domain). For instance, in [6] an approach for long term localization, stabilization, and navigation of micro-aerial vehicles (MAVs) in unknown environment is presented. This approach consists of extraction of information from pictures consequently captured using down-looking camera carried by the particular MAV. Corner-like scale invariant visual features are obtained from images of the surface under the MAV, and stored into a map that is represented by these features. The position of the MAV is then obtained through matching with previously stored features.

A general approach for multi-sensor fusion is described in [16], which allows to incorporate different kinds of sensors, either of absolute (GPS, magnetometer, altimeter) or relative (laser-based odometry and visual odometry) measurements. This sensor fusion is based on the unscented Kalman filter (UKF) with the stochastic cloning approach described in [14]. The fusion schema makes use also of a pose-only graph-based SLAM (being in fact a mixed approach using both filtering and optimization techniques) in order to cope with large uncertainty when GPS signal becomes available, after a long time offline. The limitation of the algorithm is related to the visual pose estimation which is highly affected by changes in the illumination for outdoor scenes. Also, the computational complexity of the UKF is higher than the EKF, which limits its applicability in on-board processing. The authors of [4] describe a fusion schema also based on the UKF, where the camera information is extracted from an optical flow algorithm. The main goal is to achieve a robust estimation of the velocity and angular motion of the vehicle to be applied in dynamic motion control, and not to achieve a high-precision in the estimation as it is stated. The image processing part is based on FAST features (using Shi-Tomasi score) with the KLT tracker and evaluated against the standard epipolar constraint for error determination used by the filter correction. The authors of [5] present a method for increasing the accuracy of the standard visual-inertial odometry (VIO) system by removing the angular drift. The visual-inertial filter is based on the classical EKF from the approach presented in [12], using the unit quaternion for orientation representation and IMU bias estimation. The visual part is based on a line segment classification using inertial-aided RANSAC, where detected vanishing points are used in the update stage of the estimation filter. The limitation of this approach is that it only operates in man-made indoor environments, given that the vanishing points are obtained from the lines detected in the image in corridor like scenarios. The work in [18] describes an EKF-based tightly coupled monocular VIO with direct photometric error minimization, using a sparse (10–20) set of small patches (as small as 3×3 pixels). This allows a fast camera motion estimation and does not depend on corner-like features. The presented results show the comparison against ground truth obtained from a VICON system and they show a better performance in scenes without corner-like features and also with lines structures.

On the other side, using the optimization approach, the most representative work is presented in [15], which uses an IMU-camera fusion schema based on the sliding window graph-based formulation for non-linear optimization. In more details, the algorithm estimates the position and orientation (with unit quaternion representation) based on the standard IMU integration model (without bias estimation), and the image processing is based on KLT tracker with RANSAC for epipolar constraint. The IMU integration model is the same of those used in the fusion schema. The described algorithm was evaluated in different situations including autonomous hovering, autonomous trajectory tracking (both with VICON), and in autonomous flight in indoor environments, the algorithm was also evaluated with respect to the real-time performance.

An important issue in the implementation of a filter-based pose estimation is the parametrization used to represent the orientation. Different orientation representations present some advantages and disadvantages [13]. For instance, the Euler angles representation uses the minimum of three required parameters but they present singularities. On the other hand, the commonly used rotation representation given by a 3×3 orthogonal matrix has nine components with six constraints without singularities. Unit quaternions have the minimum redundant parametrization for orientation representation, which avoids discontinuities with only one constraint. However, using unit quaternions in filter-based orientation estimation presents the dilemma of how to treat the estimation error, which can be additive or multiplicative [10,11]. Our implementation, as it will be described later, uses the multiplicative error model (multiplicative EKF) in which a non-singular representation is used for the estimated orientation, and a minimal representation for the deviation or error from this estimate.

In the present work, we describe a novel fusion schema to estimate the position and orientation of a UAV using inertial sensors and a monocular camera observing a considered flat scene. In addition, an altimeter is employed to disambiguate the scale factor of the camera measurements and to avoid the divergence of the altitude estimation resulting from the integration of the inertial sensors. The fusion is performed by an extended Kalman filter, in which the orientation is represented using unit quaternions [13,19]. The motion information from the visual algorithm is based on the plane induced homography using so called spectral features [2]. The algorithm is able to operate with images presenting small amount of corner-like features [1], which gives more robustness to the state estimation. The key contribution of the paper stands in the use of this visual algorithm in a fusion schema with inertial sensors, exploiting the complementary properties of these two sensors. The current fusion approach is an extension of the work presented in [2], where the visual algorithm only returns the yaw angle measurement. In addition, this approach incorporates the complete three dimensional pose from the camera, i.e. position and orientation measurements.

Results are presented in simulation with six degrees of freedom motion that satisfies dynamic constraints of a specific UAV, particularly a quadcopter. Virtual views are generated from this simulated motion cropped from a real floor image. In this case, simulations are useful to validate the estimation when ground truth information is not available, which for the case of experiments with real UAV is usually obtained from an external tracking system. Simulation results show that the presented algorithm would have enough precision to be used in an on-board algorithm to control the UAV in hovering operations.

The model used for the filter-based sensor fusion does not incorporate the estimation of the inertial sensor biases, which is left as future work. Also, a future work will be to compare the performance of our IMU-camera fusion approach with that described in [18]. There, as was previously stated, the image processing is based on the intensity information of small patches instead of using the frequency domain as in our approach.

The rest of the paper is organized as follows. Section 2 gives a short overview of the proposed system. The models for the Kalman filter based sensor fusion are described in Sect. 3, while Sect. 4 details the used visual algorithm. The results are described in Sect. 5, while Sect. 6 finally presents the conclusions and future work.

2   System Overview

The proposed system consists of a down-looking monocular camera and an inertial measurement unit. These sensors are rigidly attached to the UAV and their relative pose is assumed to be known. An extended Kalman filter (EKF) is used to fuse the IMU and the camera information in order to obtain a six degrees of freedom motion estimation, i.e. the three dimensional position and orientation. The orientation is represented using a unit quaternion, which presents some advantages with respect to other representations, like algebraic simplicity and numerical stability [13]. The vector state to be estimated by the filter is then composed by the position, the linear velocity and the unit quaternion. The inertial sensors (accelerometer and gyroscope) biases are not included in this vector

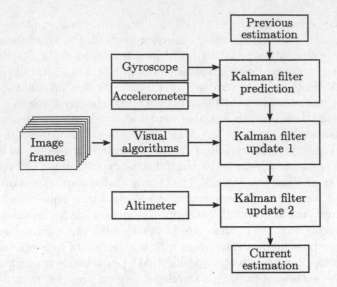

Fig. 1. Sensor fusion diagram

state, thus they are not estimated by the filter. In some applications and mainly for flights of short time, the estimation of these biases averaging accelerometer and gyroscope readings before every flight would be sufficient. However, it has to be experimentally evaluated in real platforms. The prediction stage of the fusion filter integrates the IMU readings at each time step using the classical model, and when camera information is available, the update stage uses it to correct the estimation. Figure 1 shows the block diagram of the estimation filter.

The camera motion is estimated using the homography induced by the observed floor, which is assumed to be flat, as shown schematically in Fig. 2. This is based on corresponding points which are obtained from the frequency domain. This spectral information corresponds to a fixed number of image patches distributed on each image, which we call spectral features. This kind of features performs better than interest points based on the image intensity

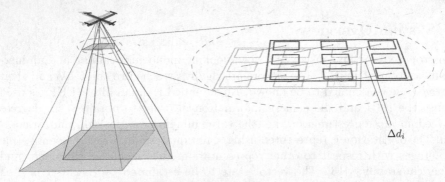

Fig. 2. Homography-based pose estimation

when observing a floor with homogeneous texture [1]. Moreover, because their positions in the image plane are previously selected, they are always well distributed. The obtained homography is then decomposed into the motion parameters, i.e. the translation vector and the rotation matrix.

3 Sensor Fusion

In order to estimate a three dimensional pose using an extended Kalman filter, the system has to be represented stochastically by means of a process and a measurement models. These two models are generally expressed as $\dot{\mathbf{x}} = f(\mathbf{x}, \mathbf{u}, \mathbf{w})$ and $\mathbf{z} = h(\mathbf{x}, \mathbf{v})$, respectively. The process model in the current implementation integrates the inertial sensor information, whilst there are two measurement models: one that incorporates the camera information, and the other one that incorporates the altimeter information.

The unknown state vector is composed of the three dimensional position, the linear velocity and the unit quaternion representing the orientation, i.e. $\mathbf{x} = \left[\mathbf{p}^T \ \mathbf{v}^T \ \mathbf{q}^T\right]^T$. The measurement of the three axial accelerometer and gyroscope acting as input signal of the process model is defined as $\mathbf{u} = \left[\mathbf{a}_m^T \ \boldsymbol{\omega}_m^T\right]^T$. On the other hand, the camera measurement is composed of relative translation vector and orientation expressed in the unit quaternion between consecutive frames, i.e. ${}^c\mathbf{z} = \left[{}^c\mathbf{p} \ {}^c\mathbf{q}\right]^T$. This is used for the first update stage, while the altimeter measurement ${}^a\mathbf{z}$ is used in the second update.

As it was previously stated, the implementation is based on the multiplicative definition of the orientation error. That is, the estimation error is

$$\mathbf{x} \ominus \hat{\mathbf{x}} = \begin{bmatrix} \delta\mathbf{p} \\ \delta\mathbf{v} \\ \delta\mathbf{q} \end{bmatrix} = \begin{bmatrix} \mathbf{p} - \hat{\mathbf{p}} \\ \mathbf{v} - \hat{\mathbf{v}} \\ \hat{\mathbf{q}}^* \otimes \mathbf{q} \end{bmatrix}, \tag{1}$$

where $\ominus$ is a general difference operator, which is the algebraic difference for the position and velocity vectors, and a Hamilton product for unit quaternion. The quaternion error in (1) for small angles can be expressed as

$$\delta\mathbf{q} = \begin{bmatrix} \delta q_w \\ \delta\mathbf{q}_v \end{bmatrix} = \begin{bmatrix} 1 \\ \frac{1}{2}\delta\boldsymbol{\theta} \end{bmatrix}, \quad \mathbf{q}_v = \left[q_x \ q_y \ q_z\right]^T, \tag{2}$$

where $\delta\boldsymbol{\theta}$ is the attitude or orientation error. Hence, the final estimation error, used to define the covariance matrix representing the uncertainty in the estimation $\mathbf{P} = \mathbb{E}[\delta\mathbf{x}\delta\mathbf{x}^T]$, is defined as $\delta\mathbf{x} = \left[\delta\mathbf{p} \ \delta\mathbf{v} \ \delta\boldsymbol{\theta}\right]^T$.

3.1 Inertial Sensor Models

The continuous-time kinematic model of three dimensional motion is given by

$$\begin{aligned} \dot{\mathbf{p}} &= \mathbf{v} \\ \dot{\mathbf{v}} &= \mathbf{R}(\mathbf{q})\mathbf{a} + \mathbf{g}^n \\ \dot{\mathbf{q}} &= \frac{1}{2}\mathbf{q} \otimes \begin{bmatrix} 0 \\ \boldsymbol{\omega} \end{bmatrix}, \end{aligned} \tag{3}$$

where $\mathbf{p}$ and $\mathbf{q}$ represent the three dimensional pose in the navigation or earth fixed frame, and the inertial measurements $\mathbf{a}$ and $\boldsymbol{\omega}$ are expressed in the body or moving frame. $\mathbf{R}(\mathbf{q})$ is the representation of the orientation given by the unit quaternion as a rotation matrix, $\mathbf{g}^n$ is the gravitational acceleration expressed in the navigation frame, and the symbol $\otimes$ represents the Hamilton product [19], using the convention of the quaternion in which the first component is the scalar part.

The models of the inertial sensors, i.e. the accelerometer and gyroscope, are given by

$$\mathbf{a}_m = \mathbf{a} + \mathbf{w}_a \tag{4}$$
$$\boldsymbol{\omega}_m = \boldsymbol{\omega} + \mathbf{w}_\omega, \tag{5}$$

where the subscript m stands for the measured value, which is equal to the true value plus an additive white Gaussian noise $\mathbf{w}_a \sim \mathcal{N}(0, \sigma_a^2 \mathbf{I})$ and $\mathbf{w}_\omega \sim \mathcal{N}(0, \sigma_\omega^2 \mathbf{I})$. Then, the continuous-time covariance matrix of the process noise of (3) is $\mathbf{Q}^c = diag(\sigma_a^2 \mathbf{I}, \sigma_\omega^2 \mathbf{I})$.

For the application of the prediction stage of an EKF based on the model given by (3), it is needed to obtain: (1) a discrete solution of (3) to propagate the mean value of the state vector, where the orientation is represented in a non-singular way [10], and (2) a linearized version of (3) to propagate the covariance matrix [17] where the orientation error is expressed with three components.

The discrete-time form of (3), as a first-order approximation with a zero-order holder for the sensor measurements, is given by

$$\begin{aligned}
\mathbf{p}_k &= \mathbf{p}_{k-1} + \Delta t \mathbf{v}_{k-1} \\
\mathbf{v}_k &= \mathbf{v}_{k-1} + \Delta t \mathbf{R}(\mathbf{q}_{k-1}) \mathbf{a}_{m,k-1} \\
\mathbf{q}_k &= \left(\mathbf{I} + \frac{\Delta t}{2} \Omega(\boldsymbol{\omega}_m) \right) \mathbf{q}_{k-1},
\end{aligned} \tag{6}$$

where

$$\Omega(\boldsymbol{\omega}) = \begin{bmatrix} 0 & -\boldsymbol{\omega}^T \\ \boldsymbol{\omega} & \lfloor \boldsymbol{\omega}_\times \rfloor \end{bmatrix} = \begin{bmatrix} 0 & -\omega_x & -\omega_y & -\omega_z \\ \omega_x & 0 & \omega_z & -\omega_y \\ \omega_y & -\omega_z & 0 & \omega_x \\ \omega_z & \omega_y & -\omega_x & 0 \end{bmatrix}, \tag{7}$$

and $\lfloor \mathbf{x}_\times \rfloor$ is the skew-symmetric matrix of the vector $\mathbf{x}$ such as $\mathbf{a} \times \mathbf{b} = \lfloor \mathbf{a}_\times \rfloor \mathbf{b}$.

On the other hand, the first term of the linearized model or the error state model, is given by

$$\begin{aligned}
\dot{\delta \mathbf{p}} &= \delta \mathbf{v} \\
\dot{\delta \mathbf{v}} &= -\mathbf{R}(\mathbf{q}) \lfloor \mathbf{a}_{m\times} \rfloor \delta \boldsymbol{\theta} - \mathbf{R}(\mathbf{q}) \mathbf{w}_a \\
\dot{\delta \boldsymbol{\theta}} &= -\lfloor \boldsymbol{\omega}_{m\times} \rfloor \delta \boldsymbol{\theta} - \mathbf{w}_\omega,
\end{aligned} \tag{8}$$

which results to be a linear model of the form $\delta\mathbf{x} = \mathbf{A}\delta\mathbf{x} + \mathbf{D}\mathbf{w}$, where the matrices $\mathbf{A}$ and $\mathbf{D}$ are independent of the state $\delta\mathbf{x}$, and are defined as

$$\mathbf{A} = \begin{bmatrix} \mathbf{0} & \mathbf{I} & \mathbf{0} \\ \mathbf{0} & \mathbf{0} & -\mathbf{R}(\mathbf{q})\lfloor \mathbf{a}_{m\times}\rfloor \\ \mathbf{0} & \mathbf{0} & -\lfloor \boldsymbol{\omega}_{m\times}\rfloor \end{bmatrix}, \quad \mathbf{D} = \begin{bmatrix} \mathbf{0} & \mathbf{0} \\ -\mathbf{R}(\mathbf{q}) & \mathbf{0} \\ \mathbf{0} & -\mathbf{I} \end{bmatrix}.$$

Using also the first order or Euler approximation, the state transition matrix of the model given in (8) is $\mathbf{F} = e^{\mathbf{A}\Delta t} \approx \mathbf{I} + \Delta t\mathbf{A}$, where Δt is the time step. This transition matrix is used in the prediction state of the filter. The discrete-time covariance matrix [17] of the process noise is then expressed as

$$\mathbf{Q}_{k-1} = \int_{t_{k-1}}^{t_k} e^{\mathbf{A}(t_k-\tau)} \mathbf{D}\mathbf{Q}^c\mathbf{D}^T e^{\mathbf{A}^T(t_k-\tau)} d\tau , \tag{9}$$

where the sub-matrices, removing time-step subscript, are given by

$$\mathbf{Q}_{11} = \frac{\sigma_a^2 \Delta t^3}{3}\mathbf{I}$$

$$\mathbf{Q}_{22} = \sigma_a^2\mathbf{I} - \frac{\sigma_\omega^2 \Delta t^3}{3}\mathbf{R}\lfloor \mathbf{a}_{m\times}\rfloor^2\mathbf{R}^T$$

$$\mathbf{Q}_{33} = \sigma_\omega^2 \Delta t\mathbf{I} - \frac{\sigma_\omega^2 \Delta t^3}{3}\lfloor \boldsymbol{\omega}_{m\times}\rfloor$$

$$\mathbf{Q}_{12} = \frac{\sigma_a^2 \Delta t^2}{2}\mathbf{I} = \mathbf{Q}_{21}, \quad \mathbf{Q}_{13} = \mathbf{Q}_{31} = \mathbf{0}$$

$$\mathbf{Q}_{23} = -\frac{\sigma_\omega^2 \Delta t^2}{2}\mathbf{R}\lfloor \mathbf{a}_{m\times}\rfloor - \frac{\sigma_\omega^2 \Delta t^3}{3}\mathbf{R}\lfloor \mathbf{a}_{m\times}\rfloor\lfloor \boldsymbol{\omega}_{m\times}\rfloor, \quad \mathbf{Q}_{32} = \mathbf{Q}_{23}^T .$$

3.2   Camera Measurement Model

The camera information, after applying the image processing algorithms, is the relative position and orientation of two consecutive frames both expressed in the first frame. This parameters are then used in the update stage of the fusion filter, where the measurement vector is defined as

$$^c\hat{\mathbf{z}}_k^- = \begin{bmatrix} ^c\hat{\mathbf{p}}_k^- \\ ^c\hat{\mathbf{q}}_k^- \end{bmatrix} = \begin{bmatrix} \mathbf{R}(\mathbf{q}_p)^T(\hat{\mathbf{p}}_k^- - \mathbf{p}_p) \\ \mathbf{q}_p^* \otimes \hat{\mathbf{q}}_k^- \end{bmatrix}. \tag{10}$$

In (10), $\mathbf{p}_p$ and $\mathbf{q}_p$ are the position and orientation of the camera in the previous frame. It should be noted that the model given in (10) has to take into account the rigid transformation between the camera and IMU coordinate systems for a real system. However, given that the presented results are based on simulated data, these two coordinate systems are considered to be coincident.

The measurement Jacobian of the camera measurement model (10) needed in the implementation of the Kalman filter is then

$$^c\mathbf{H}_k = \left.\frac{\partial h_c(\mathbf{x})}{\partial \mathbf{x}}\right|_{\mathbf{x}=\hat{\mathbf{x}}_k^-} = \begin{bmatrix} \partial^c\mathbf{p}_k/\partial \mathbf{x} \\ \partial^c\mathbf{q}_k/\partial \mathbf{x} \end{bmatrix} = \begin{bmatrix} \partial^c\mathbf{p}_k/\partial \mathbf{p}_k & \mathbf{0}_{3\times 3} & \mathbf{0}_{3\times 4} \\ \mathbf{0}_{4\times 3} & \mathbf{0}_{4\times 3} & \partial^c\mathbf{q}_k/\partial \mathbf{q}_k \end{bmatrix}, \tag{11}$$

where

$$\frac{\partial^c \mathbf{p}_k}{\partial \mathbf{p}_k} = \mathbf{R}(\mathbf{q}_p)^T, \quad \frac{\partial^c \mathbf{q}_k}{\partial \mathbf{q}_k} = Q_l(\mathbf{q}_p^*),$$

and $Q_l(\cdot)$ is the left-matrix representing the quaternion product [19].

The residual or innovation $\boldsymbol{\nu}_k = \mathbf{z}_k \ominus \hat{\mathbf{z}}_k^-$ is computed as $^c\mathbf{p}_k - {}^c\hat{\mathbf{p}}_k^-$ for the position, and as $(^c\mathbf{q}_k)^* \otimes {}^c\hat{\mathbf{q}}_k^-$ for the orientation quaternion. Then, this residual is used in the filter update stage taking into account also the multiplicative model, $\hat{\mathbf{x}}_k = \hat{\mathbf{x}}_k^- \oplus \mathbf{K}_k \boldsymbol{\nu}_k$.

3.3   Altimeter Measurement Model

The sonar measurement is the distance from the sonar position and the floor plane. Here, we assume that the sonar position is at the center of the body frame, and its orientation is such that the measured distance is in the body frame z-axis direction. In this way, the measurement to be modeled is the distance defined in a 3D line in the direction of the body frame z-axis, from the body frame center to the point where this line intersects the floor plane. This is shown schematically in Fig. 3.

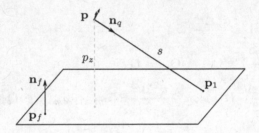

Fig. 3. Geometry of sonar measurement model

The floor plane is defined by the norm vector $\mathbf{n}_f = \begin{bmatrix} 0 & 0 & 1 \end{bmatrix}^T$ and the point $\mathbf{p}_f = \begin{bmatrix} 0 & 0 & 0 \end{bmatrix}^T$. The direction vector of the measurement is then

$$\mathbf{n}_q = \mathbf{R}(\mathbf{q}) \begin{bmatrix} 0 \\ 0 \\ 1 \end{bmatrix} = \begin{bmatrix} 2(q_x q_z + q_y q_w) \\ 2(q_y q_z - q_x q_w) \\ q_w^2 - q_x^2 - q_y^2 + q_z^2 \end{bmatrix},$$

therefore the sought distance can be obtained as

$$s = \frac{-\mathbf{n}_f \cdot (\mathbf{p} - \mathbf{p}_f)}{\mathbf{n}_f \cdot \mathbf{n}_q},$$

where $\mathbf{p} = \begin{bmatrix} p_x & p_y & p_z \end{bmatrix}^T$ is the position of the body frame. Then, the sonar measurement model, removing time-step subscript, is

$$^a z = h_a(\mathbf{x}) = \frac{p_z}{q_w^2 - q_x^2 - q_y^2 + q_z^2}. \tag{12}$$

Finally, the measurement Jacobian of the altimeter measurement model is

$$^{a}\mathbf{H}_k = \frac{\partial h_a(\mathbf{x})}{\partial \mathbf{x}}\bigg|_{\mathbf{x}=\hat{\mathbf{x}}_k^-} = \left[\frac{\partial^a z}{\partial \mathbf{p}_k} \ \mathbf{0}_{1\times 3} \ \frac{\partial^a z}{\partial \mathbf{q}_k} \right], \tag{13}$$

where

$$\frac{\partial^a z}{\partial \mathbf{p}} = \frac{1}{r}, \quad \frac{\partial^a z}{\partial \mathbf{q}} = \left[-\frac{2p_z q_w}{r} \ \frac{2p_z q_x}{r} \ \frac{2p_z q_y}{r} \ -\frac{2p_z q_z}{r} \right],$$

with $r = q_w^2 - q_x^2 - q_y^2 + q_z^2$.

4 Visual Algorithm for Pose Computation

The visual pose estimation is based on the principle that two consecutive images of a planar scene are related by a homography. The planar scene corresponds to the floor surface, which is assumed to be relatively flat, observed by the down-looking camera on the UAV. The spatial transformation of the camera, and therefore of the UAV, is encoded in this homography. Knowing the homography matrix that relates both images, the transformation parameters that describe the camera rotation and translation can be obtained.

In order to estimate the homography induced by the planar surface, a set of corresponding points on two consecutive images has to be obtained. This process is performed selecting a set of features in the first image and finding the corresponding set of features in the second one. Then, the image coordinates of each feature in both images conform the set of corresponding image points needed to calculate the homography.

The image features used in our approach are the so-called spectral features, a Fourier domain representation of an image patch. Selecting a set of patches in both images (the same number, with the same size and position), the displacement between them is proportional to the phase shift between the associated spectral features, and can be obtained using the Fourier shift theorem. This displacement, in addition to the feature center, determines the correspondence between features in both images: that is, the set of corresponding points needed to estimate the homography. An evaluation of spectral features for motion estimation can be seen in [3].

4.1 Plane-Induced Homography and Decomposition

Given a 3D scene point $\mathbf{P}$, and two coordinate systems, CS_A and CS_B, the coordinates of the point $\mathbf{P}$ on each one can be denoted by $\mathbf{X}_A$ and $\mathbf{X}_B$ respectively. If $\mathbf{R}_A^B$ is the rotation matrix that changes the representation of a point in CS_A to CS_B, and $\mathbf{T}_B$ is the translation vector of the origin of CS_A w.r.t CS_B, then the representations of the point $\mathbf{P}$ relate to each other as

$$\mathbf{X}_B = \mathbf{R}_A^B \mathbf{X}_A + \mathbf{T}_B . \tag{14}$$

We suppose now that the point $\mathbf{P}$ belongs to a plane π, denoted in the coordinate system CS_A by its normal $\mathbf{n}_A$ and its distance to the coordinate origin d_A. Therefore, the following plane equation holds

$$(\mathbf{n}_A)^T \mathbf{X}_A = d_A \qquad \Rightarrow \qquad \frac{(\mathbf{n}_A)^T \mathbf{X}_A}{d_A} = 1 \ . \tag{15}$$

Replacing (15) into (14) we have

$$\mathbf{X}_B = \left(\mathbf{R}_A^B + \frac{\mathbf{T}_B}{d_A}(\mathbf{n}_A)^T \right) \mathbf{X}_A = \mathbf{H}_A^B \mathbf{X}_A \ , \tag{16}$$

with

$$\mathbf{H}_A^B = \left(\mathbf{R}_A^B + \frac{\mathbf{T}_B}{d_A}(\mathbf{n}_A)^T \right) \ . \tag{17}$$

The matrix $\mathbf{H}_A^B$ is a plane-induced homography, in this case induced by the plane π. As can be seen, this matrix encodes the transformation parameters that relate both coordinate systems ($\mathbf{R}_A^B$ and $\mathbf{T}_B$), and the structure parameters of the environment ($\mathbf{n}_A$ and d_A).

Considering now a moving camera associated to the coordinate system CS_A at time t_A and to CS_B at time t_B, according to the central projection model the relations between the 3D points and their projections on the camera normalized plane are given by

$$\lambda_A \mathbf{x}_A = \mathbf{X}_A, \quad \lambda_B \mathbf{x}_B = \mathbf{X}_B, \tag{18}$$

where $\lambda_A, \lambda_B > 0$. Using (18) in (16) we have

$$\lambda_B \mathbf{x}_B = \mathbf{H}_A^B \lambda_A \mathbf{x}_A \qquad \Rightarrow \qquad \mathbf{x}_B = \lambda \mathbf{H}_A^B \mathbf{x}_A \ , \tag{19}$$

with $\lambda = \frac{\lambda_A}{\lambda_B}$. Given that both vectors $\mathbf{x}_B$ and $\lambda \mathbf{H}_A^B \mathbf{x}_A$ have the same direction

$$\mathbf{x}_B \times \lambda \mathbf{H}_A^B \mathbf{x}_A = \lfloor \mathbf{x}_{B \times} \rfloor \mathbf{H}_A^B \mathbf{x}_A = 0 \ , \tag{20}$$

with $\lfloor \mathbf{x}_{B \times} \rfloor$ the skew-symmetric matrix associated to $\mathbf{x}_B$. Equation (20) is known as the planar epipolar restriction, and holds for all 3D points belonging to the plane π. Assuming that the camera is pointing to the ground (downward-looking camera) and that the scene structure is approximately a planar surface, all the 3D points captured by the camera will fulfill this restriction.

The homography $\mathbf{H}_A^B$ represents the transformation of the camera coordinate systems between instant t_A and t_B, hence, it contains the information of the camera rotation and translation between these two instants. This homography can be estimated knowing at least four corresponding points of two images. In our case the correspondence between these points is calculated in the spectral domain, by means of the spectral features.

Following [9], a homography matrix $\mathbf{H}$ can be decomposed in four possible solutions, that is

$$\begin{aligned} \left\{\mathbf{R}_1, \mathbf{n}_1, \tfrac{\mathbf{T}_1}{d_1}\right\}, & \quad \left\{\mathbf{R}_1, -\mathbf{n}_1, \tfrac{-\mathbf{T}_1}{d_1}\right\}, \\ \left\{\mathbf{R}_2, \mathbf{n}_2, \tfrac{\mathbf{T}_2}{d_2}\right\}, & \quad \left\{\mathbf{R}_2, -\mathbf{n}_2, \tfrac{-\mathbf{T}_2}{d_2}\right\}. \end{aligned} \tag{21}$$

Then, in order to ensure that the plane inducing the homography $\mathbf{H}$ appears in front of the camera, each normal vector $\mathbf{n}_i$ must fulfill $n_z < 0$, and therefore only two solutions remain. These two solutions are both physically possible, but given that most of the time the camera on the UAV is facing-down, we choose the solution with the normal vector $\mathbf{n}$ closer to $[0, 0, -1]^T$ in terms of the norm L_2. A detailed description of the homography decomposition is presented in [1].

4.2   Spectral Features Correspondence

The so-called spectral feature refers to the Fourier domain representation of an image patch of $2^n \times 2^n$, where n is set accordingly to the allowed image displacement. The power of 2 of this patch size is selected based on the efficiency of the Fast Fourier Transform (FFT) algorithm. The number and position of spectral features in the image are set beforehand. Even though a minimum of four points is needed to estimate the homography, a higher number of features is used to increase the accuracy, and the RANSAC algorithm is used for outliers elimination.

Consider two consecutive frames, where spectral features on each image were computed. To determine the correspondence between features is equivalent to determine the displacement between them. This displacement can be obtained using the spectral information by means of the Phase Correlation Method (PCM). This method is based on the Fourier shift theorem, which states that the Fourier transforms of two identical but displaced images differ only in a phase shift.

Given two images i_A and i_B differing only in a displacement (u, v), such as $i_A(x, y) = i_B(x - u, y - v)$, their Fourier transforms are related by

$$I_A(\omega_x, \omega_y) = e^{-j(u\omega_x + v\omega_y)} I_B(\omega_x, \omega_y), \tag{22}$$

where I_A and I_B are the Fourier transforms of images i_A and i_B, respectively; u and v are the displacements for each axis. From (22), the amplitudes of both transformations are the same and only differ in phase which is directly related to the image displacement (u, v). Therefore, this displacement can be obtained using the cross-power spectrum (CPS) of the given transformations I_A and I_B. The CPS of two complex functions is defined as

$$\mathcal{C}(F, G) = \frac{F(\omega_x, \omega_y) G^*(\omega_x, \omega_y)}{|F(\omega_x, \omega_y)||G^*(\omega_x, \omega_y)|}, \tag{23}$$

where G^* is the complex conjugate of G. Using (22) in (23) over the transformed images I_A and I_B, gives

$$\frac{I_A I_B^*}{|I_A||I_B^*|} = e^{-j(u\omega_x + v\omega_y)} \ . \tag{24}$$

The inverse Fourier transform of (24) is an impulse located exactly in (u, v), which represents the displacement between the two images

$$\mathcal{F}^{-1}[e^{-j(u\omega_x + v\omega_y)}] = \delta(x - u, y - v) \ . \tag{25}$$

Using the discrete Fast Fourier Transform (FFT) algorithm instead of the continuous version, the result will be a pulse signal centered at (u, v) [20].

5   Results

5.1   Synthetic Dataset

A synthetic dataset is obtained from the dynamic simulation of a quadcopter based on the model described in [7]. The simulated quadcopter performs a given flight from which ground truth variables are obtained, these include position, linear velocity and orientation. The simulated flight is also used to obtain the ground truth inertial measurements, i.e. linear acceleration and angular rate in the vehicle frame, which are then affected by additive noise. Additionally, a large image represented a flat floor is cropped in order to obtain the camera image sequence, where the camera pose is also based on ground truth information. The ground truth pose of the UAV is also used to evaluate the performance of the proposed estimation filter. Figure 4 shows the data obtained from the simulation. Specially, Fig. 4a depicts the path followed by the quadcopter, whilst Fig. 4b presents the ground truth inertial sensor measurement in blue, and noisy measurement in gray.

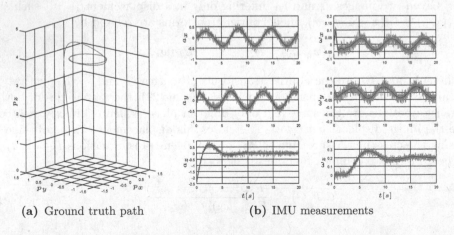

(a) Ground truth path   (b) IMU measurements

Fig. 4. Ground truth position and inertial sensor measurements

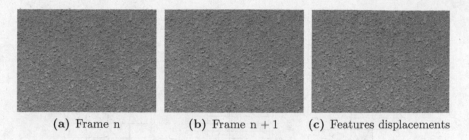

(a) Frame n   (b) Frame n + 1   (c) Features displacements

Fig. 5. Consecutive cropped images and detected feature displacements

The noise parameters of inertial sensors are the same of a real sensor, particularly the MicroStrain model 3DM-GX1, which are obtained from the vendor specifications. The continuous-time variance of the accelerometers is $\sigma_a = 0.4mg/\sqrt{Hz}$ and for the gyroscopes $\sigma_\omega = 3.5°/\sqrt{hour}$, which are converted to discrete time, dividing them by the square root of the sampling interval $\sqrt{\Delta t}$. As usually done, the accelerometer noise is affected by a factor of 10, to reflect the noise increase when the sensor is on-board a quadcopter. The simulated camera is of 640×480 with a pixel size of $5.6\mu m$. The image processing algorithm is set to use 42 patches of 128×128 pixels, equally distributed in the image, and with this setup the visual algorithms process 20 frames per second. Figure 5 shows some images obtained from the simulated camera, and processed by the visual algorithm. Figures 5a and b show two consecutive cropped images, whereas Fig. 5c shows the detected image feature displacements.

As can be seen in Fig. 4a, in this dataset the quadcopter flights from a high of 1.5 m to 4.0 m, and describes a circular path in the $x - y$ plane. The initial high is not zero in order to obtain an appropriate image from the simulated camera.

5.2 Pose Estimation

The obtained results from the estimation filter using the described dataset represented in Figs. 4 and 5, are shown in Figs. 6, 7 and 8. Figure 6 shows the estimated position, linear velocity and orientation expressed in Euler angles (ϕ, θ, ψ), whereas in Fig. 7 this orientation is represented as a unit quaternion. In these figures, the thick blue line is the ground-truth information obtained from the simulated dataset, the black line corresponds to the integration given by the inertial sensor model, and the red line is the estimation given by the filter. The integrated result is obtained from the filter prediction stage without any correction, whereas the final estimation is obtained with the correction stages, i.e. fusing all sensor measurements together. The orientation result given in Euler angles of Fig. 6 is obtained converting the unit quaternion of Fig. 7, which is a component of the filter state vector. As can bee seen in Figs. 6 and 7, the estimation obtained from the fusion of all the sensors avoids a typical unbounded integration error when using only inertial sensors.

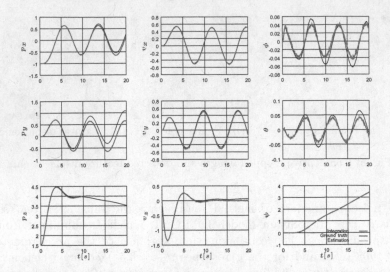

Fig. 6. Estimated position, linear velocity and orientation expressed in Euler angles

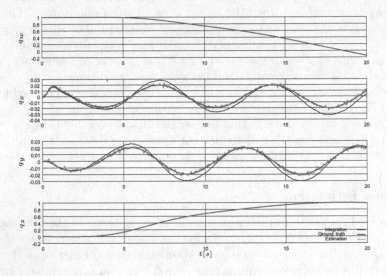

Fig. 7. Estimated orientation expressed in unit quaternion

Figure 8 shows the filter estimation error, together with the $\pm 3\sigma$ error bound given by the diagonal elements of the covariance matrix. In this case, the estimation error in orientation is expressed in Euler angles, given that the filter covariance matrix is based on this minimal representation, as previously stated. This figure shows that the initial uncertainties reach their final values in a few time steps and they remain bounded for the next time steps.

Figure 9 shows inertial sensor measurements corrupted by a constant bias. The bias for each axis of the accelerometer is $b_a = 0.5 \, m/s^2$, and for each axis of

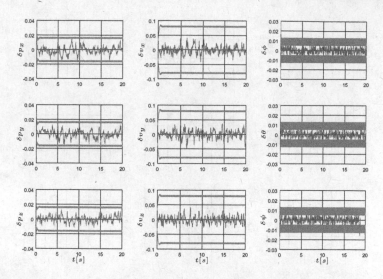

Fig. 8. Estimation error and $\pm 3\sigma$ uncertainty in position, linear velocity and Euler angles

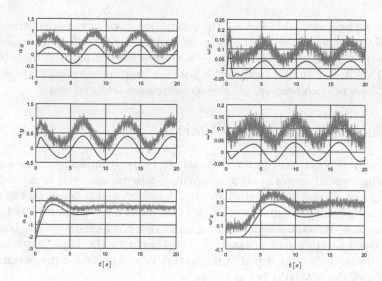

Fig. 9. IMU measurements corrupted with constant bias

the gyroscope is $b_\omega = 0.1\,rad/s$. As previously mentioned, the biases in the inertial sensors can be estimated before every flight by means of averaging accelerometer and gyroscope reading. Fig. 10 shows the estimation error for the cases in which the biases are partially and completely removed. The red line corresponds to a remaining of 25 % of the bias, whereas the blue line is for a remaining of 50 %. The gray line is the estimation error without any bias, as it was shown in Fig. 8.

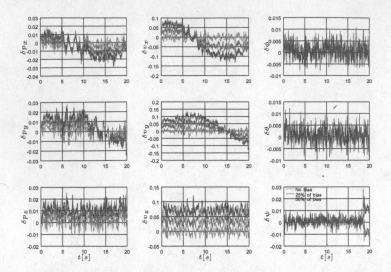

Fig. 10. Estimation error for IMU measurement corrupted constant with bias

As it can be observed in Fig. 10, the estimation error in the orientation given by the Euler angles (three rightmost plots) are negligibly affected by the gyroscope bias, whereas the linear velocity and position are affected more significantly. This is mainly due to that the position and linear velocity are affected for the biases of both sensors, i.e. the accelerometer and gyroscope.

6   Conclusion and Future Work

In this work a novel schema for estimating the position and orientation of a UAV using inertial sensors and a monocular camera has been presented. The visual algorithm uses the so called spectral features, and is based on the plane-induced homography obtained when observing a flat floor. The presented results are based on a dynamic simulation of a quadcopter, which allows to obtain the ground truth position and orientation, together with the ideal inertial sensor measurements. This ground truth information is also useful for the performance evaluation of the proposed fusion algorithm.

As the results show, the three dimensional pose estimation has a precision that seems promising to be applied in UAV onboard algorithms for control purposes. Also, it was shown that a not precise bias correction, as high as 50 % of the real bias, does not affect pose estimation considerably, specially for short time flights.

As future work, the next step is to test the proposed fusion schema with a real UAV, in order to evaluate how the estimation is affected by real sensor noise and unmodeled sensor bias. Also, a new filter model can be formulated incorporating the sensor biases in the state vector in order to be estimated. This has the main disadvantage of a high dimensional state vector requiring a higher computational power to compute the filter equations. Finally, the proposed visual algorithm can be compared with other similar approaches, particularly those that does not use corner-like features.

References

1. Araguás, G., Paz, C., Paina, G.P., Canali, L.: Visual homography-based pose estimation of a quadrotor using spectral features. In: 2015 Latin America Congress on Computational Intelligence (LA-CCI), pp. 1–6, October 2015
2. Araguás, G., Paz, C., Gaydou, D., Perez Paina, G.: Quaternion-based orientation estimation fusing a camera and inertial sensors for a hovering UAV. J. Intell. Robot. Syst. **77**(1), 37–53 (2015). doi:10.1007/s10846-014-0092-z
3. Araguás, G., Paz, C., Perez Paina, G., Canali, L.: Visual homography-based pose estimation of a quadrotor using spectral features. In: Designing with Computational Intelligence. Studies in Computational Intelligence (in press)
4. Bloesch, M., Omari, S., Fankhauser, P., Sommer, H., Gehring, C., Hwangbo, J., Hoepflinger, M., Hutter, M., Siegwart, R.: Fusion of optical flow and inertial measurements for robust egomotion estimation. In: IEEE/RSJ International Conference on Intelligent Robots and Systems (IROS), pp. 3102–3107, September 2014
5. Camposeco, F., Pollefeys, M.: Using vanishing points to improve visual-inertial odometry. In: 2015 IEEE International Conference on Robotics and Automation (ICRA), pp. 5219–5225, May 2015
6. Chudoba, J., Kulich, M., Saska, M., Báča, T., Přeučil, L.: Exploration and mapping technique suited for visual-features based localization of MAVS. J. Intell. Robot. Syst. 1–19 (2016). http://dx.doi.org/10.1007/s10846-016-0358-8
7. Corke, P.I.: Robotics, Vision and Control: Fundamental Algorithms in MATLAB. Springer, Heidelberg (2011)
8. Gaydou, D., Suarez, G., Paz, C., Perez Paina, G., Araguás, G.: Robot volador no tripulado QA3. Diseño y construcción de un cuatrirrotor para experimentación. In: Proceedings of the VIII Jornadas Argentinas de Robótica (JAR) (2014)
9. Ma, Y., Soatto, S., Kosecka, J., Sastry, S.S.: An Invitation to 3-D Vision: From Images to Geometric Models. Springer, Heidelberg (2003)
10. Markley, F.L.: Attitude error representations for Kalman filtering. J. Guidance Control Dyn. **26**, 311–317 (2003)
11. Markley, F.L.: Multiplicative vs. additive filtering for spacecraft attitude determination. In: Dynamics and Control of Systems and Structures in Space (2004)
12. Mourikis, A., Roumeliotis, S.: A multi-state constraint Kalman filter for vision-aided inertial navigation. In: 2007 IEEE International Conference on Robotics and Automation, pp. 3565–3572, April 2007
13. Pucheta, M.A., Paz, C.J., Pereyra, M.E.: Representaciones cinemáticas de orientación y ecuaciones de estimación. In: XXI Congreso sobre Métodos Numéricos y sus Aplicaciones ENIEF, vol. XXXIII, pp. 2303–2324 (2014)
14. Roumeliotis, S., Burdick, J.: Stochastic cloning: a generalized framework for processing relative state measurements. In: Proceedings of the IEEE International Conference on Robotics and Automation, ICRA 2002, vol. 2, pp. 1788–1795 (2002)
15. Shen, S., Michael, N., Kumar, V.: Tightly-coupled monocular visual-inertial fusion for autonomous flight of rotorcraft MAVS. In: 2015 IEEE International Conference on Robotics and Automation (ICRA), pp. 5303–5310, May 2015

16. Shen, S., Mulgaonkar, Y., Michael, N., Kumar, V.: Multi-sensor fusion for robust autonomous flight in indoor and outdoor environments with a rotorcraft MAV. In: 2014 IEEE International Conference on Robotics and Automation (ICRA), pp. 4974–4981, May 2014
17. Simon, D.: Optimal State Estimation: Kalman, H Infinity, and Nonlinear Approaches. Wiley-Interscience, Hoboken (2006)
18. Tanskanen, P., Naegeli, T., Pollefeys, M., Hilliges, O.: Semi-direct EKF-based monocular visual-inertial odometry. In: 2015 IEEE/RSJ International Conference on Intelligent Robots and Systems (IROS 2015) (2015)
19. Trawny, N., Roumeliotis, S.I.: Indirect Kalman filter for 3D attitude estimation. Technical report 2005–002, University of Minnesota, Department of Computer Science and Engineering, March 2005
20. Zitová, B., Flusser, J.: Image registration methods: a survey. Image Vis. Comput. **21**(11), 977–1000 (2003)

Multi-agent Poli-RRT*

Optimal Constrained RRT-based Planning for Multiple Vehicles with Feedback Linearisable Dynamics

Matteo Ragaglia, Maria Prandini, and Luca Bascetta[✉]

Politecnico di Milano - Piazza Leonardo da Vinci, 32 - 20133 Milan, Italy
{matteo.ragaglia,maria.prandini,luca.bascetta}@polimi.it

Abstract. Planning a trajectory that is optimal according to some performance criterion, collision-free, and feasible with respect to dynamic and actuation constraints is a key functionality of an autonomous vehicle. Poli-RRT* is a sample-based planning algorithm that serves this purpose for a single vehicle with feedback linearisable dynamics. This paper extends Poli-RRT* to a multi-agent cooperative setting where multiple vehicles share the same environment and need to avoid each other besides some static obstacles.

Keywords: Planning · Optimal control · Feasability · Safety · Autonomous vehicles · Multi-agent systems

1 Introduction

In the past few years the interest towards autonomous unmanned vehicles is considerably increased, mainly because they allow to perform critical tasks without endangering the life of human pilots/drivers. Their applications range from scientific exploration to provision of commercial services, from search and rescue to military operations.

Among the functionalities that make a vehicle autonomous, planning plays a crucial role. As a matter of fact, the planner not only has the responsibility to deliver a trajectory that takes the vehicle to the desired goal but it also needs to guarantee both "feasibility" (with respect to possibly nonlinear dynamics, kinodynamic and actuation constraints) and "safety" (in terms of avoiding obstacles and dangerous kinematic configurations, i.e., vehicle roll-over) of the computed trajectory. Moreover, in most practical applications, it is typically required to find trajectories that are optimal according to some cost metric.

Unfortunately, given a complex system characterized by nonlinear dynamics, moving from a standard planning problem to an optimal planning problem, or even to a constrained and optimal one, computational intractability comes at no surprise. As a consequence, sample-based planning algorithms have emerged as an appealing alternative to search-based planning techniques [1,2] and model predictive control approaches [3].

© Springer International Publishing AG 2016
J. Hodicky (Ed.): MESAS 2016, LNCS 9991, pp. 261–270, 2016.
DOI: 10.1007/978-3-319-47605-6_21

1.1 · State of the Art

The success that sample-based planners like Rapidly-exploring Random Trees (RRT) [4] have achieved in the last fifteen years is due to a rather simple yet effective idea: a set of points is sampled from the free-space and connected in order to build a tree (roadmap) of feasible trajectories, that are then used to determine the solution to the planning problem. Interestingly, probabilistic completeness has been shown for this approach in [5].

RRT-based planning algorithms [4] have been originally introduced to solve the trajectory planning problem for holonomic robots. Then, they have been extended to optimal and constrained trajectory planning. Several solutions have been proposed in the latest few years, including optimal/non-linear RRTs [6,7], Rapidly-exploring Random Graphs (RRG) and RRT* [8–13]. A generalization of the RRT* planning approach to arbitrary kino-dynamic systems is presented in [14], where the shooting method [15] is used to connect pairs of nodes, thus obtaining feasible yet inherently suboptimal trajectories.

In [16] the authors present an algorithm, named "Kinodynamic RRT*", that guarantees asymptotic optimality for systems characterised by linear differential constraints. The same approach can be applied to non-linear dynamics as well, by using their first-order Taylor approximations. Furthermore, in [17] the "LQR-RRT*" algorithm is proposed to solve planning problems with complex or under-actuated dynamics, by locally linearising the system and applying linear quadratic regulation (LQR), while in [18] a new method for applying RRT* to kino-dynamic motion planning problems is introduced, using a finite-horizon quadratic criterion to assess the cost and extend the tree.

Finally, [19] introduces the "Poli-RRT*" algorithm, which is the first RRT-based planner that takes into account vehicle constraints without either representing the vehicle dynamics with an approximate linearised model or using the shooting method. In fact, the proposed methodology relies on an exact linearisation of the model, that allows to efficiently recast the optimal control problem used to extend the tree into a quadratic program, without any model simplification.

The main contribution of this work to the field of planning for autonomous vehicles consists in extending Poli-RRT* to a multi-agent framework.

1.2 Paper Structure

The remainder of this paper is organized as follows. Section 2 briefly describes the original Poli-RRT* algorithm, while the extension to multi-agent systems is detailed in Sect. 3. Section 4 presents simulation results. Finally, some concluding remarks are drawn in Sect. 5.

2   Background on Poli-RRT* for a Single Agent

The Poli-RRT* algorithm computes a solution to the optimal constrained planning problem for a vehicle with feedback linearisable dynamics

$$\dot{x} = f(x, u)$$

subject to constraints on the actuation input $u \in \Omega$, while accounting also for collision avoidance in presence of static obstacles.

Given the initial state x_{start} and the set of goal states X_{goal} within the obstacle-free set X_{free}, Poli-RRT* builds a tree $T = (X_T, E_T)$, where $X_T \subset X_{free}$ are the nodes, and E_T are the edges that correspond to collision-free trajectories connecting two nodes in X_T. Among all sequences of m nodes $x_0, x_1, x_2, \ldots, x_m$, satisfying

$$x_i \in X_T, \ i = 0, 1, \ldots, m,$$
$$x_0 = x_{start}$$
$$x_m \in X_{goal}$$
$$e_i = (x_i, x_{i+1}) \in E_T, \ i = 0, 2, \ldots, m-1$$

Poli-RRT* chooses the one with minimal overall cost:

$$C(\rightarrow x_m) = \sum_{i=0}^{m-1} C(e_i) \tag{1}$$

with the cost per edge satisfying $C(e) \geq 0$ for any edge e.

2.1   Edge Calculation Procedure

Given two nodes x and x', the edge $e = (x, x')$ represents the optimal trajectory that connects x to x' while minimising the cost function $C(e)$ and satisfying actuation constraints. The edge calculation procedure relies on a two-step approach that combines optimal control and a receding horizon strategy.

By applying feedback linearisation we can express the original system together with the input constraints in the new state coordinates s and in the new input v as follows:

$$\dot{s} = As + Bv$$
$$h\left(g\left(s\right), v\right) \in \Omega$$

where

$$x = g\left(s\right)$$
$$u = h\left(x, v\right)$$

According to the approach proposed in [16], it is possible to compute a minimum-time optimal trajectory connecting two states s_i and s_{i+1} with respect to the cost metric

$$J_\tau(v) = \int_0^\tau \left(1 + v(t)^T R v(t)\right) dt$$

$R > 0$ being an input weight matrix, subject to

$$s\left(0\right) = s_i$$
$$s\left(\tau\right) = s_{i+1}$$

More in details, for each given final time $\tau > 0$, the optimal control input v and the corresponding cost $J_\tau^\star$ is computed analytically and the minimum time $\tau^\star$ is determined as

$$\tau^\star = \operatorname*{argmin}_{\tau > 0} \ J_\tau^\star$$

Given $\tau^\star$, the minimum-time optimal input and state variables $v^\star(t)$ and $s^\star(t)$, $t \in [0, \tau^\star]$, are given by:

$$v^\star(t) = R^{-1}B^T \exp\left(A^T\left(\tau^\star - t\right)\right) d^\star$$

$$s^\star(t) = [I_n \ 0_n] \exp\left(\begin{bmatrix} A & BR^{-1}B^T \\ 0_n & -A^T \end{bmatrix} (t - \tau^\star)\right) \begin{bmatrix} s_{i+1} \\ d^\star \end{bmatrix}.$$

where n is the dimension of the state s, I_n is the $n \times n$ identity matrix, 0_n is the $n \times n$ zero matrix and we set

$$d^\star = G(\tau^\star)^{-1} \left(s_{i+1} - e^{A\tau^\star} s_i\right)$$

with $G(\tau)$ equal to the weighted controllability Gramian of the system.

Let

$$x^\star(t) = g\left(s^\star(t)\right), \quad t \in [0, \tau^\star]$$

$$u^\star(t) = h\left(x^\star(t), v^\star(t)\right), \quad t \in [0, \tau^\star]$$

be the optimal trajectory in the original state and input variables. If the input constraints are satisfied by $u^\star(t)$, for all $t \in [0, \tau^\star]$, then, the edge e is set equal to

$$e = (x^\star(0), x^\star(\tau^\star))$$

with the understanding that the corresponding trajectory is given by $u^\star(t)$ and $x^\star(t)$, with an associated cost

$$C(e_i) = J_{\tau^\star}(u^\star)$$

If that is not the case, a receding horizon strategy is put in place so as to enforce the constraints, while keeping the resulting trajectory close to the optimal unconstrained one (see [19] for the details).

2.2 Poli-RRT* Algorithm

The steps of the Poli-RRT* algorithm are given by:

1. **Tree initialisation**: An empty tree is initialised, setting

$$X_T = \{x_{start}\}$$

$$E_T = \emptyset$$

2. **Random sampling**: A state configuration x_{rand} is randomly sampled within X_{free} according to a uniform distribution;

3. **Neighbour radius computation**: Set

$$r = \underset{x \in X_{reach}}{\text{argmax}} \left(\max \left\{ C(e_1), C(e_2) \right\} \right)$$

where $e_1 = (x_{rand}, x)$, $e_2 = (x, x_{rand})$ and

$$X_{reach} = \left\{ x \in X_T \mid ||x_{rand} - x||_2 \leq \gamma_{ball} \right\}$$

γ_{ball} being computed according to [10];

4. **Minimum-cost trajectory selection**: In order to connect x_{rand} to the tree, a minimum-cost trajectory is determined as $e_{min} = (x_{min}, x_{rand})$ where

$$x_{min} = \underset{x \in \{x \in X_T \mid C(e) \leq r \wedge CFree(e)\}}{\text{argmin}} (C(\to x) + C(e))$$

where r is the neighbour radius, $CFree(e)$ is a function that returns true when e is a collision-free trajectory, false otherwise, and $C(\to x)$ represents the cost of the current-best trajectory going from x_{start} to x. Then

$$X_T = X_T \cup \{x_{rand}\}$$
$$E_T = E_T \cup \{e_{min}\}$$

5. **Tree rewiring**: Whenever a node x_{rand} is added to the tree, in order to ensure trajectory optimality, it is necessary to check the existence of minimum-cost trajectories starting from x_{start}, passing through x_{rand} and reaching any other node within the neighbour radius r of x_{rand}. In other words, for every node $x \in X_T$, if $e = (x_{rand}, x)$ satisfies

$$CFree(e) = true, \quad C(e) \leq r, \quad C(\to x_{rand}) + C(e) < C(\to x)$$

the tree is rewired by setting

$$E_T = \{E_T \setminus \{e_{prev}\}\} \cup \{e\}$$

where e_{prev} is the edge that was previously connecting x to the tree and that is replaced by e;

6. **Termination**: The algorithm iterates steps (2), (3), (4) and (5) until $|X_T| = N$, where N is a given maximum cardinality for X_T;

7. **Optimal trajectory**: If the goal area has been reached, the minimum cost-to-go node inside X_{goal} is selected and the trajectory connecting x_{start} with x_{goal} is returned along with the entire tree T:

$$X_{goal} \cap X_T \neq \emptyset \implies x_{goal} = \underset{x \in (X_{goal} \cap X_T)}{\text{argmin}} C(\to x).$$

3   Extension to Multi-agent Systems

The main contribution of this work is the extension of the Poli-RRT* algorithm to a multi-agent setting, by adopting a priority-based approach.

All the K agents are ranked according to a priority criterion and the algorithm plans trajectories in sequence, starting from the highest-priority agent A_1 and moving to the lowest-priority one A_K, each time considering the trajectories that have already been designed as obstacles to avoid.

A pseudo-code version of the procedure is given in Algorithm 1, whose parameters are:

- N, the maximum tree cardinality;
- $AgentsSet$, the set of agents;
- $ObstaclesSet$, the set of obstacles (that initially contains only the static ones);
- $safeDist$, the minimum safe distance that the algorithm must always ensure between each couple of agents.

Clearly, once the i-th iteration of the algorithm is completed, the list of obstacles must be updated in order to keep track of the newly designed trajectory $Traj_i$ for agent i. At each iteration of the multi-agent algorithm, Poli-RRT* is run for a specific agent A_i using an updated list of obstacles that account for previously designed trajectories. Within Poli-RRT* every time a new edge is instantiated, its initial and final time instants t_0 and t_f are set, and the edge is checked against the already planned trajectories within the time window $[t_0, t_f]$. If the edge is able to ensure that the distance from the agents whose trajectories have been already set is greater than the minimum safe distance, the edge is collision-free and is added to the tree, otherwise it is discarded.

Algorithm 1. Multi-agent Poli-RRT*

1: $ObstaclesSet \leftarrow \{O_1, O_2, \ldots, O_M\}$
2: $AgentsSet \leftarrow \{A_1, A_2, \ldots, A_K\}$
3: **procedure** MULTIAGENTPOLIRRT*($N, AgentsSet, ObstaclesSet, safeDist$)
4:     $TrajList \leftarrow \emptyset$
5:     **for** $i = 1$ to K **do**
6:         $Traj_i \leftarrow PoliRRT^* (A_i, ObstaclesSet, safeDist)$
7:         $TrajList \leftarrow TrajList \cup Traj_i$
8:         $ObstaclesSet \leftarrow ObstaclesSet \cup Traj_i$
9:     **end for**
10: **return** $TrajList$
11: **end procedure**

---

4   Simulation Results

In this section an example is shown where the multi-agent version of Poli-RRT* is applied to a three-agent system.

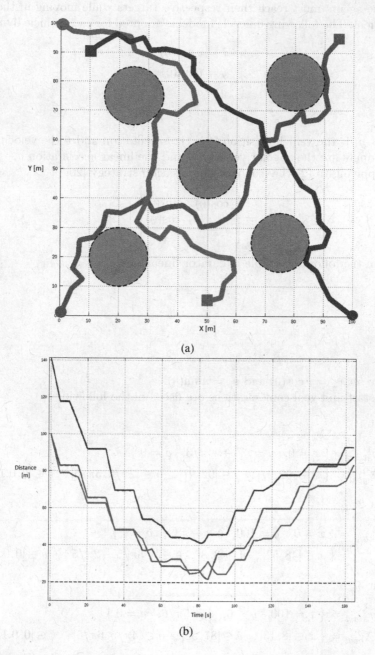

(a)

(b)

Fig. 1. A multi-agent Poli-RRT* run. 1(a) trajectories for agent 1 (blue), 2 (red), and 3 (green), circular and square markers represent starting and goal positions, respectively. 1(b): Pairwise agent distance (1–2 blue, 2–3 red, 1–3 green) and minimum safety distance (black dashed). (Color figure online)

The three agents must reach their respective targets while moving in the same environment. The following unicycle model is adopted for each vehicle dynamics:

$$\dot{x} = v\cos(\theta)$$
$$\dot{y} = v\sin(\theta)$$
$$\dot{\theta} = \omega$$
$$\dot{v} = a \qquad (2)$$

where (x, y) is the vehicle position, θ is the orientation and v the velocity. The control inputs are the angolar velocity ω and the linear acceleration a.

By applying to (2) the feedback linearisation strategy [20]

$$\begin{bmatrix} a \\ \omega \end{bmatrix} = \begin{bmatrix} \cos(\theta) & \sin(\theta) \\ -\dfrac{\sin(\theta)}{v} & \dfrac{\cos(\theta)}{v} \end{bmatrix} \begin{bmatrix} u_1 \\ u_2 \end{bmatrix},$$

we obtain the following double integrator linear model

$$\dot{x} = v_x$$
$$\dot{y} = v_y$$
$$\dot{v}_x = u_1$$
$$\dot{v}_y = u_2$$

where we set $v_x = v\cos(\theta)$ and $v_y = v\sin(\theta)$.

The start and goal configurations are listed in the following:

– Agent 1:

$$x^1_{start} = \{\, x = 0,\ y = 0,\ \theta = \pi/3,\ v = 0\,\}$$
$$X^1_{goal} = \{\, x \in [92, 97],\ y \in [92, 97],\ \theta \in [2\pi/5, 3\pi/5],\ v \in [0, 0.1]\,\}$$

– Agent 2:

$$x^2_{start} = \{\, x = 0,\ y = 100,\ \theta = -\pi/9,\ v = 0\,\}$$
$$X^2_{goal} = \{\, x \in [48, 52],\ y \in [3, 8],\ \theta \in [-3\pi/5, -2\pi/5],\ v \in [0, 0.1]\,\}$$

– Agent 3:

$$x^3_{start} = \{\, x = 100,\ y = 0,\ \theta = 5\pi/6,\ v = 0\,\}$$
$$X^3_{goal} = \{\, x \in [8, 13],\ y \in [87, 92],\ \theta \in [4\pi/5, 6\pi/5],\ v \in [0, 0.1]\,\}$$

where linear positions are expressed in m, angles in rad, and linear velocities in m/s.

State variables are subject to the following bounds

$$x \in [0, 100] \qquad y \in [0, 100] \qquad \theta \in [-\pi, +\pi] \qquad v \in [0, 1]$$

whereas actuation constraints on linear acceleration and angular velocity are given by

$$a \in A = [-0.50, +0.50] \qquad \omega \in \Omega = [-0.50, +0.50]$$

The control variables are weighted in the optimal control problem by matrix $R = 10I_2$.

Fig. 1(a) shows the simulation results obtained when the maximum tree cardinality is set equal to 200. Note that the algorithm is able to plan the required trajectories. Moreover, the minimum safety distance between each couple of agents is guaranteed (Fig. 1(b)).

5   Conclusions

This paper extends the Poli-RRT* algorithm to the case of multi-agent systems. Agents are sorted according to a given hierarchy and the Poli-RRT* algorithm is executed for each agent following the priority order. The algorithm is validated in a simulated environment. The resulting solution is sub-optimal from the perspective of the multi-agent system, as it depends on the agents ordering. In turn, single agent trajectory planning can be exploited to make the problem tractable.

References

1. Pivtoraiko, M., Knepper, R., Kelly, A.: Differentially constrained mobile robot motion planning in state lattices. J. Field Robot. **26**, 308–333 (2009)
2. Likhachev, M., Ferguson, D.: Planning long dynamically feasible maneuvers for autonomous vehicles. Int. J. Robot. Res. **28**, 933–945 (2009)
3. Tahirovic, A., Magnani, G.: General framework for mobile robot navigation using passivity-based MPC. IEEE Trans. Autom. Control **56**, 184–190 (2011)
4. LaValle, S.M., Kuffner, J.J.: Randomized kinodynamic planning. Int. J. Robot. Res. **20**, 378–400 (2001)
5. Barraquand, J., Kavraki, L., Latombe, J., Motwani, R., Li, T., Raghavan, P.: A random sampling scheme for path planning. Int. J. Robot. Res. **16**, 759–774 (1997)
6. Branicky, M., Curtiss, M., Levine, J., Morgan, S.: RRTs for nonlinear, discrete, and hybrid planning and control. In: IEEE Conference on Decision and Control (CDC), vol. 1, pp. 657–663 (2003)
7. Branicky, M., Curtiss, M., Levine, J., Morgan, S.: Sampling-based planning, control and verification of hybrid systems. IEEE Proc. Control Theory Appl. **153**, 575–590 (2006)
8. Karaman, S., Frazzoli, E.: Optimal kinodynamic motion planning using incremental sampling-based methods. In: IEEE Conference on Decision and Control (CDC), Atlanta, GA (2010)
9. Karaman, S., Frazzoli, E.: Incremental sampling-based algorithms for optimal motion planning. In: Robotics: Science and Systems (RSS), Zaragoza, Spain (2010)
10. Karaman, S., Walter, M., Perez, A., Frazzoli, E., Teller, S.: Real-time motion planning using the RRT*. In: IEEE International Conference on Robotics and Automation (ICRA) (2011)

11. Karaman, S., Frazzoli, E.: Sampling-based algorithms for optimal motion planning. Int. J. Robot. Res. **30**, 846–894 (2011)
12. Karaman, S., Frazzoli, E.: Sampling-based optimal motion planning with deterministic μ-calculus specifications. In: American Control Conference (ACC) (2012)
13. Perez, A., Karaman, S., Walter, M., Shkolnik, A., Frazzoli, E., Teller, S.: Asymptotically-optimal path planning for manipulation using incremental sampling-based algorithms. In: IEEE/RSJ International Conference on Intelligent Robots and Systems (IROS) (2011)
14. hwan Jeon, J., Karaman, S., Frazzoli, E.: Anytime computation of time-optimal off-road vehicle maneuvers using the RRT*. In: IEEE Conference on Decision and Control and European Control Conference (CDC-ECC), pp. 3276–3282 (2011)
15. Press, W., Teukolsky, S., Vetterling, W., Flannery, B.: Numerical Recipes: The Art of Scientific Computing. Cambridge University Press, Cambridge (2007)
16. Webb, D., van den Berg, J.: Kinodynamic RRT*: asymptotically optimal motion planning for robots with linear dynamics. In: IEEE Intenrational Conference on Robotics and Automation (ICRA), pp. 5054–5061 (2013)
17. Perez, A., Platt, R., Konidaris, G., Kaelbling, L., Lozano-Perez, T.: LQR-RRT*: optimal sampling-based motion planning with automatically derived extension heuristics. In: IEEE International Conference on Robotics and Automation (ICRA), pp. 2537–2542 (2012)
18. Goretkin, G., Perez, A., Platt, R., Konidaris, G.: Optimal sampling-based planning for linear-quadratic kinodynamic systems. In: IEEE International Conference on Robotics and Automation (ICRA) (2013)
19. Ragaglia, M., Prandini, M., Bascetta, L.: Poli-RRT*: optimal RRT-based planning for constrained and feedback linearisable vehicle dynamics. In: European Control Conference (ECC) (2015)
20. Stipanovic, D., Inalhan, G., Teo, R., Tomlin, C.: Decentralized overlapping control of a formation of unmanned aerial vehicles. Automatica **40**, 1285–1296 (2004)

STAM: A Framework for Spatio-Temporal Affordance Maps

Francesco Riccio[1]([⊠]), Roberto Capobianco[1], Marc Hanheide[2],
and Daniele Nardi[1]

[1] Department of Computer, Control, and Management Engineering,
Sapienza University of Rome, via Ariosto 25, Rome 00185, Italy
{riccio,capobianco,nardi}@dis.uniroma1.it
[2] Lincoln Centre for Autonomous Systems, School of Computer Science,
University of Lincoln, Brayford Pool, Lincolnshire, Lincoln LN6 7TS, UK
mhanheide@lincoln.ac.uk

Abstract. Affordances have been introduced in literature as action opportunities that objects offer, and used in robotics to semantically represent their interconnection. However, when considering an environment instead of an object, the problem becomes more complex due to the dynamism of its state. To tackle this issue, we introduce the concept of Spatio-Temporal Affordances (STA) and Spatio-Temporal Affordance Map (STAM). Using this formalism, we encode action semantics related to the environment to improve task execution capabilities of an autonomous robot. We experimentally validate our approach to support the execution of robot tasks by showing that affordances encode accurate semantics of the environment.

Keywords: Spatial knowledge · Affordances · Semantic agents

1 Introduction

The concept of affordances has been originally introduced by Gibson [4] as action opportunities that objects offer. This idea has been recently used in robotics to learn [6], represent [11] and exploit [5] object related actions in human-populated environments. However, when considering the affordances of an environment, methods proposed in literature cannot be directly applied. Differently from normal objects, the state of the environment is highly dynamic and contains the state of the robot and other dynamic entities, such as humans. This inevitably leads to a more complex problem that requires specific representation and learning approaches.

To tackle this problem, the concept of spatial affordance has been adopted in some works with the aim of supporting navigation [3] or improving the performance of a tracking system. In this work, we use this concept to encode action semantics related to the environment to improve task execution capabilities of an autonomous robot. In particular, we formalize a Spatio-Temporal Affordance

© Springer International Publishing AG 2016
J. Hodicky (Ed.): MESAS 2016, LNCS 9991, pp. 271–280, 2016.
DOI: 10.1007/978-3-319-47605-6_22

Map (STAM) as a representation that contains high-level semantic properties of an environment, directly grounded on the operational scenario. This grounding is obtained through the use of a function (the affordance function), that generates areas of the environment that afford an action, given a particular state or an equivalent observation of the world. More in detail, STAM contains generic descriptors that (if needed) provide prior information about the actions. For example, when performing a following task, we might not want the relative distance of a robot, with respect to the followed individual, to be greater than a given threshold. These descriptors are then specialized according to the environment where the robot is operating – i.e., the current state of the external world, its entities, including objects and people, and their position over time.

We evaluate an autonomous STAM agent over the execution of a following task that, as shown in Fig. 1, can be beneficial in several applications. In this example, we use expert demonstrations to teach a robot the spatial relation that holds between the environment and the task "to follow". While learning

Fig. 1. Following is a key skill in several robotic applications: swarm airdrones, robot teaming, exploration and service tasks. All of them, however, require the robot to execute the task according to different criteria, such as closeness or social acceptability. Being able to represent (and learn) the task semantics according to the specific scenario improves task execution capabilities of a robot.

from demonstration has been already used to learn object affordances [10], we provide an example of how to easily extend such techniques to the case of spatial affordances. Our tests demonstrate that affordances encode accurate semantics of the environment and that they can be used to improve robot skills in terms of efficiency and acceptability in the specific context.

The remainder of this paper is organized as follows. Section 2 presents previous research about affordances, while Sect. 3 defines the concept of Spatio-Temporal Affordances and Spatio-Temporal Affordance Maps, by also describing how they can be generated (Sect. 3.1). Additionally, Sect. 4 describes how to use STAM on a robot and Sect. 5 reports on our experimental validation. Final conclusions are presented in Sect. 6.

2   Related Work

Affordance theory has been introduced to represent possible actions that a robot can perform over a particular object. We extend affordance theory to explicitly formalize the environment itself as a combination of spatial affordances that are used to provide a semantic analysis of the space surrounding the robot. In this context, there is not a vast literature that represent spatial affordances and no prior work models affordances in a general framework. In fact, affordances are used to leverage a particular robot behavior or to adapt the routine of a specific algorithm. For example, Epstein et al. [3] exploit spatial affordances to support navigation. In this work, the leaned spatial affordance informs the robot about the most suitable action to execute for navigation. However, this approach cannot be generalized, since the affordance model strictly depends on a metric representation of the operational scenario. Hence, different representations, such as topological maps, cannot be used. Similarly to our work, Diego et al. [2] encode activities in an affordance map in order to leverage robot movements. The affordance map is used to represent the presence of people in the environment and then to avoid crowded areas not easily navigable. In a different scenario, Luber et al. [9] use affordances to improve tracking and prediction of people destinations. Also in this case, the authors exploit spatial affordances to map activities directly into the operational scenario. However, their system is not intended to run on a robot, and the activities recognized only relate to the presence of people in the scenario. The aforementioned works formalize spatial affordances to only represent navigability of the environment, and in most of the cases, the proposed approaches cannot encode spatial semantics which is a key contribution of our work.

Manifold works confirm our insights that a proper spatial semantic representation can improve robot capabilities. These works typically evaluate spatial semantics although they do not explicitly represent spatial affordances. For example, Rogers et al. [12] and Kunze et al. [7] exploit semantic knowledge to afford a search task. In [12], a robot attaches a semantic label to each room of an environment, and considers the semantic link between the object to search and locations in the indoor scenario. However, the used semantic annotation is very coarse and remains static once acquired. In [7], the authors compare different areas of the environment depending on flat surfaces and the semantic label of objects previously seen in the scene. Also in this case the proposed framework is instantiated to a particular task and the search is only influenced by objects semantics. We believe that object semantics do not provide a complete environmental knowledge and robot performance can be improved in executing these kind of tasks by integrating information about activities and areas where robot actions are performed.

All the aforementioned contributions exploit spatial affordances to model a unique task and to improve robot skills in performing that specific task. In this work, we want to introduce a general architecture that provides the possibility to model different types of spatial affordances simultaneously. To this end, we consider the remarkable contribution of Lu et al. [8]. The authors propose a layered costmap to encode different features of the environment in order to support navigation. Their architecture enables to formalize each layer independently, which is beneficial in the development of robotic systems. We borrow such paradigm and propose a modular approach in representing affordances. Additionally, we generalize our framework by not forcing our system to only represent navigability tasks. As shown in Sect. 3, we propose a system to semantically annotate the space of the environment in order to support manifold high-level tasks – of which navigability is just an instance.

3   STAM: Spatio-Temporal Affordance Map

Affordances have been originally introduced by Gibson [4] as action opportunities that objects offer, and further explored by Chemero [1] in a more recent work. This notion has been accordingly adopted in robotics to provide a different perspective in representing objects and their related actions. Here, we extend the spatial affordance theory, where the considered "object" is the environment itself, by introducing the idea of spatial semantics and spatio-temporal affordances. Spatial semantics provides a connection between the environment and its operational functionality – e.g., in a surveillance task, areas that are hidden or not entirely covered by fixed sensors present a different "risk semantics". A Spatio-Temporal Affordance (STA) is a function that defines areas of the operational environment that afford an action, given a particular state of the world.

Definition 1. *A spatio-temporal affordance (STA) is a function*

$$f_{E,\boldsymbol{\theta}} : S \times T \to A_E. \tag{1}$$

$f_{E,\boldsymbol{\theta}}$ depends on the environment E and a set of parameters $\boldsymbol{\theta}$ characterizing the affordance function. It takes as input the state of the environment $s_E(t) \in S$ at time t, a set of tasks $\{\tau(t)\} \in T$ to be performed, and outputs a map of the environment A_E that evaluates the likelihood of each area of E to afford $\{\tau(t)\}$ in s_E at time t.

The function $f_{E,\theta}$ hence characterizes spatial semantics by evaluating areas of E where the set of tasks $\{\tau(t)\}$ can be afforded. At each time t, it generates the spatial distribution of affordances within the environment and encodes them in a map A_E. Then, the STA function can be exploited by an autonomous agent as a part of a Spatio-Temporal Affordance Map (STAM) - a representation that encodes the semantics of the agent's actions related to the environment.

Definition 2. *A Spatio-Temporal Affordance Map (STAM) is a representation of the STA of an environment that can be (1) learned, (2) updated and (3) used by an autonomous agent to modify its own behavior.*

As depicted in Fig. 2, the core element of a STAM is the function $f_{E,\theta}$ introduced in Definition 1, that depends on a set of parameters θ obtained from an *affordance description module* and takes as input the current state of the world and a set of tasks from the *environment module*. In particular:

- the affordance description module (**a-module**) is a knowledge base composed by a library of parameters θ that characterize the STA and represent its *signature*. The signature modifies the spatial distribution of affordances within the environment;
- the *environment module* (**e-module**) encodes the state of the world $s_E(t)$ and provides such a state to the STA function, by coupling it with a set of tasks $\{\tau(t)\}$ to be executed in order to achieve the desired goal.

It is worth remarking that $f_{E,\theta}$, s_E and A_E refer to a common representation of the environment E that needs to be instantiated in order to enable a robot to use STAM. Such a representation can be chosen to be a metric map, a grid map, a topological map, or a semantic map. Additionally, STAM can be used to interpret relations among different affordances (if there exists) and to represent affordances individually. In fact, as shown in Fig. 3, a STA can be seen as a

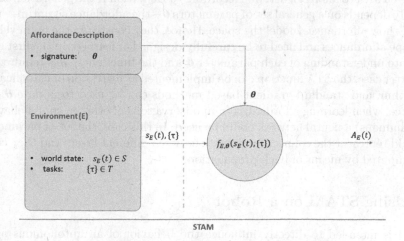

Fig. 2. Spatio-temporal affordance map – STAM.

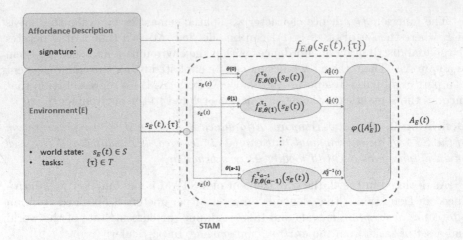

Fig. 3. Spatio-temporal affordance map – STAM.

composition of different $f_{E,\theta(i)}^{\tau_i}$ functions ($i \in [0, a-1]$, where a is the number of affordances), each modeling the spatial distribution A_E^i of a particular affordance in E. These are then combined by a function ϕ, that takes as input all the A_E^i and outputs a map A_E that satisfies $\{\tau(t)\}$, according to the considered affordances.

3.1 Generating a Spatio-Temporal Affordance Map

The affordance map A_E is a representation of the operational environment that evaluates E with respect to the current state of the world and encodes areas of E where a particular task can be afforded. For instance, in the case in which the environment is represented as a grid-map, A_E encodes in each cell the likelihood of a given area to afford an action. According to Definition 1, the generation of A_E directly depends on a general set of parameters $\boldsymbol{\theta}$ – the affordance signature – that modify how affordances model the space. Hence, they constitute the main vehicle to shape affordances and need to be carefully designed or learned. In the first case, accurate understanding of each parameter $\boldsymbol{\theta}$ and the function $f_{E,\theta}$ is required. In the latter case, the STA function can be implemented as regression or classification algorithm, and standard gradient-based methods can be used to update $\boldsymbol{\theta}$. For instance, when learning affordances from observations of other agents' behaviors (e.g., humans) a neural network could be used. In this case, the set of parameters $\boldsymbol{\theta}$ would represent the connection weights between different layers and they could be computed by means of back-propagation.

4   Using STAM on a Robot

STAM is intended to directly influence the behavior of an autonomous agent and, in particular, the navigation stack of a mobile robot. We consider the case in which the robot navigation system relies upon standard costmap-based techniques [8]. In contrast to previous work in this field, we are not interested in enabling a robot to "*go from point A to point B*", but we aim at making the agent capable to "*go from A to β*", where $\beta \in B'$ is a set of "good" poses obtained from the map A_E generated by STAM. Such poses intrinsically respect spatio-temporal constrains imposed by the considered affordances. Among these, the selection of the final pose can be based upon different criteria, such as the top scoring area in A_E, the nearest area to the robot, the biggest area, or a combination of these criteria. Nevertheless, we also want the robot to decide how to navigate the environment by selecting the path accordingly to the affordances imposed by the task. To this end, we can directly use A_E to effectively crop out all the trajectories of the robot that cross areas violating affordance constraints. In particular, we can substitute the costmap with a *gainmap* that encodes high-level information extracted from STAM. Accordingly, the robot will not follow the cheapest path, as in "usual" costmap-based systems, but it will maximize its gain over the generated gainmap. Such a map is generated as a function of the normalized cost map and the likelihood obtained from A_E.

$$m(cost, likelihood, \lambda) = \lambda(1 - cost) + (1 - \lambda)likelihood, \tag{2}$$

with $\lambda \in [0, 1]$. In this respect, we are modifying the navigation systems of an autonomous robot by transferring high-level information encoded in A_E into the navigation system.

5   Experiments

In order to evaluate of our approach we perform an analysis of the learned affordance model. To this end, we exploit expert demonstrations to teach a robot how to correctly interpret the environment when performing a following task. Then, we evaluate the learned model by reporting the affordance map A_E generated by the affordance function and the prediction error of the regression algorithm after each demonstration.

5.1   Affordance of a Following Task

We consider a robot that has to perform a following task. In this case, the areas of the environment E that afford the task depend on manifold factors such as general rules (e.g., forbidden areas), user preferences (that can be encoded in the set of parameters θ) and the position of the followed person (encoded in the state of the environment s_E). According to Definition 1, we can generate A_E and identify robot poses that support the execution of the task. To this end, we encode the pose $\langle x_T, y_T, \alpha_T \rangle$ of the target T to follow in the state $s_E(t)$. Additionally, we use Gaussian Mixture Models (GMMs) and Gaussian Mixture Regression to represent and implement the function $f_{E,\theta}$. The signature θ of the STA function is hence composed as a tuple $\theta = \langle \pi_1, \mu_1, \Sigma_1, \ldots, \pi_N, \mu_N, \Sigma_N \rangle$, where π_i is the prior, μ_i the mean vector and Σ_i the covariance matrix of a mixture of N Gaussians.

In this experiment, the signature θ is learned from demonstration of different experts. To collect expert data we setup two robots in a simulated environment – one randomly navigates, the other is controlled by an expert through a joystick and follows the target robot T by always moving between a minimum and maximum distance from it. During these sessions, the state $s_E(t)$, as defined above, is recorded at each time instant together with the pose $\langle x_F, y_F, \alpha_F \rangle$ of the follower F. The collected measurements are provided as input to the GMM and, by using Expectation Maximization, the tuple $\theta = \langle \pi_1, \mu_1, \Sigma_1, \dots, \pi_N, \mu_N, \Sigma_N \rangle$ that best fits the data is determined. In our experiments, prior to Expectation Maximization, the model has been initialized with k-means and a set of candidate GMMs has been computed with up to 8 components; the number of components has then been selected to minimize the Bayesian Information Criterion.

The learned model is used by the follower to determine, through Gaussian Mixture Regression, areas of E that enable the robot to execute the task and, hence, to generate A_E. In particular, the output of the regression consists of a mean vector and covariance matrix that enable us to infer the probability distribution (shown in Fig. 4) of the follower pose, given the target pose for the following task τ. In this example, no specific constraint is imposed to the robot for the selection of its path. Hence, the agent can select the pose that

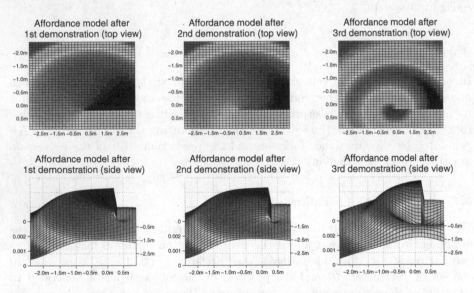

Fig. 4. Spatio-temporal affordance of a following task learned with increasing number of expert demonstrations. Here, the target is located at the origin and the plots represent the probability density function of a pose to afford the task. The plots, whose coordinates are expressed in meters, show that the model is able to represent both minimum and maximum distances from the target, in accordance with the data provided as demonstrations.

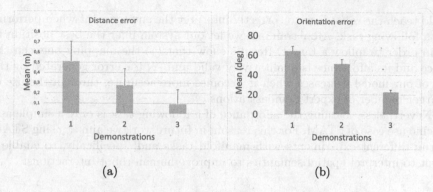

(a)   (b)

Fig. 5. Error of the best pose, selected according to the learned model, against the expert behavior. On the left we report (a) the mean and standard deviation of relative distance error between the follower and the target, while on the right (b) the mean and standard deviation of the relative orientation error are shown. These values have been obtained by running 20 experiments and incrementally using three expert demonstrations (arranged on the x-axis).

maximizes its profits over the gainmap computed according to Eq. 2, and reach it by following the shortest path.

Finally, we report an analysis of the prediction error of the affordance model generated by the regression algorithm. To this end, we use expert data collected in three different demonstrations in an incremental fashion – after each demonstration we append new training examples to the previous dataset. Then, we generate the affordance model by splitting the dataset into two distinct parts. One is used to learn the affordance model, while the other is used to compute the error of the best pose, selected according to the learned model, against the expert behavior (the ground-truth). To evaluate our model, we ran the experiment 20 times. Accordingly, Fig. 5 shows the mean and standard deviation of the prediction errors of the relative distance (a) and orientation (b) between the target and the follower position. It is worth remarking that, as soon as the affordance model becomes more accurate (Fig. 4), the prediction errors of both the distance and orientation decay.

6   Conclusion

In this paper we presented and formalized Spatio-Temporal Affordances (STA) and Spatio-Temporal Affordance Maps (STAM) as a novel framework to represent spatial semantics. This is a relevant problem since, by providing a connection between the environment and its operational functionality, spatial semantics leads to a proper interpretation of the environment and hence to a better execution of robot tasks. To test this representation, we implemented STAM and learned the affordance model of a following task by exploiting expert demonstrations. Specifically, we set up a simulated environment where human experts could teach the robot how to correctly interpret the environment when performing a following task. After training, we let our system infer the best position to be in order to follow a target. Results show that (1) the mapping between the space and its affordance is qualitatively valid and (2) the error generated by the use of our model decreases when it becomes more accurate, through the use of a larger number of expert demonstrations.

Nevertheless, learning the affordance of a following task is only a simple and specific use case of STAM. For this reason, in future work we aim at using STAM to run different experiments with manifold tasks and, specifically, to enable a robot to interpret spatial semantics to improve human-robot interactions.

References

1. Chemero, A.: An outline of a theory of affordances. Ecol. Psychol. **15**(2), 181–195 (2003)
2. Diego, G., Arras, T.K.O.: Please do not disturb! Minimum interference coverage for social robots. In: IEEE/RSJ International Conference on Intelligent Robots and Systems, pp. 1968–1973, September 2011
3. Epstein, S.L., Aroor, A., Evanusa, M., Sklar, E., Parsons, S.: Navigation with learned spatial affordances. In: COGSCI (2015)
4. Gibson, J.J.: The Ecological Approach to Visual Perception. Houghton Mifflin, Boston (1979)
5. Kim, D.I., Sukhatme, G.S.: Interactive affordance map building for a robotic task. In: 2015 IEEE/RSJ International Conference on Intelligent Robots and Systems (IROS), pp. 4581–4586. IEEE (2015)
6. Koppula, H.S., Gupta, R., Saxena, A.: Learning human activities and object affordances from RGB-D videos. The Int. J. Robot. Res. **32**(8), 951–970 (2013)
7. Kunze, L., Burbridge, C., Hawes, N.: Bootstrapping probabilistic models of qualitative spatial relations for active visual object search. In: AAAI Spring Symposium on Qualitative Representations for Robots. Stanford University in Palo Alto, California, 24–26 March 2014
8. Lu, D.V., Hershberger, D., Smart, W.D.: Layered costmaps for context-sensitive navigation. In: IEEE/RSJ International Conference on Intelligent Robots and Systems, pp. 709–715, September 2014
9. Luber, M., Tipaldi, G.D., Arras, K.O.: Place-dependent people tracking. In: Pradalier, C., Siegwart, R., Hirzinger, G. (eds.) Robotics Research. STAR, vol. 70, pp. 557–572. Springer, Heidelberg (2011)
10. Montesano, L., Lopes, M., Bernardino, A., Santos-Victor, J.: Learning object affordances: from sensory-motor coordination to imitation. IEEE Trans. Robot. **24**(1), 15–26 (2008)
11. Pandey, A.K., Alami, R.: Taskability graph: towards analyzing effort based agent-agent affordances. In: 2012 IEEE RO-MAN, pp. 791–796. IEEE (2012)
12. Rogers, J.G., Christensen, H.I.: Robot planning with a semantic map. In: 2013 IEEE International Conference on Robotics and Automation (ICRA), pp. 2239–2244, May 2013

Human-Like Path Planning in the Presence of Landmarks

Basak Sakcak[✉], Luca Bascetta, and Gianni Ferretti

Dipartimento di Elettronica Informazione e Bioingegneria,
Politecnico di Milano, Piazza L. da Vinci, 32-20133 Milano, Italy
{basak.sakcak,luca.bascetta,gianni.ferretti}@polimi.it

Abstract. This work proposes a path planning algorithm for scenarios where the agent has to move strictly inside the space defined by signal emitting bases. Considering a base can emit within a limited area, it is necessary for the agent to be in the vicinity of at least one base at each point along the path in order to receive a signal. The algorithm starts with forming a specific network, based on the starting point such that only the bases which allow the described motion are included. A second step is based on RRT*, where each edge is created solving an optimal control problem that at the end provides a human-like path. Finally the best path is selected among all the ones that reach the goal region with the minimum cost.

Keywords: Human-like path planning · Planning with landmarks

1 Introduction

Path planning is still a lively research field in robotics and autonomous vehicles, nowadays focusing on some peculiar aspects like the introduction of an accurate dynamic model of the agent, sometimes even including logical rules to govern multi-agent interaction, or a multi-objective cost function. Sampling based planners such as Rapidly-exploring Random Trees RRT [6] has enabled motion planning problem in high-dimensional spaces to be solved more efficiently. RRT incrementally samples the continuous state-space and returns a feasible solution as soon as a path from start to goal is obtained. RRT* has been introduced to tackle the optimal path planning problem and problems with complex task specifications [5]. This approach has been applied to many scenarios while guaranteeing *asymptotic optimality*. There are many variations of RRT*, such as, in [4] the authors used the same approach combined with a shooting method to obtain feasible but suboptimal solutions for any kino-dynamic system extending to systems with nonlinear dynamics, LQR-RRT* [9] locally linearizes the system in the presence of complex dynamics and applies the linear quadratic regulator. In T-RRT* [3] the evolution of the RRT* algorithm is guided by a transition function favoring the low-cost regions, conserving the asymptotic optimality. These innovative planning techniques can be applied to a context completely different from robotics, where the problem to be solved is finding a path in a complex environment a walking human can follow in order to safely reach a target. With the emergence of human-robot collaboration in the recent

© Springer International Publishing AG 2016
J. Hodicky (Ed.): MESAS 2016, LNCS 9991, pp. 281–287, 2016.
DOI: 10.1007/978-3-319-47605-6_23

years, there is a substantial interest on how humans plan their paths. Among many approaches that cover the human-like path planning some focus especially on finding a cost function that results in a human-like path [1, 7, 10].

This work proposes a path planning algorithm for scenarios where an agent has to reach a goal while always keeping in contact with other humans in the surroundings using a SDR radio. This problem can be reformulated as a multi-objective path planning problem, where the path is selected optimizing a cost function including not only path length, safety, but also distance from the path to the other radios in the surroundings, and the motion of the agent is described using a dynamic model able to generate human-like walking paths. Considering each device can emit within a limited range, the agent must keep in the vicinity of at least one device at each point along the path in order to keep the connection alive. The proposed algorithm is based on RRT* and is composed by two steps. The first step sets up a specific network, based on the starting point of the agent, such that only the emitting devices that allow the motion to the target are included in the network. In the second step, RRT* algorithm is used to generate the desired path within the space defined by the network. Each edge of this path is determined by solving an optimal control problem where the differential constraint is represented by the kinematic model of a unicycle in the space domain, and the objective function has been selected in such a way that a human-like motion is generated [7]. Finally, the best path is selected minimizing an overall cost that includes the cost of the human-like motion and the distance from the signal emitting devices. The proposed path planning method is validated by simulation using a realistic scenario.

2   Proposed Approach

The main idea of the proposed path planning approach is to be able to generate a path that a walking human can follow. It has been shown that the motion of a human can be represented by a simple unicycle model [2]

$$
\begin{cases}
\dot{x} = v \cos \theta \\
\dot{y} = v \sin \theta \\
\dot{\theta} = w
\end{cases}
\tag{1}
$$

where x, y are the Cartesian coordinates of the agent defined as a point, θ is the orientation, v represents linear velocity along the motion while w is the angular velocity. In [7], on the other hand, the authors focus solely on the geometry of the path. In this work we follow this approach, considering the dynamic model with respect to the natural coordinate instead of time as follows

$$
\begin{cases}
\dot{x} = \cos \theta \\
\dot{y} = \sin \theta \\
\dot{\theta} = \sigma
\end{cases}
\tag{2}
$$

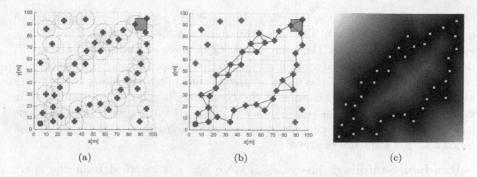

Fig. 1. Defining the connectivity zone (a) Signal emitting bases, with their emitting radii (b) Network formed using the bases that allow a motion that guarantees the connectivity condition (c) Distance transform computed on the discretized Cartesian space, darker color indicates lower cost (landmarks used are denoted with yellow color) (Color figure online)

in which $\sigma = w/v$ is the control variable while $\acute{x}, \acute{y}, \acute{\theta}$ are the derivatives with respect to the natural coordinate s, taking $s(t) = \int_0^t v(\tau)d\tau$. For instance, $\acute{x} = dx/ds$.

2.1   Connectivity Zone

The problem considered in this work restricts the agent to move strictly inside the zones defined by the signal emitting bases. Considering the starting point and the ultimate goal region of the agent, a network could be formed preliminarily, restricting this space to the union of the bases that allow a motion from start to goal (Fig. 1(a-b)). Computing the distance from each point along the path to each of the landmarks defined in the network and finding the distance to the nearest landmark is computationally inefficient. Therefore, we represent the Cartesian space as a grid and compute the *Distance Transform* of this grid (Fig. 1c) with each cell representing the Euclidean distance from the nearest landmark

$$DT(\mathbf{x}) = \min_{LM_j \in LM_{con}} ||\mathbf{x} - LM_j||$$

where LM_j, $j = 1, 2 \ldots n_{conn}$ and $\mathbf{x}$ represent the coordinates of the landmark and of each cell respectively. As a result computing the distance of the agent from the nearest landmark is converted into a look-up map.

2.2   Path Planning

The proposed approach for path planning is based on a sampling based algorithm RRT* [5]. The model defined in (2) is used to describe the motion. The *node* q is the state of system. Taking $q = [x, y, \theta]^T$, such that we can define a set $Q = [x_{min}, x_{max}] \times [y_{min}, y_{max}] \times [\theta_{min}, \theta_{max}]$ and $q \in Q$. Connection between two nodes is called an *edge* such that $e = (q, \tilde{q})$ and it represents the path obtained minimizing a cost function. Finally the cost that is assigned to an edge is denoted by $C(e)$. The algorithm builds a tree $T = (Q, E)$ with the cardinality N defined by the user, where Q is a set of nodes, and the set E defines the collision-free edges that are inside the connectivity zone. Connectivity zone Q_{conn} is defined as the union of signal emitting bases along the network and q is considered in this zone if the corresponding $DT(x)$ is smaller than r_{max}, the maximum radius that a base can emit. Tree starts with an initial node $q_0 = [x_0 \ y_0 \ \theta_0]^T \in Q$, that defines the initial dynamics of the system, and follows with a sequence of steps[1]:

- **Random Sampling:** The random state q_{rand} is sampled from the space $Q_{free} = Q_{conn} \setminus Q_{obs}$ according to a uniform distribution. Where Q_{obs} defines the space occupied by the obstacles.
- **Nearest Nodes:** Nodes that are in the vicinity of q_{rand} are selected as the ones being in the radii of $\gamma_{ball} = \gamma_{RRT*}(log(n)/n)^{1/d}$ where n is the cardinality of the tree, $d = 3$ is the dimension of the state space and γ_{RRT*} is selected according to $\gamma_{RRT*} > 2(1 + 1/d)^{1/d}(\mu((Q_{free})/\zeta d)^{1/d})$ where $\mu(Q_{free})$ is the space dimension and ζd is the unit ball volume.
- **Steering:** System is steered from the nearest nodes to q_{rand} and the *edge* e_{min} that gives out the minimum cost according to (4) is selected if all points along the edge lies in the connectivity zone and are collision free. As a result q_{rand} and e_{min} are added to the tree: $Q = q_{rand} \in Q$ and $E = e_{min} \in E$
- **Rewiring:** Every time a new node is added to the tree, it is rewired to check if an already existing node in the tree can be reached from this newly added node with a smaller cost.
- **Termination and Best Path Selection:** After the desired cardinality is reached tree incrementation terminates. For every node sequence $q_0, q_1, \ldots, q_n$ that satisfies $q_i \in Q$ where $i = 0, 1, \ldots, n$ and $2 \leq n \leq N$, the cost is cumulative over the sequence such that $C(\to q_n) = \sum_0^n C(e_i)$. At the end the best path is selected among the node sequences reaching the goal region, $q_n \in Q_{goal}$ with the minimum cost $C(\to q_n)$.

Two nodes are connected minimizing a normalized hybrid energy/goal-based cost function that is proven to generate human-like paths [7]

$$J = \frac{1}{2} \int_0^S \sigma^2 (1 + \beta^T \Gamma^2) ds \qquad (3)$$

where $\beta^T = [\beta_1 \ \beta_2]$ is a set of parameters and

$$(\Gamma^2)^T = \left[\frac{(x - x_{i+1})^2 + (y - y_{i+1})^2}{(x_i - x_{i+1})^2 + (y_i - y_{i+1})^2} \quad \frac{(\theta - \theta_{i+1})^2}{(\theta - \theta_{i+1})} \right]$$

$(x_i, y_i, \theta_i) =: \mathbf{q_i}$ and $(x_{i+1}, y_{i+1}, \theta_{i+1}) =: \mathbf{q_{i+1}}$ being the initial and the final nodes to be connected. The cost function for generating the path can be interpreted

---

[1] One can refer to [5] for the computation of the nearest nodes and the rewiring step.

as penalizing the control effort σ with a space-varying weight. Such that, as the agent approaches the goal in the state space the weight on the control effort decreases, similar to how humans plan their path. Cost of each edge includes the cost of the human-like path and the cost of being away from the nearest landmark and is defined as follows

$$C(e_i) = c \left(1 + \frac{\bar{d}_i}{r_{max}}\right) J_i^* \tag{4}$$

where J^* represents the optimal value of (3), $\bar{d}$ is the average of the distances from the nearest landmarks along the path computed, and c is a constant.

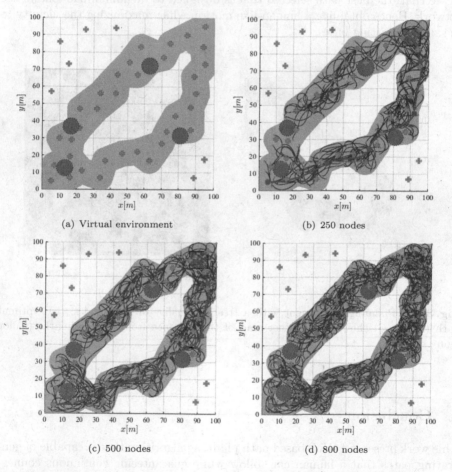

(a) Virtual environment

(b) 250 nodes

(c) 500 nodes

(d) 800 nodes

Fig. 2. Experiments: allowed zone (cyan), tree nodes (yellow), tree edges (blue), best path (red), goal region (magenta square), landmarks (magenta), discarded landmarks (yellow), obstacles (green circles) (Color figure online)

3   Results

The proposed algorithm has been developed and tested in a MATLAB implementation. State limits are chosen to be $x \in [0, 100]$, $y \in [0, 100]$, $\theta \in [0, 2\pi]$. Parameters of the objective function are taken as $\beta = [7.55 \; 0.27]$ as given in [7]. A virtual environment is used for verification that comprises 40 landmarks and 4 non-overlapping circular obstacles as represented in Fig. 2(a). We used *GPOPS-II* [8] software for MATLAB to solve the nonlinear optimization problem (3) for building the edges, taking model in (2) for differential constraints. Simulations are preformed for different numbers of cardinalities (Fig. 2(b-d)). Considering the minimum cost path obtained from a tree of 1500 vertices (Fig. 3) it is possible to see that, the best path selected that is designed to be human-like follows the network. Hence obtaining a human-like motion while maximizing the vicinity to the signal emitting bases.

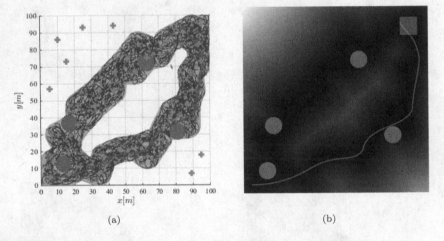

(a)   (b)

Fig. 3. (a) Planning experiment with a tree cardinality of 1500 nodes. (b) Optimal path (solid red) shown on the cost map of the distance from the landmarks (Color figure online)

4   Conclusion

This work presents a RRT-based path planning algorithm that is capable of generating paths that a human can follow while guaranteeing continuous connectivity in the environments populated with signal emitting bases. The approach can be used for various applications extending from search-rescue missions to military applications, where an agent is expected to move human-like and to be able to communicate with the surroundings.

References

1. Arechavaleta, G., Laumond, J.P., Hicheur, H., Berthoz, A.: An optimality principle governing human walking. IEEE Trans. Robot. **24**(1), 5–14 (2008)
2. Arechavaleta, G., Laumond, J.P., Hicheur, H., Berthoz, A.: On the nonholonomic nature of human locomotion. Auton. Robots **25**(1–2), 25–35 (2008)
3. Devaurs, D., Simon, T., Corts, J.: Efficient sampling-based approaches to optimal path planning in complex cost spaces. In: Akin, H.L., Amato, N.M., Isler, V., van der Stappen, A.F. (eds.) Algorithmic Foundations of Robotics XI. Springer Tracts in Advanced Robotics, vol. 107, pp. 143–159. Springer, Heidelberg (2015)
4. Jeon, J.H., Karaman, S., Frazzoli, E.: Anytime computation of time-optimal off-road vehicle maneuvers using the RRT*. In: Decision and Control and European Control Conference (CDC-ECC) (2011)
5. Karaman, S., Frazzoli, E.: Sampling-based algorithms for optimal motion planning. Int. J. Robot. Res. **30**(7), 846–894 (2011)
6. LaValle, S.M., Kuffner, J.J.: Randomized kinodynamic planning. Int. J. Robot. Res. **20**(5), 378–400 (2001)
7. Papadopoulos, A.V., Bascetta, L., Ferretti, G.: Generation of human walking paths. Auton. Robots **40**(1), 59–75 (2016)
8. Patterson, M.A., Rao, A.V.: A MATLAB software for solving multiple-phase optimal control problems using hp-adaptive Gaussian quadrature collocation methods and sparse nonlinear programming. ACM Trans. Math. Softw. (TOMS) **41**(1), 1 (2014)
9. Perez, A., Platt Jr., R., Konidaris, G., Kaelbling, L., Lozano-Perez, T.: LQR-RRT*: optimal sampling-based motion planning with automatically derived extension heuristics. In: Robotics and Automation (ICRA) (2012)
10. Puydupin-Jamin, A.S., Johnson, M., Bretl, T.: A convex approach to inverse optimal control and its application to modeling human locomotion. In: IEEE International Conference on Robotics and Automation (ICRA) (2012)

Indoor Real-Time Localisation for Multiple Autonomous Vehicles Fusing Vision, Odometry and IMU Data

Alessandro Faralli$^{(\boxtimes)}$, Niko Giovannini, Simone Nardi, and Lucia Pallottino

Research Center E. Piaggio, Faculty of Engineering,
University of Pisa, Largo Lucio Lazzarino 1, 56122 Pisa, Italy
ale.fara.90@gmail.com, nikogiovannini3@gmail.com,
nardi@mail.dm.unipi.it, lucia.pallottino@unipi.it

Abstract. Due to the increasing usage of service and industrial autonomous vehicles, a precise localisation is an essential component required in many applications, e.g. indoor robot navigation. In open outdoor environments, differential GPS systems can provide precise positioning information. However, there are many applications in which GPS cannot be used, such as indoor environments. In this work, we aim to increase robot autonomy providing a localisation system based on passive markers, that fuses three kinds of data through extended Kalman filters. With the use of low cost devices, the optical data are combined with other robots' sensor signals, i.e. odometry and inertial measurement units (IMU) data, in order to obtain accurate localisation at higher tracking frequencies. The entire system has been developed fully integrated with the Robotic Operating System (ROS) and has been validated with real robots.

Keywords: Localisation indoor · Odometry · IMU · EKF · Passive marker

1 Introduction

A fundamental problem for an autonomous mobile robot is knowing its current position and orientation by sensorial observation and previous accurate localization. This is still the subject of several researches in the mobile robot community with the aim of increasing robot autonomy. Although global positioning system (GPS) is suitable for mobile robot localization in outdoor environment, it is difficult to be used in an indoor environment. In case GPS is unavailable, localization using odometry [1] and dead reckoning using IMU sensors [2] may provide an alternative solution. However, odometry is subject to growing errors over time and it is hence insufficient for many tasks [3]. The indoor navigation is based on the exploitation of the environment and of available technologies that allow localisation even in indoor scenarios. One of the most widely used techniques is to place landmarks in known environment's points. In this way mounting

© Springer International Publishing AG 2016
J. Hodicky (Ed.): MESAS 2016, LNCS 9991, pp. 288–297, 2016.
DOI: 10.1007/978-3-319-47605-6_24

an on-board robot webcam (focused on the landmarks), the localisation system uses the information about the position of each landmark to localise the robot inside the environment [4]. Nevertheless, in presence of obstacles between robot and landmarks, the relative position can not be evaluated. Moreover, especially in industrial scenarios, it is usually not well accepted the introduction of landmarks in the environment. A possible alternative is to take advantage of a priori knowledge of the environment where the idea is to extract features from the environment and to compare them with a priori knowledge. For example, in [5] the choice of the corridor as the working environment has two important reasons. First, the corridor is a common part of most domestic environments and being able to navigate in it has potential on its own. Second, it has a very regular and simple structure, making it easier to start the development of a more general vision based solutions.

In recent years, smart buildings use wireless sensor network (WSN) as localization systems: in [6], WSN is used as an assistant for odometry and other on board sensors used by the localisation systems. The main limit of such infrastructure is its cost, that is not negligible. Another possible infrastructure is based on cameras placed in known positions in the environment. For example, in [7] a camera is placed on the ceiling of the hall. A drawback of the proposed method is the localisation failure in certain situations. For instance in case of bad illumination, markers on the robots can not be detected and localised properly.

The purpose of this work is to create a localisation system based on low cost devices, in order to verify applicability of the algorithms presented in [8–10]. We want to identify robots moving in an indoor environment, fusing vision data from the cameras mounted in the environment, odometry data from the encoders fixed on the robot's wheels and IMU data from the IMU sensor mounted on board. Based on the work proposed in [11], where a single camera is used to localise a single robot, we develop a localisation system able to manage multiple robots with multiple cameras. The developed system is environment independent and hence it does not require any a priori knowledge of the environment. Moreover, our framework is able to manage an unlimited number of robots and cameras at the same time. For this reason the system can perform in an indefinitely wide environment. In addition, a method for on line camera self-calibration is also proposed. Once the initial calibration of the cameras is done, it is possible to move each camera while a monocular visual odometry algorithm [12] performs a continuous real-time calibration of the cameras parameters. To speed up the visual localisation and to increase accuracy, vision information is combined with robots sensors using two Kalman-Filters. One of the main problems when dealing with optical cameras is the illumination of the scene that can change during robot operation. With the proposed approach failures in detection are avoided thanks to an on-line calibration of the HSV (Hue, Saturation and Value) values of the markers colour, performed by an operator. In this way we can change the colours calibration whenever lights in the environment change increasing robot autonomy.

The paper is organized as follows: in Sect. 2 we define the visual tracking system. In Sect. 3 the integration of on board sensors is detailed while Sect. 4 is devoted to the experimental set-up and results. Finally Sect. 5 presents some conclusive remarks and the planned future work, such as an extension of the system to other, more demanding, situations.

2   Visual Tracking Module

The localisation system consists of two different modules. The first is the module responsible for the localisation of the vehicle through fixed cameras while the second is dedicated to the integration of the data provided by the first one and all the other available sensors. The system has been developed so that the two modules can be implemented independently. In this Section details on the Visual Tracking Module are provided. On top of each robot are placed two coloured balls mounted at fixed known distance and such that the midpoint coincides with the centre of the robot, as shown in Fig. 1.

Fig. 1. Roomba robot equipped with front red marker and back blue marker mounted at 10 cm (Color figure online)

In order to identify each marker position, some sequential operations must be performed. First, the camera hardware must be calibrated: 8 parameters are calibrated such that the position and orientation of each camera with respect to the fixed reference system can be computed. Once images are acquired from each camera, a filtering operation starts, (e.g. see [13]):

1. Remove image's noise through a Gaussian blur filter;
2. Convert RGB (Red, Green, Blue) color model to HSV (Hue, Saturation, Value). In this way we can filter the hue, saturation and value of the negligible colours, i.e. colours different from those used for the markers;
3. Use morphological operations such as erosion and dilation. The main uses are:

– Remove noise;
– Isolate individual elements and join related elements in an image;
– Find intensity bumps or holes in an image.

Once marker contours are identified, a white rectangle is drawn around them whose center coincides with the marker position in the environment, as shown in Fig. 2.

Fig. 2. Robot is tracked by a camera and its position and orientation is marked with rectangle centered on passive markers

The center of the marker is reported in pixel coordinate of the camera reference frame. In order to allow more cameras to identify the same marker a common reference frame is chosen, e.g. the world reference system.

Marker positions, from different cameras, of the same color are collected into position arrays, so that it is possible to assign to each robot only the two position arrays related to the colors of its markers. Each robot manages a private Kalman filter, which predicts the marker position at the current time instant. Such prediction is used to reduce false assignments, through the execution of a spatial filter on the position arrays received from the cameras. Moreover, due to the fact that the distance between the markers is fixed and known, a second check is performed to select the pair of markers that respect the given distance. Once marker positions are selected, the robot position is computed as the midpoint of the selected markers. Moreover, based on this information, the heading of each robot can also be computed. A graphical scheme of the entire process described in this section is reported in Fig. 3, where the software architecture of the visual tracking module is represented.

In case of obstacles in the environment, the visual tracking module computes robot position using Kalman filter pure prediction. Such kind of computation is affected by a fast degradation of the performances decreasing the robot autonomy. To mitigate such problem and to improve the dead-reckoning computation, an integration with other sensors data can be performed as described in Sect. 3.

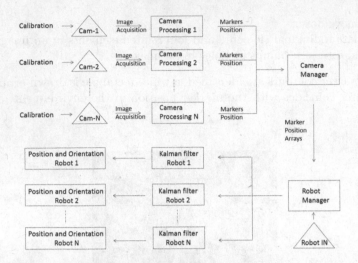

Fig. 3. Tracking Visual Module software architecture. The main steps of each camera are: camera calibration, image acquisition, marker position computation, coloured marker positions array creation, arrays sorting for each robot, robot position and orientation computation (Color figure online)

2.1   Online Calibration

In order to avoid the use of an external infrastructure, that is typically unavailable in disaster scenarios in case of search and rescue tasks, the capability of tracking passive markers with on board cameras has been also developed. More specifically, by the use of a visual odometry module such as the one proposed in [12], it is possible to have an online calibration of camera parameters. Online calibration and tracking with on board cameras allow to localise robots in environment parts not reachable by a fixed camera infrastructure, e.g. hidden areas occluded by obstacles. Moreover, this feature may also be used to avoid localisation errors due to unexpected external perturbation of the camera positions in an infrastructure.

3   On Board Sensor Integration Module

In general, localisation using odometry and dead reckoning using IMU sensors may provide an alternative solution for robot localisation purposes. Unfortunately, it is well known that odometry from encoders and dead reckoning from IMU sensors may show substantial errors in the localisation due to wheel slippage and drift respectively [14]. These errors can be overcome by integrating these sensors with the data provided by the visual tracking module proposed in the previous section. Fusing all these sensor data through two Extended Kalman filters (EKFs) reduces the robot localisation error. The integration is performed with two sequential EKFs as shown in Fig. 4. This approach combines the benefits of the three sensor typologies. The visual tracking module can be seen as a correction for the estimation obtained based on the on board sensors. On the other hand, the on board odometry information can be employed to overcome time-delays that occurs in the vision system, as well as errors due to regions where no visual markers are available. Referring to Fig. 4, the prediction operation of the first EKF is executed once a new odometry pose estimation is available. Since the on board odometry estimation is fast, the estimation of the robot's state can be performed at a high frequency. The second and subsequent EKF is used to integrate the filtered odometry obtained with the first EKF with the data provided by the visual tracking module. The update step of the second EKF is executed when a new pose estimation is obtained from the vision tracking module and it is employed to correct the estimation performed by the on board odometry. It is worth noticing that the second EKF has a lower update frequency with respect to the first one.

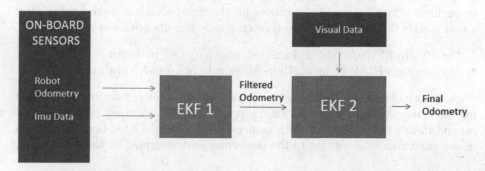

Fig. 4. Two EKFs fusing all sensors data. The first ones fuses on-board odometry data, the second one updates the pose estimation with visual data

Time-delay of the visual tracking module is also an issue which needs to be tackled. In our vision system, for example, the vision time-delay is about 300 ms and to overcome this problem, the past odometry information is saved in a buffer. When obtaining a vision estimation, this information is aligned to the robot's pose in the past. Thus, the Kalman belief state now corresponds to the (past) robot's pose and the update can be performed.

4 Experimental Results and Validation

To facilitate the evaluation of the performance of the proposed approach we developed a system fully integrated with the well known Robotic Operating System (ROS) [15]. Such integration lead us to test the framework in a simulation environment (Gazebo) and in a real world scenario without any change of the code. In this section, the results and the performances achieved by the proposed localisation system are reported. Two type of tests have been performed:

1. *Static tests* are used to verify the accuracy of the measures of the visual tracking module;
2. *Dinamic tests* are used to verify the accuracy of the measures when on board sensors are integrated with visual tracking module.

4.1 Static Tests

For the evaluation performance of the visual tracking module, two different types of cameras have been used to test the applicability of the proposed approach to different hardware:

1. Philips SPC1030NC/00;
2. Logitech HDWebcam C270.

The first test aimed to define the maximum distance from the cameras lens to perform a localisation of the robots on the floor. Cameras were mounted on a two meters tall tripod, with fixed pitch angle. Results obtained are that:

1. the Philips SPC1030NC/00 localises robots up to 5 m distance;
2. the Logitech HDWebcam C270 localises robots up to 5.5 m distance.

The second test was performed to define the measurement accuracy provided by the cameras with respect to known positions. The accuracy error obtained ranged from 2 cm to 5 cm for both cameras. The cameras have been positioned in the environment according to the performance determined by the static tests.

4.2 Dynamic Tests

Dynamic tests have been conducted to validate the performance of the proposed localisation system and in particular the integration of the data from the on board sensors with the visual tracking module. To verify the functionality of the proposed framework autonomous vehicles are moved by a remote operator along a fixed trajectory: a rectangle of 2.5 m per 1.5 m. Data are recorded once the robot starts moving until it reaches the initial position. In Fig. 5 odometry data and filtered odometry (outcomes of the first EKF described in previous section) are compared in a single rectangle tracking.

As expected, the final pose error in case of the robot odometry (red trajectory) is quite high, for the experiment reported in Fig. 5 the final pose shifted of approximately 51 cm with respect to the ground truth. On the other hand, when filtered odometry is used (white trajectory), the final position estimation is, as expected, affected by a smaller error of 33 cm compared to the ground truth. These results show that the first EKF improves the estimation of the position and orientation of the robots, but they are still not satisfactory to allow the robot operating for a significant amount of time. When visual tracking module is integrated with on board sensors, the estimation of the final position and orientation is affected by an error of 10 cm compared to the ground truth reducing the error of the 70 %.

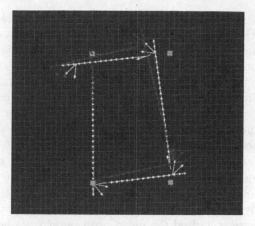

Fig. 5. The robot's trajectory using only odometry data is shown in red, the trajectory using odometry and IMU data is shown in white. The grey squares bound the perimeter of the rectangle followed by the robot (Color figure online)

A final set of experiments has been conducted to validate the localisation system in case of a single robot and multi cameras and then in case of multiple robots and multiple cameras. In the first test the robot is piloted in an indoor area of $7\,\text{m} \times 3\,\text{m}$ monitored by three cameras located in known positions that focus three different and possibly overlapping sub-areas of the experiment. In Fig. 6, a snapshot of the three cameras is reported on the left. Notice that the robot presence is detected only by the first camera. On the right the real trajectory is reported in red while the one estimated with the proposed localisation system is reported in yellow. It is worth noticing that, the proposed method allows a

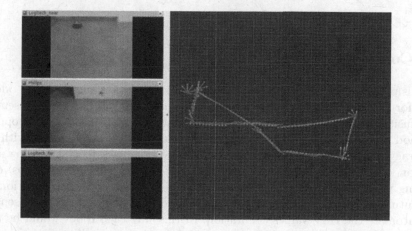

Fig. 6. In the left there are three acquired images by the cameras at the end of the experiment. In the right the real trajectory is shown in red and the estimated trajectory using all the sensors is shown in yellow (Color figure online)

smooth trajectory estimation even if the robot, while moving, is detected by different cameras. Hence, no substantial errors occur during cameras switching. In this case, the visual tracking module integrated with on board sensors, is able to estimate the robot position with errors less than 10 cm.

A final test has been performed with two different cameras and two robots. During such experiment robots occurred to be in the same camera field of view at the same time or in different camera field-of-views. In Fig. 7 it is reported a snapshot of two different cameras when more than one robots are in their field of view, at the same time. The proposed system has been able to manage robots overlapping in the captured image without compromising the robot localisation. With this experiment the localisation system demonstrates to perform well also in complex scenarios.

During experiments we have hence obtained very good results in localisation accuracy and robustness, indeed the mean position error is between 1 to 10 cm and the mean absolute heading angle error is between 1 to 5° validating the proposed method.

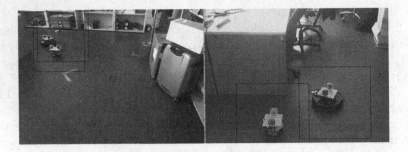

Fig. 7. Two cameras manage two robots at the same time

5   Conclusion

In this paper a simple but efficient algorithm to fuse vision and on-board odometry for accurate indoor localisation using low cost devices has been presented. For fusing sensors informations, two sequential EKFs are used. The proposed method is able to combine the high tracking frequency of the odometry with the accuracy of the vision tracking system. This work allows to create a low cost indoor localisation system that could be used also in external scenarios, converting visual data in GPS data without any substantial code modification. In the future we aim to investigate the possibility of employing brightness sensors to automate the HSV values calibration. In this way each robot would be able to adjust the HSV values calibration on their markers according to the specific brightness detected in the robot's position.

References

1. O'Kane, J.M.: Global localization using odometry. In: Proceedings IEEE International Conference on Robotics and Automation, ICRA, pp. 37–42. IEEE (2006)
2. Malyavej, V., Kumkeaw, W., Aorpimai, M.: Indoor robot localization by RSSI/IMU sensor fusion. In: 10th International Conference on Electrical Engineering/Electronics, Computer, Telecommunications and Information Technology (ECTI-CON), pp. 1–6. IEEE (2013)
3. Pereira, G.A.S., Vijay Kumar,R., Campos, M.F.M.: Localization and tracking in robot networks. In: Proceedings of the 11th International Conference on Advanced Robotics (ICAR), Coimbra, Portugal, 30 June–3 July 2003
4. Panzieri, S., Pascucci, F., Setola, R., Ulivi, G.: A low cost vision based localization system for mobile robots. Target **4**, 5 (2001)
5. Bayramolu, E., Andersen, N.A., Poulsen, N.K., Andersen, J.C., Ravn, O.: Mobile robot navigation in a corridor using visual odometry. In: International Conference on Advanced Robotics: ICAR 2009, pp. 1–6. IEEE (2009)
6. Fu, G., Zhang, J., Chen, W., Peng, F., Yang, P., Chen, C.: Precise localization of mobile robots via odometry and wireless sensor network. Int. J. Adv. Robot. Syst. **10** (2013)
7. Baatar, G., Eichhorn, M., Ament, C.: Precise indoor localization of multiple mobile robots with adaptive sensor fusion using odometry and vision data. In: The International Federation of Automatic Control Cape Town, South Africa (2014)
8. Nardi, S., Della Santina, C., Meucci, D., Pallottino, L.: Coordination of unmanned marine vehicles for asymmetric threats protection. In: OCEANS Genova. IEEE (2015)
9. Nardi, S., Fabbri, T., Caiti, A., Pallottino, L.: A game theoretic approach for antagonistic-task coordination of underwater autonomous robots in asymmetric threats scenarios. In: OCEANS Monterey. IEEE (2016)
10. Nardi, S., Pallottino, L.: NoStop: a real-time framework for design and test of coordination protocol for unmanned marine vehicles involved in asymmetric threats protection. In: Hodicky, J. (ed.) MESAS 2016. LNCS, vol. 9991, pp. 176–185. Springer, Heidelberg (2016)
11. Bischoff, B., Nguyen-Tuong, D., Streichert, F., Ewert, M., Knoll, A.: Fusing vision and odometry for accurate indoor robot localization. In: 12th International Conference on Control Automation Robotics and Vision (ICARCV), pp. 347–352. IEEE (2012)
12. Forster, C., Pizzoli, M., Scaramuzza, D.: SVO: fast semi-direct monocular visual odometry. In: IEEE International Conference on Robotics and Automation (ICRA) (2014)
13. Szeliski, R.: Computer Vision: Algorithms and Applications. Springer Science and Business Media, London (2010)
14. Lobo, A., Kadam, R., Shajahan, S., Malegam, K., Wagle, K., Surve, S.: Localization and tracking of indoor mobile robot with beacons and dead reckoning sensors. In: IEEE Students Conference on Electrical, Electronics and Computer Science (SCEECS), pp. 1–4. IEEE (2014)
15. Quigley, M., Conley, K., Gerkey, B., Faust, J., Foote, T., Leibs, J., Wheeler, R., Ng, A.Y.: ROS: an open-source robot operating system. In: ICRA Workshop on Open Source Software, vol. 3, p. 5 (2009)

Unmanned Aerial Vehicles and Remotely Piloted Aircraft Systems

Disasters and Emergency Management in Chemical and Industrial Plants: Drones Simulation for Education and Training

Agostino Bruzzone[1], Francesco Longo[2], Marina Massei[1],
Letizia Nicoletti[3], Matteo Agresta[1(✉)], Riccardo Di Matteo[1],
Giovanni Luca Maglione[1], Giuseppina Murino[1],
and Antonio Padovano[2]

[1] DIME, University of Genoa, Via Opera Pia, Genoa, Italy
{agostino,massei}@itim.unige.it, {matteo.agresta,
riccardo.dimatteo,gianluca.maglione,
giuseppina.murino}@simulationteam.com
[2] DIMEG, University of Calabria, Via P. Bucci, 45 C, 87036 Rende, Italy
{francesco,antonio}@msc-les.org
[3] Cal-Tek, Sr Via Spagna, 240, 87036 Santo Stefano, CS, Italy
letizia@msc-les.org

Abstract. The use of simulation for training is proven to be extremely effective both in term of costs and in term of its flexibility for different uses and applications, such as building situation awareness and creating scenarios for training scopes. The aim of the project proposed is to demonstrate the powerful rule of simulation in UAV pilots' cooperative training; the project presented makes use of a 3D simulation environment in order to build a realistic condition of an emergency situation in a chemical plant for the first responders. The model proposed makes use of HLA (High Level Architecture) standards in order to be potentially federated with other existing simulators.

In the solution proposed, the pilot of the drone must accomplish the mission in a given time piloting a UAV; the scenario is based inside a chemical plant where a disaster is newly occurred. Then ability of the pilot is measured by the system and several constraints are reproduced to provide a realistic training scenario (such as small spaces and barriers to overcome, battery durations, risks of damages due to high temperatures zones, etc.); the system records and tracks all the actions of the pilot and gives a feedback to the user at the end of the simulation time.

Keywords: UAV · 3D simulation · Training and education · Augmented reality

1 Introduction

The use of Remotely Piloted Aircraft Systems (RPAS) is rapidly increasing as demonstrated by recent developments in regulations; in addition RPAS are now equated as aircraft and have to comply with aviation safety rules (EASA, 2014). Certified programs for UAV (Unmanned Aerial Vehicles) pilot, including a

© Springer International Publishing AG 2016
J. Hodicky (Ed.): MESAS 2016, LNCS 9991, pp. 301–308, 2016.
DOI: 10.1007/978-3-319-47605-6_25

mandatory number of hours of simulator have been instituted both in defense domain and in civil domain; in addition, civil domain is expected to overcome the military one in term of use of drones [1].

UAV can be controlled by a pilot or can have a pre-programmed mission/task to perform; thanks to their flexibility and the different mode of use there is a number of projects in a wide variety of sectors involving UAV's and their cooperation with human. Indeed UAV simulation for civil application can be found in context that are really different: helicopter-based UAV have been fruitfully used in precision agriculture for remote thermal signals and sensor for optimizing irrigation and water consumption [2] and multiple mini UAV have been used in forest monitoring [5].

It is clear that the wide spectrum of possible use for the UAVs imply a proper training for the pilot that must be tailored for each different context; for this reason, simulation can support at best the training and operations, in particular in critical environment [7]. Simulators have different advantages compared to live simulation; are more flexible for creating training scenarios, [8] they allow to reproduce "extreme conditions" like low gravity condition in space domain, or complex operations in a lunar base by making use of a federation of different entities [3, 6]. Autonomous Systems in general opens a door for a new training paradigm. The trainees and ASs must be trained in the same synthetic environment [9].

2   UAV for Disaster Assessment

Drones, and UAVs in general, can be used effectively for disaster assessment and they represent a useful resource for speeding up the operations and increase the information available for the emergency squad.

After the occurrence of a disaster, the first respondents needs to acquire information about the infrastructure that have been damaged and what is the current status of the disaster; furthermore, they have to coordinate the assistance and the emergency operations both in terms of actions to undertake and in term of allocation of the available resources [4]. For this reason UAV, can be fruitfully used in taking measurement, area mapping and visual inspection on a chemical plant scenario, where a disaster is newly occurred. Autonomous systems can increase the security for the first responders substituting their physical presence in dangerous situation with a remote control; finally, they can be used to support triage activities with the people involved.

In this context the capability of the UAV pilots to accomplish the task fast and effectively is a primary key; this imply an high attention on the quality of the training for the pilot on the ground.

The aim of this project is a 3D simulation of a virtual environment representing an emergency situation focused on an accident inside a chemical plant. The project proposed is able to reproduce the emergency conditions inside and outside the plant and it can support:

- training both for single and multiple users
- mission planning
- support to operations.

Indeed one of the primary objective of the simulator is to reproduce the situational awareness, and for doing that, it is important to note that the forces involved should be able to do the following actions:

- undertake intelligent evaluations
- take an overview of the current situation, considering the present condition and the risk correlated
- estimate the potential risk related to the evolution of the current condition
- reach the "optimum" training level
- operate easily and in a coordinate way with the other people involved.

The trainee must define the action to undertake considering also the procedural aspect in a dynamic scenario evolving in time. Such scenario matches different chemical accident, with other ancillary failures stochastically generated (i.e. communication interruption, electrical power interruption) and drone's constraints (speed, autonomy of the batteries, wind interferences etc.) that the user need to face.

3   Model Description

This project in Fig. 1 have been developed following the following steps:

- Chemical plant 3D models (interior and exterior);
- UAV 3D model-quadcopter;
- Set of humans inside the plant;
- UAVs physics implementation;
- UAV's sensors implementation;

Fig. 1. User piloting the UAV over the simulated plant

The total number of polygons have been optimized in order to assure a sustainable workload for the graphic card for reproducing a real time simulation.

The initial scenario proposed is a chemical plant that have been damaged by a big earthquake causing an increase of the pressure in the production systems and uncontrolled chemical reactions that evolve with fire generation in different part of the plant.

Some toxic substances have been released in the atmosphere, and the toxic cloud is propagating with a certain speed and moving to the village close to the plant. The structure of the plant is damaged and the production systems and control system are out of order.

In the Fig. 2 is possible to see the diffusion of the toxic cloud: its propagation depends on different parameters that can vary during the simulation (such as wind speed, external and internal temperature, fire propagation inside the plant etc.).

The first responders can't direct access physically inside the plant due to the dangerous condition and they need to understand the situation by making use of the available drones in term of:

- what type of chemical material have been released
- what are the risks and what is the propagation speed of such kind of substances
- how many person have been involved in the disaster, what is their health condition.

The UAV is equipped with different sensors and have a predetermined autonomy of batter that is stochastically generated. Such constraint make the simulation closer to reality because the trainee should consider the total time available for his mission.

A further constraint is the wind speed limit, and the meteorological condition that are stochastically generated by the computer and that can vary during the simulated time.

Fig. 2. Toxic cloud diffusion

Fig. 3. User piloting the UAV over the plant

The simulated drone (Fig. 3) recreates the true real motion with the 6 degree of freedom (DOFz). The motion of the drone is given by the second law of Newton applied to the 6 DOFs.

Each drone is equipped by:

- a main camera installed under the drone body and the user is free to switch the different views.
- a camera following the drone.
- air contamination sensor (e.g. oxygen level, toxics substances detection such as nitrogen, etc.).
- biomedical sensor measuring the health status of injured people (life signs such as breath, voice messages, etc.).

Further additional sensors may be present or not inside the drone, or can be out of order for example:

- capability to manipulate object
- capability to activate devices
- sensor measuring distances
- capability to record video and images.

The Fig. 4 shows the drone flying within the chemical plant when the air contamination sensor is active. When contaminants are found (e.g., Methane, Ammonia, etc.), the concentration of contaminants is shown by using red parallelepipeds whose height is proportional to the contamination level (the higher the height is, the higher is the contaminant concentration).

The biomedical sensor is used to check life signs; in order to work properly the drone must be close enough (e.g., less than 1 m) from the human body. Indeed the

Fig. 4. Drone flying inside the chemical plant, in the disaster zone

drone need to approach at the right distance for a sufficient time to the man on the ground for checking his life signs in a proper way.

It is worth mentioning that the disaster scenario changes every time the simulator is started, therefore, the user can always play a different scenario. In particular, contaminant concentrations as well as the position of the injured people and their life signs change every time the simulator is restarted.

Here is described an example of the mission for the trainee:

(1) Scenario Generation:

The system generate a scenario with a partial description of the event, an estimation on the number of people involved in the accident and the type of chemical substances that have been released. It is important to note that all the information will be partial and incomplete in order to make the scenario closer to the reality.

(2) Mission Planning:

The user have a set of available UAV available, with a predetermined autonomy of battery and each one equipped with certain sensor. Based on the configuration of the plant, the sensors and the information provided by the system (i.e. number of people involved, meteorological condition, chemical substances released, distance of the village near the plant) he have to decide the most suitable UAV to use considering also the drone dimension and its capability to enter and move in small space.

(3) Mission Execution:

The user should plan his mission and his flight plan considering all the constraints and the current condition, the layout of the plant and the possibility of interruption of the communication due to the layout of the plant or other events that can occur.

The user should perform the triage operation of the people involved during the accident in the right way. Each person involved in the accident has a different health status that change and get worse during time. The ability of the operator is to understand the situation and to decide the "best sequence" for the triage by processing the information given by the drone's camera and by considering the obstacles such as fire, smoke and high temperature that can damage the drone or make extremely challenging the drive of the drone itself.

(4) Simulation Results:

When the mission is accomplished, the system provides a feedback to the trainee (Fig. 5) with:

– Total time for the mission
– Damages for the drone
– Health condition of the people involved in the disaster
– Time elapsed
– Battery level
– Triage efficiency
– Area coverage
– Sampling effectiveness

As shown in the Figure, the time elapsed is the time from the beginning of the flight. The battery level shows the percentage of remaining charge. The triage efficiency is the percentage of people identified as injured. The area coverage shows the percentage of area covered by the flight of the drone, while the sampling effectiveness shows the percentage level of contaminants found through the air contamination sensor.

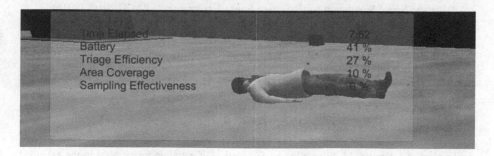

Fig. 5. Simulation results

4 Conclusions

The paper has presented a simulator developed by the University of Calabria – MSC-LES Team and University of Genova.

The simulator provides a 3D virtual environment, that involve the user reproducing the real condition in emergency situation; it is important to note that such situation are really difficult to be reproduced in reality, since the process can be time consuming, really costly, and dangerous.

The main objective is to propose an innovative instrument for training drone pilots in emergency condition in disaster relief context.

The simulation is based on discrete event; the stochastic nature of the simulator allow to test different scenarios with different conditions that change during the simulation time and that are different for every game.

Finally, the system can be federated by using an HLA-based bridge with other UAVs simulator or M&S Autonomous Systems' experimental frameworks [10] in order to support multiple training and experimentation; further development and researches are ongoing for Augmented Reality applications. Such simulator have been tested among a group of students and the results before and after the training have been compared. For brevity reasons the learning curve profile of the different users have not been reported. In average, the users have demonstrated a good improvement in the performance in particular in term of: speed in accomplishing the task, reduction of the number of mistakes and collisions, total time for the mission and area coverage.

References

1. Austin, R.: Unmanned Aircraft Systems: UAVS Design, Development and Deployment. Wiley, Hoboken (2010). ISBN 978-047005819-0
2. Berni, J.A.J., Zarco-Tejada, P.J., Suárez, L., Fereres, E.: Thermal and narrowband multispectral remote sensing for vegetation monitoring from an unmanned aerial vehicle. IEEE Trans. Geosci. Remote Sens. 47(3), 722–738 (2009)
3. Bruzzone, A.G., Longo, F., Agresta, M., Di Matteo, R., Maglione, G.L.: Autonomous systems for operations in critical environments. In: Proceedings of the Modeling and Simulation of Complexity in Intelligent, Adaptive and Autonomous Systems (MSCIAAS 2016) and Space Simulation for Planetary Space Exploration (SPACE 2016) (2016)
4. Bruzzone, A.G., Massei, M., Agresta, M., Tremori, A., Longo, F., Murino, G., De Felice, F., Petrillo, A.: Human behavior simulation for smart decision making in emergency prevention and mitigation within urban and industrial environments. In: Proceedings of the 27th EMSS European Modeling & Simulation Symposium (2015)
5. Casbeer, D.W., Beard, R.W., McLain, T.W., Li, S.M., Mehra, R.K.: Forest fire monitoring with multiple small UAVs. In: Proceedings of the American Control Conference, vol. 5, pp. 3530–3535 (2005)
6. Longo, F., Bruzzone, A.G., Vetrano, M., Padovano, A.: Drones based relief on moon disaster simulation. In: Proceedings of SpringSim, Pasadena, CA, USA, 3–6 April 2016
7. Tremori, A., Agresta, M., Ferrando, A.: Simulation of autonomous systems in the extended marine domain. Int. J. Simul. Process Modell. 11(1), 9–23 (2016)
8. Wilson, B., Mourant, R., Li, M., Xu, W.: A virtual environment for training overhead crane operators: real-time implementation. IIE Trans. 30, 589–595 (1998)
9. Hodicky, J.: Modelling and simulation in the autonomous systems' domain- current status and way ahead. In: Hodicky, J. (ed.) Modelling and Simulation for Autonomous System. LNCS, vol. 9055, pp. 17–23. Springer, Heidelberg (2015)
10. Hodicky, J.: HLA as an experimental backbone for autonomous system integration into operational field. In: Hodicky, J. (ed.) Modelling and Simulation for Autonomous System. LNCS, vol. 8906, pp. 121–126. Springer, Heidelberg (2014)

DeSIRE 2: Satcom Modeling and Simulation a Powerful Tool to Enable Cost Effective and Safe Approach to RPAS Operational Deployment

Giancarlo Cosenza[1], Alessandro Mura[2], Alessandro Righetto[1],
Fabio De Piccoli[1], Dario Rapisardi[1], and Laura Anselmi[1(✉)]

[1] Telespazio, a Leonardo and Thales Company, Rome, Italy
{giancarlo.cosenza, alessandro.righetto,
fabio.depiccoli, dario.rapisardi,
laura.anselmi}@telespazio.com
[2] Leonardo SpA, Rome, Italy
alessandro.mura@leonardocompany.com

Abstract. Drones are a breakthrough systemic solution for a number of applications, from institutional and governmental purposes to a wide range of possible commercial applications. Autonomous and remotely controlled machines, fully integrated with many devices all connected wherever they are, are going to be a major part of the Internet of Things (IoT), where satellite communication plays a pivotal role.

Modelling and Simulation (M&S) are very helpful tools in the design and risk reduction of sustainable integration of Autonomous Systems into cost effective operational activities. As matter of fact, the M&S approach is extensively used in the DeSIRE 2 (Demonstration of the use of Satellites complementing Remotely Piloted Aircraft Systems integrated in non-segregated airspace 2nd Element). The ongoing Project, recently launched by the European Space Agency and the European Defence Agency, aims to demonstrate a service based on a Remotely Piloted Aircraft (RPA) flying in Beyond Radio Line of Sight (BRLOS) using space assets (SatCom, SatNav). The project has been kicked off in April 2015, after a selective process among important European consortia, and is leaded by Telespazio.

Through Model and Simulation, within DeSIRE 2 it will be possible to:

- Decrease costs, considering the loop "designing, building, testing, redesigning, rebuilding, retesting";
- Make easier the "what-if" definition and analysis allowing the definition and experimentation and test of CONOPS;
- De-risk the overall project.

To characterize adequately the Satcom link of DeSIRE 2 against the stringent performance requirements of the aeronautical context, an intensive measurement campaign is required. Concerning flight, the testing hours for a large RPAS are very costly. Therefore, it has been decided to add to the experimental flight campaign a combination of simulated and emulated environments, which replicate, as much as possible, the real operational conditions.

© Springer International Publishing AG 2016
J. Hodicky (Ed.): MESAS 2016, LNCS 9991, pp. 309–336, 2016.
DOI: 10.1007/978-3-319-47605-6_26

The models used in the simulation will be refined during the iterations, increasing the robustness and reliability, thus, making available results otherwise difficult, costly and even dangerous to be experiment directly in the real world.

An overview of the main expected results and how they should support the European standardisation and regulatory activities in the framework of the Air Traffic Insertion (ATI), especially for the definition of future satellite-based command & control datalinks, will be given as well. The paper will explain how the project intends to characterise the Satcom command and control datalinks for both Ka and L frequency bands.

It will be described how the threefold simulation/emulation/flight campaign approach will be followed to demonstrate that the system meets or exceeds the design requirement by combining:

- Mission Simulation, including satcom, airborne, mission applications and combination of the above segments;
- (Satcom) Emulation with real satellite full communication and RPA/RPS simulators.
- Mixed simulation and emulation will also be considered and real hardware will be introduced in the simulation loop (e.g. real satellite transponders and on board satcom terminals);
- Flight Campaign.

At any stage of this iteration, the results will be fed-back into the simulation/emulation chain. For example, the measured jitter and error rates will be introduced to update the parameters for the simulators for more trustworthy results.

1 The DeSIRE 2 Project - Quick Introduction

The project started about one year ago, with a budget of 2.6 M€. The winning consortium is composed by e-GEOS, Leonardo, Piaggio Aerospace, ViaSat, Skyguide and Ædel Aerospace (Fig. 1).

After an initial design phase now concluded with its Critical Design Review held on last January, the ongoing Phase 2 of the project will pass through its manifold demonstration phases.

DeSIRE 2 will field a complex mix of national and European technologies including, as key innovation, the Piaggio Aerospace's RPAS P1.HammerHead (P1. HH), with the central collaboration of Leonardo most of the on-board avionics and of the Remote Pilot Station (RPS or Ground Control Station - GCS).

Telespazio plays the role of system integrator and, together with its subsidiary eGeos, will be the service provider for all the End Users involved.

The project can count on a User Advisory Board composed by key leading Institutions in the selected application areas such as the Italian Coast Guard (ICG), Guardia di Finanza (GdF), Department of Civil Protection (DPC), the European Fish Control Agency (EFCA) and Armasuisse.

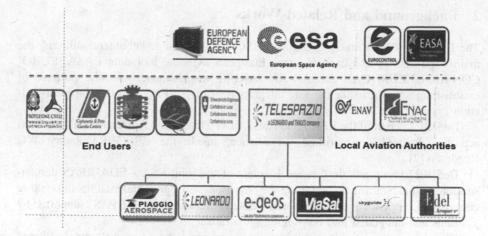

Fig. 1. DeSIRE 2 industrial team and advisory boards

It is worthwhile to note also the important contribution from the national competent Air Traffic Insertion (ATI) Stakeholders. ENAC (Ente Nazionale per l'Aviazione Civile) and ENAV (Ente Nazionale di Assistenza al Volo) that will participate along the entire project life to consolidate the operational and regulatory requirements to operate RPAS in response to institutional needs, in close coordination with the European and International ATI Stakeholders European Aviation Safety Agency (EASA), Eurocontrol; Single European Sky Air Traffic Management Research (SESAR), Joint Authorities for Rulemaking on Unmanned Systems (JARUS).

During the flight test campaign, the P.1HH will be fully integrated with the Telespazio and e-Geos satellite infrastructures and through them to the involved End User Operating Centres, to provide real time and near real time value added services.

Among the most important planned activities, Telespazio is in charge of the development of the air/ground communication system integrating a twin SatCom systems (in both L- and Ka-bands - in partnership with Viasat) for both Control and Non Payload Communication (CNPC) and Payload data links transmission. Furthermore, the Prime, is in charge of the development of innovative satellite navigation services, based on Global Navigation Satellite System (GNSS)/European Geostationary Navigation Overlay System (EGNOS) receivers, On the side of End User service provision, e-Geos will take care of the integration of the real time surveillance data acquired by RPAS with that derived from Earth Observation satellites, providing high benefit services. Leonardo will also provide the overall Mission Simulation environment for which Telespazio, in turn, is in charge of the SatCom simulator components. Telespazio is also in charge of the Emulation Platform.

The Italian Space Agency (ASI) will make available the Ka band SatCom resource from the Athena Fidus satellite.

2 Background and Related Works

The European RPAS Steering Group (ERSG), a group of stakeholders gathering the main organisations and experts of the European aviation, including EASA, EURO-CONTROL, EUROCAE, SESAR JU, JARUS, was founded with the purpose of establishing a roadmap for the safe integration of civil RPAS into the European aviation system [1].

DeSIRE2 is part of the RPAS related ESA IAP (Integrated Applications Promotion) activities focused on maritime surveillance, inside the ERSG Regulatory WG Roadmap [2].

DeSIRE2 represents the Second Element of the joint ESA - EDA RPAS demonstration roadmap aimed at supporting the development of governmental/institutional & commercial services based on Remotely Piloted Aircraft Systems (RPAS) supported by satellites and integrated into non-segregated airspace.

Objectives are to develop and demonstrate a service based on a Remotely Piloted Aircraft (RPA) flying in Beyond Radio Line of Sight (BRLOS) using space assets (SatCom, SatNav) for satellite communications, extending the work performed in Desire – First Element [3].

The project addresses the following perspectives:

- Regulatory perspective: contributing to some of the regulatory improvements in the European Regulatory Roadmap, and disseminating the results to relevant regulatory and standardisation bodies. Main contribution will be represented by the definition and validation of certification requirements (e.g. RCP - Required Communication performance - in terms of transaction time, Continuity, Availability and Integrity [6]) for RPAS C2 link satellite communication according to the approach proposed by JARUS [4, 5].
- User perspective: developing the applications and demonstrating the operational service provision shortly after the completion of the project.
- Technology perspective: demonstrating the technology required for supporting the regulatory improvements defined by the European RPAS Steering Group and satisfying user needs.

3 DeSIRE 2 Mission Simulation

3.1 Distributed Simulation Environment Implementation Using an Iterative Approach

The development of technologies and standards is the key for the full integration of Remotely Piloted Aircraft System (RPAS) in the worldwide airspace.

These types of aircraft have to be operated taking into consideration the risk of each specific task, by applying proportionate rules suitable for each different environment.

The evolution of the RPAS technology and rules cannot be carried out without a significant testing period, CONOPS studies, "what-if" scenarios, and training phases for all the involved operators. All of the above must have a large agreement among all the stakeholders, from the RPAS industry to the National and International Authorities.

Just to give an idea of the complexity of the topic, one of the most important challenges in the Instrument Flight Rule (IFR)/RPAS insertion is to demonstrate the validity and limits of:

- Ad-hoc operational procedures to operate RPAS in non-segregated airspace;
- Airworthiness rules that normally are used to "certify" an RPAS for experimental scope;
- Existing technologies and systems compared to the requirements and capabilities of the current and future ATM systems (e.g. SESAR project).

Keeping these in mind, the typical problems span from allowing the assessment of the feasibility to introduce RPAS in non-segregated airspace for each traffic density to the use of satellite communication to cope with the Beyond Radio Line of Sight (BRLOS) situation as well as from the definition and test of emergency procedures to the development of Detect and Avoid (DAA) technology. Without mentioning the paramount issues of possible cyber-attack to the whole system.

Considering the extreme practical difficulties and very high costs in setting up test and trials in a real environment, the operational simulation approach seems to be the right if not the only solution.

Furthermore, the multiple technologies involved together with a number of stakeholders, points out that the Distributed Simulation is a suitable solution to cope with a myriad of technical and user's requirements.

To face this complex situation, in the DeSIRE 2 project there are three main guidelines:

- Iterative approach;
- Extensive use of distributed simulation;
- Final user direct involvement with requirements elicitation and near-simultaneous testing.

3.2 Iterative Approach

As shown in Fig. 2 the project is evolving from a pure simulated environment to a live system where the real aircraft will fly in a real scenario. The simulated scenario was chosen taking into consideration the feasibility in terms of cost, time and permit to fly as required in a real setting.

Wherever possible, the simulated system will be completed with real components. In this way, it will be possible to "superimpose" the two environments creating a mixed exercise (real + virtual) where real actors will be able to operate together with simulated parts. Eventually, when all the constraints will be overcome, this approach will be ready for the migration from the mixed situation to the all-real one.

3.3 Extensive Use of Distributed Simulation

The simulation architecture will be the cradle for all the exercises foreseen in the DeSIRE 2 project and it is intended to:

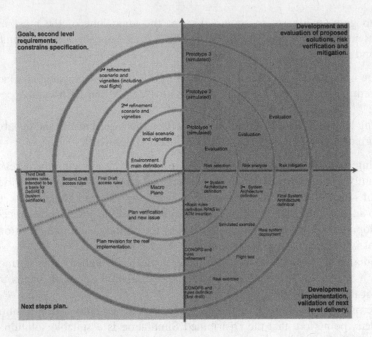

Fig. 2. Iterative approach

- Decrease costs, in particular considering the loop "designing, building, testing, redesigning, rebuilding, retesting, etc.". All the phases that can be simulated are taken off the loop of real tests by using the models created in the initial design. The iterative approach allows for the refining of the models used in the simulation, increasing their robustness and reliability as the project proceeds collecting data coming from the emulation and real flight.
- Obtain results that would be costly, difficult or even dangerous to experiment in the real world (e.g. system complexity and the number of the actors make too expensive and/or physically impossible the real exercise). By using simulation, also critical situations can be investigated without risk. In these cases, simulation will allow the project to run at any level of detail for as many times as needed, being constrained only by the intrinsic hardware limitation. Moreover, a fine tune of time control can be available speeding up or slowing down the experiment according to specific needs.
- Facilitate the "what-if" definition and analysis. In the DeSIRE 2 project, this is particularly important for all the preparatory phases including the definition, experimentation and tests of CONOPS, and the state of related rules. Specific tools to measure the most significant exercises' parameters are in place to facilitate the data gathering and their analysis.
- Investigate the effects of several changes by simply changing the parameters and/or the environmental conditions.
- De-risk the overall project. The simulation will take a key part in all the de-risking steps including the preparation, design and implementation of the real experiments.

In the current implementation each mission's goal is fulfilled by using a simulated aircraft, operating in an ATM sky generated by an IFR traffic simulator integrated with other simulated and real objects while the evolution of the mission simulation is carried out. Examples of these objects are: RPAS ground station; vessel traffic controlled and displayed by a VTS real system, ATM Control Working Positions, other cooperative actors, test targets.

Afterwards, the chain of events recorded will be used to:

- Guide the experiment in the real environment;
- Suggest maneuvers to challenge the real system;
- Compare the results coming from the real field with the previous one.

The latter bullet will have consequently the possibility of fine-tuning the simulation system that will be available for further, more trustworthy, exercises.

3.4 The Distributed Approach

The simulation approach will include the use of single equipment as well as whole systems, depending on the level of needed analysis.

Because of the extreme heterogeneity of the technology and equipment involved, a distributed approach has been adopted. A dedicated network is used, allowing constructive, virtual and, wherever possible, live simulations. Each participating working group, specialised in a specific operation, contributes delivering its portion of virtual simulation.

3.5 The Simulation Network: SimLabs

The Leonardo's Simulation Network (SimLabs in the following) is a scalable and reconfigurable on-demand operating network among simulation laboratories, which establishes a synthetic environment that allows constructive and virtual simulation systems.

The test bed, instead of having a single monolithic simulator able to represent all the characteristics of the overall system, is composed of a network-based federation of simulators. Each involved lab manages and maintains the complete control of its simulator.

The simulation network has been implemented as configurable and scalable environment in which it is possible to:

- Design a synthetic environment where scenarios, objects and related relationships can be defined;
- Design and test equipment, systems behaviour, rules, doctrines, strategies and tactics;
- Allow people to operate on any object, the object's action or rules put in place for the defined scenario;
- Integrate and validate systems.

Each lab is able to participate, in real-time, to the evolution of a specific shared operational scenario, making available simulators, together with people and related expertise without increasing the costs by avoiding equipment duplication. Moreover, each institution is able to maintain all the IPR on the specific piece of software and/or the simulated or real component.

SimLabs could be also seen as a technological asset through which various expertise, skills and tools, available across several Labs can be shared.

Since the co-development and testing with partners have become increasingly common, the technology has been designed to make available the shared environment not only internally but also to industrial, academic or institutional partners in a "hosting service mode".

The subsystems are implemented as federates exchanging data via HLA (High Level Architecture protocol).

The network may also provide the connected sites with a specific support to their system development and performance evaluation activities in a "System of Systems" fashion.

During the last decade, multiple joint events have highlighted the flexibility and the effectiveness of the implementation of a real-time Virtual-Constructive-Live simulation, involving various systems and laboratories.

The network has been connected with several institutions: not only other Leonardo's Divisions but also partners and customers facilities (e.g. the Rome NATO Center of Excellence of M&S, the Italian Navy facilities in Taranto, the Italian Army in different sites).

In its implementation, SimLabs is also used to provide a Proof of Concepts tool offering an environment in which Concepts of Operation can be designed and experimented. Furthermore, it is possible to train and verify the ability of operators, to exercise operational procedures and to interact with command and control systems. Finally, it can be used as a reconfigurable demonstration tool for customers' prospect.

To facilitate the integration, the architecture concept is scalable, starting from the single site is then extended in a step-by-step approach to reach a geographical distributed configuration.

In this way, each group can start working independently on its own portion of project just having in common the local SE.

The capability to grant connection and interoperability is one of the main characteristics of these laboratories. Their high-configurable and scalable architecture allow them to be very adaptable to a wide spread of tests and trials from systems design/analysis to activities including portion of real scenarios.

It is noteworthy that this approach is well known by most of the participating groups and already used in other distributed simulations in previous programmes.

A portion of this network is already available for DeSIRE 2 and a specific set-up and integration among Leonardo's labs is under construction considering the possible extension to other participants in the future projects.

3.6 The Scenario and the Simulated Actors

Following the spiral structure depicted in the Fig. 2 the first step will be to define and implement the simulated scenario.

The zone has been chosen according to the following considerations:

- Significant exercises consistent with real current emergency situations can be carried out;
- A number of possible flight corridors for RPAS are already defined;
- It is relatively easy to define a non-segregated zone for the final exercise.

In the Fig. 3 the zone is shown in the official map of Italian Air Forces.

Among all these possible corridors, a specific subset will be cut out in order to focus only on the itinerary needed for the exercise.

The corridors, currently used in the DeSIRE 2 mission simulation exercise, are shown in Fig. 4.

They include portions of the "Decimo corridor", "Victor corridor", "Trapani corridor", (including "GHOST Areas" (1 and 2), "TC2" and "TC3"), "HESPO corridor", "TANGO corridor".

A new possible corridor starting from the Grottaglie Airport and finishing in the Taranto southern littoral will be also considered.

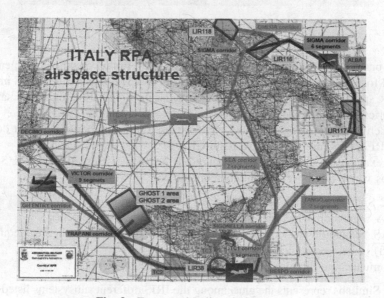

Fig. 3. Zones and Italian air fore map

3.7 The IRIS Environment

To cope with all the previous requirements, for the implementation of the DeSIRE 2 scenario in the distributed synthetic environment, has been chosen a product currently under development in the Leonardo Company.

The IRIS (IFR/RPAS Integration Simulator) is a Simulation Environment that aims at replicating substantial aspects of real RPAS operations in an ATM sky under realistic operating conditions and in a fully interactive fashion.

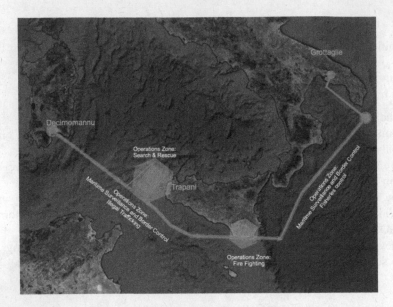

Fig. 4. Simulated scenario

It is based on SimLabs technology and is intended, in this specific implementation, as a tool for Experimentation and Test, Evaluation and Training for the RPAS insertion in a IFR space, including CONOPS studies, Mission preparation and rehearsal, brief and debrief sessions, basic, intermediate and advanced training.

The environment is agnostic and could be used in a number of different domains where IRF/RPAS insertion will be required.

An example is the recently configured Blue Border Surveillance and Security scenarios where the most relevant components are:

- ATC Simulator (which has an interface with the real equipment);
- MDA Simulator (which has an interface with the real equipment);
- RPAS Simulator (which may have both an interface with the real equipment (RPS) or being completely simulated);
- Communication Simulator, which includes a satellite segment).

The SimLabs represents the glue among the IRIS different subsystems listed above.

In Fig. 5 an example is given of the test cases that will be performed before starting the real Mission exercises.

3.8   The ATC Simulator

This is an essential part of the IRIS infrastructure and represents one of these subsystems.

The ATC Simulator system provides a support for the ATC environment, including workload evaluation, flow control, optimum airspace configuration and new control procedure for RPAS.

Test	Description
Test 1	Entire flight plan Switch from RLOS to BRLOS BRLOS communication monitoring Change of flight level to verify ATC Voice and CPDLC (UC1+UC2+UC3)
Test 2	Flight until the first waypoint. meteorological condition will be degraded. Record the performances of ATC (Voice e CPDLC) communications and satellite channels (Ka-band and L-band) (UC1+UC2+UC4)
Test 3	Flight until the first waypoint and clear sky RPIL changes the position and the asset of RPA, sending C2 command through BRLOS: modify immediately the pitch angle and climb's speed to the P1HH dynamic limit values (UC1+UC2+UC3)
Test 4	Flight until the first waypoint and clear sky RPIL commands the same acrobatic maneuvers of test 3, repeating them with all the degraded meteo conditions (UC1+UC2+UC4)
Test 5	Flight until the first waypoint and clear sky Ka-band o L-band are alternately disabled and the emergency procedures are monitored (UC5)

Fig. 5. Simulation tests description (example)

Its primary function is the realistic simulation of an ATC environment where a predefined group of aircrafts are automatically flown by the System. This is followed by controlled Pseudo-Pilots and the insertion of a RPA controlled by RPS according to the ATC rules and Controllers instructions.

It is a flexible and powerful system having the capability of running a wide range of ATC Simulation Scenarios for advanced training of Controllers. This allows investigations in which RPAS may be able to use a technical capability or procedural means to comply with ATC instructions, including current and new concepts to be conceived and tested in the simulation.

As an example: ATC Simulator shall be used to determine the impact of integration of RPAS on ATM in some areas assuming RPAS may be unable to comply with all existing manned operations rules, particularly in case of C2 (Command & Control) data-link loss between RPAS and the remote pilot, and other emergency cases.

The simulation scenarios shall be used also for assessment of whether RPAS might, in the early phases of ATM integration, not behave exactly in the same way as manned aircraft. The latency and a different flight awareness of the crew, will impact on separation provision. Moreover, by means of ATC simulation scenarios, shall be possible to better evaluate the sensitivity of RPAS in different weather conditions and the capacity to react to these by simulating a specific coordination between ATC and the Remote Pilot especially for immediate maneuver, level changes and rerouting.

3.9   The Maritime Domain Awareness (MDA) Simulator

This is the second main subsystem of IRIS representing the specialisation of this application for the Blue Border Surveillance.

In its completed implementation, it includes simulators of:

- Distributed sensors: radar, electro-optical sensors, transponders (AIS) and radio equipment (voice, communication intelligence-COMINT), airborne sensors (UAV, Airplane, helicopter), buoys sensors;
- Satellite surveillance providing radar images relevant to the whole extended EEZ including the continental shelf;
- Protection systems for coastal infrastructures (e.g. ports, oil terminals) and offshore platforms;
- Local C4I canters performing sensor data collection and processing, sensor management, compilation and broadcasting of Common Operational Picture (COP);
- Regional C4I canters that receive and merge data from local C4I, protection systems as well as other legacy systems and satellite imagery, compile the high level COP and manage operations.

3.10   The RPAS Simulator

It is composed by a synthetic environment and several objects, including a number of RPAS models, represented in a 2D/3D scenario.

SYENA (Synthetic Environment Animator) is a Leonardo Simulation Environment Suite designed to create, run and manage complex tactical scenario with a high level of realism.

Syena is also meant to provide the user with the maximum level of flexibility in the creation of elaborated scenario and mission planning. Scenarios with thousands of entities can be generated rapidly and their run-time evolution can be monitored and easily modified by the user.

Syena is here used to implement the RPAS operational environment "inserted" in the ATC Simulation.

3.11   Integrated Communication

Simulated by the SVC (namely "Simulatore e Valutatore delle Comunicazioni"). Developed by the Leonardo Company, it is a simulation environment dedicated to the communication network analysis and validation.

The application fields of SVC range from the evaluation of new architectures and solution to Acquisition Support and Training.

Specifically, its advantages are to model and simulate new communication techniques and technologies before their introduction "in the field. Verify their applicability and operational benefits can be obtained in complex scenarios.

4   The RPAS Satcom Challenge: Complementary Approach

To allow a Remotely Piloted Aircrafts System (RPAS) to be safely integrated into non-segregated airspace, from the perspective of the Air Traffic Management (ATM) system, entails RPAS to behave as any other manned aircrafts. This principle implies that, the performance required for the communication capabilities, expressed as RCP/RCTP (Required Communication Performance/Required Communication Technical Performance") meet challenging requirements in particular for the C2/ATC links between the RPS (Remote Pilot Station) and the RPA (remoted Piloted Aircraft) [4, 7].

Due to limits on RPA availability, risk mitigation requirements and budget constraints the time for flight trials are limited to 30 flight hours. This limited duration is not sufficient to exercise and demonstrate the performance requirements under all the nominal and contingency situations. Even to prove that error rate does not exceed the expected value would require thousands of hours of flight campaign.

M&S are very helpful tool also in this context for characterizing the RPAS communication links. DeSIRE 2, in particular, will address the Beyond Radio Line of Sight (BRLOS) case where satcom is mandatory. As matter of fact a twin satcom link solution is foreseen, combining an L band channel for C2/ATC purposes with a wider Ka band channel for both C2/ATC and Payload data transmission.

In the first phase a pure simulation of both Satcom components, integrated with the other mission elements (airborne, ATC and mission applications already described) will be provided. Considering the iterative approach, this phase will be followed by a mixed simulation and emulation, where real hardware is introduced into the satcom simulation loop (e.g. real satellite terminals and transponders) using a full flight emulation platform with a motion test bench, reducing the need of a flying RPA.

At any stage of this communication iteration, the results will be fed-back into the simulation/emulation chain. As an example, the measured jitter and error rates will be introduced as updated parameters for the simulators for more realistic results (Fig. 6).

The advantages of this approach are:

- Higher confidence on simulation results;
- Higher confidence on overall design;
- Much richer set of test conditions and performance statistics than would be attainable with sole flight campaigns.

A series of field tests, through flight trials, will close the demonstration campaign.

Satcom Simulation, emulation and flights measurement campaign will allow to measure some specific parameters (e.g. BER/PER, latency, etc.) that will have to be related with the RCP/RTCP parameters (availability, integrity, continuity, transaction time).

In particular, for the Satcom link, the following parameters will be measured:

- BER Bit Error Rate or PER Packet Error Rate
- Satellite link Quality (Eb/No or C/N)
- Latency

Fig. 6. DeSIRE 2 threefold complementary approach

4.1 Satcom Simulation

The Satcom module simulates the Satcom communication channels among RPA, RPS and Teleport. It is used to propagate satellite over the time scenario, simulate the on-board antenna pointing dynamics, subject to the aircraft attitude changes, and compute the geometries of the scenario, e.g. distance to satellite, azimuth and elevation angles (Fig. 7).

The geometric engine computes the geometric parameters for the link budget, among which distances (e.g. RPA Sat, Sat gateway, RPS-RPA,), visibilities (e.g. RPS-RPA), visibilities interference (e.g. RPA Sat during operations), azimuth and elevation of satellites as seen by SATCOM antennas (e.g. on-board RPA, on the Teleport-gateway, RPS).

Satcom module computes information on propagation channel characteristics, related to propagation delay, C/N, data rate, BER/PER, mainly derived from geometric and link budget calculations, and sent to the simulation environment so that the degradation of the propagation channel can be applied to the sensor data flows.

All the information is used to estimate the propagation channel characteristics of Ka band and L band frequencies (e.g. free space loss, total loss, propagation delay, C/N, data rate, BER/PER, Doppler effect), and consequently the link budget. The total latency also takes into account the ground network latency, estimated from the characteristics of the different trunks of the satellite networks.

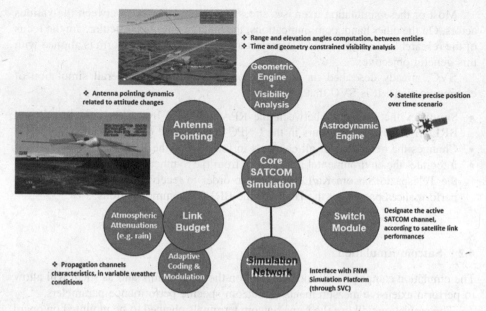

Fig. 7. DeSIRE 2 satcom simulation concept

The main differences between Ka and L band SATCOM simulator components is in the following areas:

- Link budget calculation, L-band is much more resilient to rain/snow/ice/cloud/ scintillation events.
- Antenna pointing characteristics, the L-band antenna is a phased array type, therefore mechanical inertia is negligible.

The integration module automates the management of the other modules of the platform and handles the information flow of simulation parameters from and to the UDP server. This module needs to be adapted/extended to suit the specific needs of the simulation.

Satcom module communicates exclusively with SVC, through a dedicated UDP socket. From SVC, Satcom module receives all pertinent scenario information, in particular simulation time, aircraft data (position, velocity, acceleration, and attitude), simulated sensors data characteristics, weather conditions on aircraft and on HUB/gateway generated by the synthetic environment.

Satcom module sends to SVC information on propagation channel characteristics, among which propagation delay, C/N, data rate, BER/PER, mainly derived from geometric and link budget calculations, so that SVC can apply the degradation of the propagation channel, if present, to the sensor data flows.

The Ka – L band Switch Module, using the link budget information and an internal algorithm for Ka-L band switching, is responsible to designate the active SATCOM channel to be used for CNPC data transmission. This information is timely transmitted to the SVC every time the simulation scenario is updated.

Most of these simulation exercises stress the communications between the various actors. On the other hand, communications, the Satcom ones in particular, are the focus of the research addressed within the project and the simulation platform is aligned with this general objective.

SVC, already described, is in charge of orchestrating the overall simulation of communications. It is SVC that:

- Simulates the data flow between the RPA and RPS by putting the RLOS and BRLOS channels behaviours in the CNPC and Payload communications;
- Changes the behaviour of all channels in function of the RPA state;
- Integrates the environmental information from the Synthetic Environment (SE) with the Telespazio Satcom Ka/L simulator in order to receive and use the parameters performances passed by the latter for the BRLOS communications.

4.2   Satcom Emulation

The emulation campaign will focus mainly on the Satcom link and as such, will allow to perform extensive measurements of Satcom specific performance parameters.

The emulation will use the same Satcom terminals planned to be mounted on board the RPA, fastened to a motion platform, a hexapod equipped with six electric actuators that give it six degrees of freedom, and the ability to mimic the attitude changes of the RPA (Fig. 8).

The motion system will allow to replicate the same conditions that on-board antennas encounter during a typical flight phase, e.g. misalignment of Ka band antenna after an emergency maneuver.

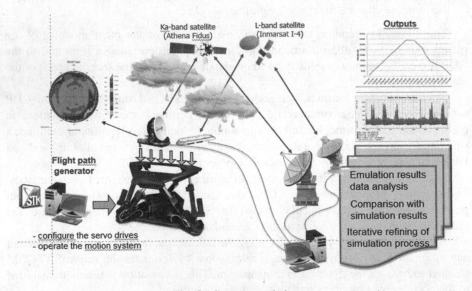

Fig. 8. Satcom emulation

The emulation test phase gives the project the significant opportunity to test the antennas extensively without limitations imposed by a real flight test, especially due to time and cost limits.

The emulation testbed guarantees many hours of data that can be analyzed for statistical purposes and so for RCTP derivation.

In addition, tests on switch between the L band and Ka-band will be performed. Several degraded performance will be induced on Ka band link to force the system to switch to L-band link, more resilient to rain outages. Also the reverse switch will be tested.

The switch tests will help to evaluate the dual link switch process, in order to refine the switch logic algorithm.

In this case the motion platform will not be required. Both terminals will be positioned on ground to ensure the complete visibility to the satellites.

The emulation phase will allow bypassing some limitations imposed by the flight campaign.

In fact, the emulation testbed will allow testing a second L-band antenna that will not be possible to mount and test, for reason of costs and design complexity, on board.

The performances of two L band antennas will be compared to determine if differences exist and so the best solution to offer to the end-users.

Besides the emulation test phase will allow testing the antennas in variable weather conditions, therefore also in rainy conditions, contrarily to the flight campaign, during which the RPA will flown only when the weather conditions permit, so-called clear sky conditions, especially for safety issues.

The emulation platform will remain in operation for a long period, during which the antenna/s mounted on it will be subjected to the normal variations of weather conditions.

The measurement of satellite link performances will be mainly based on the collection and statistical analysis of the following type of data:

- Satellite Link Quality & Performances of both the Ka-band and L-band links, with measurements derived directly from Satcom modem through the SNMP Protocol (Simple Network Management Protocol), aimed at "physical" characterization of the satellite link;
- IP Data flows transmission performances for both UDP and TCP Protocols, with measurements derived from Network Monitoring tools, aimed at evaluating end-to-end performances of a specific data flow over the satellite link path (i.e. measuring the speed of the network, the elapsed time for a particular network transaction, the IP packet loss rate/percentage) in both directions (forward link and return link – see note below).

Note:

- "RX link" is intended as downlink channel from Satcom terminal viewpoint, that corresponds to the "Forward Link" transmitted from the Gateway to the Satcom terminal (GW to RPA);
- "TX link" is intended as uplink channel from Satcom terminal viewpoint, that corresponds to the "Return Link" transmitted from the Satcom terminal to the Gateway (RPA to GW).

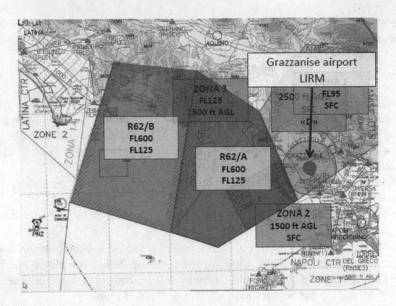

Fig. 9. Grazzanise airspace

Performance Measurement analysis will be also correlated, when applicable, with motion platform "maneuvers" and meteorological conditions.

5   The DeSIRE 2 Flight Demonstration

5.1   The Airspaces

The airspace involved in the demonstration are shown in Fig. 9:

- Grazzanise ATZ
- Grazzanise CTR
- LI-R62A
- LI-R62B

R-62 is a restricted area and during flight tests, it will not be accessible to other civil airspace users for safety reasons. Nevertheless, during demonstration the RPA will be under control of civil ATC (ENAV) and will follow real ATM procedures, including:

- Preparation of an actual IFR flight plan (FPL) and submission through the Aeronautical Information System;
- Operation under military control for airport operations (Grazzanise TWR) and handoff to civil ATC (ENAV) for departure, climb, en-route and arrival phases;
- Use of SIDs and STARs procedures specifically designed by ENAV for the flight campaign;

- Continuous radio contact with ATC during OAT phase for mandatory reports of normal operations.
- The typical flight demonstration mission will be divided in four phases:
- Planning and preparation: mission is planned by pilots, ground crew and involved end-users. The RPA is prepared and checked for flight.
- Departure and deployment: the RPA will depart from base, climb and reach the target area for use-case demonstration. During this phase the RPA operates as a GAT (General Air Traffic, following ICAO civil aviation rules). After departure RPA control is typically switched from RLOS to Satcom BRLOS.
- Operation: the RPA performs the operational task (e.g. S&R, law-enforcement, etc.) acquiring the status of OAT (Operational Air Traffic) if necessary. The RPA is controlled through Satcom BRLOS datalinks.
- Return to base: the RPA returns to the base and lands. This phase of flight is again conducted as GAT and before landing RLOS, links are re-activated.

The base for the flight campaign is Grazzanise airport (ICAO code LIRM) and neighbouring "R-62" (ROMEO-62) areas, from sea level up to around 20.000 ft (Fig. 10). The operational theatre is representative of a real scenario and covers both land and sea areas.

Fig. 10. Grazzanise airbase

Flight missions will mainly be conducted over the sea, but sorties along the coast or with the coast in-sight could also be possible if required by the use-case scenario.

The mission will be conducted between FL200 and a minimum altitude varying between 2500 and 4500 ft. The difference in minimum altitude is caused by mountains obstructing RLOS datalinks at low altitude in some areas. A survey campaign is currently being conducted (at the time of writing) to characterize such obstruction area.

The typical duration of a flight will be between 1.5 and 3 h.

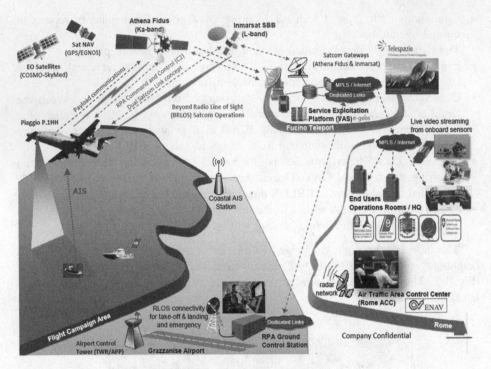

Fig. 11. DeSIRE 2 system demonstration architecture

5.2 The DeSIRE 2 System Demonstration Architecture

The Demonstration System Architecture (DSA) that will be set up during the project is presented in Fig. 11. From a logical point of view, this architecture can be structured in three major segments:

- **Space Segment** composed by the SatCom Satellites Athena Fidus (made available by ASI), operating in Ka Band and Inmarsat I-4, operating in L band: Ka will support both aero safety services and real time payload data dissemination; L band will be used only for CNPC to increase its overall availability. The EO Satellites based on COSMO-SkyMed constellation and ESA Sentinel satellites are included, providing both Synthetic Aperture Radar (X and C bands) and Optical data.
- **Ground Segment** composed by elements needed to control the operation of the mission, the integration of the RPA in the airspace and the mission data exploitation:
  - **The Fucino Teleport** where both Athena Fidus and Inmarsat L band Gateways are located. For Ka band data link, a dedicated Viasat Mini-Hub is integrated with the ASI Athena Fidus Gateway.
  - **The RPS** located at the airport and connected to the Fucino Teleport through a dedicated, secure and redundant terrestrial link.
  - **The Value Added Services (VAS) Processing centre**, in Rome (e-GEOS and Telespazio headquarter), connected to the Fucino Teleport, The VAS processing

center will take advantage of Matera Ground Station, to acquire EO satellite data and operate information extraction and integration with available ancillary data (maritime Automatic Information System - AIS, Vessel monitoring system - VMS, Long-Range Identification and Tracking - LRIT and met-ocean data).
- **The SatNav centre** based in Telespazio headquarter of Rome will be able to process data coming from on board GNSS/EGNOS receiver.
- **The End User Interface Networks** to transfer real time RPA payload and value added data to the End User system at their operational premises.
- RPA segment. The Piaggio P.1HH prototype will be incorporating all the equipment necessary to perform the DeSIRE 2 mission tasks:
  - satellite terminals (both Viasat Ka and Inmarsat L band)
  - EO/IR video camera, AIS and EGNOS receivers integrated with the Payload Management subsystem,
  - The Voice comm, ATC connection and other safety critical items (Air Data, Traffic Collision Avoidance System -TCAS 1 and the transponder Mode S), or Nose Cams and Datalinks.

5.3   M&S as Support to Plan the Most Effective Demonstration Phase Vs. the ATI and User Mission Requirement

The project will provide an important step forward for the «safety critical» RPAS CNPC Services, by defining a first set of RCPs applicable to both the RPAS C2 and ATC links following the JARUS C2 link RCP Concept [R2] to define a certification path for the RPAS category above the threshold of 150 kg:

M&S, as far as ATI Requirements are concerned, will support DeSIRE 2 to demonstrate the following major requirement by allowing to create **the storyboard** of the fights dedicated to this particular requirement section that includes:

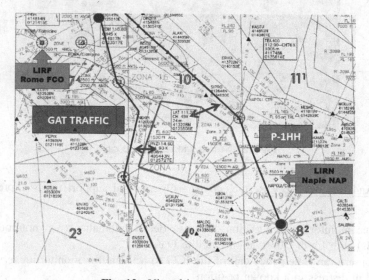

Fig. 12. Virtual intruder exercise

- Dual satcom link concept (L-band and Ka-band links) for •increased availability
- Cost-efficiency
- BRLOS satcom link performance measurements for CNPC and Payload data transmission
- End-to-End Voice Communication latency and QoS evaluation (RPIL -ATC)
- ATC procedures execution:
- RPIL-ATC interaction with ATC Relay over Satcom link and
- Implementation of C2 commands to RPA following ATC instructions
- Situation Awareness based on TrAw Data
- Virtual intruder exercise (Fig. 12)

As far as the User Mission Requirements, are concerned, DeSIRE 2 is going to provide interoperable, state-of-the-art real time services, to major institutional End Users operating in one of more of the following operational sectors:

- Search and Rescue
- Law Enforcement
- Fishery Control
- Fire Crisis Management

Modelling and Simulation will support to define **the storyboards** of the flights dedicated to demonstrate the major requirements identified in the following Use Cases.

Fig. 13. Search and rescue use case

Search And Rescue Use Case Objectives - Operational support needs expressed by the ICG:

- Routine monitoring of maritime areas to detect anomalies (e.g. not-cooperative vessels) with Earth Observation Satellite Data
- Response to an Emergency call of the ICG to activate the monitoring service of a vessel in distress in a known position

- Detection of vessels not transmitting their position in a given area of operation, this includes the integration of vessels identification data (AIS as a minimum)
- The target vessel type to be detected by the service shall have the following characteristics:
- Metallic and non-metallic materials, such as wooden or rubber boats
- Length of 5 to 80 m (Fig. 13)

<u>Law Enforcement Use Case Objectives</u> - Operational support needs expressed by the Guardia di Finanza (GdF):

- Monitoring of commercial lanes to support anomalies detection (not-cooperative vessels, rendezvous, etc.)
- Service activation by the GdF to monitor a vessel in a given area of operation, based on GdF intelligence information
- Detection of vessels not transmitting their position in a given area of operation with integration of vessels identification data (AIS as a minimum)
- Target vessel type to be detected by the service shall have the following characteristics:
- Metallic and non-metallic materials, such as wooden or rubber boats
- Length of 5 to 30 m
- Certified localization reference to provide legal evidence in case of infringements detection (Fig. 14)

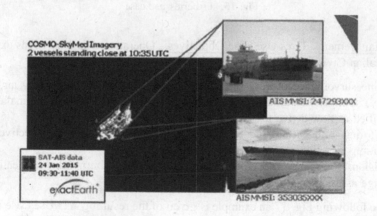

Fig. 14. Law enforcement use case

<u>Fisheries Use Case Objectives</u> - Operational support needs expressed by the ICG and EFCA:

- Routine monitoring of maritime areas subjected to illegal fishing activities to support anomalies detection (not-cooperative vessels, rendezvous, etc.).
- Detection of vessels not transmitting their position in a given area of operation (AIS as a minimum)

- The target vessel type to be detected by the service shall have the following characteristics:
- Fishing vessels
- Length of 5 to 80 m
- Identification of the used fishing methods
- Certified localization reference to provide legal evidence in case of infringements detection (Fig. 15)

Fig. 15. Fisheries use case

<u>Crisis Management - Fires Use Case Objectives</u> - Operational support needs expressed by the Italian Civil Protection Department (ICPD) and CEREN:

- Routine surveillance of very risk areas, under weather condition (dry air, worm, windy) strongly favourable to ignition, in order to detect thermal anomalies to be identified as new active fires.
- Monitoring, after an emergency call, of active fires to verify the effectiveness of operations and firefighting coordination support.
- Provision, soon after the emergency fire events, of burn scar delineation and damage assessment (Fig. 16).

In the following Fig. 17 an example is given of the resulting ATI Use Case analysis that will be performed in detail with the full support of the DeSIRE 2 User Community, according to what has been agreed in the DeSIRE 2 User Consultation Meeting (UCM) of Rome of last May 24th 2016.

Each User presented relevant Entity's assets and workflows, confirmed high interest on the RPAS and proposed service model and willingness to take part in the Flights campaign making available Personnel to assist and validate the results, on field support and real time data gathered from other sources. (e.g. VTS, AIS,..).

The Users confirmed their availability to build precise storyboards for the flights in cooperation with the Project team.

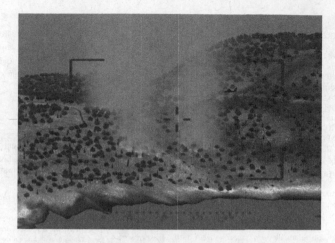

Fig. 16. Fires use case

ID	ATI Use Cases	Description
UC1	ATC Voice	Evaluate impact on ATCo-Remote Pilot voice communication of High Latency, introduced by Satcom
UC2	CPDLC	Evaluate ATCo-Remote Pilot interaction via CPDLC in BRLOS
UC3	BRLOS Comms performance in clear sky conditions	Evaluate BRLOS System Performance operating in L-band/Ka-band in "clear sky" conditions
UC4	BRLOS Comms System performance in degraded meteo conditions	Evaluate BRLOS System Performance operating in L-band/Ka-band in "degraded meteo" conditions

Fig. 17. ATI use cases (example)

The generation of the storyboards of the entire 30 h DeSIRE 2 Flight Demonstration Campaign has, as its main objective, to allocate all elementary flight test building blocks (see an example in Fig. 18) derived from the use case detailed requirement analysis.

The DeSIRE 2 Industrial Consortium, fully assisted by the entire DeSIRE 2 User Community and with the powerful support of the Mission Simulation tools described in the above sections, will generate the storyboards of each of the planned flights by making meaningful each elementary component of the P1.HH flight (Fig. 19).

ID	ATI Flight Tests
FT-ATI-001	BRLOS performance on Ka-band Satcom link (CNPC data)
FT-ATI-002	BRLOS performance on L-band Satcom link (CNPC data)
FT-ATI-003	CNPC (C2 and ATC Voice) End-to-End Communication latency / QoS evaluation (incl. C2, ATC)
FT-ATI-004	Payload Data End-to-End Communication latency / QoS evaluation
FT-ATI-005	BRLOS dual satcom link operations (for CNPC)
FT-ATI-006	RLOS-BRLOS handover
FT-ATI-007	ATC procedures
FT-ATI-008	virtual intruder
FT-ATI-010	Situational awareness based on D&A data (i.e. traffic information).
FT-ATI-010	Situational awareness based on D&A data (i.e. traffic information).

ID	Mission Flight Tests
FT-UR-001	Vessel detection Capability
FT-UR-002	Vessel recognition Capability
FT-UR-003	Vessel identification Capability
FT-UR-004	Vessel Tracking Capability
FT-UR-005	Multiple vessels detection capability within the AOO
FT-UR-006	AIS data reception and transmission capability
FT-UR-007	Fire detection Capability
FT-UR-008	Fire recognition Capability
FT-UR-009	Fire identification Capability
FT-UR-010	Sensors detection capability in bad visibility conditions
FT-UR-011	Specific Maneuvers Request from the User
FT-UR-012	Onboard Sensors looking direction modification request from the User
FT-UR-013	Real Time Data service delivery
FT-UR-014	VA products Near Real Time service delivery

Fig. 18. Flight tests building blocks (example)

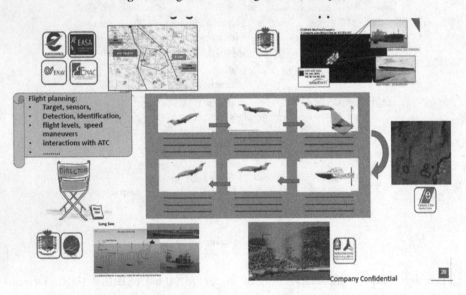

Fig. 19. ATI and mission flight storyboards

The Storyboard will include in details parameters like:

- Flight altitude,
- RPA manoeuvres,
- Sensor to be used and relevant operations,
- Intruders Aircraft maneuvers,
- Deployment of supporting assets, e.g. target to be identified, User Operational Vessels and so on.

These elements, necessary to demonstrate the requirements mentioned above, will be addressed in order to optimise the limited fight hours and to reach the demonstration target in the most effective and efficient way.

The storyboard will take care also of the different flight execution phases, including:

- **Departure and deployment**: the RPA will depart from base, climb and reach (Transit phase) the target area for use-case demonstration. During this phase the RPA operates as a GAT (General Air Traffic, following ICAO civil aviation rules). After departure RPA control is typically switched from RLOS to Satcom BRLOS;
- **Operation**: the RPA performs the operational task subdivided in Target identification and Recognition (to be identified for each type of mission, e.g. S&R, law-enforcement, etc.) acquiring the status of OAT (Operational Air Traffic) if necessary. The RPA is controlled through Satcom BRLOS datalinks.
- **Return to base**: the RPA returns to the base and lands. This phase of flight is again conducted as GAT and before landing RLOS, links are re-activated.

6   Conclusions

Results from simulation, emulation and flight campaign will be compared and analyzed, will help to consolidate the safety requirements and establish the CONOPS for a Satellite based Data Link service for RPAS.

The service delivery concept will be refined and consolidated thanks to the feedbacks from the involved users.

The main results of the project and recommendations will be disseminated to the relevant stakeholders, including European standardisation and regulatory organisations, especially for the definition of future satellite-based command & control datalinks, in order to contribute to the process of the integration of the RPAS into non-segregated airspace.

7   Future Work

The project represents a significant step into the European Roadmap for the integration of RPAS into the civil airspace.

Future activities will build on the work performed in the framework of the project simulation and emulation campaigns aiming to assess and compare the performances of different types of satellite connectivity, in order to support RPAS C2 datalink for BRLOS operations. More in detail, future activities may extend the assessment to:

- Other types of satellite connectivity and terminals.
- Different classes of RPAS platforms and associated CONOPS.

Future measurement campaign will allow also to increase the statistic relevance of the test results, to refine the measurement methodology and to provide further elements supporting the definition of the target RCP applicable to the satcom component of the C2 datalink chain.

Main target will be represented by the assessment and optimization of:

- Latency and availability values on the technical/performance side, and of
- Satellite connectivity costs on the operational/economical side.

References

1. EUROPEAN COMMISSION: Towards a European strategy for the development of civil applications of Remotely Piloted Aircraft Systems (RPAS)
2. ERSG: European RPAS Roadmap
3. DESIRE D13 Final Report
4. JARUS: RPAS C2 link Required Communication Performance (C2 link RCP) Concept
5. JARUS: Guidance on RPAS C2 link Required Communication Performance
6. ICAO: Doc 9869 AN/462, Manual on Required Communication Performance (RCP)
7. ICAO: Doc 10019 AN/507, Manual on Remotely Piloted Aircraft Systems (RPAS)

Modelling of the UAV Safety Manoeuvre for the Air Insertion Operations

Jan Mazal[1](✉), Petr Stodola[1], Dalibor Procházka[1], Libor Kutěj[2],
Radomír Ščurek[3], and Josef Procházka[1]

[1] University of Defence, Brno, Czech Republic
{jan.mazal, petr.stodola, dalibor.prochazka,
josef.prochazka}@unob.cz
[2] Ministry of Defence of the Czech Republic, Prague, Czech Republic
libor.kutej@centrum.cz
[3] Faculty of Security Engineering, VŠB-Technical University Ostrava,
Ostrava, Czech Republic
radomir.scurek@vsb.cz

Abstract. Tempo and complexity of the contemporary asymmetric battlefield is on the increase and time for a certain component delivery (ammunition, medical kit, vaccine and so on), for instance in the special operations, could be critical. Usually, the only way in these situations is a fast air delivery of concrete material to the "hot" destination zone. Contemporary air insertion in that case is usually performed by manned or unmanned (if available) system with human intuitive manoeuvre planning supported by information from ISR systems. In this case, there is almost impossible to achieve a fast, detailed and mathematically optimal solution with the real time implementation to the UAV control system (autopilot). The article describes a modelling approach which leads to high automation and optimal (autonomous) reasoning in case of 3D UAV path planning, respecting the operational situation in the area, manoeuvre limits of the UAV and potential threat in the operational area. The solution is based on detailed operational area 3D modelling, known and unknown probabilistic threat simulation and its capability estimation, quantification of safety area parameters and large 3D (multi-criteria) safety matrix development, criterial function and boundary condition specification, UAV air manoeuvre and constraints algorithm development, optimal UAV path search and operational evaluation.

Keywords: UAV · Safety manoeuvre modelling · ISR · Optimization · Air insertion

1 Introduction

In many branches, especially technically or technologically oriented, the approach of successful modelling as well as finding inverse solutions to generally set output requirements, is common and successful (with accuracy corresponding up to 95 % to real tests – statics, aerodynamics, hydrodynamics etc.). It is possible due to high level of exactness and little uncertainty in the model. Uncertainty is unfortunately presented in socio-economical domains, where military operational-tactical processes belong.

© Springer International Publishing AG 2016
J. Hodicky (Ed.): MESAS 2016, LNCS 9991, pp. 337–346, 2016.
DOI: 10.1007/978-3-319-47605-6_27

Therefore it is difficult to model a process of combat activities with accuracy corresponding to technological processes, nevertheless it is possible to model conditions accompanying a specific tactical situation successfully. After optimization of solution to these conditions we can use the results as a starting point for selection of variants of friendly or enemy forces activities (courses of actions). This approach is commonly used in the process of an operational task solution, where aspects of this problem should create a backbone of commander's and staff's decision making process [1].

A solutions of an operational-tactical task is realized through an initial mathematical model (operational environment) of the task that is an object of an application of additional methods and procedures, usually aggregated in partial geographical-tactical tasks in a way leading to the solution to the given task. A character of operational-tactical tasks is usually pragmatic-statistical or probabilistic, related to its solution assignment and its goals, setting ideal conditions, position, maneuver, reaction etc. for a specific task accomplishment. Thus, solutions to operational-tactical tasks support commander's decision making process during preparation and execution of military operations. Geographical-tactical analyses can be considered as basic building blocks of operational-tactical tasks solutions [2], aggregating military-geographical battlefield assessment into thematically unified algorithmic processes applicable to tactics, namely decomposition of operational-tactical tasks, which is the aim of the paper.

2 Analyses

The importance of automation of an optimal manoeuvre selection is crucial in actual dynamic conditions of digitalized battlefield. Automation is also possible in conditions of communication and computing infrastructure. In an actual command and control process architecture arrangement, automation of optimal manoeuvre selection belongs so far to support of a commander's or an operator's decision making process. Nevertheless, due to algorithmic character of the task and the need for continuous re-computing, based on operational space changes, i.e. due to changes in the state graph of a manoeuvre during an operation, we can suppose that full integration of the process into an automated low-level UAV control process under an operator supervision will take place in near future – Man on the Loop [3].

There can be more approaches to the solutions and they can give different results. Our approach to optimization is based on approximation of a 3D safety space of a manoeuvre that is transformed into a 3D non-oriented graph, where the minimal path is evaluated by the sum of all safety coefficients of all individual intersected subareas. The path topology is subordinated to another criteria, which have to be met. In general, these criteria are related to constraints of manoeuver capabilities of the UAV.

3 State of the Art

Relatively a lot of work has been done and published in the area of UAV manoeuvre optimization recently and it is undoubtedly an actual topic. Based on a literature research it can be stated that most of publications deals with UAW swarm optimization or UAV reconnaissance optimization, where the objective function is usually set on time or fuel consumption minimization during a selected manoeuvre type accomplishment (trajectory planning [4], safe trajectory [5], cooperative path planning [6], Ant colony approach [7, 9], heuristic and genetic algorithms [8]).

In many cases the third dimension of the air space (a fixed altitude operation) [4] and possibly other flight or aircraft parameters and options are omitted, as a velocity variation etc. An integration of given parameters significantly increases complexity of calculation models and these parameters are often approximated or neglected during modelling and simulation.

From the terminology point of view, a safe manoeuvre or path planning are usually defined as trajectories respecting selected criteria and integrating a collision avoidance features at the same time [10]. The presented concept of a operational safe manoeuvre or its equivalent considering a complex 3D model of a battlefield including variable and dynamical threats has not been found within a literature research yet and it represents a substantial innovation [11–13].

4   Solution

Taking into account main criteria, factors influencing the solving process and the context of the approach described above, O_{UAV} criterial function was constructed. We suppose optimization by minimizing the sum of all possible safety threats that the UAV faces during task accomplishment. The task accomplishment means a flight through a 3D operation space, from an issuing point to a specified destination point. The Fig. 1 demonstrates the "experimental displacement" of the operational area.

The trajectory can be evaluated by the purpose function:

$$UAV_{path} = \min \rightarrow \sum_{i=1}^{M} K_{I_i, J_i, K_i};$$
(1)

where:

$K_{x,y,z}$ – 3D safety matrix of operational area, derived from the set of analyses (3)
I_i, J_i, K_i – are the mathematical progressions coding the individual components/axes of the 3D path

The condition:

$$\forall i \in (1 \ldots M) = > (|I_{i+1} - I_i| + |J_{i+1} - J_i| + |K_{i+1} - K_i|) < 3,$$
(2)

means that that two following elements of K matrix are adjacent and:

$K_{I_i, J_i, K_i}; i = 1$ – starting point of the UAV flight, represented by a particular matrix element
$K_{I_i, J_i, K_i}; i = M$ – destination point of the UAV flight, represented by a particular matrix element

A calculation of the 3D safety space should consider an actual situation in the operation space – COP – and it can be fully or mostly automated by means of C4ISR

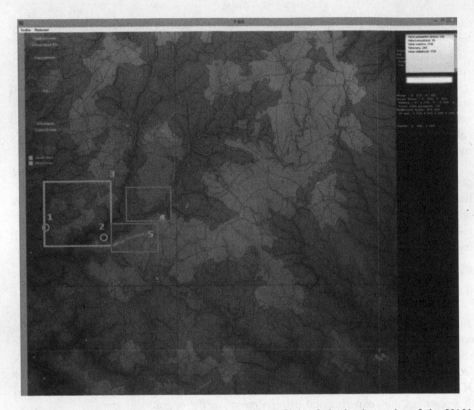

Fig. 1. Operational area, 1-issuing point of the UAV flight, 2-destination point of the UAV flight, 3-desired area of safety evaluation, 4-operational area of enemy – 2 option, 5-operational area of enemy – 1 option, from application developed by the authors. (Color figure online)

systems. Criteria definitions and a system of operational-tactical analyses, from which the target safety coefficient of operational space 3D matrix can be derived, are crucial for the task solutions:

$$K_{i,j,k} = \sum_{l=1}^{N} \left(TV_l \cdot An_l(i,j,k) \right) \tag{3}$$

$K_{x,y,z}$ – 3D safety matrix of operational area
$An_l(i,j,k)$ – geo-tactical or operational analyses
TV_l – tactical weights defining the priorities in particular case of operational task solution

The number of analyses influencing coefficients of the safety matrix is not limited, nevertheless it is necessary to set rates among A_i weight coefficients. Setting key parameters and requirements on the task is usually commander's or operator's decision. Setting A_i coefficients is an operational task and it is based on manoeuvre requirements and a supposed threat character. The sum of the A_i weight coefficients is normalized, i.e.

$$\sum_i A_i = 1. \tag{4}$$

To demonstrate the chosen approach we suppose following scenario. Tactical enemy entities are equipped by two type of weapons that can engage UAV, namely heavy and light weapons. The entities equipped by heavy weapons are mounted on vehicles that can move only on roads. Positions of the entities equipped by light weapons are not limited, so we can suppose them to be in the operation area, with respect to tactical rules influencing a threat probability in a point of operational space.

So for this purpose we suppose:

- Defined space for the threat matrix computing, denoted by D_{OR}, see Fig. 1 - *for the first demonstration (Figs. 4 and 5) we took in account area 5.*
- Defined area of enemy entities movement, denoted by S_{OR}.
- Analysis of visibility from the area of enemy entities occurrence, denoted by S_{OR}.
- Analysis of the threat for the area of interest D_{OR} from the S_{OR} area by light weapons.
- Analysis of the threat for the D_{OR} area from selected positions in the S_{OR} area by heavy weapons.
- Definition of UAV manoeuvre limitations.

The following algorithm, Fig. 2, describes schema of sequence of individual processes:

For calculations of individual analyses following relations were derived:

Analysis of D_{OR} (area of interest) threat from S_{OR} area by "light weapons" A_{lk}:

$$A_{lk} = C_{alk} \cdot F_v(S,D) \cdot P_{zlk}(S,D), \tag{5}$$

analysis of D_{OR} threat from selected positions in S_{OR} area by "heavy weapons" A_{tk}:

$$A_{tk} = C_{atk} \cdot F_v(S,D) \cdot P_{ztk}(S,D) \tag{6}$$

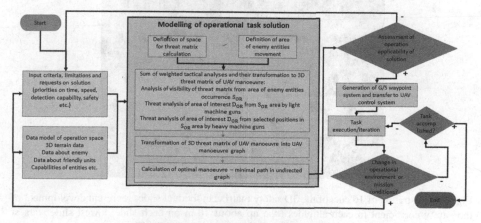

Fig. 2. General algorithm of the solution.

Fig. 3. 3D visualization of operational area, application developed by the authors.

where:

- C_{alk} is a tactical (pragmatic) coefficient of a multi-criteria evaluation defined for A_{lk} analysis.
- C_{atk} is a tactical (pragmatic) coefficient of a multi-criteria evaluation defined for A_{tk},
- $F_v(S, D)$ is a visibility function from the S point to the D point in a digital terrain model, $0 \leq F_v(S, D) \leq 1$. This function can reflect also level of clouds, fog or daylight.

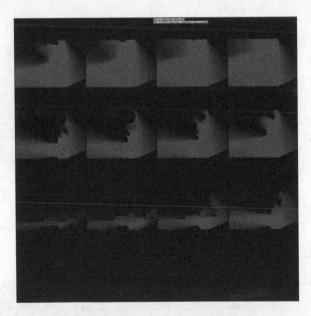

Fig. 4. Illustration of 16 cuts of the 3D safety matrix, individual slides represent development of the safety coefficient in each altitudes (rise up about 10 m on each slide, lowest slide stars at 80 m), from application developed by the authors.

- $P_{zlk}(S, D)$ is a hit probability of a slowly flying target at the position of $D(x, y, z)$ by a "light weapon" from the point of $S(x, y, z)$ in a digital terrain model (in ideal conditions).
- $P_{ztk}(S, D)$ is a hit probability of a slowly flying target at the position of $D(x, y, z)$ by a "heavy weapon" from the point of $S(x, y, z)$ in a digital terrain model (in ideal conditions).
- $S(x, y, z)$ is the initial point in a digital terrain model.
- $D(x, y, z)$ is the target point in a digital terrain model.

To demonstrate solution of the task, a standalone application was programmed in C++, where algorithms explained above were implemented and terrain data of the Czech Republic were used for digital terrain model creation. Virtual 3D look on operational area is demonstrated in the following picture (Fig. 3):

The results of operational analyses, supporting the 3D safety matrix development, are visible in the next Fig. 4.

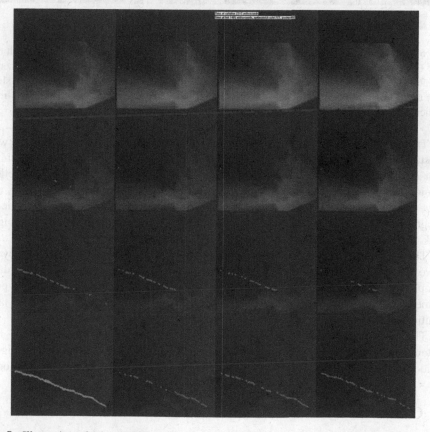

Fig. 5. Illustration of 16 cuts of the 3D safety **MANEUVER** matrix, with the best UAV route highlight in each layers/altitudes, integration of all waypoint from all slides (red dots), creates the continuous path as it is demonstrated in the left corner (yellow) individual slides represent of the safety **MANEUVER** coefficient distribution in each altitudes (rise up about 10 m on each slide, lowest slide stars at 80 m), from application developed by the authors. (Color figure online)

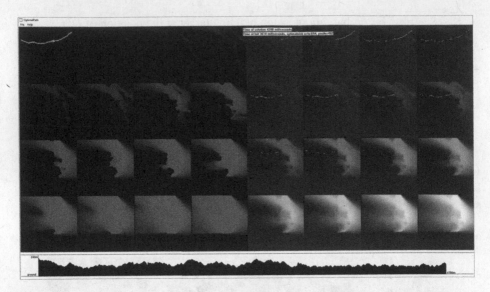

Fig. 6. Illustration of 16 cuts of the 3D safety matrix and safe **MANEUVER** matrix, with the best UAV route highlight in each layers/altitudes, this analyses took in an account enemy operational area 2 - Fig. 1 – red rectangle no. 4, (rise up about 10 m on each slide, lowest slide stars at 80 m), altitude flight profile – 240 m top line, 4780 - flight "horizontal" length, from application developed by the authors. (Color figure online)

Taking into account the previous analyses and criteria, the 3D threat matrix was constructed. From this matrix a 3D maneuver space graph was derived and a minimal path calculation in a non-oriented weighted graph was applied on it (26-direction topology of connecting neighbouring cells was chosen - in 3D). After computing, the value of the best possible safety/cost maneuver (to that point) is stored in every node of the graph (total of $512 \times 512 \times 16$ nodes). Choosing a target point and by running a back search, a concrete path is found, that is demonstrated in Fig. 5.

The approach explained above and the algorithms demonstrate a possible way to solve the discussed problem. It is possible to develop the solution with regard to completeness and adaptation to a concrete application. The calculations were performed on a PC with AMD A10-5800 K (3.8 GHz) processor and the whole task solution, including geo-tactical analyses, took approximately 10 min.

The same processes were executed also for enemy operational area 2 (Fig. 1 – red rectangle no. 4) with identical criteria and constrains. The result is presented on Fig. 6 including altitude profile of the flight. Optimal path change is apparent at the first look.

5   Conclusion

In many cases an algorithm schema can be applied to pragmatic aspects of tactical activities, so the decision making process of their execution can be automated at a quite high level. Taking into account this fact, it is possible to formulate a generic starting point, based on a new philosophical perspective on a computer support tactical decision making process and a system approach to operational-tactical tasks solutions. This topic is related to a mathematical solution to problems dealing with modelling, algorithm development, automation and optimization of decision making problems of command and control bodies (commanders) in uncertain operational environment.

Issues of a decision making process rationalization based on solution to complex operational-tactical tasks are very broad and they include sets of sub-problems concerning multi-criterial decisions, game theory, probability theory, operation research, graph theory, linear algebra, mathematical analysis etc. Ways of solutions are usually not trivial and final results require further analysis from a stability point of view and assessment of their practical usability. Anyway, this innovative approach shifts a static concept of commander's decision support at a tactical level, incoming only from a technological-distribution platform, to a higher level and it provides a powerful tool for planning and execution of a combat activity.

Presented approach differs from other optimization ways based on seeking the highest probability (for instance given in [5]) of a variant task accomplishment, while the matter of the suggested approach is seeking for a system of the best conditions, within which the given task can be accomplished. In this regard, there is a connection between these approaches at a philosophical level (both of them seek for the best accomplishment of the task), but the approach based on the highest probability usually faces reality problem of key parameters, used for probability computing concerning operational activities realization, including sociological, physiological and psychological factors. The presented solution is related to exact parameters of a battlefield and individual tactical entities and it represents an approach providing better preconditions for real implementation in C4ISR systems or in direct control systems of end systems (i.e. UAV in our case). Some ideas and inspirations concerning the algorithmic approaches were also taken from [14–16].

Growing need for military information systems (C4ISR), which actually reach their limits determined by current technologies, stimulate continuous development and implementation of methods and tools using modelling and simulation support to decisions processes. Optimization of tactical activities in an area of a combat operation, especially operational UAV path optimization, which is merit of this paper, becomes integral part of it. This is a presumable trend to the tactical-technological future of the 21st century battlefield. This concept creates prerequisites for effective involvement of automatic and robotic systems into command and control processes and it contributes to time, force and equipment economy during military operations. Further development of this concept and its application and operational deployment will enable to gather adequate amount of necessary information for realization of fully autonomous and robotic operational-tactic systems, towards which technologically advanced armies aim.

References

1. Hodicky, J., Frantis, P.: Decision support system for a commander at the operational level. In: Dietz J.L.G. (ed.) KEOD 2009 - Proceedings of International Conference on Knowledge Engineering and Ontology Development, Funchal - Madeira, October 2009, pp. 359–362. INSTICC Press (2009). ISBN 978-989-674-012-2

2. Hodicky, J., Frantis, P.: Using simulation for prediction of units movements in case of communication failure. World Acad. Sci. Eng. Technol. Int. J. Electr. Comput. Energ. Electr. Commun. Eng. **5**(7), 796–798 (2011)

3. Hodicky, J.: Modelling and simulation in the autonomous systems' domain- current status and way ahead. In: Hodicky, J. (ed.) MESAS 2015. Lecture Notes in Computer Science, vol. 9055, pp. 17–23. Springer, Heidelberg (2015)

4. Geiger, B.: Unmanned aerial vehicle trajectory planning with direct methods. A dissertation in Aerospace Engineering, The Pennsylvania State University, Pennsylvania, USA (2009)

5. Kamal, W.A.: Safe trajectory planning techniques for autonomous air vehicles. A dissertation work, University of Leicester, United Kingdom (2005)

6. Tsourdos, A., White, B., Shanmugavel, M.: Cooperative Path Planning of Unmanned Aerial Vehicles, pp. 1–214. Wiley, Hoboken (2010). ISBN 978-0-470-74129-0

7. Duan, H.B., Ma, G.J., Wang, D.B., Yu, X.F.: An improved ant colony algorithm for solving continuous space optimization problems. J. Syst. Simul. **19**(5), 974–977 (2007)

8. Yao, H.Q., Quan P., Jian, G.Y.: Flight path planning of UAV based on heuristically search and genetic algorithms. In: Proceedings of IEEE 32nd Annual Conference, pp. 45–50 (2005)

9. Liu, C.A., Li, W.J., Wang, H.P.: Path planning for UAVs based on ant colony. J. Air Force Eng. Univ. **2**(5), 9–12 (2004)

10. Kress, M.: Operational Logistics: The Art and Science of Sustaining Military Operations. Springer, Berlin (2002)

11. Rybar, M.: Modelovanie a simulacia vo vojenstve. Ministerstvo obrany Slovenskej republiky, Bratislava (2000)

12. Washburn, A., Kress, M.: Combat Modeling. International Series in Operations Research & Management Science. Springer, Berlin (2009)

13. Mokrá, I.: Modelový přístup k rozhodovacím aktivitám velitelů jednotek v bojvých operacích. Disertační práce. Univerzita obrany v Brně, Fakulta ekonomiky a managementu, Brno (2012). 120 s

14. Binar, T., Sukáč, J., Šilinger, K., Zatloukal, M., Rolc, S.: The steel ballistic resistance directly affecting logistics-related expenditures. In: 16th International Conference on Advanced Batteries, Accumulators and Fuel Cells, ABAF 2015, pp. 187–196. Electrochemical Society Inc., USA (2015). ISSN 1938-5862. ISBN 978-1-60768-539-5

15. Binar, T., Dvořák, I., Kadlec, J., Sukáč, J., Rolc, S., Křesťan, J.: Material characteristics of plastic deformation in high-strength steel. Adv. Mil. Technol. **9**(2), 33–39 (2014). ISSN 1802-2308

16. Michálek, J., Sedlačík, M., Doudová, L.: A comparison of two parametric ROC curves estimators in binormal model. In: Proceedings of 23rd International Conference Mathematical methods in Economics 2005. : GAUDEAMUS Univerzita Hradec Králové, Hradec Králové, pp. 256–261 (2005). 11 s, ISBN 80-7041-53

UAV as a Service: A Network Simulation Environment to Identify Performance and Security Issues for Commercial UAVs in a Coordinated, Cooperative Environment

Justin Yapp, Remzi Seker$^{(\boxtimes)}$, and Radu Babiceanu

Electrical, Computer, Software, and Systems Engineering,
Embry-Riddle Aeronautical University, Daytona Beach 32114, USA
{yappj,sekerr,babicear}@erau.edu
http://daytonabeach.erau.edu/about/labs/cybase/

Abstract. UAV as a Service (UAVaaS) is a proposed cloud orchestration framework aiming to provide efficient coordination and cooperation of commercial Unmanned Aerial Vehicles (UAVs). This work proposes a simulated environment to perform analysis and testing for UAVaaS integration. The environment is realized using off-the-shelf frameworks such as Flight Gear and Ardupilot's Software In The Loop to simulate real world UAV hardware, as well as web service and messaging API's such as RabbitMQ and Java Spring Framework to simulate UAVaaS cloud coordinator and client functionality. This simulation environment is devised to conduct further research into the network performance and security issues associated with UAVaaS configurations.

Keywords: UAV as a service · Unmanned Aerial Vehicles · Software Defined Networks · Network simulation

1 Introduction

Unmanned Aerial Vehicles (UAVs) have been impacting on multiple domains, including defense, business, societal, and legal domains. Although UAV technology was traditionally used in military applications, it has quickly become a practical solution for a wide range of commercial and industrial problems. Today, UAVs can be registered and certified to fly commercial operations involving structural inspections, wildlife protection, emergency management, land surveying, real estate, film production, border patrol, and agriculture, while simultaneously allowing users to upload and share visual data into the cloud [1]. As a consequence of the wide-range of solutions suggested by UAV applications, many organizations and research groups have been working on cloud-based solutions for UAV operations [2].

Increased application areas and proliferation of low-cost UAVs started posing problems for public safety and privacy. In order to address these challenges, the

© Springer International Publishing AG 2016
J. Hodicky (Ed.): MESAS 2016, LNCS 9991, pp. 347–355, 2016.
DOI: 10.1007/978-3-319-47605-6_28

US Federal Aviation Administration (FAA) established rules and guidelines for registering and operating UAVs [3,4].

UAV as a Service (UAVaaS) is a cloud-provided, pay-as-you-go utility for commercial Unmanned Aerial Vehicles (UAVs) that eliminates the need for owning and bearing operating risks of UAVs associated with business solution integration. UAVaaS operations take place mostly in heavily populated areas with communication channels that span over multiple, wide-area networks using heterogeneous "on-the-wire" interfaces. Because of the risk of causing harm to individuals and property, the system must inherently be treated as real-time and safety critical where network reliability, security, and resiliency pose as major factors that need further investigation. Since it is not feasible to perform thorough operational testing on live systems, a simulation approach that models UAVaaS topology and behavior is taken.

2 UAV as a Service Overview

The cloud computing concept of UAV as a Service is not new, but rather analogous to the more widely known Infrastructure as a Service (IaaS) model [5]. In IaaS, third party providers host hardware, software, servers, storage, and other components on behalf of their customers. Infrastructure maintenance, backups and updates are performed behind-the-scenes, providing a hassle free, user experience. Other characteristics of IaaS include scalable resources that adjust on-demand and allow billing on a pay-per-use basis.

The IaaS concepts mentioned in previous paragraph can be mapped to UAV as a Service model where server and storage infrastructure is replaced by UAV clusters. With regards to maintenance, UAVs are repaired and serviced by trained employees of the UAVaaS provider and is performed behind the scenes. Customers who use the service will only be charged for flight time used per each UAV as well as the amount and quality of data recorded.

UAVs, while heterogeneous in design and hardware, share common network interfaces and tightly coupled software components that enable standardized communication to UAVaaS providers. This feature allows multiple vendors and manufacturers to connect customized, mission specific UAVs that can be automatically tasked and deployed into the field.

Typically, UAVs will be assigned to particular service area hubs, based on demand. Figure 1 depicts how these hubs may be located for their respective service areas. As illustrated, a particular geographical area may contain different UAV requirements across multiple domains. Three UAV hubs are implemented in order to provide sufficient coverage area for agriculture, construction, emergency management, and mining while simultaneously allowing management and news reporting entities to spectate operations from anywhere outside service area coverage.

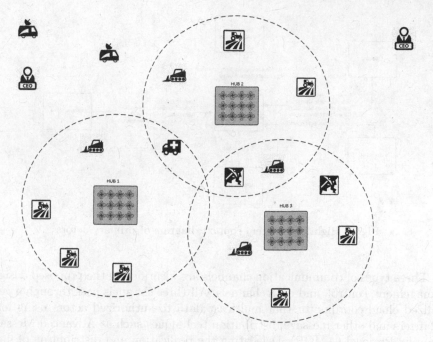

Fig. 1. A presentation of hubs for UAVaaS

3 Components of UAVaaS System and Communication Channels

We identify five primary actors who would be interacting with the UAVaaS system. These actors are operators, spectators, emergency services personnel, UAV ground crew personnel, and third party UAV vendors. Figure 2 depicts the interaction of these actors with a UAVaaS Coordinator, the primary cloud service that acts as a liaison for all operations.

Operators are the primary users who require access to UAVs to satisfy business requirements. Operators plan and control flight operations, while spectators only require access to collected data (e.g. imagery). Emergency Service Personnel represent privileged higher priority organizations such as fire departments, police departments, and other emergency first responders that re-task UAVs mid-flight or on ground for the purpose of using them in high-risk situations. For example, fire fighters trying to extinguish a major forest fire may need aerial assistance of nearby UAVs for reconnaissance, planning and detection of human life within the area. Fire fighters may need current UAVs nearby re-tasked (with current customer's permission). The ground crew maintains and operates strategically located UAV hubs. Their role is to monitor the safety of all UAVs during take-off, while en-route, and landing as well as to respond to any accidents within specified service areas. UAV Vendors represent manufacturers who supply UAVs to the UAVaaS system.

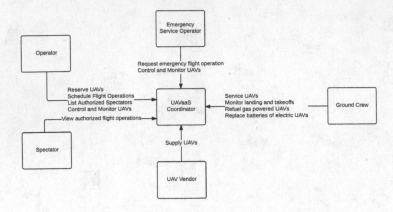

Fig. 2. High level system context diagram of primary actors

Three types of communication channels are identified in the proposed design: management, control, and data channels. All three channels pass through a centralized cloud coordinator that multicast data to authorized actors using load balancers and other message distribution techniques such as Advanced Message Queuing Protocol (AMQP). Delegating the replication and distribution of messages to a cloud coordinator, overhead and bandwidth requirements necessary for managing large amounts of spectators, controllers, and ground crew personnel for a given mission are reduced. This delegation can enable using simpler UAVs and have them use their resources on the mission.

Data messages contain telemetry, logs, and sensory information sent back to the UAVaaS Coordinator (as depicted in Fig. 3). Data messages are distributed to appropriate controllers and spectators as needed. These messages may include high resolution imagery or some environmental data, real-time altitude, speed, and location information needed by the controller to make decisions about a current mission.

Control messages are relatively light-weight and provide controllers an interface to send control signals to UAVs. Since the UAVs will be flying autonomously for the entire duration of the operation, these messages will be simple control commands for altitude and speed changes, uploading new waypoints or points of interest, or control camera and other payload features.

Management messages provide the coordination and administration properties of UAVaaS. Before any flight operation and any communication between customers and UAVs can begin, authorization, access control, mission tasking and session negotiation need to be handled. Similarly, when flight operations are finished, termination of sessions, and disassociation of UAVs, controllers and spectators must be performed.

Controllers communicate via management messages to authenticate to the UAVaaS cloud provider, create mission plans, reserve and schedule UAVs, and request specific session keys needed to communicate with UAVs. Controllers also retrieve data when a mission starts. Spectators communicate via management

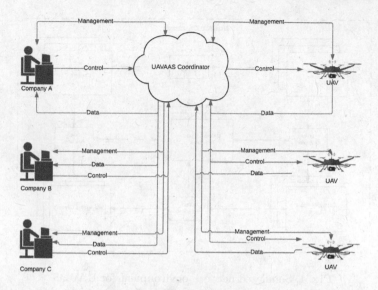

Fig. 3. Communication topology between for UAVaaS

messages to authenticate to the UAVaaS cloud provider and to retrieve session keys needed to collect UAV data by controllers. UAVs communicate via management messages to send status and availability updates to the UAVaaS cloud provider for tasking/re-tasking purposes and to retrieve session keys needed to communicate with controllers and to send collected data back.

The UAVaaS Coordinator is designed with two key services that work together to satisfy all communication requirements. Two services are needed because of differing natures of management, control, and data messages. Management messages are sent and received as a request-response pair, meaning that when a request is received by the UAVaaS Coordinator, a response is sent directly back to the sender. Such messages may include logging into the system, requesting a list of currently available mission plans, paying bills, and starting missions. Control and data messages work differently. Instead of the original sender receiving a response, the message is forwarded to its appropriate receiver(s). Such messages include control commands that are forwarded to one or more UAVs and video feeds that are forwarded to one or more spectators. Management messages can therefore be processed using a simple REST service [6], and control and data messages can be processed using a forwarding/messaging service. A third type of communication occurs in which the messaging service is dynamically configured by the management service based on requests sent to it on behalf of UAVs or operators and spectators.

4   Simulation Scope and Test Environment

The scope of the simulation comprises data producing and consuming agent clusters that represent four identified actors (UAV vendors are omitted due to

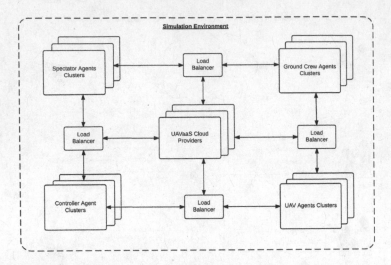

Fig. 4. Simulated network environment for UAVaaS

lack of direct interaction). By prioritizing communication channels, adjusting factors such as cluster sizes and data production rates, it is possible to study the effects on bandwidth contention and overall availability of the system. The simulated network environment is presented in Fig. 4.

The testing environment consists of 24 Dell OptiPlex desktop computers (8 GB RAM) connected to an HP ProLiant Server via a Cisco Catalyst switch that is networked in an isolated environment (*i.e.*, without connectivity to the outside world). Simulated components such as the UAVaaS cloud coordinator's messaging and management services, UAVs and controllers are developed on virtualized guest operating systems using Virtual Box where they are cloned and deployed across the network to appropriate host machines. This setup provides a consistent and controlled environment for future testing as external noise to the network is removed, each simulated device is given its own physical network card, and allowing for changes to components on the fly through cloning. The test environment is presented in Fig. 5.

5   Simulation

Three components are simulated for this testing environment: (1) UAVs, (2) UAVaaS Coordinator, and (3) Clients. Note that clients collectively include controllers, spectators and ground crew personnel, as they share common implementation to generate and retrieve data, to and from the UAVaaS Coordinator.

5.1   UAV Simulation

This component simulates real world UAVs that operate within a UAVaaS environment. Its scope is limited to a simulation of basic hardware components such

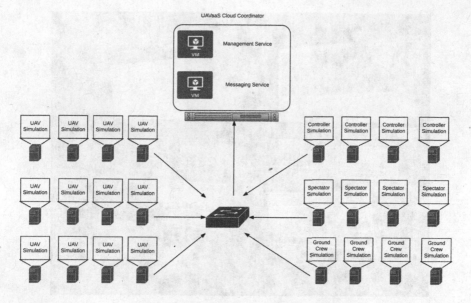

Fig. 5. Test environment for UAVaaS

as motors, GPS, altimeter, batteries, cameras, companion board software, and 4G LTE uplink and downlink. It also emulates the on-board flight controller to send and receive Micro Air Vehicle Communication Protocol (MAVLink) messages.

The UAV simulation is developed using Ardupilot's Software In The Loop Simulator (SITL). This is a complete, out-of-the-box utility implemented in C++ that emulates a quad copter's flight controller without the need for any hardware. It natively supports communication of MAVLink messages and properly simulates hardware components such as GPS and batteries. To communicate with SITL, Ardupilot's DroneKit API is used to provide a programmatic interface to control simulated UAVs. The DroneKit API is written in Python and can easily issue the simulated quad copter navigation and flight commands. To better visualize the UAV simulation, Flight Gear, an open sourced flight simulator is connected to SITL, captures flight information, and accurately displays the UAV model in a 3D environment as shown in Fig. 6. All components are neatly packaged into a Ubuntu virtual machine where it is deployed onto 12 physical host machines in the test environment.

5.2   UAVaaS Coordinator Simulation

This component simulates instances of cloud coordinators that provide management and messaging services across multiple geographical locations. Load balancers and DNS services assist UAVs to locate and contact the closest cloud coordinator service available to improve overall network performance.

Fig. 6. UAV models running on 12 workstations controlled by the UAVaaS controller

The UAVaaS Coordinator simulation is accomplished using the Java Spring Framework to develop a RESTful web server for the management service and the RabbitMQ API for the messaging service. MongoDB is used as a lightweight NoSQL database to store user authorization and access control policy information. The RESTful web server associates with the messaging service to configure messaging sessions on behalf of users and UAV requests. All components are packaged into a Ubuntu Server virtual machine where it is deployed onto the HP Proliant Server's VMWare hypervisor.

5.3   Client Simulation

This component simulates controllers, spectators, and ground crew personnel using UAVaaS services by passing messages. Client simulation generates requests and pass and retrieve messages to and from UAVaaS cloud coordinators. These messages simulate authentication, authorization, and administrative tasks. More bandwidth intensive messages may include video streams and live telemetry updates for controllers and authorized spectators.

Simulation is accomplished using native Java libraries to make RESTful requests to the management service. The RabbitMQ API is used to subscribe to various data messages and publish control messages to appropriate UAVs. Java mapping API collects telemetry data and plots UAVs in real time as demonstrated on the overhead projector display in Fig. 6.

6   Concluding Remarks and Future Work

This research has proposed a simulated environment to perform analysis and testing on UAV as a Service integration. This is accomplished using off-the-shelf frameworks such as Flight Gear and Ardupilot's Software In The Loop to simulate real world UAV hardware, as well as web service and messaging API's such as RabbitMQ and Java Spring Framework to simulate UAVaaS cloud coordinator and client functionality. The results of future testing will be used to generate Software Defined Networking (SDN) requirements and uncover underlying network availability issues. SDN will allow for greater scalability and higher reliability of the UAVaaS network. Once implemented, UAVs (conforming to a UAVaaS specification) can be openly shared by stakeholders that wish to utilize UAV services, without the legal and financial overheads associated with traditional upfront capital expenditure.

Using this simulated environment, further study will investigate network performance at scale by simulating multiple instances of UAVaaS components as shown in Fig. 5. Important performance metrics such as bandwidth, latency and throughput will be measured and determine potential bottlenecks that exist within the proposed design. Messages will be prioritized based on type, source, destination, client type and bandwidth consumption needs to generate requirements for future Software Defined Networking integration. Security aspects such as system availability will also be analyzed by determining whether the proposed design may be vulnerable to Denial of Service(DOS) and Distributed Denial of Service (DDOS) attacks.

References

1. Yapp, J.: UAV as a service: providing on-demand access and on-the-fly retasking of multi-tenant UAVs using cloud services. MSc thesis, Embry-Riddle Aeronautical University, Daytona Beach, FL, (2016)
2. Mahmoud, S., Mohamed, N.: Collaborative UAVs Cloud, 1st edn. In: International Conference on Unmanned Aircraft Systems (ICUAS), Orlando, FL, USA, pp. 365–373 (2014)
3. Civil Operations (Non-Governmental) Faa.gov (2016). http://www.faa.gov/uas/civil_operations/. Accessed 02 Apr 2016
4. Public Guidance for Petitions for Exemption Filed Under Section 333, 1st edn. Federal Aviation Administration (2016)
5. Mell, P.M., Grance, T.: SP 800–145. The NIST definition of cloud computing. National Institute of Standards and Technology, Gaithersburg, MD, United States (2011)
6. Fielding, R.T.: Architectural styles and the design of network-based software architectures. Ph.D. dissertation, University of California, Irvine (2000)

Modelling and Simulation Application

Sniper Line-of Sight Calculations for Route Planning in Asymmetric Military Environments

Ove Kreison[✉] and Toomas Ruuben

Department of Radio and Communication Engineering,
Tallinn University of Technology, Tallinn, Estonia
ove.kreison@gmail.com, toomas.ruuben@ttu.ee

Abstract. Situation aware route planning plays a key role in modern urban warfare. While planning routes to military convoys decision support systems have to take into account multiple environmental conditions to find safe routes and minimize the risk of convoy being attacked during mission. Considering that nowadays battles are fought in asymmetric conditions where red forces almost always have an upper hand then all systems aiding soldiers must try to take into account as much of those conditions as possible. This paper proposes a way how snipers locations and their line-of-sight can be added to dynamic threat assessment which in turn is an input for route planning. Risk minimization is done by using well known A* route planning algorithm where threat is presented as one of graph edge parameters that is in added to other parameters describing the surrounding environment.

Keywords: Multi-objective optimization · Military route planning · Military environment risk assessment · Route planning · A* algorithm · Situation aware route planning · Sniper calculation · Haversine formula · Situational awareness · Environment orientation · 3D risk assesment

1 Introduction

During urban military operations military commanders and team leaders are faced with complicated and time critical decisions. For example, when a military convoy is travelling through a previously planned route it might be stopped by the occurrence of an asymmetric threat. Urban military environments are filled with different types of asymmetric threats (for example improvised explosive devices, snipers, military booby traps) and finding routes in a military environment in a way that would help to avoid previously mentioned threats is defined as Military Unit Path Finding Problem (MUPFP) [1]. Therefore all Decision Support Systems (DSS) that aim to help commanders and team leaders have to solve MUPFP. Route planning algorithms are usually studied from the viewpoint of algorithmic optimality and efficiency, but the success in solving a MUPFP also relies heavily on modelling the surrounding environment and its constraints accurately enough so that they describe the actual environment as closely as possible. In addition to describing the environment effectively enough one also has to consider military units own parameters (such as vehicles width

© Springer International Publishing AG 2016
J. Hodicky (Ed.): MESAS 2016, LNCS 9991, pp. 359–370, 2016.
DOI: 10.1007/978-3-319-47605-6_29

and weight) because their interaction with environmental parameters defines MUPFP solution. For example if it is known that convoy contains a vehicle weighing 5000 kilograms then roads that do not support such weight should be eliminated from possible routes.

Describing the surrounding environment using a graph in a way that would be adequate enough for solving MUPFP is an extremely complicated task because one needs to transform a variety of information (such as units hostility and road type) into a numerical representation and combine all that information together in a meaningful way. In the context of route planning these bits of information are called parameters. As route planning algorithms expect that all graph edges are described numerically then all different parameters can be combined using weighted sums, but as their magnitudes usually differ then firstly they should be normalized to a range [0, 1] and then their importance can be adjusted using weights. In [2] we found that for solving MUPFP it is possible to describe every graph edge and therefore model the surrounding environment using the following ten parameters: length, width, ground type, environment, road type, road infrastructure, maximum speed, maximum bearing capacity, units hostility and threat for describing graph edges representing the digital terrain. By combining these parameters under three properties categories: shortness, fastness and safety one is able to use well known A* search algorithm with Manhattan distance as a heuristic function or genetic algorithm for finding routes in a graph [2]. Test results presented in [2] showed that our model of the environment using already mentioned ten parameters was able to model the surrounding environment with sufficient precision for finding routes in a graph.

Most parameters described in [2] are static and therefore do not change that often. Only units hostility and threat values depend on whether there are any blue or red units located nearby. This in turn means that previously mentioned values can change in minutes and therefore DSS has to update its underlying parameters and aggregations describing the environment accordingly. For example, the threat value takes into account gatherings of crowds, IED's current and historical locations, sniper locations, locations of schools/hospitals/police stations/gas stations etc. Evaluating the risk to soldiers emanating from different threats is filled with uncertainties because all of its components could change in time and these changes could be unpredictable. For example a sniper on the rooftop may start to look on the other direction and therefore its line-of-sight will change and also the threat emanating from it will change and therefore the underlying graph parameters will change. But sniper changing its position is one thing, its surroundings can also change and they also in turn affect line-of-sight. As an example a large lorry might block its view. This means that in addition to taking into account objects the current state of an object, one also has to simulate interactions of a collection of objects to create actual situation awareness. On the other hand snipers line-if-sight depends on the altitude where sniper is located and the height of buildings surrounding it. Sniper on the top floor of a high building can in this context do much more damage than a sniper on the middle floor of medium sized building surrounded with high buildings. The example demonstrates effectively that in order to understand and to evaluate situations numerically we have to solve MUPFP taking into account spatiotemporal properties and their changes in real-time.

This paper proposes an approach how threats emanating from snipers in asymmetric warfare situations can be taken into account in a way that would allow to embed dynamic risk assessment into MUPFP. Firstly an overview of different parameters that are used for modelling the environment using a graph is given based on the results of [2]. Then a theoretical solution for assessing the threat from snipers and its coverage is given which is succeeded by the testing results. The result is achieved by using a separate process which constantly polls data about sniper locations, calculates the area size affected by them and modifies the road graph values so that route planning algorithm could find routes to avoid known sniper locations.

2   Routing Graph

As part of European Defence Agencies project CARDINAL (CApability study to investigate the essential man-machine Relationship for improved Decision making IN urbAn miLitary operations) we developed an approach which uses ten parameters to describe one graph edge. Since some of those parameters can vary in a large range which in turn affects the resulting route, the graph has to be constructed in a way, where most of these parameters are homogenous for the entire length of the edge.

Parameters describing one graph edge are following:

1. Length – Length describes the physical distance between two graph vertices and is presented in meters. Usually when graphs of urban networks are constructed, vertices are but on intersections and therefore length describes the distance between two intersections. Length is the only value that doesn't have to be homogenous and consequently its values can range from a few dozen meters to thousands of meters. The latter case usually occurs outside urban areas, because other parameters don't change so often out there.
2. Width – Width describes the physical width of the road segment that is represented as a graph edge. It is a very dispersive parameter and can range from less than a meter to a few dozen meters. Width should be kept homogenous for the entire length of the edge, but if for some reason that should prove to be impossible then the smallest value should be chosen to represent width because in the context of military route planning wider roads are preferred. For one reason, choosing the smaller width helps to eliminate unsuitable graph edges before they are even given to the route planning algorithm. For instance if the widest vehicle in the convoy is 2.5 m wide then it would be reasonable to eliminate edges whose width is smaller than that to speed up route planning algorithms work. Narrow roads can also be very dangerous because if an improvised explosive device (IED) is planted beside the road then the convoy would be much closer to the epicenter of explosion than in the case of a wider road.
3. Ground type – Ground type describes the ground on which the convoy is driving on. This parameter describes if the road segment is even passable and if it is, then how fast the convoy can drive on it. In this study seven values are used to describe ground type: unknown value, tarmac, gravel, soil, water, swamp and impassable. If road segments ground type is set equal to swamp, water or impassable then the route planning algorithm will know that this segment is very hardly passably, in the

case of swamp, or totally impassable, in the case of water and the impassable value. The reason, why ground type influences convoys speed is due to the fact that different ground types have different friction coefficients. Because of this, machines can drive faster on tarmac than on gravel or soil and therefore choosing slower road segments into the route will affect total travel time.

4. Environment – Term is used to describe the environment surrounding road segments. This study uses four different values for describing it: unknown value, urban, flat and forest. Urban is used to describe an area with higher building and population density. Flat on the other hand describes an area with low or non-existent building and population density (for instance a desert or a steppe). Finally forest is used to describe an area with plenty of trees, but low or non-existent human density. In general, the probability of being attacked in an urban area or forest is much larger than the probability of being attacked in a flat land because the first two offer more opportunities for an unexpected attack and an easy getaway. Since this study is focused on improving decision making in urban military operations, it is impossible to avoid urban areas or forests, if they are surrounding the one road between two cities, and therefore to ensure convoys safety, other parameters have to be considered in addition to environment. More thorough definition of environment types and on topic of how to measure them can be found in [10].

5. Road type – Road type describes the road based on its type. Seven different parameters are used to describe road type: unknown value, highway, road, lane, track, drive and causeway. Different types are mainly distinguished by their travelling speed, but choosing the right road type can also have an effect on routes safety. On the one hand using the highway or road can be safer than crossing a causeway because the latter could be rigged with explosives, but on the other hand, one can join or exit the highway only at certain points. Furthermore, highway lanes are usually separated from each other, which in turn means that if a convoy is attacked on a highway, its chances of getting to an alternative route or retreating are very limited. To prevent previously mentioned incidents, other parameters have to be considered together with road type.

6. Road infrastructure – Road infrastructure is used to describe the road segments based on their structure. Four values are used to describe it: unknown value, open structure, bridge and tunnel. Open structure is used to describe all sorts of different road types that are already mentioned in the previous point. Although the word open might suggest that besides the structure, the convoy would be open to different sorts of threats that suggestion is not completely true. Using a bridge or a tunnel is far more dangerous because they both have only one entrance and one exit and if both of them are blocked then the convoy is trapped. In addition, by blowing up the bridge or a tunnel it is possible to destroy the entire convoy at once. Due to historical reasons a lot of cities are located at riverbanks or in mountainous areas and therefore it might be impossible to avoid using bridges or tunnels because the only way in or out of an urban area can be via bridge or tunnel.

7. Maximum speed – Maximum speed describes how fast a convoy can travel on specific road segments and is measured in kilometers per hour or miles per hour. This value can be the legal speed limit or a value which is specifically calculated by military personnel.

8. Maximum bearing capacity – Maximum bearing capacity describes the maximum weight that the road segment supports and is usually presented in tons. Considering maximum bearing capacity in route planning comes even more important when there is at least one heavy machine in the convoy because if this machine collapses through the road, a roadblock problem is automatically created. This is an extremely difficult situation which could break the machine and make the entire convoy an easily attackable standing target. It follows that considering maximum bearing capacity is of couse more important for heavier machines than for jeeps but it has to be considered in the case of them as well because with equipment those jeeps can weigh more than 3 tons.

9. Units hostility – Units in military operations are usually divided into two categories which are denoted by different colors: red denotes enemy units and blue allies and own units. For route planning it is wise to use more than two categories. Authors found that for better performance it is suitable to use five values: unknown, no units, uncertain (used to mark civilians), blue and red. It is important to force the route planning algorithms to find routes that pass through areas filled with blue units or with no units at all. The probability of an armed conflict becomes extremely large when the convoy is directed close to red units and therefore these situations have to be avoided. Unfortunately it is impossible to plan routes in a city without passing by civilians. The reason why this is unfortunate is that it is practically impossible to assess the hostility of a single person. However to some extent it is possible to probabilistically evaluate the threat emanating from civilians by assessing the number of attacks made against soldiers in a specific region during a certain time interval. This means that units hostility, when not dealing with blue or red units, should always assessed together with the tenth parameter.

10. Threat – Threat is a numerical value, which is based on military intelligence and relevant information. Information for evaluating the threat of an area could be collected using unmanned aerial vehicles (UAV) and unmanned ground vehicles (UGV), but one should also consider information coming from blue units based on area of interest, previously known information about red units (for example coordinates, direction and speed of movement), historical data about attacks against soldiers in that region, the number of IEDs found in that area and other information that could be used to form an objective evaluation of threat in a specific area. Thales Groups MYRIAD system [7] was used to to evaluate the threat level in range from 0 to 10, where 10 stands for highest threat possible and 0 on the other hand denotes that the area is safe. Sniper calculations proposed in this article have a direct effect on the threat parameter value which is set to 10 if a graph edge or vertex is in direct line-of-sight from the sniper.

11. Altitude – Altitude describes graph edges, vertices or objects height from sea level in meters and is used to calculate line of site between different objects and graph vertices and nodes.

As some of the parameters are not numerical then they have to be factorized and normalized before they can be added together. The complete methodology can be found in [2], but for clarity the numerical representation of previous parameters is given in Table 1.

Table 1. Numerical representation of parameters

Parameter	Numerical representation
Length	Value in meters
Width	Value in meters
Ground type	0 – unknown value 1 – tarmac 2 – gravel 3 – soil 4 – swamp 5 – water 6 – impassable
Environment	0 – unknown value 1 – flat 2 – forest 3 – urban
Road type	0 – unknown value 1 – highway 2 – road 3 – lane 4 – track 5 – drive 6 – causeway
Road infrastructure	0 – unknown value 1 – open structure 2 – bridge 3 – tunnel
Maximum speed	Value in kilometers per hour
Maximum bearing capacity	Value in tons
Units hostility	0 – unknown value 1 – no units 2 – uncertain (civilians) 3 – blue 4 – red
Threat	Value in range from 0 to 10
Altitude	Value in meters

As one can see from Table 1 then when the parameters are added together, some of them will dominate in the sum because their values are much larger (for example length, width, threat, altitude). In order to add the parameters together using a weighted sum they have to be normalized to a range [0, 1] and then added together using weights to spotlight the parameters that affect certain properties. Only parameters that is not normalized is altitude which is used to calculate threat parameter values. The process of snipers threat calculations is given in the succeeding paragraphs. The properties that are used for finding routes can be found in Table 2.

Table 2. Parameters relationship to route properties

Properties	Parameters
Shortness	• Length
Fastnss	• Length
	• Ground type
	• Road type
	• Maximum speed
Safety	• Width
	• Environment
	• Road infrastructure
	• Maximum bearing capacity
	• Units hostility
	• Threat

As every graph edge can be described by only one numerical values then all ten values are added together using a weighted sum: calculated using methodology presented in [4]:

$$a_{i,j} = \sum_{n=1}^{10} w_n x_n, \tag{1}$$

where $a_{i,j}$ denotes graph edge value between vertices i and j, n denotes the specific parameter, w_n is the weight given to the parameter and x_n is the parameter value. Using (1) a N x N weight matrix is constructed for the entire domain that is in turn used by the A* algorithm for finding optimal routes. As threat and units hostility values are dynamic then the matrix itself has to be cached so that it could be updated in real-time. As current papers aim is to demonstrate how snipers locations affect route planning results then we will always be finding the safest route.

Current paper uses A* algorithm for finding routes because of its performance over other greedy best-search first algorithms and the fact that it can find the optimal path if an admissible heuristic is used [8]. A* is a best-first search algorithm in which evaluation function is of the form:

$$f(n) = g(n) + h(n), \tag{2}$$

where f(n) is distance-plus-cost heuristic function, which determines path cost through vertex n, g(n) is the cost from start vertex to vertex n and h(n) is the estimated minimum cost from vertex n to goal vertex [3]. Manhattan distance between geographical coordinates is used as a heuristic functions and it can be presented in the form:

$$h(n) = |n.lat - goal.lat| + |n.lon - goal.lon|, \tag{3}$$

where n.lat and goal.lat are the latitude values of vertex n and goal vertex and n.lon and goal.lon are the longitude values of vertex n and goal vertex. Manhattan distance was chosen as a heuristic function because it is admissible and therefore it never overestimates the actual cost of the route, i.e. the cost it estimates to reach the goal is not higher than the lowest possible cost from the current vertex in path [9]. During our tests in [2], A* algorithm showed excellent performance and accuracy; however one major drawback of this algorithm is its memory requirement. Since two lists of graph vertices are used during the calculation: open list and closed list, the amount of memory required to store open lists (at initialization all graph vertices are stored at open list) for large areas, containing multiple urban areas, can be extremely large. Because the purpose of our application is to help soldiers in urban military situations, we only need to store a graph describing one city and its surrounding areas into the open list, which in turn means that memory requirements can be satisfied by most of the computers on the market today.

3   Sniper Calculation

Taking into account sniper line of sight in a battlefield is an extremely complicated task and can be accomplished using different methods. One can either calculate snipers actual line-of-sight very precisely by for example taking into account every small obstacle and every building feature or it can be done using more robust methods. This paper use a robust approach because predicting snipers movement on their locations is filled with too much uncertainty and therefore is not practical in real life situations. Therefore we choose a way where snipers line-of-sight is modelled as a circle and all graph edges and vertices that fall into these circle will have a maximum threat value [2]. Previously mentioned approach has been used and has also been proven to be useful in military practice. This is due to the fact that when dealing with soldiers lives in warfare situations then it is safer to avoid sniper shooting zones entirely rather than trying to cut corners and put the entire convoy at risk.

As our main aim is to calculate new threat values for graph elements using sniper locations then all elements must have longitude and latitude coordinates. This is true for graph vertices and segments that are used for route planning as well as for sniper locations. The approach is useful because it is universal and is not dependent on the underlying map. We also know that average sniper shooting range is usually between 600–1000 [m] although there have been occasions when shots have been made from as far as 2 [km]. The actual shooting range depends on the rifle used and weather conditions. If the sniper rifle type used is known then its shooting range can be loaded to a database and loaded from there. As the coordinates of snipers location and its average shooting range are known and the coordinates of graph vertexes are known then we can use Haversine formula to calculate great circle distances between two points.

We previously stated that every object has geographical and coordinates and therefore distances between them can be calculated using methodology presented in [4]:

$$dLon = lon2 - lon1, \tag{4}$$

$$dLat = lat2 - lat1, \tag{5}$$

$$a = (\sin\left(\frac{dLat}{2}\right))^2 + \cos(lat1) * \cos(lat2) * \left(\sin\left(\frac{dLon}{2}\right)\right)^2, \tag{6}$$

$$c = 2 * \text{atan2}\left(\sqrt{a}, \sqrt{1-a}\right), \tag{7}$$

$$d = R*c. \tag{8}$$

where dLon and dLat are longitude and latitude differences, c is earth radius 6367 km and atan2 is an arctangent function with two arguments [4]. To model the environment more accurately then we also added an altitude parameter to graph edges described in [2]. This way it is possible to extend the model to take into account higher objects and their ability to reduce snipers line-of-sight. Currently the algorithm checks if there are higher objects in direct sight from snipers location to graph edge. Graphs describing entire cities and countries can have millions of vertices and segments and if we want to model the surrounding environment as accurately as we can then our models can turn very complex which sets high requirements to computation and storage. As we are dealing with urban military situations then we have to find routes in real-time or near real-time conditions to have an effect on situational awareness. This in turn means that the solution to the problem lies in finding a suitable practical model that allows to model the surrounding environment with a suitable accuracy while following real-time constraints. Together with results presented in [2] we are moving in direction of finding the maximum practical model still allowing real-time constraints.

Our solution, which currently is only for demonstration purposes, follows classical service oriented architecture and consists of a user interface that uses Google Maps for map engine, an agent who communicates with user interface and different services. This services include route planning application introduced in [2] which uses A* algorithm and handles combining the ten parameters together and sniper calculation service introduced in this paper. Currently as the underlying map is not very large and does not contain that many objects then the steps of the algorithm can be described as following:

1. Find all graph vertices in range from sniper location using previously described Haversine formula where lon1 and lat1 describe snipers location and lon2 and lat2 describe graph vertices coordinates.
2. If graph vertex is in snipers shooting range then its altitude is compared to snipers altitude and road infrastructure parameter is checked to determine if it is not a bridge or tunnel [2].
3. Find all graph segments that are connected to the vertex and change their threat value to maximum which is 10 [2].
4. Save the results and send them back to broker agent.

In the future all the calculations should be done in parallel to reduce time spent on calculations. One way to achieve that is to use cluster computing frameworks that are based on MapReduce algorithms [5]. For example we could use Apache Spark framework to distribute the map graph as resilient distributed datasets over a cluster and find vertices affected by snipers. To speed the process even more up then vertices can be sent to driving node which can forward the results to other worker nodes that can be used in parallel to find segments connected to vertices [6].

4 Testing

For testing purposes the sniper range is read from a properties file, but in productions environments the values are stored in database for different sorts of weapons. According to [2] the aim is always to find the safest route meaning that A* tries to find a route by minimizing threat value. As mentioned previously then all graph vertices that are in direct sight from snipers locations have a threat value 10 and also all segments that are connected to these vertices have a maximum threat value.

All tests are done in the area surrounding Tallinn University of Technology campus. Scenario is that a safe route is planned for a military convoy, but after gathering some intelligence information two snipers are sighted at region. Snipers line-of-sight is calculated and a new route is found for the convoy. As previously stated then snipers range is actually much longer, but for testing purposes it was set to 250 m. Figure 1. illustrates the route found when there is only one blue force object and no red forces objects.

Figures 1 and 2 demonstrate that sniper ranges are effectively taken into account. The route found on Fig. 1 is now in snipers line-of-sight and is therefore too dangerous. From Fig. 2 we can see that A* managed to find a route that avoids both snipers. As we are dealing with a greedy algorithm then it tries to minimize all the route values which in case of Fig. 2 leads to a situation where convoy can take an unnecessary risk by driving too close to the danger zone. This can be avoided by adding an extra buffer zone to the calculation. For example one could make the sniper danger zone wider than it actually is. Another interesting research opportunity comes from the situation described in Fig. 2 where there is an overlapping area between two snipers. For example if there is a situation where snipers cannot be avoided then algorithms should try to find a route that passes only the line-of-sight of one sniper rather than two. This means that data model has to be changed by adding a new value which describes how many threats and which affect certain vertices and segments. This approach also helps to improve risk analysis because then you can for example score different threat sources and make route planning more situation aware [7].

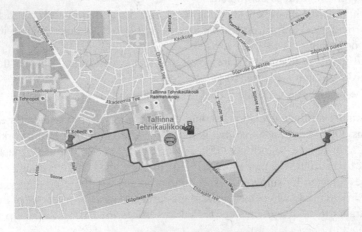

Fig. 1. Route without red forces objects (Color figure online)

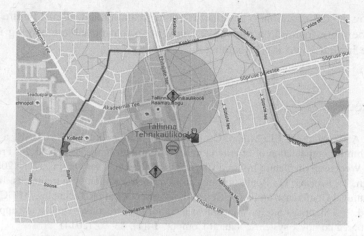

Fig. 2. Route with two red forces snipers (Color figure online)

Next research topics for us will be how radio communication parameters can be taken into account in route planning. For example modelling radio spectrum usage in real-time might give an indication whether snipers might have gotten a hint about convoy movement and might try to change their location. Also radio propagation modelling can be used in predictive analysis to avoid areas where convoy might not get any new information from decision support systems.

5 Conclusion

This paper proposes a new approach for including snipers line-of-sight modelling into route planning tasks in in asymmetric urban warfare situations. A Java application was developed which can be interfaced to already existing Battlefield Management Systems (BMS) for modelling and evaluating snipers threat. Developed solution was integrated to the agent oriented system built in [2] and route planning tests were done using popular A* algorithm. In the near future we will move our demonstrating platform to an actual BMS engine. As sniper calculation is done in a separate daemon process then all calculations can be done in real-time. Tests show that snipers line-of-sight is taken into account correctly but as the algorithm itself is greedy then it tries to minimize the route which in turn can lead to a situation where military convoys can pass the snipers too closely. To avoid that a special buffer zone can be simply added to the algorithm.

The DSS-s described before are heavily dependent on radio communication and therefore the next parameters that we will add to our model will describe radio wave propagation such as signal strength, interference etc. This will also allow to solve jammer avoidance and radio path problems. In the case of snipers we choose a robust approach, but in the case of radio wave propagation it cannot be done because for example vehicles in the convoy itself can block radio signals to other vehicles. Our current research is mainly focused on describing the surrounding environment with a data model that is practical enough for asymmetric warfare situations in a way that would allow all optimization to be done by route planning algorithms. Future research will also be more focused on predictive analysis so that possible emerging risks can already be included into route planning.

References

1. Mora, A.M., Merello, J.J., Millan, C., Torrecillas, J., Laredo, J.L.T.: CHAC, a MOACO algorithm for computation of bi-criteria military unit path in the battlefield. In: Proceedings of the Workshop on Nature Inspired Cooperative Strategies for Optimization (2006)
2. Ruuben, T., Kreison, O.: Route planning in asymmetric military environments. In: Second International Conference on Future Generation Communication Technology (FGCT) (2013)
3. Hoverd, T., Stepney, S.: Environment orientation: a structured simulation approach for agent-based complex systems. Natural Comput. 14(1), 83–97 (2014)
4. Sinnott, R.W.: Virtues of the Haversine. Sky Telescope 68(2), 158–159 (1984)
5. Lämmel, R.: Google's MapReduce programming model—Revisited. Sci. Comput. Program. 70(1), 1–30 (2008)
6. Zaharia, M., Chowdhury, M., Franklin, M.J., Shenker, S., Stoica, I.: Spark: cluster computing with working sets. In: Proceedings of the 2nd USENIX Conference on Hot Topics in Cloud Computing, vol. 10, p. 10 (2010)
7. Labreuche, C., Le Huédé, F.: MYRIAD: a tool suite for MCDA. In: EUSFLAT, vol. 5, pp. 204–209 (2005
8. Nilsson, N.: Principles of Artificial Intelligence. Morgan Kaufmann Publishers, Burlington (1982). 476 p.
9. Russel, S.J., Norwig, P.: Artificial Intelligence: A Modern Approach, 3rd edn. Prentice Hall, New Jersey (2009). 1152 p.
10. Hodicky, J., Frantis, P., Litvaj, O.: Validation of simulator supporting movement of small group or individuals in different terrains. In: 2012 15th International Symposium, MECHATRONIKA, Prague, pp. 1–3 (2012)

The Design of 3D Laser Range Finder for Robot Navigation and Mapping in Industrial Environment with Point Clouds Preprocessing

Petr Olivka[1]([✉]), Milan Mihola[2], Petr Novák[2], Tomáš Kot[2], and Ján Babjak[2]

[1] Department of Computer Science, FEECS, VŠB – Technical University of Ostrava,
Ostrava, Czech Republic
`petr.olivka@vsb.cz`
[2] Department of Robotics, FME, VŠB – Technical University of Ostrava, Ostrava,
Czech Republic
{`milan.mihola,petr.novak,tomas.kot,jan.babjak`}`@vsb.cz`
`http://www.vsb.cz`

Abstract. This article describes the design of 3D Laser range finder (LRF) for industrial and mine environment. The 3D LRF is designed for usage on middle size robots and can be used for environment mapping and navigation. The design reflects heavy and dirty working conditions in industrial environment and it is equipped by own methane sensor for usage in mine. The process of design started with definition of requirements, follows by dynamic analysis and selection of suitable parts. The housing is designed from stainless steel and it encloses all electrical and mechanical components. The internal control unit is designed to suit modern trends of fog computing. It is equipped with four cores ARM CPU and IMU and it is able to preprocess the acquired point clouds in real time.

Keywords: Robot · Mapping · Navigation · Laser range finder · Fog computing · Point clouds

1 Introduction

The navigation and mapping subsystem of mobile robot is integral part of a robot control system. Many various methods are used in a practice and their algorithms depend on used type of sensors. One of the most suitable sensor for navigation and mapping is a laser range finder (LRF).

Nowadays on the market many types of 3D LRF are available. One of the most known 3D LRF producer is Velodyne. Its products are very often used for autonomous control of cars. The Velodyne Lidar HDL-64E is visible in Fig. 1. This lidar has the horizontal field of view (FOV) 360° but the vertical FOV is only 27°. Its measurement range is up to 120 m and power consumption 60W. These technical parameters are suitable for the outdoor usage, especially in the traffic environment, but disadvantaging it for indoor usage. The high power consumption is limiting factor for power supply from batteries. The narrow vertical

© Springer International Publishing AG 2016
J. Hodicky (Ed.): MESAS 2016, LNCS 9991, pp. 371–383, 2016.
DOI: 10.1007/978-3-319-47605-6_30

Fig. 1. Velodyne LIDAR HDL-64E [9]   **Fig. 2.** Raw data from HDL-64E [9]

FOV allows to fully recognize obstacles with size of adult person from distance approximately 4 m. In Fig. 2 is an example of data captured by HDL-64E and there is visible that the first points of ground are detected by this lidar at distance about 3 m. Any large obstacles at closer range can be only detected, but not recognized. Moreover the overall coverage of a surrounding environment is only 15 %. The large blind space is above and below this lidar. The last but not least disadvantage is the very high price of this lidar – around $70000. The smaller version of Velodyne lidar HDL-32E costs around $29000.

On the opposite side to professional industrial 3D LRF devices, solutions for office and home usage are available. The examples are Kinect, visible in Fig. 3 and Xtion showed in Fig. 4. These devices are mass-produced, therefore they are cheap, but they are unusable for industrial applications.

The high price of high-quality 3D LRFs is still the main limiting factor for their wider use in industrial applications.

Fig. 3. Kinect [http://www.microsoft. com]   **Fig. 4.** Xtion PRO LIVE [http://www. asus.com]

A number of designers are therefore thinking about cheaper design. The market offers the an alternative – the 2D LRF. There are two well-known producers of 2D LRF on the market with relative wide range of product lines – Sick and Hokuyo.

Fig. 5. First know design of 3D LRF with servo [8]

Fig. 6. Zebedee design of 3D LRF with 2D LRF mounted on spring [1]

For the 2D LRF usage in 3D applications is only necessary to add the third dimension. Probably the first documented design of 2D LRF used for 3D measuring, introduced in 2009, is visible in Fig. 5. The main weakness of this design is the mounting of the carrier directly to the servo. The servo is not able to capture all inertial forces of the mounted LRF and this design will damage very soon the gears and their bearings inside the servo.

The different approach to 3D LRF design is shown in Fig. 6 and this design was introduced in [1]. The 2D LRF is mounted on a spring and the third spatial dimension is added by swinging. This design has two main disadvantages. At first it is the requirement of manual swinging which causes the irregular coverage of environment. The second disadvantage is necessity of using IMU, which is mounted below the LRF, and the perfect time synchronization of IMU and LRF.

The design with LRF mounted on the horizontal axis was presented in [2] and its design is shown in Fig. 7. Nevertheless this design has limited rear visibility.

The own design of 3D LRF was developed in our lab, inspired by [8]. The 2D LRF Hokuyo URG-04LX is mounted on a step motor which captures all inertial forces of the carrier and LRF in their ball bearings. The vertical orientation of the rotatable axis guarantees the same views to all sides and this laser is able to measure 66 % of space. The blind space is under this 3D LRF. The overall design of 3D LRF is depicted in Fig. 8.

The first version of 3D LRF required a special microstepping unit [4], but the latest design uses a step motor with 400 physical steps per revolution and a common circuit DRV8825 is used for the control. The main control unit is composed of Raspberry Pi 2 computer and real-time control circuit is realized by Arduino Nano. For reliable usage of the short range LRF Hokuyo, it is necessary to calibrate it. The calibration process is described in [6].

This 3D LRF was successfully used in a few applications and the gained experiences were used for design of new industrial version of 3D LRF, introduced herein below.

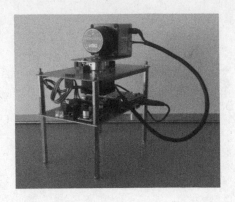

Fig. 7. LRF mounted on the horizontally oriented axis [2]

Fig. 8. LRF Hokuyo URG-04LX mounted
on the vertically oriented step motor

2   Desired Parameters of 3D LRF Design for the Industrial Environment

For the proper design of industrial 3D LRF it is necessary to define a set of
parameters, which is required for good and perspective design. The main requirements to 2D LRF are: measured distance up to 20 m, frequency of scanning at
least 25 Hz, measuring angular range at least 240°, data interface USB or Ethernet for fast data transfer and power supply and data line in one cable. Because
it is planned to use this 3D LRF even in mine, the good black surface detection
must be preferred too.

For the autonomous usage the unit must be equipped with its own power
supply in the form of batteries. The dust and water proof design is expected
naturally. Additionally, for the potential underground work it will be necessary
equip the device with methane sensor.

Most of the required parameters are related to the main part: the 2D LRF.
On the market are available many products in product lines of Hokuyo and
Sick producers. But only a few of them fulfill the required parameters. The main
problem is the detection of black surface. This requirement considerably narrows
the assortment of suitable LRF.

Both the producers mentioned above have in their product lines only one
LRF designed for black surface. But only the Sick LRF was available from our
supplier and therefore we had to use it.

The compliant scanner is Sick LMS111. Its main technical characteristics can
be found in [10].

The selection of the most important parameters: dimensions $105 \times 102 \times 162$ mm, weight 1.1 kg, scanning frequency 25 or 50 Hz, resolution 0.5 or 0.25°,
measuring angular range 270° and operating range up to 20 m. Power consump-
tion is 8 W, enclosure IP67 and communication interface Ethernet 10/100Mbit/s,
systematic error of measuring is ±30 mm.

The power and the Ethernet cables of the LMS111 are from production separated. But there is an easy possibility to integrate them together in the PoE (Power over Ethernet) form.

The first testing of the LMS111 discovered an impossible combination of measurement resolution and scanning frequency. The resolution 0.25° cannot be used at frequency 50 Hz. This problem was not explained in the documentation, neither by the supplier. Therefore at 50 Hz the only possible resolution is 0.5°.

The design of the positioning unit for the relatively large and heavy LMS111 will be described in following sections.

3   Dynamic Analysis of Positioning Unit Design

It is not possible to mount the LMS111 in such an easy way as it was shown in Fig. 8. This scanner is relatively heavy and it is not possible to mount it directly on the step motor. Moreover the step motor is not suitable for design of a battery-powered device because of its high and continuous power consumption.

The rotatable mounting of the LMS111 has to be designed to capture all inertial forces that may occur during movement. Therefore the shaft for the carrier with the LMS111 is mounted in two ball bearings inside a sleeve. The overall design is depicted in Fig. 9. The LSM111 is mounted in its centroid for the maximal elimination of inertial forces. The centroid position is not listed in technical documentation, it had to be found experimentally.

For the proper selection of a rotating actuator it is necessary to perform the dynamic analysis of the designed rotatable mounting with the LMS111. But the design is not sufficient for analysis. Some additional information is needed.

The first unknown parameter is the rotating motion sequence. The theoretical course of the angular velocity between two positions is visible in Fig. 10. Here

Fig. 9. Rotatable mounting of LMS111 on axis with pair of ball bearings inside sleeve

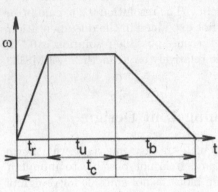

Fig. 10. Course of angular velocity between two angular positions [3]

Fig. 11. Valve model of LMS111 for dynamic analysis

it is necessary to know the time t_c of rotation and angle between two positions. The time can be easily computed from the known parameters of the LMS111. The highest frequency of scanning is 50 Hz. The time period for this frequency is $t_1 = 20$ ms. The angular range of scanning is 270° and blind space is the rest of a turn, which is 90°.

The LMS111 has to be rotated in the blind space, that is one quarter of t_1. Thus the time of rotation t_c should be 5 ms or less.

The angle between two scanning position, during the LMS111 rotation, should be the same as the LMS111 resolution. The maximal angle is 0.5°. Now the time t_c and angular distance between two scanning position are known.

The penultimate unknown parameter for dynamic analysis is the LMS111 mass moment of inertia. This information is not available even in 3D model of the LMS111 supplied by its producer. Thus for the simulation the LMS111 can be replaced by a virtual valve with the similar dimensions as the LMS111 metal body and with the same weight. The virtual valve model is visible in Fig. 11.

The last unknown parameter of rotatable mounting showed in Fig. 9 is the friction torque between the radial shaft seal and the shaft itself. According to the known material of the proposed seal and the shaft surface quality the friction torque 1000 N·mm can be used.

The PTC Creo Parametric software [13] was used for the dynamic analysis. This software automatically computes every necessary moment of inertia of all parts from the 3D model. The additional input parameters are the course of movement, depicted in Fig. 10, and the angle between two positions, described above. The whole time t_c of the movement can be divided to three phases: the time of acceleration t_r, the time of constant velocity rotation t_u and the time of deceleration t_b.

The result of dynamic analysis is shown in Figs. 12 and 13.

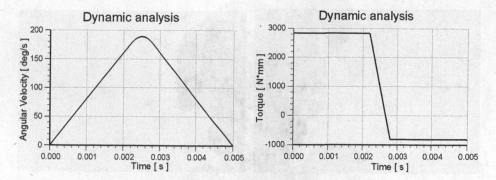

Fig. 12. Course of angular velocity   **Fig. 13.** Course of required torque

The course of angular velocity is depicted in Fig. 12. This course corresponds to the theoretical course in Fig. 10. Because of the very small angle between two positions the phase with constant velocity is missing. The angular movement contains only the acceleration and deceleration phases.

The course of the torque computed by Creo is visible in Fig. 13. This course corresponds to the theoretical angular velocity with a short phase of acceleration and a short deceleration. The difference between the acceleration and deceleration torque is caused by the internal friction in the rotatable mounting.

The dynamic analysis found two main important parameters for actuator selection. The maximal required angular velocity is 200°/s and the maximal torque is 3000 N·mm.

The market offers many suitable rotating actuators which fulfill the required parameters for the design proposed earlier. The additional parameters for selection should be: small dimensions, low power consumption, easy control, good angular position control and the same power supply voltage as the LMS111.

The servo Dynamixel MX-64R was selected as a suitable actuator. The list of its technical parameters is in the e-manual or data sheet [11]. The range of power supply is 12–14.8 V, maximum current 4 A, quiescent (standby) current 100 mA, communication interface RS-485, maximum torque 6000 N·mm, angular resolution 4096 steps per turn guaranteed by inner magnetic sensor, maximum rotating speed 63 rpm and weight only 126 g.

4   Positioning Unit Design

The design of the only moving part of the positioning unit was depicted in Fig. 9. For the overall design it is at first necessary to organize spatially all the internal parts into the smallest volume, while preserving enough manipulation space for the assembly process.

Fig. 14. Arrangement of all internal parts of positional unit

The proposed internal arrangement is depicted in Fig. 14. There are visible the four largest components: the not-yet-mentioned methane sensor SC-CH4 [12], the rotatable mounting with the servo and two batteries on the bottom. On the top is the LMS111, but it will be outside the positioning unit. The rest of the space is occupied by the electronic equipment, switches, LEDs and connectors.

All parts will be encapsulated in a metal housing. The overall design of this housing is visible in Figs. 15 and 16.

The housing is composed of two parts: bottom pan and top lid. These two parts are assembled together by 16 screws and the sleeve is mounted on the lid by 4 screws.

The first prototype of 3D LRF was made using rapid prototyping – printed on a 3D printer from polycarbonate. On this prototype the functionality and interoperability of all parts were verified. Subsequently the final prototype was completely made from stainless steel. The overall view of the welded prototype is visible in Figs. 17 and 18.

Fig. 15. Overall design of 3D LRF

Fig. 16. Overall design of 3D LRF

Fig. 17. Welded prototype of 3D LRF

Fig. 18. Welded prototype of 3D LRF

5   Control System Unit of 3D LRF

The overall block diagram of the 3D LRF control system is depicted in Fig. 19. It is clear from this figure that the control system is relatively complex.

In Fig. 19 all parts of the control system are divided to two group separated by the horizontal dotted line. On the bottom of this diagram are power parts and above them are the control parts. The thicker solid lines represents the power supply from batteries. The thinner solid lines represent the 5 V power supply. This lower voltage power supply is generated by a DC/DC converter. All dashed lines denote data lines for communication. All parts in the diagram are marked according to their type or purpose.

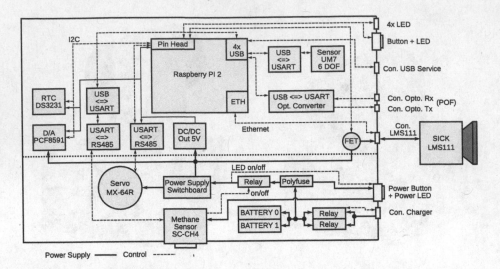

Fig. 19. Diagram of control system inside 3D LRF

The main control node is the SoC computer Raspberry Pi 2. This computer contains 4 ARM cores operating at frequency 1 GHz, 1 GB of DRAM memory, Ethernet 100 Mbit/s, 4 USB connectors, HDMI and a pin head. The pin head allows to connect devices with USART, SPI or I²C interface. It contains also a few GPIO pins.

The power supply of the servo MX-64R is connected directly to batteries. Its internal control unit allows to switch the servo on and off and set current limit.

The interconnection between the LMS111 and the positioning unit is realized by a single cable with PoE, see Fig. 18. The power of the LMS111 has to be controlled by a power transistor.

Three USB interfaces are used for communication with three independent devices and the fourth USB interface is dedicated for service and diagnostic purposes.

The positional sensor UM7 detects inclination of the whole 3D LRF. The internal control unit of this sensor has implemented a Kalman filter.

The communication with another system is realized by Plastic Optical Fiber (POF) to achieve fully galvanic insulation between the connected systems and the POF guarantees safe functioning in a mine environment. This communication is also required for the exploration mobile robot [5].

6   Measuring Process and Captured Data Preprocessing

The measuring process will be described now. The LMS111 measures in a vertical plane with frequency 50 Hz. The resolution of this measuring is 0.5° in range 270°. The blind gap 90° is used for horizontal rotation of the LMS111 to a new position. This small rotation corresponds with LMS111 resolution and it is also 0.5°. This measuring process is repeated until the whole environment around the device is captured, which occurs after half a horizontal revolution of the LMS111. The measuring process is in detail described in [6].

The measurement precision is derived from technical parameters of the LMS111 [10]. Because of measurement in rotating vertical plane the 3D LRF has the same precision in the horizontal and vertical direction. As was mentioned herein above, the precision is ±30 mm.

The required time for one measuring t_s can be computed from the known parameters by the following formula:

$$t_s = 180/(f_s \cdot \alpha_r) = 180/(50 * 0.5) = 7.2 \ [s], \tag{1}$$

where f_s is scanning frequency and α_r is horizontal angular resolution. It is also possible to measure with resolution 0.25° in both axes, but the LMS111 must be slowed down to scanning frequency 25 Hz and the resulting time of one measuring will be 28.8 s.

The main computer inside the 3D LRF has to control many devices. Even so, it still has a sufficient surplus computing power (4 cores) which can be used for preprocessing of captured data in real time. This preprocessing performs a few successive tasks:

- Estimation of physical measuring ability of the LMS111. It depends on quality of the surface and its reflection.
- Detection of weak points and their removal.
- Detection and removal of outliers.
- Evaluation of information from the positioning sensor UM7 and compensation of measured data to the proper horizontal position.
- Transformation of captured data from spherical to Cartesian coordinate system.

After the preprocessing the data are passed to the main control system of the robot, which uses the 3D LRF. This principle, when cooperating systems perform data preprocessing and then they are passing data with increased value, is nowadays called "fog computing". In practise it is a principle of computing power distribution between cooperating systems. The result is easier usage of data in the system which requested these data. For the testing is nowadays used the earlier developed control system for mobile robot [7].

7   3D LRF Testing

The testing of new industrial prototype was performed at first in a laboratory and then in a real underground environment in Gliwice (Poland) in the coal mine Queen Luiza. Because we tested carefully the functionality of the proposed 3D LRF design on the previous polycarbonate prototype, the final welded stainless steel industrial prototype was working well without problems.

Up to one hundred point clouds in 200 m long corridor were captured in the coal mine. All point clouds were automatically compensated to proper horizontal position and every point cloud was filtered during preprocessing. One example

Fig. 20. Underground corridor of the coal mine Queen Luiza

Fig. 21. Point cloud captured in coal mine Queen Luiza (Color figure online)

of a point cloud captured in the corridor shown in Fig. 20 is visible in Fig. 21. In this figure is visible Y-shaped juntion of corridors. The height of individual points is there differentiated by colour.

8   Conclusion

In this article was described the design of 3D LRF for the industrial environment. At first the dynamic analysis of the design was performed to properly select a rotatable actuator.

Then the arrangement of all parts, including a methane sensor, into the smallest volume was showed, followed by the design of the positioning unit housing. The diagram of control system showed complexity of this important part of 3D LRF. The surplus of computing power of the used main computer with 4 ARM cores is used for data preprocessing to simplify the subsequent point cloud processing in robotic systems. One welded stainless steel prototype was made and it was tested in real underground environment in a coal mine in Gliwice (Poland). In the end is presented an example of captured point cloud from this coal mine. The designed 3D LRF is working well and it is possible to use it on any robot in real industrial environment.

Acknowledgement. The project has been carried out in a framework of an EU programme of the Research fund for Coal and Steel under the grant agreement No. RFCR-CT-2014-00002 [14].

References

1. Bosse, M., Zlot, R., Flick, P.: Zebedee: design of a spring-mounted 3-D range sensor with application to mobile mapping. IEEE Trans. Robot. **28**(5), 1104–1119 (2012)
2. Zhang, J., Singh, S.: LOAM: lidar odometry and mapping in real-time. In: Robotics: Science and Systems Conference (RSS), pp. 109–111 (2014)
3. Cubero, S.: Industrial Robotics: Theory, Modelling and Control. Pro Literatur Verlag, Augsburg (2006). ISBN: 3866112858
4. Krumnikl, M., Olivka, P.: PWM nonlinearity reduction in microstep- ping unit firmware. Przegld Elektrotechniczny **88**(3a), 232–236 (2012)
5. Novák, P., Babjak, J., Kot, T., Olivka, P., Moczulski, W.: Exploration mobile robot for coal mines. In: Hodicky, J. (ed.) MESAS 2015. LNCS, vol. 9055, pp. 209–215. Springer, Heidelberg (2015)
6. Olivka, P., Krumnikl, M., Moravec, P., Seidl, D.: Calibration of short range 2D laser range finder for 3D SLAM usage. J. Sens. **501**, 3715129 (2016)
7. Kot, T., Krys, V., Mostyn, V., Novak, P.: Control system of a mobile robot manipulator. In: 2014 15th International Carpathian Control Conference (ICCC), pp. 258–263. IEEE (2014)
8. I Heart Robotics: More Hokuyo 3D Laser Scanner Images (2009). http://www.iheartrobotics.com/2009/06/more-hokuyo-3d-laser-scanner-images.html
9. Velodyne LiDAR, HDL-64E (2016). http://www.velodynelidar.com/
10. Sick, 2D Laser Scanner LMS111, Online Data Sheet. https://www.sick.com/media/pdf/2/42/842/dataSheet_LMS111-10100_1041114_en.pdf. Accessed 05 May 2016
11. Robotis, Servo Dynamixel MX-64R, e-Manual. http://support.robotis.com/en/product/dynamixel/mx_series/mx-64.htm. Accessed 10 May 2016
12. ZAM Service, Stationary Gas Detectors. http://www.zam-service.cz/www/index.php/en/produkty-3/detektory-plynu/stacionarni-detektory-zam
13. PTC Creo Parametric. http://www.ptc.com/cad/creo/parametric. Accessed 15 Apr 2016
14. TeleRescuer. http://www.telerescuer.eu/

Accuracy of Robotic Elastic Object Manipulation as a Function of Material Properties

Vladimír Petrík[1]([✉]), Vladimír Smutný[2], Pavel Krsek[1], and Václav Hlaváč[1]

[1] Czech Institute of Informatics, Robotics, and Cybernetics,
Czech Technical University in Prague, Prague, Czech Republic
{vladimir.petrik,krsek,hlavac}@ciirc.cvut.cz
[2] Center for Machine Perception, Department of Cybernetics,
Faculty of Electrical Engineering, Czech Technical University in Prague,
Prague, Czech Republic
smutny@cmp.felk.cvut.cz

Abstract. We deal with the problem of thin string (1D) or plate (2D) elastic material folding and its modeling. The examples could be metallic wire, metal, kevlar or rubber sheet, fabric, or as in our case, garment. The simplest scenario attempts to fold rectangular sheet in the middle. The quality of the fold is measured by relative displacement of the sheet edges. We use this scenario to analyse the effect of the inaccurate estimation of the material properties on the fold quality. The same method can be used for accurate placing of the elastic sheet in applications, e.g. the industrial production assembly.

In our previous work, we designed a model simulating the behavior of homogeneous rectangular garment during a relatively slow folding by a dual-arm robot. The physics based model consists of a set of differential equations derived from the static forces equilibrium. Each folding phase is specified by a set of boundary conditions. The simulation of the garment behavior is computed by solving the boundary value problem. We have shown that the model depends on a single material parameter, which is a weight to stiffness ratio. For a known weight to stiffness ratio, the model is solved numerically to obtain the folding trajectory executed by the robotic arms later.

The weight to stiffness ratio can be estimated in the course of folding or manually in advance. The goal of this contribution is to analyse the effect of the ratio inaccurate estimation on the resulting fold. The analysis is performed by simulation and in a real robotic garment folding using the CloPeMa dual-arm robotic testbed. In addition, we consider a situation, in which the weight to stiffness ratio cannot be measured exactly but the range of the ratio values is known. We demonstrate that the fixed value of the ratio produces acceptable fold quality for a reasonable range of the ratio values. We show that only four weight to stiffness ratio values can be used to fold all typical fabrics varying from a soft (e.g. sateen) to a stiff (e.g. denim) material with the reasonable accuracy. Experiments show that for a given range of the weight to stiffness ratio one has to choose the value on the pliable end of the range to achieve acceptable results.

© Springer International Publishing AG 2016
J. Hodicky (Ed.): MESAS 2016, LNCS 9991, pp. 384–395, 2016.
DOI: 10.1007/978-3-319-47605-6_31

Keywords: Robotic soft material folding · Physical elastic flat material model · Robotic fold accuracy

1   Introduction

The robotic manipulation with the soft material remains a challenging task due to the high degree of freedom of the soft material. One of the studied manipulation skills is the ability to fold the material accurately. The folding requires a folding trajectory which depends on several material properties. Estimation of these properties is inaccurate or omitted in real environment and then the folding itself is inaccurate as well. The folding inaccuracy as a function of the material properties is studied in this contribution.

The fold is specified by the folding line as shown in Fig. 1. The folding line divides the sheet into two parts. The goal of the folding is to move the left part on the top of the right part. The folding is achieved by following the folding trajectory. In the simplest scenario, the folding is aligned with the sheet edges and divides the sheet into two equally sized parts (Fig. 1). In this paper, all performed experiments assume the simplest scenario. The correct folding in the simplest scenario results in aligned edges of the sheet. The quality of the fold can be quantified by the distance between edges, which is zero if folding was accurate.

The goal of this paper is to analyse the fold quality for different robotic folding methods. In robotic folding, the folding trajectory is generated for the given sheet properties. The folding trajectory starts with grasping of the one side of garment while the opposite side lies freely on the folding surface. The trajectory depends on several sheet properties, for instance the size, density and stiffness. Generated trajectory is used to perform the folding by a robot. If the unsuitable trajectory is generated, the resulting fold is inaccurate. In practice, the sheet properties are measured or estimated in advance. The estimation might be inaccurate and the designed trajectory is thus unsuitable for the real material.

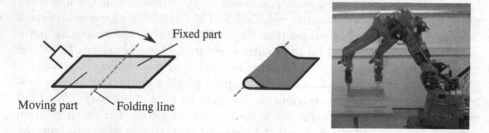

Fig. 1. The accurate folding visualization for the simplest scenario, where folding line (green, dashed) divides the sheet into two equally sized parts. The one side of the sheet is grasped and folding trajectory is followed in order to move the moving part on the top of the fixed part. One or two grippers are required for grasping depending on the width of the sheet. (Color figure online)

In the following two sections, the methods used for generation of the folding trajectory are described. The rest of the paper examines several experiments performed both in simulation and in real robotic testbed. These experiments analyze the effect of the properties estimation inaccuracy on the resulting fold.

The key contribution of the paper is a methodology, which select a folding trajectory for a given range of the material properties. This trajectory provides the satisfactory folding results for all materials from a given range. It also gives a possibility to pre-compute the trajectories and thus provides a fast planning algorithm for the folding trajectory design. This is demonstrated for all typical fabrics used for garments, where we will show that only four trajectories are required to fold all fabrics.

2   Related Work

To the author's knowledge, there are four different approaches for the folding trajectory design. Two of them are independent of material properties and the trajectory is described by a set of simple curves. The other two approaches depend on the material properties and are planned based on simulation.

The first approach for trajectory design is gravity based folding method [2], denoted as linear trajectory hereinafter. The trajectory shape was derived assuming the infinitely flexible material and infinite friction between the garment and the folding surface. Such assumptions are unrealistic and lead to imprecise fold as shown in work [6], where the linear trajectory was compared to the circular trajectory. The circular trajectory proved to be more accurate when the folding was performed on jeans. The derivation of the circular trajectory was build on the assumption of the rigid material with frictionless joint located in the folding line. The linear as well as circular trajectory do not depend on the material properties. The design of these trajectories is thus fast and it is the preferable solution if the folding accuracy requirement is not high.

The other two approaches relay on the simulation and requires the material properties to be known in advance. The first method was designed in [5], where the simulation software Maya was used. Authors described the material by a single parameter called shear resistance. In the simulated environment, the garment with a known material is folded and the resulting shape is analyzed. The folding trajectory is parametrized by a Bézier curve and the curve parameters were optimized until a sufficiently accurate fold was obtained. The shear resistance was measured by an operator before the actual folding.

In our previous work [7], we have designed another method for folding trajectory design. Our model describes the garment by a set of ordinary differential equations derived based on the static equilibrium of forces. The linear relation between the bending moment and the garment curvature is assumed, ignoring the effect of hysteresis [4]. Single parameter is required to characterize the material properties and this material parameter is a weight to stiffness ratio. The several methods for an estimation of this parameter were described in [8] and we use technique called a free fold test, originally described in [9]. The folding trajectory is found by solving a Boundary Value Problem [1,3], where boundaries characterize the folding requirements. Our method design a single trajectory for a given material and this trajectory results in the zero displacement from the expected position. In this work, an effect of the weight to stiffness ratio estimation inaccuracy is analyzed with respect to this approach for a folding trajectory design.

The methods presented here are not restricted for analysing of the garment folding only. Our model describes a wide range of materials and the accuracy analysis can be used in other fields as well. For example, the similar model was used for the task of undersea pipes laying using the J-lay method [10] or for a pipeline installation and recovery in deepwater [11].

3   Model

The model described in [7] will be briefly introduced in this section. The model is valid for homogeneous rectangular sheets and for homogeneous 1D strings. We have shown [7], that the material can be described by a single parameter called weight to stiffness ratio and denoted by a symbol η. The weight to stiffness ratio η is a combination of the material density ρ and the material bending stiffness K in a form:

$$\eta = \frac{\rho_a\, b\, g}{K}, \tag{1}$$

where ρ_A is area density, b is a width of a rectangle and g stands for a gravitational acceleration. In a case of a 1D string, the term $\rho_A\, b$ is replaced by a length density. The density as well as the bending stiffness are constant due to the assumed homogeneity of the material. The larger weight to stiffness ratio represents softer and/or heavier material.

According to [7], the string element (see Fig. 2) is modeled by a set of following differential equations:

$$\frac{\mathrm{d}}{\mathrm{d}s}\left(\tilde{T}(s)\cos\theta(s) + \frac{1}{\eta}\frac{\mathrm{d}^2\theta(s)}{\mathrm{d}s^2}\sin\theta(s)\right) = 0, \tag{2}$$

$$\frac{\mathrm{d}}{\mathrm{d}s}\left(\tilde{T}(s)\sin\theta(s) - \frac{1}{\eta}\frac{\mathrm{d}^2\theta(s)}{\mathrm{d}s^2}\cos\theta(s)\right) = 1 - f(y(s)), \tag{3}$$

$$\frac{\mathrm{d}x(s)}{\mathrm{d}s} = \cos\theta(s), \tag{4}$$

$$\frac{\mathrm{d}y(s)}{\mathrm{d}s} = \sin\theta(s), \tag{5}$$

where $\mathrm{d}s$ is an element of a string, $\theta(s)$ is an angle between the element and the horizontal axis, $\tilde{T}(s)$ is a scaled tension force $T(s)$ and $f(y(s))$ is a force used to incorporate the contact of the element s with the folding surface. The variables $x(s)$ and $y(s)$ stand for the position of the element. The scaled tension force acts in a direction, which is tangent to the element and is related to the tension force as:

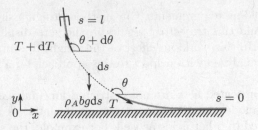

Fig. 2. The model of the string.

$$\tilde{T}(s) = \frac{T(s)}{\rho_A \, b \, g}.$$ (6)

The contact force $f(y(s))$, which supports the part of the string laying on the table is modeled as:

$$f(y(s)) = \frac{1}{y^2} 10^{-6},$$ (7)

which implies that the folding surface is horizontal with the zero height. The force is already normalized by the term $\rho_A \, b \, g$.

3.1 State of the Model

The model differential Eqs. (2), (3), (4) and (5) could be transformed to the six first order ordinary differential equations. Six boundary conditions (BCs) are thus required to specify the state of the model. For the string of the length l, the boundary conditions restrict the start ($s = 0$) or the end ($s = l$) of the string to be e.g. on the specific position or to have zero tension force. The BC at the position $s = 0$ are denoted by superscript '$-$' and the BC at $s = l$ are denoted by superscript '$+$'. When six BCs are specified, the BVP solver [3] is used to find the state of the model.

During the manipulation, there are many states of the model, which have to be solved. One such state is a completely folded string. It can be found by specifying the following boundary conditions:

$$\theta^- = 180°, \quad \frac{d\theta^-}{ds} = 0, \quad x^- = l, \quad \frac{d\theta^+}{ds} = 0, \quad x^+ = l, \quad y^+ = 0.$$ (8)

The folded states will differ depending on the weight to stiffness ratio η. The several folded states for different weight to stiffness ratio are shown in Fig. 3. It can be seen, that the string curvature located in the folding line is changing according to η. In our experiments, we have measured the maximal height of the string in the folded state, and denoted it as h_m. This height was used to estimate η for the given material [8]. The relation between η and h_m, which was used for the estimation, is shown in Fig. 4.

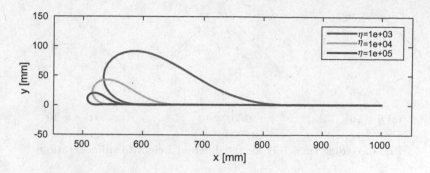

Fig. 3. Folded states for different weight to stiffness ratio η.

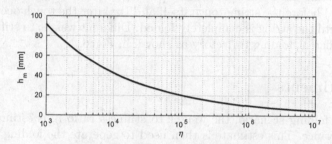

Fig. 4. Relation between weight to stiffness ratio η and maximal height of the folded string.

3.2 Folding Trajectory

The folding trajectory describes the pose of the robot gripper in time. In our model, the garment states satisfying the folding requirements are found and the trajectory is computed from these states. Two different types of boundary conditions were used and are denoted as the forward and the backward folding phase. Both folding phases are shown in Fig. 5. In the forward folding phase, the string is lifting until the touchdown point reaches its final position. The

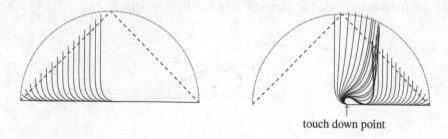

touch down point

Fig. 5. Folding phases. The linear and circular trajectories are shown in blue and green, respectively. The forward folding phase is shown on the left side and backward phase is shown on the right side. (Color figure online)

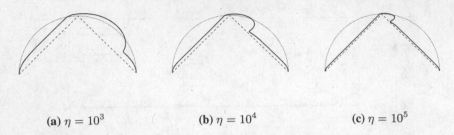

(a) $\eta = 10^3$ **(b)** $\eta = 10^4$ **(c)** $\eta = 10^5$

Fig. 6. Folding trajectory for the different weight to stiffness ratio η.

backward folding has a fixed touchdown point position and can be divided into two parts: (a) before the string touch itself and (b) after the touch occurs, which continues until the string is completely folded. Different weight to stiffness ratio results in different folding trajectory as shown in Fig. 6.

4   Experiments

In the ideal folding scenario, the weight to stiffness ratio η, is estimated accurately in advance. This estimate is then used to generate the folding trajectory which is executed by the robot. In reality, the estimation of the weight to stiffness ratio might be inaccurate and then the designed folding trajectory is not suitable for the given material. The purpose of these experiments is to analyse the quality of the fold when η_t, used for trajectory generation, differs from the material weight to stiffness ratio η_m. We fold several materials both in simulation and in real robotic testbed and the resulting folds were analysed based on the displacement d (Fig. 7). Displacement measures the oriented distance between the expected and real position of the grasped side of the string.

Two undesirable events influence the displacement: the slipping of the strip and the bending behaviour. In this paper, the effect of bending behaviour is studied and the slipping is avoided by considering several assumptions. It is assumed, that the friction between the garment and the folding surface is high enough so the slippage of the non grasped side is zero. Furthermore, it is assumed that the friction between the garment layers is high enough as well, so the upper

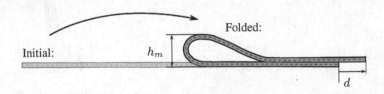

Fig. 7. The displacement measurement. The displacement d measures the quality of the fold and the maximal height h_m is used to estimate the material weight to stiffness ratio η_m.

layer cannot slip on the lower layer. The slipping of the upper layer is unfavorable because it is hard to predict the amount of the slippage due to the elasticity of the real material and due to the high variance of the soft material friction behavior. Furthermore, it is not decidable in our model whether the upper layer will slip on the lower layer or the both layers will slip on the folding surface.

4.1   Simulated Displacement

To obtain the simulated displacement, the boundary conditions have to be modified such that the given trajectory $\boldsymbol{u}(t) = \left[u_x(t),\, u_y(t),\, u_\theta(t)\right]^\top$ can be followed. The slippage of the upper layer is forbidden in the simulation and the after touch correction of the displacement is not possible. The simulation is described by the following BCs:

$$\theta^- = 180°, \quad \frac{\mathrm{d}\theta^-}{\mathrm{d}s} = 0, \quad x^- = l, \quad \theta^+ = u_\theta, \quad x^+ = u_x, \quad y^+ = u_y. \quad (9)$$

The simulation is stopped when the upper layer touches the lower layer and the displacement is computed.

For the purpose of the experiments, 24 different trajectories were generated. Two of these trajectories were linear [2] and circular [6]. Other trajectories were generated for η_t interpolated logarithmically between the values: 10^3 and 10^6. These trajectories were then used to fold several materials, which differ in weight to stiffness ratio η_m in a range from 10^3 to 10^6. The measured displacements are shown in Fig. 8. It can be seen, that the displacement is zero in the case where $\eta_t = \eta_m$. It represents the situation in which the weight to stiffness ratio was estimated accurately before trajectory generation - i.e. the ideal scenario. The displacement is more or less enlarging as the estimation is moving away

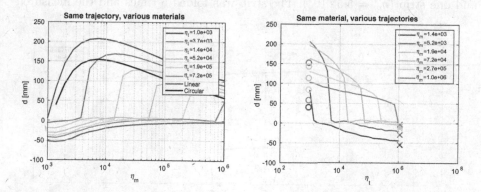

Fig. 8. Simulated displacements - two different visualizations of the same experiment. The displacements for the selected trajectories (generated with η_t) are shown for all simulated materials η_m on the left side. On the right side, the displacements of the selected materials are shown for all trajectories. The cross and circle marker stand for the linear and circular trajectory, respectively.

from the ideal scenario. Furthermore, the displacement is not symmetric. For the situation where $\eta_t > \eta_m$, the displacement is lower then for the situations where $\eta_t < \eta_m$. It suggests that one should select the trajectory on the pliable end of the known range of the material weight to stiffness ratio η. It means, that for the given η_m, we should use the larger η_t for the trajectory generation. It will results in the satisfactory folding for all materials in the range. Moreover, the smaller range will results in smaller displacement.

4.2 Real Displacement

We performed a real experiment with the CloPeMa testbed, where an industrial arm was used to fold the fabric strips. Strips with different weight to stiffness ratios were folded by each generated trajectory. The weight to stiffness ratios were estimated using the maximal height of the folded strips. To avoid the slipping of the strips on the table, the non grasped side was fixed to the table with the tape. The measured displacement together with simulated displacements for the estimated material are shown in Fig. 9. The measurements show, that simulation overestimated the oriented displacement for all situations except one, where $\eta_t = \eta_m$. Nevertheless, the hypothesis that trajectory on the pliable end should be selected is confirmed for the real displacements too.

4.3 Model Inconsistency

The simulated displacements overestimation suggests that there is an inconsistency in our model. To analyse this inconsistency, we performed two experiments: the first to check the repeatability of the real displacement and the second to compare simulated and real shapes of the strips during folding.

The repeatability experiment was performed for one trajectory ($\eta_t = 3.7{\cdot}10^5$) and one strip ($\eta_m = 5.5 \cdot 10^4$). The strip was folded 5 times and the measured

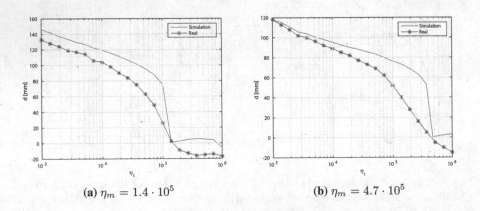

(a) $\eta_m = 1.4 \cdot 10^5$ (b) $\eta_m = 4.7 \cdot 10^5$

Fig. 9. Measured real displacement.

   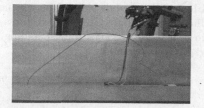

(a) Inconsistency start   **(b)** Inconsistency touch real

Fig. 10. The inconsistency in the model bending behaviour. The real strip is red, the simulated is shown in green color and the followed trajectory is blue. The difference between the simulation and the real strip was negligeble until the situation shown in 10a was reached. During the situation 10a, the simulatated model skips in a single step considerably. The real strip catches up the simulation with a small delay but the touch point was shifted w.r.t. shown in simulation 10b. (Color figure online)

variance of the displacement was 0.5 mm. It shows satisfactory repeatability of the real robotics folding.

The second experiment compares the simulated and real strip states. For the comparison purposes, the camera was added to the testbed and its field of view was geometrically calibrated. The calibration was used to project the simulated model into the image. The simulated state and the real state were compared visually. We observed, that the model is inconsistent in the states shown in Fig. 10. The inconsistency is probably caused by the missing hysteresis model between the bending moment and the curvature. The hysteresis modeling in the bending of fabrics was described in work [4]. In our future work, we will add the hysteresis component into our simulation in order to resolve this inconsistency. The bending model will then be nonlinear and the more complex estimation technique for material properties will need to be developed. Nevertheless, this inconsistency in the model does not influence the selection of the folding trajectory for the fabrics.

4.4   Fabric Folding

Our last experiment measured the displacement for whole range of typical fabrics when folded by four trajectories only. We divided the fabrics strips into four categories based on the estimated weight to stiffness ratios η_m. For these categories, the trajectory on the pliable end of the range (generated by η_t) is selected and the folding is performed on the CloPeMa testbed. The measured displacements are shown in Table 1. The table shows, that displacement is maximally 10 mm for all used fabric strips of length 1000 mm. For the purpose of robotic garment folding, this is an acceptable displacement. The displacement can be further reduced if more categories are used.

Table 1. Measured displacements when only four trajectories are used for fabric strips folding. The estimated weight to stiffness ratio is denoted η_m and the weight to stiffness ratio η_t was used to generate the folding trajectory. The height of folded strip h_m was used for the estimation.

Material	h_m [mm]	η_m	η_t	d [mm]
Georgette	12	$4.7 \cdot 10^5$	$5.2 \cdot 10^5$	-5
Chiffon	14	$3.2 \cdot 10^5$	$5.2 \cdot 10^5$	-9
Acetate lining	16	$2.1 \cdot 10^5$	$5.2 \cdot 10^5$	-10
Twill	17	$1.7 \cdot 10^5$	$1.9 \cdot 10^5$	-8
Wool suiting	18	$1.6 \cdot 10^5$	$1.9 \cdot 10^5$	-6
Herringbone pattern	19	$1.3 \cdot 10^5$	$1.9 \cdot 10^5$	-7
Coating	20	$1.0 \cdot 10^5$	$1.9 \cdot 10^5$	-9
Terry cloth	21	$9.0 \cdot 10^4$	$1.0 \cdot 10^5$	-7
Denim	22	$7.7 \cdot 10^4$	$1.0 \cdot 10^5$	-4
Plain weave	22	$7.7 \cdot 10^4$	$1.0 \cdot 10^5$	-6
Chanel	25	$5.2 \cdot 10^4$	$7.2 \cdot 10^4$	-3

5   Conclusions

This contribution examined the robotic folding accuracy as a function of the material weight to stiffness ratio η. Several experiments were conducted in simulation as well as in real robotic testbed. The experiments measured the folding accuracy based on the displacement of the excepted and the real position of the grasped side of the completely folded strip. Different materials, varying in weight to stiffness ratio η were folded and we observed that the trajectory on the pliable end of the known range provides the satisfactory folding accuracy. Based on the observation, we proposed a methodology for folding of the materials with roughly estimated weight to stiffness ratio. The methodology designs a trajectory for the range of the weight to stiffness ratio and accurate estimation is thus not necessary. The demonstration of the methodology was provided for the fabric strips. We shown, that only four trajectories are required to fold all typical fabrics used for the garments.

In the experiments, we observed the inconsistency between the simulation and real strips. This inconsistency causes an overestimation of the simulated displacement. We think, the inconsistency can be resolved by adding the hysteresis into the model and we will address this task in the future work.

Acknowledgment. This work was supported by the Technology Agency of the Czech Republic under Project TE01020197 Center Applied Cybernetics, the Grant Agency of the Czech Technical University in Prague, grant No. SGS15/203/OHK3/3T/13.

References

1. Bellman, R.E., Kalaba, R.E.: Quasilinearization and nonlinear boundary-value problems. Technical report, RAND Corporation, Santa Monica (1965)
2. van den Berg, J., Miller, S., Goldberg, K.Y., Abbeel, P.: Gravity-based robotic cloth folding. In: Hsu, D., Isler, V., Latombe, J.-C., Lin, M.C. (eds.) Algorithmic Foundations of Robotics (WAFR), vol. 68, pp. 409–424. Springer, Heidelberg (2010)
3. Kierzenka, J.A., Shampine, L.F.: A BVP solver that controls residual and error. J. Numer. Anal. Ind. Appl. Math (JNAIAM) 3, 1–2 (2008)
4. Lahey, T.: Modelling hysteresis in the bending of fabrics (2002)
5. Li, Y., Yue, Y., Xu, D., Grinspun, E., Allen, P.K.: Folding deformable objects using predictive simulation and trajectory optimization. In: Proceedings of International Conference on Intelligent Robots and Systems (IROS). IEEE/RSJ (2015)
6. Petrík, V., Smutný, V., Krsek, P., Hlaváč, V.: Robotic garment folding: precision improvement and workspace enlargement. In: Dixon, C., Tuyls, K. (eds.) TAROS 2015. LNCS, vol. 9287, pp. 204–215. Springer, Heidelberg (2015)
7. Petrík, V., Smutný, V., Krsek, P., Hlaváč, V.: Physics-based model of rectangular garment for robotic folding. Research report CTU-CMP-2016-06, Center for Machine Perception, K13133 FEE Czech Technical University, Prague, Czech Republic, May, 2016
8. Plaut, R.H.: Formulas to determine fabric bending rigidity from simple tests. Text. Res. J. 85(8), 884–894 (2015)
9. Stuart, I.: A loop test for bending length and rigidity. Br. J. Appl. Phys. 17(9), 1215 (1966)
10. Wang, L.Z., Yuan, F., Guo, Z., Li, Ll: Numerical analysis of pipeline in J-lay problem. J. Zhejiang Univ. Sci. A 11(11), 908–920 (2010)
11. Zeng, X.G., Duan, M.L., An, C.: Mathematical model of pipeline abandonment and recovery in deepwater. J. Appl. Math. 2014, 1–7 (2014)

Tactical Decision Support System to Aid Commanders in Their Decision-Making

Petr Stodola[✉] and Jan Mazal

University of Defence, Brno, Czech Republic
{petr.stodola, jan.mazal}@unob.cz

Abstract. This paper deals with the Tactical Decision Support System (TDSS) being developed at University of Defence, Brno, since 2006. TDSS is a command and control system designed for commanders of the Czech Army to support them in their decision-making processes on the tactical level. In the first part of the article, the basic characteristics and functions of the system are introduced. Next, advanced models of military tactics are presented including the model of optimal logistics on the battlefield, model of optimal cooperative reconnaissance by a fleet of unmanned aerial vehicles, and model of optimal cooperative reconnaissance by a fleet of ground elements. The last part of the article discusses the basic metaheuristic methods and approached used in our models. Finally, the paper summarizes some perspectives of our future work.

Keywords: Tactical decision support system · Command and control system · Decision-making · Models of military tactics · Metaheuristic methods

1 Introduction

Decision Support Systems (DSS) have been used in many domains recently. The main goal of such a computer-based information system is to aid the process of decision-making. DSS are used mainly by managers in organizations to improve the control of their organization, decide about the best investment strategy, etc. In the last decade, the use of DSS have increased dramatically not only by managers but also in many other areas.

In the military, DSS are used for command and control of military units. They support a commander on the battlefield in his/her decision-making process [1]. The basic function of such a system is to provide information to the commander. This information needs to be correct, early, processed, and delivered only to a competent person. The advanced function is to help the commander with planning his/her mission, predict the potential actions of the enemy and provide variants of friendly units' tactics along with their evaluation by computing the probability of their success. If DDS is not real time connected with the battlefield, the technique of prediction may be used to overcome communication failure [2, 3].

This paper deals with the Tactical Decision Support System (TDSS) which has been developed at University of Defence in Brno, Czech Republic, since 2006. TDSS is a command and control system intended for commander on the tactical level to support them in their decision-making.

© Springer International Publishing AG 2016
J. Hodicky (Ed.): MESAS 2016, LNCS 9991, pp. 396–406, 2016.
DOI: 10.1007/978-3-319-47605-6_32

2 Basic Features

2.1 Process of the Decision-Making Support

Figure 1 presents the basic architecture of TDSS. The commander is a user communicating with the system via some user interface. The system itself is composed of two main parts as follows:

- Database which includes all the data connected with the problem to be solved (combat elements database).
- Models of military tactics designed to solve the specific classes of problems. Models takes necessary data and information from the database.

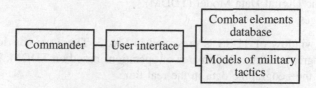

Fig. 1. Tactical decision support system architecture

The process of the decision-making support when using the system by commanders is shown in Fig. 2. The commander who has some mission at hand to be conducted turns his/her intention into a plan description via the user interface.

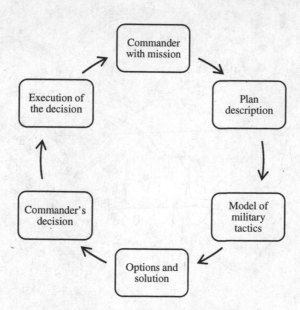

Fig. 2. TDSS process of the decision-making support

Next, the appropriate model is launched which tries to find the optimal solution to the commander's problem. The solution (solutions) to the problem is presented to the commander along with the second-order effects. Then, the commander chooses one of the solutions and the subordinates execute the decision.

2.2   Geographic Data and Coordinate Systems

One of the most important sources of data in the database is geographic data from the area of operations. TDSS processes and visualizes geographic data as follows (more information about the types of geographic data used in the system can be found in [4]):

- Digital Elevation Model (DEM).
- Topographic Digital Data Model (TDDM).
- Aerial images.

The main window of TDSS is presented in Fig. 3. There we can see 2D visualization of topographic objects of an area of operations based on TDDM. The system is able to render the geographic data in the real time.

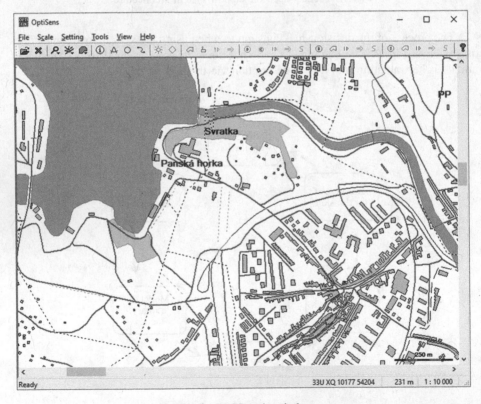

Fig. 3. TDSS main window

TDSS supports three coordinate systems. Conversion of coordinates between any coordinate systems can be done. The supported systems are as follows:

- Geographic coordinate system (latitude, longitude).
- WGS84/UTM used in NATO armies.
- MGRS use in the US Army.

2.3   Basic Tools

Figure 4 shows the basic tools and functions of the system which the commander can use. These features provide basic information and computations and also they serve when the commander needs to insert his/her own data concerning the battlefield.

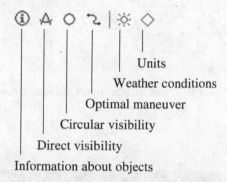

Fig. 4. Basic tools and functions of TDSS

Information about objects tool ⓘ provides information about geographic data in the area of operations. Direct ⚔ and circular ○ visibility tools allow to compute visibility as shown in Fig. 5.

Optimal maneuver tool ⟲ computes the best route of a unit from the initial position to the target destination. The three types of vehicles are supported: persons, wheeled vehicles and tracked vehicles. The model consists of five independent layers influencing the optimal route: topographic layer, elevation data layer, weather layer, hostile units layer and friendly units layer. Thus, the optimal route is computed not only as the shortest path between the initial and target positions but also from the safety point of view. Figure 6 presents an example of movement of a unit in regard to the known position of the enemy in the area of operations. More information about the optimal maneuver can be found in [5].

Weather conditions ☼ specify some important parameters influencing the behavior of various models: e.g. temperature, atmospheric pressure, humidity, visibility, precipitation, snow cover. Units tool ◇ is here to add, edit and delete hostile, friendly, neutral and unknown units in the area of operations. We can also compute the visibility or fire range of these units.

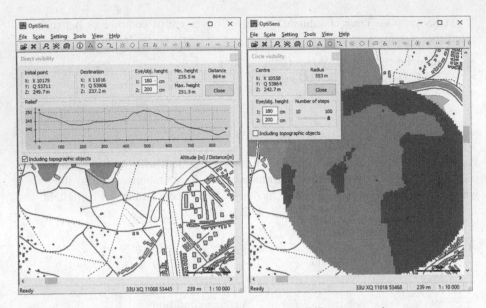

Fig. 5. Direct (left) and circular (right) visibility computation

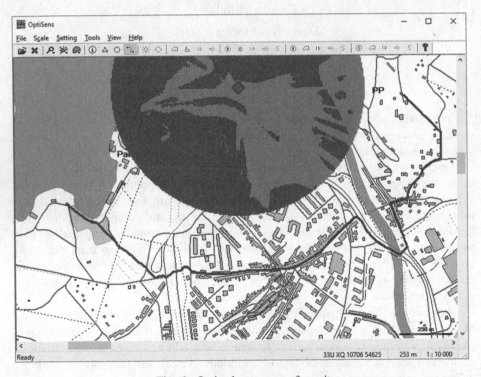

Fig. 6. Optimal maneuver of a unit

3   Advanced Models

There have been four advanced models implemented in TDSS (see Fig. 7). Each model is described briefly in the following subsections.

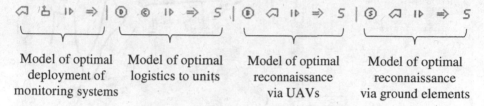

Model of optimal	Model of optimal	Model of optimal	Model of optimal
deployment of	logistics to units	reconnaissance	reconnaissance
monitoring systems		via UAVs	via ground elements

Fig. 7. Advanced models in TDSS

3.1   Model of Optimal Deployment of Monitoring Systems

Monitoring system is a system composed of unattended ground sensors (UGS). The goal is to guard the area of interest against intruders. The optimal deployment of individual sensors ensures the protection of as large area as possible by as small number of sensors as possible. More information about this model can be found in [6]. TDSS supports deployment of several monitoring systems as follows:

- CLASSIC (Covert Local Area Sensor System for Intruder Classification) used in NATO armies.
- REMBASS (Remote Battlefield Sensor System) used in the US Army.
- OASIS (Optical Acoustic SATCOM Integrated Sensor).
- System developed at University of Defence.

3.2   Model of Optimal Logistics to Units

Model of optimal logistics to units on the battlefield is about optimal supply distribution to a group of units on the battlefield by a fleet of supply vehicles. The order of units (customers) to be supplied is computed for each supply vehicle. The maximum transport capacity of supply vehicles is also of importance. If the capacity is exceeded, the vehicle needs to return to its depot before continuing with the supply operation.

The optimal routes between individual customers are computed according to the optimal maneuver model (see Sect. 2.3, Fig. 6). The optimal criterion can be set by a commander as follows:

- Shortest time for the whole supply operation.
- Shortest distance travelled by all supply vehicles.
- Minimum fuel consumed by all supply vehicles.

Figure 8 presents an example with 3 supply vehicles (hexagons marker by letters) and 15 units/customers (circles marked by numbers). In the top right corner, we can see

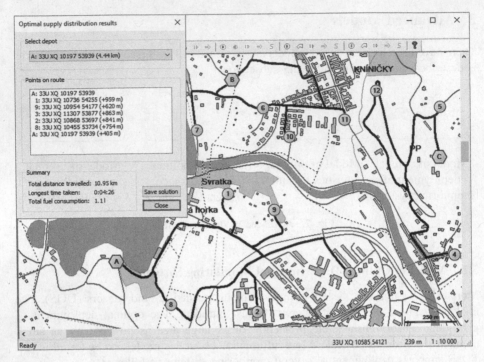

Fig. 8. Model of optimal logistics to units on the battlefield

the order of customers to be visited by vehicle A, below that is the information about the time needed to conduct the whole supply operation. More information about this model can be found in [4].

3.3 Model of Optimal Cooperative Reconnaissance via UAVs

The goal of the model of optimal cooperative reconnaissance via unmanned aerial vehicles is to explore the area of interest by a fleet of UAVs as fast as possible. If a commander has one or more UAVs at his/her disposal, he/she can use this model to plan the reconnaissance operation optimally.

The area of interest is bounded by an arbitrary polygon created by the commander. The positions of UAVs are set manually by the commander or are updated according to their GPS. Also the average velocity of each UAV is of importance (faster vehicles can explore more area than slower ones).

The model works based on the following principle. The area of interest is filled by uniformly positioned waypoints (the average distance between individual waypoints can be set according to the commander's requirement). The area of interest is assumed to be explored when every waypoint is visited by at least one of the UAVs.

Figure 9 shows an example where there are 3 UAVs. On the left, we can see detailed information about the route of vehicle B composed of the order of waypoints to be visited. If we have autonomous UAVs, we can upload this route into the vehicle, and the reconnaissance is conducted autonomously. More information about this model can be found in [4].

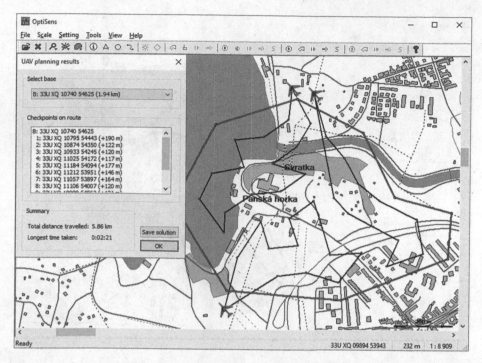

Fig. 9. Model of optimal cooperative reconnaissance via UAVs

3.4   Model of Optimal Cooperative Reconnaissance via Ground Elements

This last model is similar to the previous one. The difference consists in the types of vehicles used for reconnaissance. In this model, exploration of the area of interest is done via a group of ground elements which can be scouts or unmanned ground vehicles (UGVs).

Ground elements conduct exploration of the area of interest from specific waypoints positioned by the model. The aim of the model is to find optimal positions of these waypoints in the area of operations, the order of waypoint to be visited by each element and the optimal route for each element. The area explored from each waypoint is computed by our algorithms of circular visibility.

The principle of this model consists of three steps as follows:

- Finding the number of waypoints needed to explore most of the area of interest (e.g. more than 90 %).
- Finding the positions of waypoints in the area of operations so that the explored area is as large as possible.
- Finding the order of waypoints to be visited by elements with regard to the optimal criterion (minimum time needed to conduct the whole operation or the shortest distance travelled by all elements).

Figure 10 presents an example where there are 4 ground elements (marked by letters). The model determined the necessary number of waypoints to be deployed to

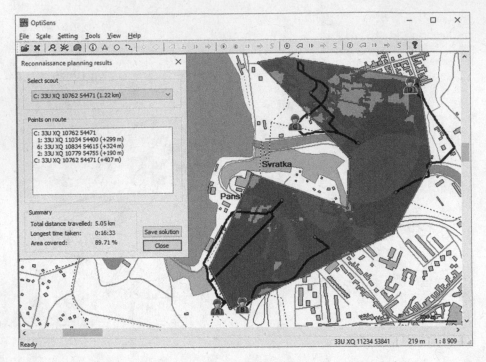

Fig. 10. Model of optimal cooperative reconnaissance via ground elements

cover about 90 % of the area of interest (6 waypoints in this case) and found the best positions for these waypoints to cover as large area as possible (89.71 %). Then the optimal routes for each element were computed. On the left, we can see the route for element C, below that is the information about the total distance and time needed to conduct the whole operation.

4   Metaheurictic Methods

This section discusses some of the methods used in the models mentioned above. We use the metaheuristic approach to find the solution to the problem at hand. The two main principles which have been used in our models are as follows:

- Stochastic and evolutionary methods.
- Ant Colony Optimization.

Stochastic and evolutionary approach is used when finding the best positions of sensors in the area of interest (see Sect. 3.1) or positions of waypoints in the cooperative reconnaissance model (see Sect. 3.4). Three main methods used are as follows [6]:

- Genetic algorithm.
- Algorithm SOMA (Self Organizing Migration Algorithm).
- Simulated Annealing algorithm.

Ant Colony Optimization (ACO) algorithm is used in models to find the order of points to be visited by multiple elements (see Sects. 3.2, 3.3 and 3.4). It is the well-known problem called Multi-Depot Vehicle Routing Problem (MDVRP) [8]. We modified the basic principles of the ACO algorithm to solve the MDVRP problem along with proposing some new parameters. With this algorithm, we managed to achieve very good solutions verified on benchmark instances (see [9] for more details).

5 Conclusion

This article presents the Tactical Decision Support System proposed to commanders to aid them in their decision-making on the tactical level. This system started in 2006, and since then its development has been carried on.

At present, we have been working on the implementation of several new models into TDSS as follows:

- Model of optimal deployment of observation posts in the area of operations.
- Model of artillery fire support.

One of the most important aspects when developing models is their verification. Generally, we use two approaches to do that as follows:

- Verification via computer simulations.
- Verification via experiments in the real environment.

Now, we are planning to enhance the verification process by conducting experiments in several real operations of the Czech Army.

References

1. Hodicky, J., Frantis, P.: Decision support system for a commander at the operational level. In: Dietz, J.L.G. (ed.) Proceedings of the International Conference on Knowledge Engineering and Ontology Development, KEOD 2009, Funchal - Madeira, October 2009, pp. 359–362. INSTICC Press (2009). ISBN 978-989-674-012-2
2. Hodicky, J., Frantis, P. Online versus offline critical geographic information system. In: Proceedings of the Informatics, Wireless Applications and Computing and Telecommunications, Networks and Systems 2011. Part of the IADIS Multi Conference on Computer Science and Information Systems 2011, Roma, July 2011, pp. 127–131. IADIS Press (2011). ISBN 978-972-8939-39-7
3. Hodicky, J., Frantis, P.: Using simulation for prediction of units movements in case of communication failure. World Acad. Sci. Eng. Technol. Int. J. Electr. Comput. Energ. Electron. Commun. Eng. 5(7), 789–796 (2011)
4. Stodola, P., Mazal, J.: Tactical and operational software library. In: International Conference on Military Technologies, University of Defence, Brno, pp. 347–350 (2015)
5. Nohel, J.: The possibilities of information support in the planning of the maneuver of units. Dissertation thesis, University of Defence, Brno (2015)

6. Stodola, P.: Position optimization of cooperative arrays of adaptive ground unattended sensors. Adv. Mil. Technol. **2**(2), 13–32 (2007)

7. Stodola, P., Mazal, J.: Tactical models based on a multi-depot vehicle routing problem using the ant colony optimization algorithm. Int. J. Math. Models Methods Appl. Sci. **9**, 330–337 (2015)

8. Dantzig, G.B., Ramser, J.H.: The truck dispatching problem. Manag. Sci. **6**(1), 80–91 (1959)

9. Stodola, P., Mazal, J., Podhorec, M.: Improving the Ant Colony Optimization Algorithm for the Multi-depot Vehicle Routing Problem and Its Application Modelling and Simulation for Autonomous Systems, pp. 376–385. Springer, Rome (2014)

10. Blaha, M., Šilinger, K.: Setting a method of determination of "fire for effect" firing data and conversion of the METCM into the METEO-11. Int. J. Circ. Syst. Sig. Process. **9**, 306–313 (2015)

11. Kozůbek, J., Flasar, Z.: Possibilities of verification the required capabilities according to NATO network enabled capabilities concept. Croatian J. Educ. **14**(1), 87–98 (2012)

12. Dubec, R., Hrůza, P.: Military concept of modularity. Croatian J. Educ. **14**(1), 35–41 (2012)

13. Ščurek, R., et al.: System of management of uncertainty and risk of renewable resources. Adv. Mater. Res. **1001**, 492–497 (2014)

Author Index

Printed in the United States
By Bookmasters